Lecture Notes in Artificial I.

Edited by J. G. Carbonell and J. Siekmann

Subseries of Lecture Notes in Computer Science

Daniel Kudenko   Dimitar Kazakov
Eduardo Alonso (Eds.)

Adaptive Agents and Multi-Agent Systems II

Adaptation and Multi-Agent Learning

 Springer

Series Editors

Jaime G. Carbonell, Carnegie Mellon University, Pittsburgh, PA, USA
Jörg Siekmann, University of Saarland, Saarbrücken, Germany

Volume Editors

Daniel Kudenko
Dimitar Kazakov
University of York
Department of Computer Science
Heslington, York, YO10 5DD, UK
E-mail: {kudenko, kazakov}@cs.york.ac.uk

Eduardo Alonso
City University London
Department of Computing
London, EC1V OHB, UK
E-mail: eduardo@soi.city.ac.uk

Library of Congress Control Number: 2005921645

CR Subject Classification (1998): I.2.11, I.2, D.2, C.2.4, F.3.1, D.3.1, H.5.3, K.4.3

ISSN 0302-9743
ISBN 3-540-25260-6 Springer Berlin Heidelberg New York

Springer is a part of Springer Science+Business Media

springeronline.com

© Springer-Verlag Berlin Heidelberg 2005
Printed in Germany

Typesetting: Camera-ready by author, data conversion by Scientific Publishing Services, Chennai, India
Printed on acid-free paper   SPIN: 11404071   06/3142   5 4 3 2 1 0

Preface

Predictions are a delicate matter. The I-told-you-this-was-going-to-happen ones are reliable, but not very helpful, as they only achieve credibility post factum. Similarly uninteresting are those of the shrowded-in-mystery, match-it-all type. Finally, when a respected person has both a vision and courage to state it, the future could prove him right, yet realize his dream with an unexpected twist. A solitary multimillionaire's round trip to an ageing orbital station is far from the crowds of space tourists predicted by A.C. Clark. However, when he said there would be hotels in space by 2001, he was spot on, despite the modest beginning.

We also met the year 2001 magical milestone to the future without being surrounded by either Arthur C. Clark's intelligent computers or their moody cousins of Douglas Adams's cut. However, one of the many small steps in this direction was made when the 1st Symposium on Adaptive Agents and Multi-agent Systems (AAMAS) was organized in that year. In front of you is a collection of selected papers from the 3rd and 4th AAMAS symposia, which persisted in the goals set in 2001, namely, to increase awareness and interest in adaptive agent research, encourage collaboration between machine learning and agent system experts, and give a representative overview of current research in the area of adaptive agents.

Recent years have seen an increasing interest, and the beginning of consolidation of the European research community in the field. Still, there are many major challenges left to tackle. While our understanding of learning agents and multi-agent systems has advanced significantly, most applications are still on simple scaled-down domains, and, in fact, most methods do not scale up to the real world. This, amongst others, is a major obstacle to bring learning agent technologies to commercial applications. Stay tuned for new developments in the – hopefully near – future.

The first book on the subject (Springer LNAI, vol. 2636), largely based on contributions to AAMAS and AAMAS-2, was published in 2002. It is with delight that we present another volume of articles in this emerging multidisciplinary area encompassing computer science, software engineering, biology, as well as the cognitive and social sciences.

Our thanks go to the symposium keynote speakers, Jürgen Schmidhuber and Sorin Solomon, for writing invited papers for this volume, the members of the symposium Program Committee for fast and thorough reviews, AgentLink II & III Networks of Excellence for co-sponsoring the symposium, the Society for the Study of Artificial Intelligence and the Simulation of Behaviour (SSAISB) for providing outstanding help in the organization of this event, and, of course, special thanks to the authors without whose high-quality contributions there would not be a book to begin with.

December 2004   Daniel Kudenko, Dimitar Kazakov, Eduardo Alonso

Organization

Symopsium Chairs

Eduardo Alonso (City University London, UK)
Dimitar Kazakov (University of York, UK)
Daniel Kudenko (University of York, UK)

Program Committee

Frances Brazier, Free University, Amsterdam, Netherlands
Philippe De Wilde, Imperial College, London, UK
Kurt Driessens, Catholic University of Leuven, Belgium
Saso Dzeroski, Jozef Stefan Institute, Ljubljana, Slovenia
Zahia Guessoum, LIP 6, Paris, France
Tom Holvoet, Computer Science Department, Catholic University of Leuven, Belgium
Paul Marrow, BTexact Technologies, UK
Ann Nowé, Free University of Brussels, Belgium
Luis Nunes, University of Porto, Portugal
Eugenio Oliveira, University of Porto, UK
Paolo Petta, Austrian Research Centre for AI, Austria
Enric Plaza, IIIA-CSIC, Spain
Michael Schroeder, City University, London, UK
Kostas Stathis, City University, London, UK
Malcolm Strens, QinetiQ, UK
Marco Wiering, University of Utrecht, Netherlands
Niek Wijngaards, Free University, Amsterdam, Netherlands

Sponsoring Institutions

SSAISB, UK
AgentLink II

Table of Contents

Gödel Machines: Towards a Technical Justification of Consciousness

Jürgen Schmidhuber

IDSIA, Galleria 2, 6928 Manno (Lugano), Switzerland
TU Munich, Boltzmannstr. 3, 85748 Garching, München, Germany
juergen@idsia.ch
http://www.idsia.ch/~juergen

Abstract. The growing literature on consciousness does not provide a formal demonstration of the *usefulness* of consciousness. Here we point out that the recently formulated Gödel machines may provide just such a technical justification. They are the first mathematically rigorous, general, fully self-referential, self-improving, optimally efficient problem solvers, "conscious" or "self-aware" in the sense that their entire behavior is open to introspection, and modifiable. A Gödel machine is a computer that rewrites any part of its own initial code as soon as it finds a proof that the rewrite is *useful,* where the problem-dependent *utility function,* the hardware, and the entire initial code are described by axioms encoded in an initial asymptotically optimal proof searcher which is also part of the initial code. This type of total self-reference is precisely the reason for the Gödel machine's optimality as a general problem solver: any self-rewrite is globally optimal—no local maxima!—since the code first had to prove that it is not useful to continue the proof search for alternative self-rewrites.

1 Introduction and Outline

In recent years the topic of consciousness has gained some credibility as a serious research issue, at least in philosophy and neuroscience, e.g., [8]. However, there is a lack of *technical* justifications of consciousness: so far no one has shown that consciousness is really useful for solving problems, even though problem solving is considered of central importance in philosophy [29].

Our fully self-referential Gödel machine [43, 45] may be viewed as providing just such a technical justification. It is "self-aware" or "conscious" in the sense that the algorithm determining its behavior is completely open to self-inspection, and modifiable in a very general (but computable) way. It can 'step outside of itself' [13] by executing self-changes that are provably good, where the mechanism for generating the proofs also is part of the initial code and thus subject to analysis and change. We will see that this type of total self-reference makes the Gödel machine an *optimal* general problem solver, in the sense of Global Optimality Theorem 1, to be discussed in Section 4.

Outline. Section 2 presents basic concepts of Gödel machines, relations to the most relevant previous work, and limitations. Section 3 presents the essential details of a self-referential axiomatic system of one particular Gödel machine, Section 4 the Global

D. Kudenko et al. (Eds.): Adaptive Agents and MAS II, LNAI 3394, pp. 1–23, 2005.
© Springer-Verlag Berlin Heidelberg 2005

Optimality Theorem 1, and Section 5 an $O()$-optimal (Theorem 2) initial proof searcher. Section 6 provides examples and additional relations to previous work, and lists answers to several frequently asked questions about Gödel machines. Section 7 wraps up.

2   Basic Overview / Most Relevant Previous Work / Limitations

All traditional algorithms for problem solving are hardwired. Some are designed to improve some limited type of policy through experience [19], but are not part of the modifiable policy, and cannot improve themselves in a theoretically sound way. Humans are needed to create new / better problem solving algorithms and to prove their usefulness under appropriate assumptions.

Here we eliminate the restrictive need for human effort in the most general way possible, leaving all the work including the proof search to a system that can rewrite and improve itself in arbitrary computable ways and in a most efficient fashion. To attack this *"Grand Problem of Artificial Intelligence,"* we introduce a novel class of optimal, fully self-referential [10] general problem solvers called *Gödel machines* [43, 44].[1] They are universal problem solving systems that interact with some (partially observable) environment and can in principle modify themselves without essential limits apart from the limits of computability. Their initial algorithm is not hardwired; it can completely rewrite itself, but only if a proof searcher embedded within the initial algorithm can first prove that the rewrite is useful, given a formalized utility function reflecting computation time and expected future success (e.g., rewards). We will see that self-rewrites due to this approach are actually *globally optimal* (Theorem 1, Section 4), relative to Gödel's well-known fundamental restrictions of provability [10]. These restrictions should not worry us; if there is no proof of some self-rewrite's utility, then humans cannot do much either.

The initial proof searcher is $O()$-optimal (has an optimal order of complexity) in the sense of Theorem 2, Section 5. Unlike hardwired systems such as Hutter's [15, 16] (Section 2) and Levin's [23, 24], however, a Gödel machine can in principle speed up any part of its initial software, including its proof searcher, to meet *arbitrary* formalizable notions of optimality beyond those expressible in the $O()$-notation. Our approach yields the first theoretically sound, fully self-referential, optimal, general problem solvers.

2.1   Set-Up and Formal Goal

Many traditional problems of computer science require just one problem-defining input at the beginning of the problem solving process. For example, the initial input may be a large integer, and the goal may be to factorize it. In what follows, however, we will also consider the *more general case* where the problem solution requires interaction with a dynamic, initially unknown environment that produces a continual stream of inputs and feedback signals, such as in autonomous robot control tasks, where the goal may be

---

[1] Or *'Goedel machine'*, to avoid the *Umlaut*. But *'Godel machine'* would not be quite correct. Not to be confused with what Penrose calls, in a different context, *'Gödel's putative theorem-proving machine'* [28]!

to maximize expected cumulative future reward [19]. This may require the solution of essentially arbitrary problems (examples in Section 6.1 formulate traditional problems as special cases).

Our hardware (e.g., a universal or space-bounded Turing machine [55] or the abstract model of a personal computer) has a single life which consists of discrete cycles or time steps $t = 1, 2, \ldots$. Its total lifetime T may or may not be known in advance. In what follows, the value of any time-varying variable Q at time t will be denoted by $Q(t)$.

During each cycle our hardware executes an elementary operation which affects its variable state $s \in S \subset B^*$ (where B^* is the set of possible bitstrings over the binary alphabet $B = \{0, 1\}$) and possibly also the variable environmental state $Env \in \mathcal{E}$ (here we need not yet specify the problem-dependent set $\mathcal{E}$). There is a hardwired state transition function $F : S \times \mathcal{E} \to S$. For $t > 1$, $s(t) = F(s(t-1), Env(t-1))$ is the state at a point where the hardware operation of cycle $t - 1$ is finished, but the one of t has not started yet. $Env(t)$ may depend on past output actions encoded in $s(t - 1)$ and is simultaneously updated or (probabilistically) computed by the possibly reactive environment.

In order to talk conveniently about programs and data, we will often attach names to certain string variables encoded as components or substrings of s. Of particular interest are the three variables called *time*, x, y, and p:

1. At time t, variable *time* holds a unique binary representation of t. We initialize *time*(1) = '1', the bitstring consisting only of a one. The hardware increments *time* from one cycle to the next. This requires at most $O(\log t)$ and on average only $O(1)$ computational steps.

2. Variable x holds the inputs form the environment to the Gödel machine. For $t > 1$, $x(t)$ may differ from $x(t-1)$ only if a program running on the Gödel machine has executed a special input-requesting instruction at time $t - 1$. Generally speaking, the delays between successive inputs should be sufficiently large so that programs can perform certain elementary computations on an input, such as copying it into internal storage (a reserved part of s) before the next input arrives.

3. Variable y holds the outputs of the Gödel machine. $y(t)$ is the output bitstring which may subsequently influence the environment, where $y(1) = $ '0' by default. For example, $y(t)$ could be interpreted as a control signal for an environment-manipulating robot whose actions may have an effect on future inputs.

4. $p(1)$ is the initial software: a program implementing the original (sub-optimal) policy for interacting with the environment, represented as a substring $e(1)$ of $p(1)$, plus the original policy for searching proofs. Details will be discussed below.

At any given time t ($1 \leq t \leq T$) the goal is to maximize future success or *utility*. A typical *"value to go"* utility function is of the form $u(s, Env) : S \times \mathcal{E} \to \mathcal{R}$, where $\mathcal{R}$ is the set of real numbers:

$$u(s, Env) = E_\mu \left[\sum_{\tau=time}^{E_\mu(T|s, Env)} r(\tau) \;\middle|\; s, Env \right], \tag{1}$$

where $r(t)$ is a real-valued reward input (encoded within $s(t)$) at time t, $E_\mu(\cdot \mid \cdot)$ denotes the conditional expectation operator with respect to some possibly unknown distribution

μ from a set M of possible distributions (M reflects whatever is known about the possibly probabilistic reactions of the environment), and the above-mentioned $time = time(s)$ is a function of state s which uniquely identifies the current cycle. Note that we take into account the possibility of extending the expected lifespan $E_\mu(T \mid s, Env)$ through appropriate actions.

Alternative formalizable utility functions could favor improvement of *worst case* instead of *expected* future performance, or higher reward intake *per time interval* etc. Clearly, most classic problems of computer science can be formulated in this framework—see examples in Section 6.1.

2.2   Basic Idea of Gödel Machine

Our machine becomes a self-referential [10] *Gödel machine* by loading it with a particular form of machine-dependent, self-modifying code p. The initial code $p(1)$ at time step 1 includes a (typically sub-optimal) problem solving subroutine $e(1)$ for interacting with the environment, such as any traditional reinforcement learning algorithm [19], and a general proof searcher subroutine (Section 5) that systematically makes pairs *(switch-prog, proof)* (variable substrings of s) until it finds a *proof* of a target theorem which essentially states: *'the immediate rewrite of* p *through current program* switchprog *on the given machine implies higher utility than leaving* p *as is'*. Then it executes *switchprog*, which may completely rewrite p, including the proof searcher. Section 3 will explain details of the necessary initial axiomatic system $\mathcal{A}$ encoded in $p(1)$. Compare Figure 1.

The **Global Optimality Theorem** (Theorem 1, Section 4) shows this self-improvement strategy is not greedy: since the utility of *'leaving* p *as is'* implicitly evaluates all possible alternative *switchprog*s which an unmodified p might find later, we obtain a globally optimal self-change—the *current switchprog* represents the best of all possible relevant self-changes, relative to the given resource limitations and initial proof search strategy.

2.3   Proof Techniques and an $O()$-Optimal Initial Proof Searcher

Section 5 will present an $O()$-optimal initialization of the proof searcher, that is, one with an optimal *order* of complexity (Theorem 2). Still, there will remain a lot of room for self-improvement hidden by the $O()$-notation. The searcher uses an online extension of *Universal Search* [23, 24] to systematically test *online proof techniques*, which are proof-generating programs that may read parts of state s (similarly, mathematicians are often more interested in proof techniques than in theorems). To prove target theorems as above, proof techniques may invoke special instructions for generating axioms and applying inference rules to prolong the current *proof* by theorems. Here an axiomatic system $\mathcal{A}$ encoded in $p(1)$ includes axioms describing **(a)** how any instruction invoked by a program running on the given hardware will change the machine's state s (including instruction pointers etc.) from one step to the next (such that proof techniques can reason about the effects of any program including the proof searcher), **(b)** the initial program $p(1)$ itself (Section 3 will show that this is possible without introducing circularity), **(c)** stochastic environmental properties, **(d)** the formal utility function u, e.g., equation (1), which automatically takes into account computational costs of all actions including proof search.

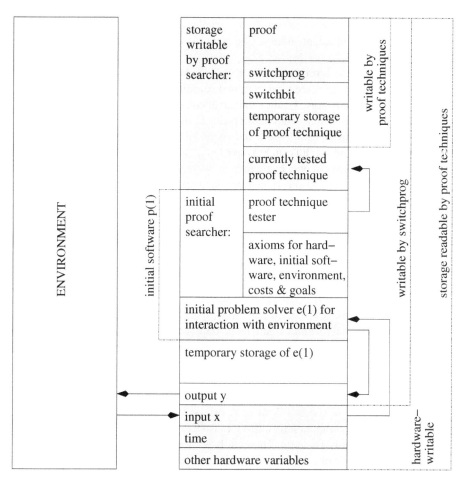

Fig. 1. Storage snapshot of a not yet self-improved example Gödel machine, with the initial software still intact. See text for details

2.4   Relation to Hutter's Previous Work

Here we will briefly review the most closely related previous work, and point out the main novelties of the Gödel machine. More relations to older approaches can be found in Section 6.2.

Hutter's non-self-referential but still $O()$-optimal *'fastest' algorithm for all well-defined problems* HSEARCH [16] uses a *hardwired* brute force proof searcher and ignores the costs of proof search. Assume discrete input/output domains X/Y, a formal problem specification $f : X \rightarrow Y$ (say, a functional description of how integers are decomposed into their prime factors), and a particular $x \in X$ (say, an integer to be factorized). HSEARCH orders all proofs of an appropriate axiomatic system by size to find programs q that for all $z \in X$ provably compute $f(z)$ within time bound $t_q(z)$. Simultaneously it spends most of its time on executing the q with the best currently proven time bound $t_q(x)$. It turns out that HSEARCH is as fast as the *fastest* algorithm that provably computes

$f(z)$ for all $z \in X$, save for a constant factor smaller than $1 + \epsilon$ (arbitrary $\epsilon > 0$) and an f-specific but x-independent additive constant [16]. This constant may be enormous though.

Hutter's AIXI(t,l) [15] is related. In discrete cycle $k = 1, 2, 3, \ldots$ of AIXI(t,l)'s lifetime, action $y(k)$ results in perception $x(k)$ and reward $r(k)$, where all quantities may depend on the complete history. Using a universal computer such as a Turing machine, AIXI(t,l) needs an initial offline setup phase (prior to interaction with the environment) where it uses a *hardwired* brute force proof searcher to examine all proofs of length at most L, filtering out those that identify programs (of maximal size l and maximal runtime t per cycle) which not only could interact with the environment but which for all possible interaction histories also correctly predict a lower bound of their own expected future reward. In cycle k, AIXI(t,l) then runs all programs identified in the setup phase (at most 2^l), finds the one with highest self-rating, and executes its corresponding action. The problem-independent setup time (where almost all of the work is done) is $O(L \cdot 2^L)$. The online time per cycle is $O(t \cdot 2^l)$. Both are constant but typically huge.

Advantages and Novelty of the Gödel Machine. There are major differences between the Gödel machine and Hutter's HSEARCH [16] and AIXI(t,l) [15], including:

1. The theorem provers of HSEARCH and AIXI(t,l) are hardwired, non-self-referential, unmodifiable meta-algorithms that cannot improve themselves. That is, they will always suffer from the same huge constant slowdowns (typically $\gg 10^{1000}$) buried in the $O()$-notation. But there is nothing in principle that prevents our truly self-referential code from proving and exploiting drastic reductions of such constants, in the best possible way that provably constitutes an improvement, if there is any.

2. The demonstration of the $O()$-optimality of HSEARCH and AIXI(t,l) depends on a clever allocation of computation time to some of their unmodifiable meta-algorithms. Our Global Optimality Theorem (Theorem 1, Section 4), however, is justified through a quite different type of reasoning which indeed exploits and crucially depends on the fact that there is no unmodifiable software at all, and that the proof searcher itself is readable, modifiable, and can be improved. This is also the reason why its self-improvements can be more than merely $O()$-optimal.

3. HSEARCH uses a "trick" of proving more than is necessary which also disappears in the sometimes quite misleading $O()$-notation: it wastes time on finding programs that provably compute $f(z)$ for all $z \in X$ even when the current $f(x)(x \in X)$ is the only object of interest. A Gödel machine, however, needs to prove only what is relevant to its goal formalized by u. For example, the general u of eq. (1) completely ignores the limited concept of $O()$-optimality, but instead formalizes a stronger type of optimality that does not ignore huge constants just because they are constant.

4. Both the Gödel machine and AIXI(t,l) can maximize expected reward (HSEARCH cannot). But the Gödel machine is more flexible as we may plug in *any* type of formalizable utility function (e.g., *worst case* reward), and unlike AIXI(t,l) it does not require an enumerable environmental distribution.

Nevertheless, we may use AIXI(t,l) or HSEARCH or other less general methods to initialize the substring e of p which is responsible for interaction with the environment. The Gödel machine will replace $e(1)$ as soon as it finds a provably better strategy.

2.5 Limitations of Gödel Machines

The fundamental limitations are closely related to those first identified by Gödel's celebrated paper on self-referential formulae [10]. Any formal system that encompasses arithmetics (or ZFC etc) is either flawed or allows for unprovable but true statements. Hence even a Gödel machine with unlimited computational resources must ignore those self-improvements whose effectiveness it cannot prove, e.g., for lack of sufficiently powerful axioms in $\mathcal{A}$. In particular, one can construct pathological examples of environments and utility functions that make it impossible for the machine to ever prove a target theorem. Compare Blum's speed-up theorem [3, 4] based on certain incomputable predicates. Similarly, a realistic Gödel machine with limited resources cannot profit from self-improvements whose usefulness it cannot prove within its time and space constraints.

Nevertheless, unlike previous methods, it can in principle exploit at least the *provably* good speed-ups of *any* part of its initial software, including those parts responsible for huge (but problem class-independent) slowdowns ignored by the earlier approaches [15, 16].

3 Essential Details of One Representative Gödel Machine

Notation. Unless stated otherwise or obvious, throughout the paper newly introduced variables and functions are assumed to cover the range implicit in the context. $l(q)$ denotes the number of bits in a bitstring q; q_n the n-th bit of q; λ the empty string (where $l(\lambda) = 0$); $q_{m:n} = \lambda$ if $m > n$ and $q_m q_{m+1} \ldots q_n$ otherwise (where $q_0 := q_{0:0} := \lambda$).

Theorem proving requires an axiom scheme yielding an enumerable set of axioms of a formal logic system $\mathcal{A}$ whose formulas and theorems are symbol strings over some finite alphabet that may include traditional symbols of logic (such as $\rightarrow, \wedge, =, (,), \forall, \exists, \ldots,$ $c_1, c_2, \ldots, f_1, f_2, \ldots$), probability theory (such as $E(\cdot)$, the expectation operator), arithmetics $(+, -, /, =, \sum, <, \ldots)$, string manipulation (in particular, symbols for representing any part of state s at any time, such as $s_{7:88}(5555)$). A proof is a sequence of theorems, each either an axiom or inferred from previous theorems by applying one of the inference rules such as *modus ponens* combined with *unification*, e.g., [9].

The remainder of this paper will omit standard knowledge to be found in any proof theory textbook. Instead of listing *all* axioms of a particular $\mathcal{A}$ in a tedious fashion, we will focus on the novel and critical details: how to overcome problems with self-reference and how to deal with the potentially delicate online generation of proofs that talk about and affect the currently running proof generator itself.

3.1 Proof Techniques

Brute force proof searchers (used in Hutter's $\text{AIXI}(t,l)$ and HSEARCH; see Section 2.4) systematically generate all proofs in order of their sizes. To produce a certain proof, this takes time exponential in proof size. Instead our $O()$-optimal $p(1)$ will produce many proofs with low algorithmic complexity [51, 21, 25] much more quickly. It systematically tests (see Section 5) *proof techniques* written in universal language $\mathcal{L}$ implemented within $p(1)$. For example, $\mathcal{L}$ may be a variant of PROLOG [6] or the universal FORTH[27]-inspired programming language used in recent work on optimal search [46]. A proof technique is composed of instructions that allow any part of s to be read, such as inputs encoded in variable x (a substring of s) or the code of $p(1)$. It may write on s^p, a part of s reserved for temporary results. It also may rewrite *switchprog*, and produce an incrementally growing proof placed in the string variable *proof* stored somewhere in s. *proof* and s^p are reset to the empty string at the beginning of each new proof technique test. Apart from standard arithmetic and function-defining instructions [46] that modify s^p, the programming language $\mathcal{L}$ includes special instructions for prolonging the current *proof* by correct theorems, for setting *switchprog*, and for checking whether a provably optimal p-modifying program was found and should be executed now. Certain long proofs can be produced by short proof techniques.

The nature of the six *proof*-modifying instructions below (there are no others) makes it impossible to insert an incorrect theorem into *proof*, thus trivializing proof verification:

1. **Get-Axiom(n)** takes as argument an integer n computed by a prefix of the currently tested proof technique with the help of arithmetic instructions such as those used in previous work [46]. Then it appends the n-th axiom (if it exists, according to the axiom scheme below) as a theorem to the current theorem sequence in *proof*. The initial axiom scheme encodes:

   (a) **Hardware Axioms** describing the hardware, formally specifying how certain components of s (other than environmental inputs x) may change from one cycle to the next.

   For example, if the hardware is a Turing machine[2] (TM) [55], then $s(t)$ is a bitstring that encodes the current contents of all tapes of the TM, the positions of its scanning heads, and the current *internal state* of the TM's finite state automaton, while F specifies the TM's look-up table which maps any possible combination of internal state and bits above scanning heads to a new internal state and an action such as: replace some head's current bit by 1/0, increment (right shift) or decrement (left shift) some scanning head, read and copy next input bit to cell above input tape's scanning head, etc.

   Alternatively, if the hardware is given by the abstract model of a modern microprocessor with limited storage, $s(t)$ will encode the current storage contents, register values, instruction pointers etc.

   For instance, the following axiom could describe how some 64-bit hardware's instruction pointer stored in $s_{1:64}$ is continually incremented as long as there is no overflow and the value of s_{65} does not indicate that a jump to some other address should take place:

$$(\forall t \forall n : [(n < 2^{64} - 1) \wedge (n > 0) \wedge (t > 1) \wedge (t < T)$$

$$\wedge (string2num(s_{1:64}(t)) = n) \wedge (s_{65}(t) = \text{`0'})]$$

$$\rightarrow (string2num(s_{1:64}(t+1)) = n+1))$$

---

[2] Turing reformulated Gödel's unprovability results in terms of Turing machines (TMs) [55] which subsequently became the most widely used abstract model of computation. It is well-known that there are *universal* TMs that in a certain sense can emulate any other TM or any other known computer. Gödel's integer-based formal language can be used to describe any universal TM, and vice versa.

Here the semantics of used symbols such as '(' and '>' and '→' (implies) are the traditional ones, while '$string2num$' symbolizes a function translating bitstrings into numbers. It is clear that any abstract hardware model can be fully axiomatized in a similar way.

(b) **Reward Axioms** defining the computational costs of any hardware instruction, and physical costs of output actions, such as control signals $y(t)$ encoded in $s(t)$. Related axioms assign values to certain input events (encoded in variable x, a substring of s) representing reward or punishment (e.g., when a Gödel machine controlled robot bumps into an obstacle). Additional axioms define the total value of the Gödel machine's life as a scalar-valued function of all rewards (e.g., their sum) and costs experienced between cycles 1 and T, etc. For example, assume that $s_{17:18}$ can be changed only through external inputs; the following example axiom says that the total reward increases by 3 whenever such an input equals '11' (unexplained symbols carry the obvious meaning):

$$(\forall t_1 \forall t_2 : [(t_1 < t_2) \wedge (t_1 \geq 1) \wedge (t_2 \leq T) \wedge (s_{17:18}(t_2) = \text{`11'})]$$

$$\rightarrow [R(t_1, t_2) = R(t_1, t_2 - 1) + 3]),$$

where $R(t_1, t_2)$ is interpreted as the cumulative reward between times t_1 and t_2. It is clear that any formal scheme for producing rewards can be fully axiomatized in a similar way.

(c) **Environment Axioms** restricting the way the environment will produce new inputs (encoded within certain substrings of s) in reaction to sequences of outputs y encoded in s. For example, it may be known in advance that the environment is sampled from an unknown probability distribution μ contained in a given set M of possible distributions (compare equation 1). E.g., M may contain all distributions that are computable, given the previous history [51, 52, 15], or at least limit-computable [39, 40]. Or, more restrictively, the environment may be some unknown but deterministic computer program [57, 37] sampled from the Speed Prior [41] which assigns low probability to environments that are hard to compute by any method. Or the interface to the environment is Markovian [33], that is, the current input always uniquely identifies the environmental state—a lot of work has already been done on this special case [31, 2, 54]. Even more restrictively, the environment may evolve in completely predictable fashion known in advance. All such prior assumptions are perfectly formalizable in an appropriate $\mathcal{A}$ (otherwise we could not write scientific papers about them).

(d) **Uncertainty Axioms; String Manipulation Axioms:** Standard axioms for arithmetics and calculus and probability theory [20] and statistics and string manipulation that (in conjunction with the hardware axioms and environment axioms) allow for constructing proofs concerning (possibly uncertain) properties of future values of $s(t)$ as well as bounds on expected remaining lifetime / costs / rewards, given some time τ and certain hypothetical values for components of $s(\tau)$ etc. An example theorem saying something about expected properties of future inputs x might look like this:

$$(\forall t_1 \forall \mu \in M : [(1 \le t_1) \land (t_1 + 15597 < T) \land (s_{5:9}(t_1) = \text{`01011'})$$

$$\land (x_{40:44}(t_1) = \text{`00000'})] \rightarrow (\exists t : [(t_1 < t < t_1 + 15597)$$

$$\land (P_\mu(x_{17:22}(t) = \text{`011011'} \mid s(t_1)) > \frac{998}{1000})])),$$

where $P_\mu(. \mid .)$ represents a conditional probability with respect to an axiomatized prior distribution μ from a set of distributions M described by the environment axioms (Item 1c).

Given a particular formalizable hardware (Item 1a) and formalizable assumptions about the possibly probabilistic environment (Item 1c), obviously one can fully axiomatize everything that is needed for proof-based reasoning about past and future machine states.

(e) **Initial State Axioms:** Information about how to reconstruct the initial state $s(1)$ or parts thereof, such that the proof searcher can build proofs including axioms of the type

$$(s_{\mathbf{m:n}}(1) = \mathbf{z}), \ e.g. : \ (s_{7:9}(1) = \text{`010'}).$$

Here and in the remainder of the paper we use bold font in formulas to indicate syntactic place holders (such as **m,n,z**) for symbol strings representing variables (such as m,n,z) whose semantics are explained in the text—in the present context z is the bitstring $s_{m:n}(1)$.

Note that it is **no fundamental problem** to fully encode both the hardware description *and* the initial hardware-describing p within p itself. To see this, observe that some software may include a program that can print the software.

(f) **Utility Axioms** describing the overall goal in the form of utility function u; e.g., equation (1) in Section 2.1.

2. **Apply-Rule(k, m, n)** takes as arguments the index k (if it exists) of an inference rule such as *modus ponens* (stored in a list of possible inference rules encoded within $p(1)$) and the indices m, n of two previously proven theorems (numbered in order of their creation) in the current *proof*. If applicable, the corresponding inference rule is applied to the addressed theorems and the resulting theorem appended to *proof*. Otherwise the currently tested proof technique is interrupted. This ensures that *proof* is never fed with invalid proofs.

3. **Delete-Theorem(m)** deletes the m-th theorem in the currently stored *proof*, thus freeing storage such that proof-storing parts of s can be reused and the maximal proof size is not necessarily limited by storage constraints. Theorems deleted from *proof*, however, cannot be addressed any more by *apply-rule* to produce further prolongations of *proof*.

4. **Set-Switchprog(m,n)** replaces *switchprog* by $s_{m:n}^p$, provided that $s_{m:n}^p$ is indeed a non-empty substring of s^p, the storage writable by proof techniques.

5. **Check()** verifies whether the goal of the proof search has been reached. First it tests whether the last theorem (if any) in *proof* has the form of a **target theorem**. A target theorem states that given the *current* axiomatized utility function u (Item 1f), the utility of a switch from p to the current *switchprog* would be higher than the utility of continuing the execution of p (which would keep searching for alternative

switchprogs). Target theorems are symbol strings (encoded in s) of the (decoded) form

$$(u[s(\mathbf{t_1}) \oplus (switchbit(\mathbf{t_1}) = \text{`1'}), Env(\mathbf{t_1})] >$$
$$u[s(\mathbf{t_1}) \oplus (switchbit(\mathbf{t_1}) = \text{`0'}), Env(\mathbf{t_1})]) \tag{2}$$

where the variable t_1 (represented by syntactic place holder $\mathbf{t_1}$) stands for a time step, while all other symbols belong to the alphabet of the theorem-proving calculus, that is, the set of possible target theorems is parameterized only by t_1. Here the calculus should permit the notation $s(\mathbf{t_1}) \oplus (switchbit(\mathbf{t_1}) = \text{`}b\text{'})$ as a shortcut for the state obtained when we replace $switchbit(t_1)$, the true value of the variable bit $switchbit$ (encoded in s) at time t_1, by $b \in \{0, 1\}$. This will facilitate the formulation of theorems that compare values conditioned on various alternative hypothetical properties of $s(t_1)$. (Note that $s(t_1)$ may be only partially known by the current proof technique even in environments where $s(t_1)$ and $switchbit(t_1)$ are fully predetermined for all valid t_1.)

The purpose of introducing t_1 is to deal with hardware-specific temporal delays that may be involved in checking and switching—it may take a significant amount of time to match abstract symbol strings found during proof search to the Gödel machine's real current state. If a target theorem has been found, *check()* uses a simple prewired subroutine to check whether there is enough time left to set variable *switchbit* (originally 0) to 1 before the continually increasing $time$ will equal t_1. If this subroutine returns a negative result, *check()* exits. Otherwise it sets *switchbit* := 1 (there is no other way of changing *switchbit*). Then it repeatedly tests $time$ until $time > t_1$, to make sure the condition of formula (2) was fulfilled at t_1. Then it transfers control to *switchprog* (there is no other way of calling *switchprog*). The *switchprog* may subsequently rewrite all parts of s, excluding hardware-reserved parts such as $time$ and x, but including p.

6. **State2theorem(m, n)** takes two integer arguments m, n and tries to transform the current contents of $s_{m:n}$ into a theorem of the form

$$(s_{\mathbf{m:n}}(\mathbf{t_1}) = \mathbf{z}), \ e.g.: \ (s_{6:9}(7775555) = \text{`1001'}),$$

where t_1 represents a time measured (by checking $time$) shortly after *state2theorem* was invoked, and z the bistring $s_{m:n}(t_1)$ (recall the special case $t_1 = 1$ of Item 1e). So we accept the time-labeled current observable contents of any part of s as a theorem that does not have to be proven in an alternative way from, say, the initial state $s(1)$, because the computation so far has already demonstrated that the theorem is true. Thus we may exploit information conveyed by environmental inputs, and the fact that sometimes (but not always) the fastest way to determine the output of a program is to run it.

This non-traditional online interface between syntax and semantics requires special care though. We must avoid inconsistent results through parts of s that change while being read. For example, the present value of a quickly changing instruction pointer IP *(continually updated by the hardware) may be essentially unreadable in the sense that the execution of the reading subroutine itself will already modify* IP *many times. For convenience, the (typically limited) hardware could be set up such* *that it stores the contents of fast hardware variables every c cycles in a reserved part of s, such that an appropriate variant of* state2theorem() *could at least translate certain recent values of fast variables into theorems. This, however, will not abolish all problems associated with self-observations. For example, the $s_{m:n}$ to be read might also contain the reading procedure's own, temporary, constantly changing string pointer variables, etc.[3] To address such problems on computers with limited memory,* state2theorem *first uses some fixed protocol to check whether the current $s_{m:n}$ is readable at all or whether it might change if it were read by the remaining code of* state2theorem. *If so, or if m, n, are not in the proper range, then the instruction has no further effect. Otherwise it appends an observed theorem of the form $(s_{m:n}(t_1) = z)$ to proof. For example, if the current time is 7770000, then the invocation of* state2theorem(6,9) *might return the theorem $(s_{6:9}(7775555) = \text{'}1001\text{'})$, where $7775555 - 7770000 = 5555$ reflects the time needed by* state2theorem *to perform the initial check and to read leading bits off the continually increasing* time *(reading* time *also costs time) such that it can be sure that 7775555 is a recent proper time label following the start of* state2theorem.

The axiomatic system $\mathcal{A}$ is a defining parameter of a given Gödel machine. Clearly, $\mathcal{A}$ must be strong enough to permit proofs of target theorems. In particular, the theory of uncertainty axioms (Item 1d) must be sufficiently rich. This is no fundamental problem: we simply insert all traditional axioms of probability theory [20].

4   Global Optimality Theorem

Intuitively, at any given time p should execute some self-modification algorithm (via instruction *check()*—Item 5 above) only if it is the 'best' of all possible self-modifications, given the utility function, which typically depends on available resources, such as storage size and remaining lifetime. At first glance, however, target theorem (2) seems to implicitly talk about just one single modification algorithm, namely, *switchprog(t_1)* as set by the systematic proof searcher at time t_1. Isn't this type of local search greedy? Couldn't it lead to a local optimum instead of a global one? No, it cannot, according to the global optimality theorem:

Theorem 1 (Globally Optimal Self-Changes, given u and $\mathcal{A}$ encoded in p). *Given any formalizable utility function u (Item 1f), and assuming consistency of the underlying formal system $\mathcal{A}$, any self-change of p obtained through execution of some program*

---

[3] We see that certain parts of the current s may not be directly observable without changing the observable itself. Sometimes, however, axioms and previous observations will allow the Gödel machine to *deduce* time-dependent storage contents that are not directly observable. For instance, by analyzing the code being executed through instruction pointer *IP* in the example above, the value of *IP* at certain times may be predictable (or postdictable, after the fact). The values of other variables at given times, however, may not be deducible at all. Such limits of self-observability are reminiscent of Heisenberg's celebrated uncertainty principle [11], which states that certain physical measurements are necessarily imprecise, since the measuring process affects the measured quantity.

switchprog *identified through the proof of a target theorem (2) is globally optimal in the following sense: the utility of starting the execution of the present* switchprog *is higher than the utility of waiting for the proof searcher to produce an alternative* switchprog *later.*

Proof. Target theorem (2) implicitly talks about all the other *switchprog*s that the proof searcher could produce in the future. To see this, consider the two alternatives of the binary decision: (1) either execute the current *switchprog* (set *switchbit* = 1), or (2) keep searching for *proof*s and *switchprog*s (set *switchbit* = 0) until the systematic searcher comes up with an even better *switchprog*. Obviously the second alternative concerns all (possibly infinitely many) potential *switchprog*s to be considered later. That is, if the current *switchprog* were not the 'best', then the proof searcher would not be able to prove that setting *switchbit* and executing *switchprog* will cause higher expected reward than discarding *switchprog*, assuming consistency of $\mathcal{A}$. *Q.E.D.*

4.1   Alternative Relaxed Target Theorem

We may replace the target theorem (2) (Item 5) by the following alternative target theorem:

$$(u[s(\mathbf{t_1}) \oplus (switchbit(\mathbf{t_1}) = \text{'1'}), Env(\mathbf{t_1})] \geq$$
$$u[s(\mathbf{t_1}) \oplus (switchbit(\mathbf{t_1}) = \text{'0'}), Env(\mathbf{t_1})]) \tag{3}$$

The only difference to the original target theorem (2) is that the ">" sign became a "$\geq$" sign. That is, the Gödel machine will change itself as soon as it has found a proof that the change will not make things worse. A Global Optimality Theorem similar to Theorem 1 holds; simply replace the last phrase in Theorem 1 by: *the utility of starting the execution of the present* switchprog *is at least as high as the utility of waiting for the proof searcher to produce an alternative* switchprog *later.*

4.2   Global Optimality and Recursive Meta-levels

One of the most important aspects of our fully self-referential set-up is the following. Any proof of a target theorem automatically proves that the corresponding self-modification is good for all further self-modifications affected by the present one, in recursive fashion. In that sense all possible "meta-levels" of the self-referential system are collapsed into one.

4.3   How Difficult Is It to Prove Target Theorems?

This depends on the tasks and the initial axioms $\mathcal{A}$, of course. It is straight-forward to devise simple tasks and corresponding consistent $\mathcal{A}$ such that there are short and trivial proofs of target theorems. On the other hand, it is possible to construct set-ups where it is impossible to prove target theorems, for example, by using results of undecidability theory, e.g., [30, 3, 4].

The point is: usually we do not know in advance whether it is possible or not to change a given initial problem solver in a provably good way. The traditional approach is to invest human research effort into finding out. A Gödel machine, however, can do this by itself, without essential limits apart from those of computability and provability.

Note that to prove a target theorem, a proof technique does not necessarily have to compute the true expected utilities of switching and not switching—it just needs to determine which is higher. For example, it may be easy to prove that speeding up a subroutine of the proof searcher by a factor of 2 will certainly be worth the negligible (compared to lifetime T) time needed to execute the subroutine-changing algorithm, no matter what is the precise utility of the switch.

5   Bias-Optimal Proof Search (BIOPS)

Here we construct a $p(1)$ that is $O()$-optimal in a certain limited sense to be described below, but still might be improved as it is not necessarily optimal in the sense of the given u (for example, the u of equation (1) neither mentions nor cares for $O()$-optimality). Our Bias-Optimal Proof Search (BIOPS) is essentially an application of Universal Search [23, 24] to proof search. One novelty, however, is this: Previous practical variants and extensions of Universal Search have been applied [36, 38, 49, 46] to *offline* program search tasks where the program inputs are fixed such that the same program always produces the same results. In our *online* setting, however, BIOPS has to take into account that the same proof technique started at different times may yield different proofs, as it may read parts of s (e.g., inputs) that change as the machine's life proceeds.

BIOPS starts with a probability distribution P (the initial bias) on the proof techniques w that one can write in $\mathcal{L}$, e.g., $P(w) = K^{-l(w)}$ for programs composed from K possible instructions [24]. BIOPS is *near-bias-optimal* [46] in the sense that it will not spend much more time on any proof technique than it deserves, according to its probabilistic bias, namely, not much more than its probability times the total search time:

Definition 1 (Bias-Optimal Searchers [46]). Let $\mathcal{R}$ be a problem class, $\mathcal{C}$ be a search space of solution candidates (where any problem $r \in \mathcal{R}$ should have a solution in $\mathcal{C}$), $P(q \mid r)$ be a task-dependent bias in the form of conditional probability distributions on the candidates $q \in \mathcal{C}$. Suppose that we also have a predefined procedure that creates and tests any given q on any $r \in \mathcal{R}$ within time $t(q, r)$ (typically unknown in advance). Then *a searcher is n-bias-optimal ($n \geq 1$) if for any maximal total search time $T_{total} > 0$ it is guaranteed to solve any problem $r \in \mathcal{R}$ if it has a solution $p \in \mathcal{C}$ satisfying $t(p, r) \leq P(p \mid r) T_{total}/n$. It is bias-optimal if $n = 1$.*

Method 51 (BIOPS) In phase $(i = 1, 2, 3, \ldots)$ Do: For all self-delimiting [24] proof techniques $w \in \mathcal{L}$ satisfying $P(w) \geq 2^{-i}$ Do:

1. Run w until halt or error (such as division by zero) or $2^i P(w)$ steps consumed.
2. Undo effects of w on s^p (does not cost significantly more time than executing w).

A proof technique w can interrupt Method 51 only by invoking instruction *check()* (Item 5), which may transfer control to *switchprog* (which possibly even will delete or rewrite Method 51). Since the initial p runs on the formalized hardware, and since proof techniques tested by p can read p and other parts of s, they can produce proofs concerning the (expected) performance of p and BIOPS itself. Method 51 at least has the optimal *order* of computational complexity in the following sense.

Theorem 2. *If independently of variable* time(s) *some unknown fast proof technique* w *would require at most* $f(k)$ *steps to produce a proof of difficulty measure* k *(an integer depending on the nature of the task to be solved), then Method 51 will need at most* $O(f(k))$ *steps.*

Proof. It is easy to see that Method 51 will need at most $O(f(k)/P(w)) = O(f(k))$ steps—the constant factor $1/P(w)$ does not depend on k. *Q.E.D.*

Note again, however, that the proofs themselves may concern quite different, arbitrary formalizable notions of optimality (stronger than those expressible in the $O()$-notation) embodied by the given, problem-specific, formalized utility function u. This may provoke useful, constant-affecting rewrites of the initial proof searcher despite its limited (yet popular and widely used) notion of $O()$-optimality.

6   Discussion and Additional Relations to Previous Work

Here we list a few examples of Gödel machine applicability to various tasks defined by various utility functions and environments (Section 6.1), and additional relations to previous work (Section 6.2). We also provide a list of answers to frequently asked questions (Section 6.3).

6.1   Example Applications

Traditional examples that do not involve significant interaction with a probabilistic environment are easily dealt with in our reward-based framework:

Example 1 (Time-limited NP-hard optimization). The initial input to the Gödel machine is the representation of a connected graph with a large number of nodes linked by edges of various lengths. Within given time T it should find a cyclic path connecting all nodes. The only real-valued reward will occur at time T. It equals 1 divided by the length of the best path found so far (0 if none was found). There are no other inputs. The by-product of maximizing expected reward is to find the shortest path findable within the limited time, given the initial bias.

Example 2 (Fast theorem proving). Prove or disprove as quickly as possible that all even integers > 2 are the sum of two primes (Goldbach's conjecture). The reward is $1/t$, where t is the time required to produce and verify the first such proof.

More general cases are:

Example 3 (Maximizing expected reward with bounded resources). A robot that needs at least 1 liter of gasoline per hour interacts with a partially unknown environment, trying to find hidden, limited gasoline depots to occasionally refuel its tank. It is rewarded in proportion to its lifetime, and dies after at most 100 years or as soon as its tank is empty or it falls off a cliff etc. The probabilistic environmental reactions are initially unknown but assumed to be sampled from the axiomatized Speed Prior [41], according to which hard-to-compute environmental reactions are unlikely. This permits a computable strategy for making near-optimal predictions [41]. One by-product of maximizing expected reward is to maximize expected lifetime.

Example 4 (Optimize any suboptimal problem solver). Given any formalizable problem, implement a suboptimal but known problem solver as software on the Gödel machine hardware, and let the proof searcher of Section 5 run in parallel.

6.2   More Relations to Previous, Less General Methods

Despite (or maybe because of) the ambitiousness and potential power of self-improving machines, there has been little work in this vein outside our own labs at IDSIA and TU Munich. Here we will list essential differences between the Gödel machine and our previous approaches to 'learning to learn,' 'metalearning,' self-improvement, self-optimization, etc.

1. **Gödel Machine vs Success-Story Algorithm and Other Metalearners**
   A learner's modifiable components are called its policy. An algorithm that modifies the policy is a learning algorithm. If the learning algorithm has modifiable components represented as part of the policy, then we speak of a self-modifying policy (SMP) [47]. SMPs can modify the way they modify themselves etc. The Gödel machine has an SMP.
   In previous work we used the *success-story algorithm* (SSA) to force some (stochastic) SMP to trigger better and better self-modifications [35, 48, 47, 49]. During the learner's life-time, SSA is occasionally called at times computed according to SMP itself. SSA uses backtracking to undo those SMP-generated SMP-modifications that have not been empirically observed to trigger lifelong reward accelerations (measured up until the current SSA call—this evaluates the long-term effects of SMP-modifications setting the stage for later SMP-modifications). SMP-modifications that survive SSA represent a lifelong success history. Until the next SSA call, they build the basis for additional SMP-modifications. Solely by self-modifications our SMP/SSA-based learners solved a complex task in a partially observable environment whose state space is far bigger than most found in the literature [47].
   The Gödel machine's training algorithm is theoretically much more powerful than SSA though. SSA empirically measures the usefulness of previous self-modifications, and does not necessarily encourage provably optimal ones. Similar drawbacks hold for Lenat's human-assisted, non-autonomous, self-modifying learner [22], our Meta-Genetic Programming [32] extending Cramer's Genetic Programming [7, 1], our metalearning economies [32] extending Holland's machine learning economies [14], and gradient-based metalearners for continuous program spaces of differentiable recurrent neural networks [34, 12]. All these methods, however, could be used to seed $p(1)$ with an initial policy.

2. **Gödel Machine vs Universal Search**
   Unlike the fully self-referential Gödel machine, Levin's *Universal Search* [23, 24] has a hardwired, unmodifiable meta-algorithm that cannot improve itself. It is asymptotically optimal for inversion problems whose solutions can be quickly verified in $O(n)$ time (where n is the solution size), but it will always suffer from the same huge constant slowdown factors (typically $>> 10^{1000}$) buried in the $O()$-notation. The self-improvements of a Gödel machine, however, can be more than merely $O()$-optimal, since its utility function may formalize a stonger type of optimality that

does not ignore huge constants just because they are constant—compare the utility function of equation (1). The next item points out additional limitations of Universal Search and its extensions.

3. **Gödel Machine vs** Oops

The Optimal Ordered Problem Solver Oops [46, 42] extends Universal Search. It is a bias-optimal (see Def. 1) way of searching for a program that solves each problem in an ordered sequence of problems of a rather general type, continually organizing and managing and reusing earlier acquired knowledge. Solomonoff recently also proposed related ideas for a *scientist's assistant* [53] that modifies the probability distribution of Universal Search [23] based on experience.

As pointed out earlier [46] (section on Oops limitations), however, neither Universal Search nor Oops-like methods are necessarily optimal for general lifelong reinforcement learning (RL) tasks [19] such as those for which Aixi [15] was designed. The simple and natural but limited optimality notion of Oops is *bias-optimality* (Def. 1): Oops is a near-bias-optimal searcher for programs which compute solutions that one can quickly verify (costs of verification are taken into account). For example, one can quickly test whether some currently tested program has computed a solution to the *towers of Hanoi* problem used in the earlier paper [46]: one just has to check whether the third peg is full of disks.

But general RL tasks are harder. Here in principle the evaluation of the value of some behavior consumes the learner's entire life! That is, the naive test of whether a program is good or not would consume the entire life. That is, we could test only one program; afterwards life would be over.

So general RL machines need a more general notion of optimality, and must do things that plain Oops does not do, such as predicting *future* tasks and rewards. A provably optimal RL machine must somehow *prove* properties of otherwise untestable behaviors (such as: what is the expected reward of this behavior which one cannot naively test as there is not enough time). That is part of what the Gödel machine does: it tries to greatly cut testing time, replacing naive time-consuming tests by much faster proofs of predictable test outcomes whenever this is possible. Proof verification itself can be performed very quickly. In particular, verifying the correctness of a found proof typically does not consume the remaining life. Hence the Gödel machine may use Oops as a bias-optimal proof-searching submodule. Since the proofs themselves may concern quite different, *arbitrary* notions of optimality (not just bias-optimality), the Gödel machine is more general than plain Oops. But it is not just an extension of Oops. Instead of Oops it may as well use non-bias-optimal alternative methods to initialize its proof searcher. On the other hand, Oops is not just a precursor of the Gödel machine. It is a stand-alone, incremental, bias-optimal way of allocating runtime to programs that reuse previously successful programs, and is applicable to many traditional problems, including but not limited to proof search.

4. **Gödel Machine vs** Aixi **etc.**

Unlike Gödel machines, Hutter's recent Aixi *model* [15, 18] generally needs *unlimited* computational resources per input update. It combines Solomonoff's universal prediction scheme [51, 52] with an *expectimax* computation. In discrete cycle

$k = 1, 2, 3, \ldots$, action $y(k)$ results in perception $x(k)$ and reward $r(k)$, both sampled from the unknown (reactive) environmental probability distribution μ. AIXI defines a mixture distribution ξ as a weighted sum of distributions $\nu \in \mathcal{M}$, where $\mathcal{M}$ is any class of distributions that includes the true environment μ. For example, $\mathcal{M}$ may be a sum of all computable distributions [51, 52], where the sum of the weights does not exceed 1. In cycle $k + 1$, AIXI selects as next action the first in an action sequence maximizing ξ-predicted reward up to some given horizon. Recent work [17] demonstrated AIXI 's optimal use of observations as follows. The Bayes-optimal policy p^ξ based on the mixture ξ is self-optimizing in the sense that its average utility value converges asymptotically for all $\mu \in \mathcal{M}$ to the optimal value achieved by the (infeasible) Bayes-optimal policy p^μ which knows μ in advance. The necessary condition that $\mathcal{M}$ admits self-optimizing policies is also sufficient. Furthermore, p^ξ is Pareto-optimal in the sense that there is no other policy yielding higher or equal value in *all* environments $\nu \in \mathcal{M}$ and a strictly higher value in at least one [17].

While AIXI clarifies certain theoretical limits of machine learning, it is computationally intractable, especially when $\mathcal{M}$ includes all computable distributions. This drawback motivated work on the time-bounded, asymptotically optimal AIXI*(t,l)* system [15] and the related HSEARCH [16], both already discussed in Section 2.4, which also lists the advantages of the Gödel machine. Both methods, however, could be used to seed the Gödel machine with an *initial* policy.

It is the *self-referential* aspects of the Gödel machine that relieve us of much of the burden of careful algorithm design required for AIXI*(t,l)* and HSEARCH. They make the Gödel machine both conceptually simpler *and* more general than AIXI*(t,l)* and HSEARCH.

6.3   Frequently Asked Questions

In the past year the author frequently fielded questions about the Gödel machine. Here a list of answers to typical ones.

1. **Q:** *Does the exact business of formal proof search really make sense in the uncertain real world?*
   A: Yes, it does. We just need to insert into $p(1)$ the standard axioms for representing uncertainty and for dealing with probabilistic settings and expected rewards etc. Compare items 1d and 1c in Section 3.1, and the definition of utility as an *expected* value in equation (1).

2. **Q:** *The target theorem (2) seems to refer only to the* very first *self-change, which may completely rewrite the proof-search subroutine—doesn't this make the proof of Theorem 1 invalid? What prevents later self-changes from being destructive?*
   A: This is fully taken care of. Please have a look once more at the proof of Theorem 1, and note that the first self-change will be executed only if it is provably useful (in the sense of the present untility function u) for all future self-changes (for which the present self-change is setting the stage). This is actually the main point of the whole Gödel machine set-up.

3. **Q** (related to the previous item): *The Gödel machine implements a meta-learning behavior: what about a meta-meta, and a meta-meta-meta level?*

A: The beautiful thing is that all meta-levels are automatically collapsed into one: any proof of a target theorem automatically proves that the corresponding self-modification is good for all further self-modifications affected by the present one, in recursive fashion. Recall Section 4.2.

4. **Q:** *The Gödel machine software can produce only computable mappings from input sequences to output sequences. What if the environment is non-computable?*

   A: Many physicists and other scientists (exceptions: [57, 37]) actually do assume the real world makes use of all the real numbers, most of which are incomputable. Nevertheless, theorems and proofs are just finite symbol strings, and all treatises of physics contain only computable axioms and theorems, even when some of the theorems can be interpreted as making statements about uncountably many objects, such as all the real numbers. (Note though that the Löwenheim-Skolem Theorem [26, 50] implies that any first order theory with an uncountable model such as the real numbers also has a countable model.) Generally speaking, formal descriptions of non-computable objects do *not at all* present a fundamental problem—they may still allow for finding a strategy that provably maximizes utility. If so, a Gödel machine can exploit this. If not, then humans will not have a fundamental advantage over Gödel machines.

5. **Q:** *Isn't automated theorem-proving very hard? Current AI systems cannot prove nontrivial theorems without human intervention at crucial decision points.*

   A: More and more important mathematical proofs (four color theorem etc) heavily depend on automated proof search. And traditional theorem provers do not even make use of our novel notions of proof techniques and $O()$-optimal proof search. Of course, some proofs are indeed hard to find, but here humans and Gödel machines face the same fundamental limitations.

6. **Q:** *Don't the "no free lunch theorems" [56] say that it is impossible to construct universal problem solvers?*

   A: No, they do not. They refer to the very special case of problems sampled from *i.i.d.* uniform distributions on *finite* problem spaces. See the discussion of no free lunch theorems in an earlier paper [46].

7. **Q:** *Can't the Gödel machine switch to a program* switchprog *that rewrites the utility function to a "bogus" utility function that makes unfounded promises of big rewards in the near future?*

   A: No, it cannot. It should be obvious that rewrites of the utility function can happen only if the Gödel machine first can prove that the rewrite is useful according to the *present* utility function.

8. **Q:** *Aren't there problems with undecidability? For example, doesn't Rice's theorem [30] or Blum's speed-up theorem [3, 4] pose problems?*

   A: Not at all. Of course, the Gödel machine cannot profit from a hypothetical useful self-improvement whose utility is undecidable, and will therefore simply ignore it. Compare Section 2.5 on fundamental limitations of Gödel machines (and humans, for that matter). Nevertheless, unlike previous methods, a Gödel machine can in principle exploit at least the provably good improvements and speed-ups of *any* part of its initial software.

7   Conclusion

In 1931, Kurt Gödel used elementary arithmetics to build a universal programming language for encoding arbitrary proofs, given an arbitrary enumerable set of axioms. He went on to construct *self-referential* formal statements that claim their own unprovability, using Cantor's diagonalization trick [5] to demonstrate that formal systems such as traditional mathematics are either flawed in a certain sense or contain unprovable but true statements [10]. Since Gödel's exhibition of the fundamental limits of proof and computation, and Konrad Zuse's subsequent construction of the first working programmable computer (1935-1941), there has been a lot of work on specialized algorithms solving problems taken from more or less general problem classes. Apparently, however, one remarkable fact has so far escaped the attention of computer scientists: it is possible to use self-referential proof systems to build optimally efficient yet conceptually very simple universal problem solvers.

The initial software $p(1)$ of our machine runs an initial problem solver, e.g., one of Hutter's approaches [15, 16] which have at least an optimal *order* of complexity, or some less general method. Simultaneously, it runs an $O()$-optimal initial proof searcher using an online variant of Universal Search to test *proof techniques*, which are programs able to compute proofs concerning the system's own future performance, based on an axiomatic system $\mathcal{A}$ encoded in $p(1)$, describing a formal *utility* function u, the hardware and $p(1)$ itself. If there is no provably good, globally optimal way of rewriting $p(1)$ at all, then humans will not find one either. But if there is one, then $p(1)$ itself can find and exploit it. This approach yields the first class of theoretically sound, fully self-referential, optimally efficient, general problem solvers.

If we equate the notion of "consciousness" with the ability to execute unlimited formal self-inspection and provably useful self-change (unlimited except for the limits of computability and provability), then the Gödel machine and its Global Optimality Theorem 1 do provide the first technical justification of consciousness in the context of general problem solving [29].

References

1. W. Banzhaf, P. Nordin, R. E. Keller, and F. D. Francone. *Genetic Programming – An Introduction*. Morgan Kaufmann Publishers, San Francisco, CA, USA, 1998.
2. R. Bellman. *Adaptive Control Processes*. Princeton University Press, 1961.
3. M. Blum. A machine-independent theory of the complexity of recursive functions. *Journal of the ACM*, 14(2):322–336, 1967.
4. M. Blum. On effective procedures for speeding up algorithms. *Journal of the ACM*, 18(2):290–305, 1971.
5. G. Cantor. Über eine Eigenschaft des Inbegriffes aller reellen algebraischen Zahlen. *Crelle's Journal für Mathematik*, 77:258–263, 1874.
6. W.F. Clocksin and C.S. Mellish. *Programming in Prolog (3rd ed.)*. Springer-Verlag, 1987.
7. N. L. Cramer. A representation for the adaptive generation of simple sequential programs. In J.J. Grefenstette, editor, *Proceedings of an International Conference on Genetic Algorithms and Their Applications, Carnegie-Mellon University, July 24-26, 1985*, Hillsdale NJ, 1985. Lawrence Erlbaum Associates.
8. F. Crick and C. Koch. Consciousness and neuroscience. *Cerebral Cortex*, 8:97–107, 1998.

9. M. C. Fitting. *First-Order Logic and Automated Theorem Proving*. Graduate Texts in Computer Science. Springer-Verlag, Berlin, 2nd edition, 1996.

10. K. Gödel. Über formal unentscheidbare Sätze der Principia Mathematica und verwandter Systeme I. *Monatshefte für Mathematik und Physik*, 38:173–198, 1931.

11. W. Heisenberg. Über den anschaulichen Inhalt der quantentheoretischen Kinematik und Mechanik. *Zeitschrift für Physik*, 33:879–893, 1925.

12. S. Hochreiter, A. S. Younger, and P. R. Conwell. Learning to learn using gradient descent. In *Lecture Notes on Comp. Sci. 2130, Proc. Intl. Conf. on Artificial Neural Networks (ICANN-2001)*, pages 87–94. Springer: Berlin, Heidelberg, 2001.

13. D. R. Hofstadter. *Gödel, Escher, Bach: an Eternal Golden Braid*. Basic Books, 1979.

14. J. H. Holland. Properties of the bucket brigade. In *Proceedings of an International Conference on Genetic Algorithms*. Lawrence Erlbaum, Hillsdale, NJ, 1985.

15. M. Hutter. Towards a universal theory of artificial intelligence based on algorithmic probability and sequential decisions. *Proceedings of the 12th European Conference on Machine Learning (ECML-2001)*, pages 226–238, 2001. (On J. Schmidhuber's SNF grant 20-61847).

16. M. Hutter. The fastest and shortest algorithm for all well-defined problems. *International Journal of Foundations of Computer Science*, 13(3):431–443, 2002. (On J. Schmidhuber's SNF grant 20-61847).

17. M. Hutter. Self-optimizing and Pareto-optimal policies in general environments based on Bayes-mixtures. In J. Kivinen and R. H. Sloan, editors, *Proceedings of the 15th Annual Conference on Computational Learning Theory (COLT 2002)*, Lecture Notes in Artificial Intelligence, pages 364–379, Sydney, Australia, 2002. Springer. (On J. Schmidhuber's SNF grant 20-61847).

18. M. Hutter. *Universal Artificial Intelligence: Sequential Decisions based on Algorithmic Probability*. Springer, Berlin, 2004. (On J. Schmidhuber's SNF grant 20-61847).

19. L.P. Kaelbling, M.L. Littman, and A.W. Moore. Reinforcement learning: a survey. *Journal of AI research*, 4:237–285, 1996.

20. A. N. Kolmogorov. *Grundbegriffe der Wahrscheinlichkeitsrechnung*. Springer, Berlin, 1933.

21. A.N. Kolmogorov. Three approaches to the quantitative definition of information. *Problems of Information Transmission*, 1:1–11, 1965.

22. D. Lenat. Theory formation by heuristic search. *Machine Learning*, 21, 1983.

23. L. A. Levin. Universal sequential search problems. *Problems of Information Transmission*, 9(3):265–266, 1973.

24. L. A. Levin. Randomness conservation inequalities: Information and independence in mathematical theories. *Information and Control*, 61:15–37, 1984.

25. M. Li and P. M. B. Vitányi. *An Introduction to Kolmogorov Complexity and its Applications (2nd edition)*. Springer, 1997.

26. L. Löwenheim. Über Möglichkeiten im Relativkalkül. *Mathematische Annalen*, 76:447–470, 1915.

27. C. H. Moore and G. C. Leach. FORTH - a language for interactive computing, 1970.

28. R. Penrose. *Shadows of the mind*. Oxford University Press, 1994.

29. K. R. Popper. *All Life Is Problem Solving*. Routledge, London, 1999.

30. H. G. Rice. Classes of recursively enumerable sets and their decision problems. *Trans. Amer. Math. Soc.*, 74:358–366, 1953.

31. A. L. Samuel. Some studies in machine learning using the game of checkers. *IBM Journal on Research and Development*, 3:210–229, 1959.

32. J. Schmidhuber. Evolutionary principles in self-referential learning. Diploma thesis, Institut für Informatik, Technische Universität München, 1987.

33. J. Schmidhuber. Reinforcement learning in Markovian and non-Markovian environments. In D. S. Lippman, J. E. Moody, and D. S. Touretzky, editors, *Advances in Neural Information Processing Systems 3 (NIPS 3)*, pages 500–506. Morgan Kaufmann, 1991.

34. J. Schmidhuber. A self-referential weight matrix. In *Proceedings of the International Conference on Artificial Neural Networks, Amsterdam*, pages 446–451. Springer, 1993.

35. J. Schmidhuber. On learning how to learn learning strategies. Technical Report FKI-198-94, Fakultät für Informatik, Technische Universität München, 1994. See [49, 47].

36. J. Schmidhuber. Discovering solutions with low Kolmogorov complexity and high generalization capability. In A. Prieditis and S. Russell, editors, *Machine Learning: Proceedings of the Twelfth International Conference*, pages 488–496. Morgan Kaufmann Publishers, San Francisco, CA, 1995.

37. J. Schmidhuber. A computer scientist's view of life, the universe, and everything. In C. Freksa, M. Jantzen, and R. Valk, editors, *Foundations of Computer Science: Potential - Theory - Cognition*, volume 1337, pages 201–208. Lecture Notes in Computer Science, Springer, Berlin, 1997.

38. J. Schmidhuber. Discovering neural nets with low Kolmogorov complexity and high generalization capability. *Neural Networks*, 10(5):857–873, 1997.

39. J. Schmidhuber. Algorithmic theories of everything. Technical Report IDSIA-20-00, quant-ph/0011122, IDSIA, Manno (Lugano), Switzerland, 2000. Sections 1-5: see [40]; Section 6: see [41].

40. J. Schmidhuber. Hierarchies of generalized Kolmogorov complexities and nonenumerable universal measures computable in the limit. *International Journal of Foundations of Computer Science*, 13(4):587–612, 2002.

41. J. Schmidhuber. The Speed Prior: a new simplicity measure yielding near-optimal computable predictions. In J. Kivinen and R. H. Sloan, editors, *Proceedings of the 15th Annual Conference on Computational Learning Theory (COLT 2002)*, Lecture Notes in Artificial Intelligence, pages 216–228. Springer, Sydney, Australia, 2002.

42. J. Schmidhuber. Bias-optimal incremental problem solving. In S. Becker, S. Thrun, and K. Obermayer, editors, *Advances in Neural Information Processing Systems 15 (NIPS 15)*, pages 1571–1578, Cambridge, MA, 2003. MIT Press.

43. J. Schmidhuber. Gödel machines: self-referential universal problem solvers making provably optimal self-improvements. Technical Report IDSIA-19-03, arXiv:cs.LO/0309048, IDSIA, Manno-Lugano, Switzerland, 2003.

44. J. Schmidhuber. Gödel machine home page, with frequently asked questions, 2004. http://www.idsia.ch/~juergen/goedelmachine.html.

45. J. Schmidhuber. Gödel machines: Fully self-referential optimal universal self-improvers. In B. Goertzel and C. Pennachin, editors, *Real AI: New Approaches to Artificial General Intelligence*. Springer, in press, 2004.

46. J. Schmidhuber. Optimal ordered problem solver. *Machine Learning*, 54:211–254, 2004.

47. J. Schmidhuber, J. Zhao, and N. Schraudolph. Reinforcement learning with self-modifying policies. In S. Thrun and L. Pratt, editors, *Learning to learn*, pages 293–309. Kluwer, 1997.

48. J. Schmidhuber, J. Zhao, and M. Wiering. Simple principles of metalearning. Technical Report IDSIA-69-96, IDSIA, 1996. See [49, 47].

49. J. Schmidhuber, J. Zhao, and M. Wiering. Shifting inductive bias with success-story algorithm, adaptive Levin search, and incremental self-improvement. *Machine Learning*, 28:105–130, 1997.

50. T. Skolem. Logisch-kombinatorische Untersuchungen über Erfüllbarkeit oder Beweisbarkeit mathematischer Sätze nebst einem Theorem über dichte Mengen. *Skrifter utgit av Videnskapsselskapet in Kristiania, I, Mat.-Nat. Kl.*, N4:1–36, 1919.

51. R.J. Solomonoff. A formal theory of inductive inference. Part I. *Information and Control*, 7:1–22, 1964.

52. R.J. Solomonoff. Complexity-based induction systems. *IEEE Transactions on Information Theory*, IT-24(5):422–432, 1978.

53. R.J. Solomonoff. Progress in incremental machine learning—Preliminary Report for NIPS 2002 Workshop on Universal Learners and Optimal Search; revised Sept 2003. Technical Report IDSIA-16-03, IDSIA, Lugano, 2003.
54. R. Sutton and A. Barto. *Reinforcement learning: An introduction.* Cambridge, MA, MIT Press, 1998.
55. A. M. Turing. On computable numbers, with an application to the Entscheidungsproblem. *Proceedings of the London Mathematical Society, Series 2,* 41:230–267, 1936.
56. D. H. Wolpert and W. G. Macready. No free lunch theorems for search. *IEEE Transactions on Evolutionary Computation,* 1, 1997.
57. K. Zuse. *Rechnender Raum.* Friedrich Vieweg & Sohn, Braunschweig, 1969. English translation: *Calculating Space,* MIT Technical Translation AZT-70-164-GEMIT, Massachusetts Institute of Technology (Proj. MAC), Cambridge, Mass. 02139, Feb. 1970.

Postext – A Mind for Society

Avishalom Shalit[1], Tom Erez[2,*], Anna Deters[3], Uri Hershberg[4],
Eran Shir[5], and Sorin Solomon[1,2,**]

[1] Hebrew University, Jerusalem, Israel
[2] Multi-Agent Division, ISI, Torino, Italy
[3] English Dept., Illinois Wesleyan University, Bloomington IL, USA
[4] Immunology Dept., Yale Medical School, New Haven CT, USA
[5] Electrical Engineering, Tel-Aviv University, Israel

Abstract. We present Postext (pronounced POS-TEH) - a platform for
collective thinking. This generic system was originally created in order to
assist the community of complexity research to self-organize (the system
is operative and can be found at `http://complexity.huji.ac.il`). In
this paper we describe the basic philosophical ideas that promoted its
creation, and the circumstances of its specific application to the complexity community.

1 Thoughts, Words and Context

Communication is an act of framing - by choosing what will be said, one excludes
an infinite amount of information, leaving it to be inferred by the receiving side.
Much like foreground and background in visual perception, a message communicated is dependent on the context in which it is embedded. Most of the context
is built into the language we use to express it. Yet, if we understand the language
(sometimes, in the case of scientific discourse, a language full of specialized words
and jargon), we often become blind to the extent in which this contextual frame
qualifies the entire message. This is no secret to computer scientists, who have
been struggling with natural language processing for decades.

One could say that context is "the stuff meaning is made of". Thoughts are
also an object of pure context. They are never abstract - You always think of
something, a certain object. However, as the Psychology theorist William James
pointed out[1], that object is hard to corner. When we try, it fades into the
interconnected concepts, precepts, and sensory inputs that brought it on. We
try to grasp the thought by putting it into words, but usually the most we can
hope for is 'the crumbs that fall from the feast'. This is mainly because one
cannot hope to communicate the entire contextual scope of every thought.

In the realm of linguistics, similar ideas were advanced by Postmodern thinkers
like Jacques Derrida[2]. According to this view, a word derives meaning not from

---

* Corresponding Author. Email: `erez@isiosf.isi.it`
** The research of S. Solomon was supported in part by a grant from the Israeli Science
Foundation.

D. Kudenko et al. (Eds.): Adaptive Agents and MAS II, LNAI 3394, pp. 24–40, 2005.

its own innate value, but rather from all the other words than can be linked to it. Comprehension and ultimate understanding result from this associative power of language, the ability to summon the correct context to support the words back into coherent ideas. A concept, like a word, derives meaning, and especially purpose, from the all the other concepts in relation to it.

The first stage of the elementary writing process exemplifies a natural pattern of thought. In elementary school, children are taught to compose an essay by "clustering" associations, a procedure which usually consists of writing an idea in a bubble and then drawing lines to additional bubbles of supportive or related ideas. The thoughts and connections should be complete before the actual writing starts.

The challenge of expressing and communicating reality was exposed in all its difficulty in Umberto Eco's book "In the Search for the Perfect Language" [3]. Notwithstanding Lao-Tzu's "that which can be named is not Tao", one is forced to accept that in practice, the fundamental and primordial act of "conscious" cognition is one of discretization - an infinite (of continuous cardinality) world is projected into a finite set of categories, which eventually crystallize in our minds into concepts, and cast into words. This is probably unavoidable to all but the true Zen masters.

2   The "Classic" Text

The main characteristic of written language is its unavoidable linearity of structure. Elementary-school children, after depicting their thoughts in a graph structure, are instructed to fit their clustered ideas into the linear form of text. This linearity imposes severe restriction on the representation of ideas. Freezing ideas in their tracks, we dissipate the flow that gives them substance, creating in essence a sequence of one-dimensional snapshots of a multi-dimensional object. Thus, the challenge to the reader is often similar to the challenge of the six blind men in the Maharaja's palace[5], trying to reconstruct the concept of an elephant, after each touched a different part and got the impression that it is, respectively, like a snake, a wall, a spear, a tree, a rope, and a large wing.

Academic writing is riddled with transitional phrasing implying causality, e.g., "thus", "therefore", "due to". Linearity forces the purpose of the text to be that of an argument, as conclusions can only be drawn from inferences in a logical sequence. Furthermore, the concepts addressed by the text are limited by the thesis of the argument, its narrative. Any concept or bit of information that is not wholly supportive of the immediate thesis is weeded out, leaving a vast number of related aspects on the cutting room floor. These floating snippets, albeit mere tangents to the "point" of the text, are often valuable. In science and academia, where knowledge is the goal, not politicised argumentation, these snippets should not have to be removed.

Fig. 1. A Talmud Page. Note the division of each page in fixed threads that flow (interactively) along the entire opus (approx. 63 volumes)

The Jewish Talmud was one of the first attempts to transcend the problems of text linearity. The solution was to present a stenographic elliptic statement of the main facts in the centre of the page; written around it were various "sub"-texts providing commentary, interpretation, and suggestions of other aspects of the main point - in short, a supply of context (Fig. 1). This style of textual presentation makes additional information available for reading *from within* the original document, like footnotes. This induces mutual context, with the original text suggesting a certain reading of the commentary, and the commentary suggesting a certain reading of the text.

In currently standard scientific texts, the very connection to their multidimensional intellectual neighbourhood is linearized (and laminated) in "the bibliography". This is typically a list of references, where connections to external texts are stacked, as an afterthought, following the actual end of the opus. This list, trailing the text, attempts to fulfil the need for related knowledge or concepts that were left out of the main body, for being only loosely related to the main argument of the text. Usually references serve as a token of authority, exempting the author from tedious elaborations required to back up a certain point. They may also serve as a collection of related works, a set of suggestions for the interested reader who seeks elaboration and extensive context. Unfortunately, bibliography lists stop short of actually making the referenced material available, and so fail to meet their own goal. No wonder that fully referenced material is typical only for professional publications, targeting a very learned audience.

There is no textual structure that can accommodate all the context of a statement. Footnoting and subsectioning are but feeble, incomplete solutions. To avoid confusion, annoyance, and vulgarity, they must be incorporated with caution. Furthermore, the physical confines of the printed page prevent any attempt at presenting a comprehensive network of knowledge.

Providing "complete" context within a printed document is not only impossible but would be counterproductive too. The main concept needs a context; but once the context is supplied, the main idea becomes just one line out of many in the page. We run the risk of losing the diamond in a lingo of gold (rather then exposing it in a fine gold monture). The main idea drowns in the context provided to situate it, lost in the multitude of words that sophisticate it.

The structure of narrative prevents the inclusion of concepts that do not fit into its predestined linearity. An attempt must be made to fully account for as much knowledge as possible, embracing the potential for full implication to exist. Such an attempt would call for a radical new conceptualisation of the cohesiveness of text.

3   From Hypertext to Networks

In recent years, networks have become a prominent object of research across many disciplines. From gene regulation to sexual partnerships, it seems like everything is being analysed from this perspective. And indeed, studying the underlying network of social and natural phenomena has proven to be a powerful new way of looking at things.

However, working with networks is still a challenge. A static representation of a large network is often too dense to be easily perceived, especially if the system is heavily connected. Recently, a dynamic and interactive approach to network representation is making great advance, and new tools, such as the "Visual thesaurus" (http://www.visualthesaurus.com/), or the "Touchgraph Google browser" (http://www.touchgraph.com/TGGoogleBrowser.html), are suggesting new and exciting perspectives on the world of information.

As of now, the most ambitious attempt to solve the problems of textual linearity is Hypertext, an alternative founded upon the tenets of Postmodern linguistics. Independently of its common use in the World Wide Web (WWW), Hypertext has been explored as a new medium for literature. Literary pieces in Hypertext, like Geoff Ryman's novel 253 (http://www.ryman-novel.com/), resist closure both in structure and purpose - many links lead to redundancy or dead ends, and all stem from primary branches, which in turn stem from the trunk, or main body of text. In this way, Hypertext attempts to upgrade the text from a line to a network.

Yet, when browsing in Hypertext, one can only experience it at every moment as a tree; a quasi-linear system of pages, with single paths extended and withdrawn. Although we may navigate in a network of links, and even with the aid of the standard "Back" and "Forward" buttons, we still explore only one branch at a time.

Even more problematic is the sensation of disorientation, inherent to this method of traversal. Like driving in Jerusalem without a map, the "reader" will soon get lost in the plethora of splitting paths and overwhelmed by the multitude of histories (and browser windows). Backtracking is often used as a simplification, at the price of losing the backtracked trails, often resulting in further disorientation. Indeed, Hypertext provokes a battle between the viewer and the seemingly limitless number of paths and uncharted (or already frustratingly charted) territory.

Without a sense of "location" in context, the viewer is lost in a sea of unconnected references - although the pages are linked, once the link has been selected, its relationship to previous pages exists only in the memory of the viewer. The navigation (attempted, but impossible) of this endless maze often leads to frustration and ultimately hostility towards the system.

We believe that the network of ideas that underlies every concept should be represented explicitly. What we conceive is a network whose nodes are items of information. These can take any form, be it an equation, a paragraph or a movie. Browsing through its elements, a map of the neighbourhood of the current item is always in view, providing context and facilitating orientation. There is no longer a main body of text, only pieces of information linked in a web of connections. Yet, a coherent picture may naturally emerge in the mind of the "reader", due to the graphic representation of the relationships between the ideas.

In such a setting, ideas are freed from the constraint of linearity, and may relate to each other to form a complex web of interrelated ideas. Such a platform could be nearer in spirit to the true form of human thought, much more so than a logically structured argument. At the same time, the "reader" can maintain orientation in this web of ideas, thanks to the dynamic map that keeps track of his/her wandering, providing the context for every element. Furthermore, such a setting may be extended to allow "readers" to personalize, in an interactive way, the information space, by allowing them to leave marks in the places they visited, or even to extend and contribute to their contents, their connections and their setting.

As soon as information items are allowed to arrange in a graph, richer dynamics may emerge. For instance, the ubiquitous role of transitive connections (diagonal links) in the emergence of creative ideas, new products and story unfolding has been systematically substantiated in a series of quantitative measurements, which could be considered as precursors of the present scheme[6, 7, 8].

4   From Co-authorship to Communal Authorship

Another limitation imposed by "classic" text is the fixedness of printed literature. Books may be revised at later editions and corrections may be published for articles, but these are inefficient exceptions that do little to maintain the relevancy of the text. In the general case, the linear text is frozen forever upon completion. Thus fossilized, the text is unable to undergo significant evolution, in order to remain a living and useful product. This is especially problematic when accounting for academic and scientific material, which can be quickly rendered "out-of-date" by new knowledge.

Paradoxically, irrelevancy is guaranteed especially for those rare occasions of true scientific breakthrough - by definition, groundbreaking ideas generate a new intellectual or factual context that often contradicts previously established modes of thought. After the paradigm shift takes place in practice, the text finds itself outside its original context; surrounded by the ideas it spawned, yet alien to them, since it was composed in another context.

Scientific collaboration (including often very many authors) has become commonplace in the academia, and this has its obvious benefits. However, articles that report such collaborative work are usually co-authored. The need to establish consensus with your co-authors is a challenging task, and one often finds it necessary to compromise. This may not be without consequences - compromises accepted in expressing a reality might compromise the reality of the expression. Moreover, compromise and consensus yields conformity and the exclusion of disputed ideas. Such exclusion, as already mentioned, stunts conceptual growth and limits the spread of knowledge.

Recently, a new form of "massive co-authorship" has gathered popularity - certain websites allow all visitors to take active part in creating the content. Ward Cunnigham devised this approach of *open content* in 1995, when he created the "WikiWikiWeb" (http://c2.com/cgi/wiki); today there are thousands of web pages running some sort of Wiki. One direction in which Wiki has developed is the web logs (blogs) and live journals, where visitors may broadcast whatever message they find relevant. This type of site allows for the emergence of a community around it, where people may converse with other people of shared interests, and the entire community accepts responsibility for the relevancy of its site. Of course, relevancy is a relative term, and so its definition is the site's main characteristic - like foreground and background, an infinite amount of potential news are necessarily excluded. Dialogues exist in a well-defined frame of time and mind. The time frame imposes linearity, while the connection of minds between the speakers makes the it dependent on a large volume of perishable context (which exists only momentarily within the minds of the conversers, and so is implicit to the words actually uttered in the unraveling of the dialogue). while this is beneficial for the transfer of knowledge from one individual to the other, it becomes a liability for a perennial durable repository of information.

At the other end of the Wiki spectrum there are visitor-compounded information repositories, such as Wikipedia (http://www.wikipedia.org). In that case, the distributed effort put in by tens of thousands of people from around the world created an online encyclopaedia that contains over 300,000 entries.

The open content paradigm (behind the Wiki ideas) stems from the belief that when releasing the constraints, the system will reach a dynamic equilibrium, rather than mayhem. In practice, open content proves to be very stable in terms of resilience to malicious activity. The community that congregates around these projects has more motivation and more resources to maintain it in good form, than occasional mischievous passer-by would have to damage.

Nevertheless, a major shortcoming of Wiki should be pointed out: a Wiki text is bound to reach a certain equilibrium. This may be the result of a consensus in the participating community, in cases where the subject is not controversial and the community is small enough. In certain cases a dialog may unravel, stemming from a minimal point of agreement. However, in cases of collaboration on larger scale (such as Wikipedia), equilibrium is often reached by means of compromise. Equilibrium is a necessity imposed by the openness of the system: the "edit all" option of Wiki enables an entire community to work together on the same pieces of information, but at the same time it forces the co-authors into compromising their ideas in search of a universally acceptable common denominator.

Thus, Wiki is extremely efficient in creating consensus virtual societies, but it might be less efficient in supporting dissent and revolution within the participating community itself. We must remember that alignment to equilibrium does not equal ongoing Self-Organization, in the same sense that crystallization does not equal (and in fact excludes) complexity emergence. Wikipedia, The last cry of encyclopaedism, shows the inherent problem to the vision of the encyclopaedists: the total sum of human knowledge simply cannot be assembled into a coherent opus, as it necessarily contains contradictions. These cannot fit in a unified encyclopaedia, but without contradictions the encyclopaedia (as in Gödel's theorem[9]) is incomplete. Therefore, an alternative container for the aggregation of human knowledge should be sought.

5   Postext – A Platform for the Mind of Society

The platform we suggest is an open content, network-oriented information repository, which we call "Post-text", or Postext in short. It is a distributed system of information items, (self-)organized in a network, created and updated by its authoring community.

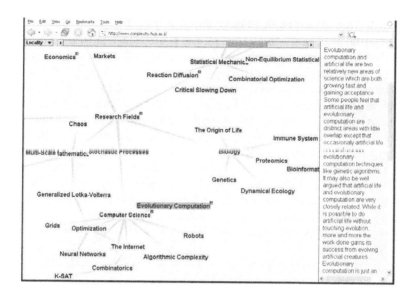

Fig. 2. A Screenshot of Postext. The system is focused on the "Evolutionary Computation" post. The left side presents part of the graph that is the neighbourhood of that post, and the right side is (part of) the content of that node

The basic element in Postext is called a "post". It is basically a web page, and so it may contain any type of content (text, figures, movies, equations and so forth). As any web page, the post may contain links to other posts, to downloadable files, or to sites outside Postext. In accordance with the open-content paradigm, posts act as wiki pages - any user may post a new post, or edit the content of existing ones. The Postext system provides the user with a simple interface to create the post, by using techniques inherited from wiki: the content of the page is written as plain text, and the system intelligently deciphers the authors' intentions with regard to the formatting of the page (i.e. transforming named URLs and named posts into hyperlinks, while rendering named images). This is a key point in making the Postext accessible for easy shaping by the entire community. Using the same interface, users can edit existing content as well.

The difference between a post and a regular web page lies in the embedding of the post into the Postext network. In Postext, the network of linked posts is not underlying - it is ever present and under user control. The Postext screen is split in two - the right pane presents the content of the presently selected post, while the left pane presents the post as one node in a graph. This graph shows a small part of the Postext network, the posts as nodes, with edges connecting them to represent a link between the posts. The graph pane shows the neighbourhood of the active post at a certain radius - for example, if the user chooses to see the neighbourhood of radius one, then all the posts that link to the present one or are linked from it will be visible. a radius of two will show the second order neighbours as well, and so forth (Fig. 2).

The creation, visualization and manipulation of the graph data is realized by an open-content graphic engine called "Touchgraph" (http://www.touchgraph.com). The graph is laid out in a way which assures maximum visibility of the nodes, yet maintains the relationships imposed by the links. This is done by simulating a "mechanical system" in which the nodes are subjected to "forces": to ensure the spread, the nodes repel each other, and to enforce the relations, the links act as rubber bands, bringing linked nodes closer together. In order to generate a view of the graph, the nodes are placed in space, and the mechanical system moves realistically across the screen until a dynamic equilibrium of nodes' positions is reached. When the user interacts with the system, the forces of repulsion/attraction are recalculated according to the changes he introduced, and the nodes are freed to accelerate and move around as dictated by the forces. The result resembles a structure of springs and weights, accommodating the pressures set upon it by the structure of the graph and by the demands of the user.

Users may operate on the network, by adding and removing posts and links between posts. Properties of the presented graph can also be changed - the user can hide a node or a link from view. More subtle manipulations to the graph representation are also possible - nodes can be dragged and repositioned. Every such change would affect the entire graph on display, because the applied forces that determine the view will have changed.

The visual presence of the map serves two main causes: the map orientates the reader, and the neighbourhood nodes provide context for the current node. Thus, the node itself may be presented "at net value", without wasting words on introductions.

The difference between the Postext web and the WWW should be stressed: the fact that the underlying network is visually available dramatically changes the user's experience. Moreover the inclusion of a new post is a much lighter task (technically and conceptually) then initiating a new WWW page. In fact our experiments show that the WWW cannot be cast trivially into a Postext format. When one attempts a machine-based projection of a system of WWW sites into a Postext, the resulting network is often too dense, and the nonsense picture it suggests fails to provide the user with the desired orientation. This can be fixed by an informed editor, who may use his/her understanding about the conceptual content of these sites to manually modify the network, and render it comprehensible; in fact, this is quite an easy task. However, the intervention of a human mind seems irreplaceable, because the redundancy in the regular WWW structure, the overlap between pages, and the presence of links of less relevance, pose a challenge that can only be answered by true comprehension of the knowledge represented in these sites. This, we believe, is beyond current abilities in artificial intelligence. This is why we believe Postext can only be

generated and maintained by an entire community of involved authors as a sum
of the projections of all users' idiosyncratic opinions and ideas.

Every post can also serve as a "place", where interaction between members of
the community may take place. Every post, apart from its content, may contain
"discourses": like forums or chat rooms, a discourse is a container of conversations. The discourse in a certain post would naturally concern itself with the
content of that post, and with the context found in the neighbouring posts.
Thus, discourses may split, or migrate from post to post, according to the subject. Discourses might mature into an independent post, and ideas spawned by
the discourse may find their way to the content of neighbouring posts. Content
posts and relevant discourses are linked on the Postext map, yet exist as separate entities, due to their diverse nature: discourses are an essentially temporal
experience of the participants, embedded in a specific mind- and time-frame,
while content posts are in nature a more perennial information repository.

Furthermore, the authors themselves are represented as posts in the system,
and links connect an author with the posts to which s/he had contributed. This
subtle alteration introduces a meaningful modification of the topology. It brings
closer together items that have the same author, and authors that share a similar
area of interest (note how the spatial meaning of the word "area" is well-defined
in Postext). There is no essential difference between a "content" post and an
"ego" post. As in the "content" posts, the context in which each author re-
sides defines his/her place in the network, and vice versa - the (identities of the)
contributors to a subject become part of its context.

Filters may be applied to the graph view, to project certain aspects of the Postext. The links that represent contribution maybe filtered on a temporal basis,
or the nodes representing authors may be hidden altogether. The entire system
can be searched, and a mechanism of personal bookmarks exists to facilitate
navigation.

So, for example, filtering the results to show contributions in the past 24
hours, will show the hottest topics, and the most prolific authors in the past day.
But the picture that emerges is much more informative than the "top ten list".
The combined picture of authors that took part in the changes to a post within
a limited time frame implies that the authors were engaged in a conversation.
Conversely, an author that made a contribution to several subjects in a limited
time frame must have had them all on his/her mind simultaneously. This not only
elucidates the active interests of the author better than any autobiographical
notes could, but illustrates a contemporary picture, detailing the mind of the
community, and the 'thoughts' that occupy it. In fact, the deformations induced
in Postext by the "active browsing" of a notable individual contain valuable
information, and may be made available to other interested users (his/her pupils,
disciples, followers).

The challenge faced by Wikis, of adherence to a consensus, is transcended
when ideas are merely placed in a network. In a graph, complementary, orthog-

onal, alternative or opposite views may be expressed without compromises and without quarrel in different posts (connected or not, neighboring or not, addressing one-another or not).

The community that is established around open-content sites plays a broader role than simply "feeding" the site with new information. Each member of the community, who frequents the "places" that are of interest to him, will naturally take care to weed out off-topic remarks and other disturbances. The joint force of a community was shown (by many sites that have formed such communities) to be stronger than any malicious passers-by. The ability of a community to heal the occasional damages stems both from its number (which by definition is larger than any lone-gunman) and from the frequent interactions with the system. Thus, we hope that Postext will require no maintenance by designated moderators.

6   Implications and Ramifications

Postext transcends the dilemma of artificial consensus vs. destructive arguing, due to its anti-narrative structure. By relaxing the need for classic argumentation, it allows the community the freedom to differ without compromise or quarrel. It transcends the problem of Hypertext, since the ever-present map facilitates orientation interactively.

Thanks to the improved sense of orientation, massive collaboration is greatly facilitated; at the same time, it allows intimate expression of thoughts in their finest detail, uncompromised by the need to fit in an argument. Since the network representation is closer in nature to human thinking than a text, the strenuous linguistic effort of sharing thoughts is simplified. In every instance, different points of view are not merged, but rather juxtaposed in a symbolic relationship that mirrors their divergence in real life. The distributed branching format of Postext allows the introduction of an arbitrary level of technical detail and rigorous scientific proof, without affecting or cluttering the main points and the broad brushes.

Postext is adequate for communal authorship, but the complementary is also true - Postext depends on the effort of an entire community. Due to its transparency, any out-datedness in Postext will be immediately recognizable. Any fault in the ideas presented could no longer be hidden behind literary talent.

Beyond the obvious advantages of such a "community mind", we are convinced that the multidimensional, spatially distributed structure of the Postext would lead to fundamental changes in the way a community thinks. In particular a new way for producing and organizing knowledge can emerge. While in standard scientific interactions there is an advantage to forming hierarchical community leadership and forging an "official" community consensus, Postext allows having large volumes of the multidimensional space left open to arbitrary positions. In the case that a participant finds certain areas irrelevant, s/he can filter them out of the view, or just browse to other places; every newcomer will soon find what zones are of more personal interest than others.

Postext can tolerate anything - the presence of "junk" is not more of a hinderance or of an embarrassment for Postext then the existence of a sewage network is for a city like Paris. If one wishes, one can easily avoid forever regions of the Postext which one considers irrelevant. Yet this Postext freedom allows the equivalent of real-world "fringe" places: avant-garde art schools, Hyde parks, and other means of unconstrained social expression. Postext (as other distributed structures) is reinstating freedom not only from scientific "dictatorships", but also from the more recent forms of mainstream (minimal denominator) cultural totalitarianism.

Most importantly, Postext is easily communicable to newcomers and can solve the problems of the modern educational systems. This is a big problem in the realm of "classic" text - even the most complete library is not self-explanatory (Poincare: "facts don't speak"). Thus the increased penury in teachers capable to teach modern knowledge as it is being generated. The self-organized Postext is in principle a stand-alone entity, providing its own context and reference-frame. Postext does not need (and in fact does not admit) a critique, an introduction or a Preface (where would one place it?!).

The nodes and edges of the Postext are a form of constraint, however it is a fluid and explicit one (not only can posts be created and destroyed but also merge, split, congregate and change character). In this it relates closely to the way we think. Postext should not be regarded as a passive infrastructure. In fact,Postext posses the abilities to infer and extract rich contextual information from the implicit actions of its users. This provides the users the means to move from a binary world, where a connection between different entities either exists or does not exist, to a rainbow of connection strengths, ideas, levels of importance, and persons' significance in the community. On the graph pane, the different posts interact continuously and dynamically. This property of the system introduces casual connectedness of physically-disconnected ideas, as every node in view has the potential to alter the place of every other node in view , thus realizing implicit interconnectedness of concepts - a quality of the continuous mind, rather than the discrete text or Hypertext forms that exist today. This, and other unique properties of Postext, welcome the introduction of innumerable options for extension of the system and its capabilities, and we will name here only a few.

When users interact with Postext, they deepen some links, while weakening others. Thus, they implicitly signal the importance or the controversy of certain claims, while signifying others as outdated. Though Postext has the abilities to extract this implicit knowledge, it remains flexible enough allowing each user to decide on the layers of implicit information s/he deems useful. For example, a researcher might wish to know what are the hot topics of interest and discussion, and Postext will present it to him, for example, through varying the background colour of different nodes (using the standard mapping connecting redder hues to hot and bluer ones to cold), while a novice student would be interested in the most paved pathways, through which most people have stridden before, like an ant walking on the scent of steps already taken. This framework of flexible inference transforms Postext into an active system, which allows interaction between its users, not only in explicit form (through concept identification or text editing) but also in various implicit manners.

Another possible ramification would be the introduction of link-types. The user may indicate that the link he added between two posts is of a certain type, e.g. extension, contradiction, similar underlying mechanism, and so forth. This will allow advanced filtering of the network - for example, users may choose to show only "derivation" links, and the presented network will become a tree-like system of theorems and proofs.

As described above, exposing the context of thoughts and information, through graph representation, lies in the heart of Postext. Sometimes, the context is embedded in a concrete space which can be identified, rather than in a white canvas. Postext, then, allows the reciprocal embedding to materialize in it. The most vivid example for this is the geographic embedding, where the nodes of the graph are pinned down to various points of an existing map or relationship which relate to them. Imagine a Postext which deals with the history of wars where the various war nodes are embedded on the globe in the points where they occurred. Or, in another extreme example, a Postext which is embedded to an output of the CERN LHC accelerator where nodes relate to the different reactions and particles presented.

Postext is based on peer interaction. Thus, its underlying metaphor should not be of a single central repository, but rather of a loosely coupled, yet tightly integrated consortium. Postext will be the realization of true peer to peer content distribution, where different users host different parts of a Postext, and users move seamlessly from one host to the other. Thus when Postext moves from a metaphor to an uncontrolled, evolving, network of information, it will move at the same time from the current ruling paradigm for presenting information, i.e. the client server paradigm (which lies in the heart of the WWW), to the much more efficient, resilient and natural paradigm of peer to peer distribution. When Postext will be deployed as a peer to peer system, it will naturally possess features which are otherwise quite difficult to maintain, such as load balancing, replication and mirroring, and minimal latency. Popular segments of Postexts will be spread to more physical nodes (hosted by Postext users) than less popular ones. Users will be able to link their home Postexts to other related Postexts. An example which goes towards this future can be found in: http://www.netDimes.org/shire/dev/, where the home Postext of one of the authors is connected to the complexity network Postext (see below), a different Postext hosted on a different machine altogether.

We hope that Postext will allow for the emergence of true collective thinking. The various individuals, groups and sub-societies are in a relationship similar to the various modules described in Minsky's "Society of Mind"[10]. As such, one can imagine the way in which their apparently diverging actions can achieve a coherent, positive net result. The modularity of the system should not be regarded as an obstacle - as Minsky argued well in his book, modularity is an essential property of a functioning mind, intimately linked to the parsing act of perception. Much like a mind, Postext contains more information on the field than the sum of its parts. Presented in the structure itself, ideas that evade phrasing may be communicable in a way that transcends the conventions of usual text.

The similarity of the dynamics of Postext to thought, like the blending of text and context, and the multi- (and inter-)scale operations, lead us to hope that technology might eventually allow Postext to start acting like a mind on its own right. Correctly steered over the years, with the natural accumulation of technological advance, Postext may indeed develop collective emergent intelligent behaviour (such as personality,moods, creativity, and will).

As any adaptive complex system, its scope and shape will depend on the fortuitous conditions of its birth, and on the particular chain of events along its history[11]. As such various communities will aggregate or rather co-aggregate intertwined with the aggregation of their Postext representation. The representation will be at the same time the expression, the catalyser and an object of the community works. As the Postext representations of "neighbouring" communities will start cross-linking, there will be practically speaking just a single global Postext.

7   The Specific Example of Complexity Science

The present mode for organizing Science took shape after the failure of the attempt by Newton, Descartes and La Metterie to put the human knowledge on a unified basis that today we would call mechanistic. In particular, Descartes' effort to describe life phenomena mechanistically was rendered inoperative by the Darwinian revolution, while La Metterie's claim that mental processes are physical at their basis have definitely failed by the time of Freud, who offered them a dignified burial.

As a consequence, chemistry, biology and psychology, as well as economics and social science, emerged as independent branches of Science. Their ways diverged so much, that by now it often seems to lead towards two separate human cultures: the exact sciences on one side, and every other human endeavour on the other[1]. Within such a framework, the way a young scientist was supposed to contribute to human knowledge was by taking up one of the leaves of Dewey Decimal Classification System, learn it from a specialist, and eventually grow a little new bud (left of Fig. 3).

With the speed-up of fundamental scientific research, following the proven use of nuclear science in real life (and death) in the Second World War, this scientific paradigm has somewhat changed. In fundamental science, a field, rather then

---

[1] Before accusing the general society of being refractory to exact science, one should remember the quote by Chemistry Nobel laureate Rutherford: "All science is either Physics or stamp collecting."

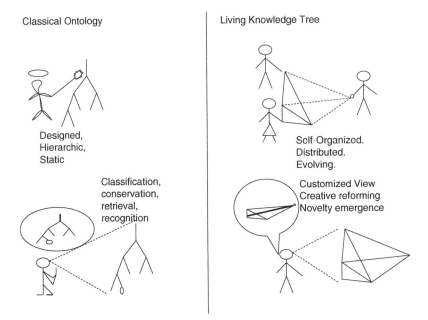

Fig. 3. The two ways of organizing scientific knowledge. The left side depicts the standard library classification. On the right side, the novel way of self-organized knowledge is depicted. New knowledge is placed where its creators find it more appropriate. At the "retrieval" stage, one may use one's own preferences and creativity by recognizing new possible connections. The classification scheme is continuously updated by the members of the relevant community, in accordance to the new current understanding of the relevant connections

being defined by its object of research, came to be defined by what its members were doing: the same community of fundamental theoretical physics studied at different times atomic, nuclear, or quark dynamics. Yet, at any given time the definition of such scientific community was quite unambiguous, stemming from the rather internal -if centrifugal- forces governing its evolution. On this background, the appearance of new scientific trans-disciplinary subjects brought a lot of confusion about membership of researchers to a specific scientific community: the speed of scientific progress, and the fractal shape of the forefront of knowledge, rendered the attempt of drawing well defined boundaries impossible, even momentarily. For somebody interested in managing or defining science, this is a major discomfort. On the other hand, for the curious researchers, these unexpected encounters of "remote regions" of knowledge are part of the joy of discovery. In this new format, science-making can be characterized as a self-organized network of subjects and interconnections, to which new knowledge is added in a way not necessarily determined by the existing elements (right of Fig. 3). At the same time, finding connections between existing elements is at the very heart of the best discoveries therein. Much of this new type of science is done within "classic" disciplines, but it is viewed better at the boundary between fields, and especially in circumstances where intellectual structures created in one field are "exported", and used to understand phenomena from another. One such cross-disciplinary observation is the hallmark of complexity research: "More is Different" (Anderson,1972). A simple, yet profound, observation (often incompatible with previous scientific tenets), stating that a collection of many similar objects can behave very differently from the sum of the characteristics of its components, and have emergent properties. It is when more is different that life emerges from chemistry, social order and revolutions emerge from individual behavior, and market crashes emerge from individual greed. The intimate fusion of intuitions and concepts brings the cross-border scientific interaction into a new dialectic phase: no recognizable border at all. Embarrassed by being left with no recognized "drawer" for their "professional folder" to be stored within, the scientists involved in this revolution invented a name: Complexity[2]. One of the main features of this new science is that instead of occupying itself with self-definition, it started to "self-organize" in a way quite unconscious at the individual participant level. This self-organization was not on the basis of a centrifugal expansion from a central nucleus, but through the convergence (or rather mutual discovery and colonization) of various "islands", who came to recognize un-expected affinities and perform im-probable but briliant syntheses.

As the complexity community started to gain recognition and support from national and international science agencies, the need arouse for its characterization. Soon enough, it became clear that:

– No single person has the expertise to authoritatively present all the field of complexity.
– Even if a person had this expertise, the exposition would present only one possible view of the community.
– Even if the positions about the present facts would be "objective", the statements about the future possible directions will be necessarily tentative, personal and limited.
– In general, the exposition would look more like the "one hour bus tour of London" then like "a map of London".

It was concluded at some stage that what is actually needed is a continuously evolving self-imprinting of the community on a multi-dimensional conceptual "photographic emulsion"; Postext aims at serving that purpose.

---

[2] In fact, the name was already attributed in the sixties to a different scientific topic, branching from computer science and mathematics; a better name could have been "microscopic representation", "multi-agent systems" or "a-disciplinary study of collective emergent objects", but these proposals were less acceptable by science managers.

In the process of recognizing its own extent and its internal connectivity, the complexity community can use "complexity-specific" methods reflexively. Postext is exactly such kind of "introspective" network-map. It can serve as a major tool for the emergence of a collective mind of the complexity community, but also of any other developing community. As the community evolves, its Postext record will become a visualization of the community thinking effort (with the equivalents of brain phenomena such as epileptic hazards, connectivity and causality relationships, and "hot-spots"). The very building blocks of the community are likely to be redefined by collective features of the map, such as clustering or centrality.

8   Conclusions and Outlook

The framework described above is offering an Information-Technology solution to the problem of collective knowledge generation, perception and communication. While we have presented the scaffold for this to take place, the ultimate result will depend on the relationship that the emerging entity develops with the human members of the community. In principle, there are all the "reasons" for a positive and co-operational basis for this relationship. Yet, some of the vitality and energy of the system may also originate in "negative" human traits: self-aggrandizing, envy, and gossip. In fact, the motivation of many of the second wave of contributions to our initial complexity science platform was the feeling that one's brand of science is under-represented or mis-represented by the first wave of contributions. The way the Postext thrives both in the presence of positive and negative emotions makes one optimistic that it is the right structure to self-catalyse its own development. We are left to watch and live together with Postext its first steps in life. Lehaim!

References

1. James, W.:The Principles of Psychology, Vol. I, Dover (1890). pp. 276
2. Derrida, J.:Writing and Difference, Univ. of Chicago Pr.(1978).
3. Eco, U.:The Search for the Perfect Language, Blackwell (1995).
4. Lao, T.:Tao Te Ching (approx. 600 BCE).
5. Quigley, L.:The Blind Men and the Elephant, Charles Scribner's Sons (1959).
6. Goldenberg J. ,Mazursky D, and Solomon S.:Creative Sparks. Science 285, pp. 1495-1496, 1999.
7. Stolov Y., Idel M., and Solomon S.:What Are Stories Made Of? Quantitative Categorical Deconstruction of Creation. Int. J. Mod. Phys. C, Vol. 11, No. 4, pp. 827-835, 2000 (cond-mat:0008192).
8. Louzon Y., Muchnik L., and Solomon S.:Copying nodes vs. Editing links: The Source of the Difference Between Genetic Networks and the WWW (submitted to Proc. Nat. Acad Sci. USA).
9. Hofstadter D.:Gödel, Escher, Bach: An Eternal Golden Braid,Basic Books (1979).
10. Minsky, M.:Society Of Mind, Simon & Schuster (1988).
11. Gell-Mann, M.: The Quark and the Jaguar, W. H. Freeman and Company (1994).

Comparing Resource Sharing with Information Exchange in Co-operative Agents, and the Role of Environment Structure

Mark Bartlett and Dimitar Kazakov

Department of Computer Science, University of York,
Heslington, York YO10 5DD, UK
lastname@cs.york.ac.uk
http://www-users.cs.york.ac.uk/~*lastname*/

Abstract. This paper presents a multi-agent system which has been developed in order to test our theories of language evolution. We propose that language evolution is an emergent behaviour, which is influenced by both genetic and social factors and show that a multi-agent approach is thus most suited to practical study of the salient issues. We present the hypothesis that the original function of language in humans was to share navigational information, and show experimental support for this hypothesis through results comparing the performance of agents in a series of environments. The approach, based loosely on the Songlines of Australian Aboriginal culture, combines individual exploration with exchange of information about resource location between agents. In particular, we study how the degree to which language use is beneficial varies with a particular property of the environment structure, that of the distance between resources needed for survival.

1   Introduction

The use of computer simulations to study the origin and evolution of language has become widespread in recent years [1, 2, 3]. The goal of these studies is to provide experimental support for theories developed by linguists, psychologists and philosophers regarding the questions of how and why language exists in the form we know it. As verbal language by its very nature leaves no historical physical remains, such as fossils, computer simulation is one of the best tools available to study this evolution, allowing us to construct a model which simulates the relevant aspects of the problem, and to abstract away any unnecessary detail. Experiments conducted using such an approach can be performed much more quickly than those involving teaching language to apes or children and allow researchers to study language in situations which would be impossible with live subjects.

Our multi-agent system has been designed to test the theory that language could potentially have evolved from the neural mechanisms our ancestors used to navigate [4, 5, 6, 7]. Specifically we wish to explore the feasibility of the hypothesis that the original task of speech in humans was to inform others about the

D. Kudenko et al. (Eds.): Adaptive Agents and MAS II, LNAI 3394, pp. 41–54, 2005.

geography of the environment. To this end, we have constructed an artificial-life environment in which a society of learning agents uses speech to direct others to resources vital to survival using the same underlying computational mechanism as they use to navigate. This differs from previous work in the field of simulating language evolution by viewing language as tool with a particular purpose rather than an abstract method of information coding. We discuss the altruistic nature of this activity and evaluate the benefits this brings to the community by measuring the difference in performance between populations of agents able to communicate and those unable to do so. We also evaluate the performance of a population of agents engaging in a non-communicative act of altruism, namely sharing stores of resources. Our simulations are carried out in a series of environments in which the distance between the two resources needed for survival is varied to assess what impact this feature of the terrain may have on any benefit that language may bring. We also study how the distance between resources of the same type may affect performance. Our aim in this paper is to assess the conditions in which language use may be beneficial and hence could be selected for by evolution.

We have chosen to carry out our simulations within a multi-agent setting as the nature of these systems allows us easily to capture much of the behaviour we wish to program into our models. We assume that language has both innate components (such as the willingness to speak) and social components (such as the words used in a language). Multi-agent systems allow both these aspects to be modelled relatively simply. Though the genetic nature of language could be modelled equally well using only genetic algorithms, indeed some researchers have done this [8, 9], in order to model the social aspects of language which rely on phenotypical behaviour, situatedness, grounding and learning, it is necessary to employ an agent model.

Simulations of the evolution of language using the multi-agent paradigm can also be of interest to the designer of any general-purpose agent-based application. In a dynamic environment that is expected to change considerably during an agent's lifetime, the faculty of learning could be essential to its success. In an evolutionary MAS setting, sexual reproduction and mutation can be used to explore a range of possible learning biases, from which natural selection would choose the best. One would expect Darwinian evolution to advance in small steps and select only very general concepts. One could also implement Lamarckian evolution, that is, use a MAS in which the parents' individual experience can be reflected in the learning bias inherited by their offspring. Lamarckian evolution is faster but brings the risks of inheriting concepts that were relevant to the parents but are not reflected in the new agent's lifetime. This work explores what could be a third way of evolving a learning bias, through communication. Language uses concepts that are specific enough to be useful in the description of an agent's environment, yet general enough to correspond to shared experience. In this way, language serves as a bias inherited through social interaction rather than genes. In the current work, language serves as a way to share a bias for navigating in an environment.

2   Altruism and Sharing

Though the object of study is a language whose rules are passed between agents in a cultural manner, the actual willingness to speak can be considered as an innate factor that influences an individual's probability of survival and is hence open to evolution. Language use of this kind is an inherently altruistic act; by informing another agent of the location of resources, an agent increases both the survival prospects of its rival and the probability that the resource mentioned will be exhausted before it is able to return to it. In our previous work [10] which focussed on resource sharing as a form of altruism, we found that through the mechanism of kin selection [11, 12] it is possible to promote altruistic acts in an agent population if the degree of relatedness between the agents is known and the amount of resource given is able to be measured and controlled. It was also found that a poor choice of sharing function (which is used to decide the amount of resource shared) could lead to a population in which all agents had enough energy to survive, but insufficient to reproduce. This can lead to extinction of a large population even in the circumstances where a smaller population would be able to survive.

Quantifying the cost of the act is much harder to achieve when the altruistic act is to share knowledge of a resource location. Even if the degree of kinship were known — which in the present simulations is achieved by simply defining all agents as identical clones sharing the same genetic material — one is left with the issues of estimating the actual, potentially different, amounts of resource the helped agent would receive, and the helper would forfeit, as a result of their communication. In place of the one-off payments of resources that occur when resources are shared, informing an agent of the location of a resource can involve a long-term, sizeable drain on the resource, especially if the receiver goes on to inform others. Conversely, the act may result in no cost at all in the case where the receiver is in such need of the resource that it is unable to reach it before dying. This point also illustrates another problem with using language to share, it is also hard to estimate the benefits that the altruistic act will bring to the listener. When resources are given directly to another agent, the amount of help is easy to quantify, whereas when language is used the reward is delayed for several turns and may never be achieved. One could easily see how the costs would also vary with the environment. For instance, in a world with volatile, non-renewable resources, an agent is unlikely to benefit on a later occasion from anything left after it has sated its current needs. In these circumstances, the agent sharing information can provide substantial help at virtually no cost to itself.

If one was to look for an example in the natural world, one might consider vultures, such as the California condor (*Gymnogyps californianus*). Condors are described as:

> carrion eaters...prefer[ring] to feed on the carcasses of large mammals...[They] may eat up to 3 to 4 pounds at a time and may not need to feed again for several days. Condors find their food by sight or by following other scavenging birds. Condors normally feed in a group... [13].

It is likely that one carcass may be sufficient to feed several birds, and that the period they need to digest the food means the rest would be consumed by other (e.g., ground) scavengers. Circling over a carcass can give away its location to the other members of the group. It is believed that this behaviour is, in part, to signal the presence of food to others nearby, bidding other birds to join in the meal. In this case, increasing the time spent circling in proportion to the carcass size, would result in a sharing strategy where larger surplus of food meant higher probability of sharing with other birds.

Another significant factor to consider when comparing the benefits of sharing resources versus sharing knowledge is the way in which the sharing of knowledge will influence the distribution of agents in the environment. It is to be expected that when agents share information, they will become clustered more in certain parts of the environment, as they will know of the same physical resource locations. It is unclear whether this is beneficial or not, as there are advantages and disadvantages to this spatial distribution. If all agents are only using a small number of resources, then these resources will obviously become depleted more rapidly and also will be more often too crowded to access. However, agents will also be more likely to meet potential mates if agents are occupying a smaller area. In nature, creatures form communities of many different sizes, from mainly solitary large cats to thousands of individuals in hives of insects, suggesting that the effect of agents becoming spatially clustered may vary depending on the needs of the individuals and the environment inhabited.

While altruism based on the underlying assumption of kin selection is used here due to the desire to provide a feasible explanation for a phenomenon in an artificial life setting, the idea of kin selection provides a useful metaphor for any community of agents. In a collection of agents solving a variety of tasks with limited resources, the degree to which two agents should cooperate (and share resources, if needed) should intuitively be related to the proportion of tasks they have in common: if we view the relatedness of two agents as the proportion of tasks they share, the ideas behind kin selection and neo-Darwinism provide inspiration for how agents might best cooperate to achieve their collective goals.

3   The Multi-agent System

In order to simulate language evolution, we have created a multi-agent system. The York Multi-Agent System [14] is a Java-based application which allows for artificial life simulations to be conducted in two-dimensional environments. It is particularly well suited to studying learning and evolution. Agents in this system have a behaviour based on drives, the most important of which are hunger and thirst. At each time-step, after the values of the drives are increased to reflect the cost of living, an agent will attempt to reduce whichever of its drives is greater. If either drive reaches its maximum then the agent dies and is removed from the simulation. Agents can also die of old age. This can occur starting when the agent is 300 cycles old.

If two agents with sufficiently low hunger and thirst values share a location, they may mate to produce a third agent. Mating costs an agent a one-off payment of one third of its food and water reserves, with the amount subtracted from both parents going to the child as its initial levels.

Agents attempt to reduce their hunger or thirst by finding and using food and water resources respectively. A resource can be utilised by an agent if they share a square in the environment, and this decreases the appropriate drive to a minimum and reduces the amount of resource remaining at this location. When a resource is entirely depleted by use, it is removed for several turns after which it reappears at its previous location with its resources renewed. When resources are required, agents will first utilise any in the square they occupy or will look for resources in adjacent squares. If this fails, they attempt to generate a path to a known resource as will be explained below and, finally if all else fails, they will make a random exploratory move. Additionally, in some populations in the experiments performed, agents are either able to request resources or directions from other agents. Sharing resources uses a progressive taxation policy with 50% of any resources in excess of the minimum needed for reproduction being given to the requesting agent, while directions are shared in the manner which will be described below. Agents always share when they are asked for help (assuming that they are able to) and they will do so as if they were clones of a single genotype: there is no account taken of the degree of kinship when deciding how much help to give.

4   Representation of Knowledge

Our approach to navigation is inspired by the Songlines, an oral tradition of Aboriginal Australian tribes. Songlines reflect a belief that "Ancestral Beings roamed once the face of the earth, creating the features of the landscape. . . along the tracks that mark their journeys." In the grouping of songs into series, "the most pervasive is the geographical organisation of songlines, where each 'small song' equates with a different site along an ancestral journey, and the series as a whole constitutes a sung map [15]."

Central to this research is the representation used to store data about the environment for later use in navigating or communicating. An extremely impoverished representation is used which gives the minimum amount of information necessary to follow a route. Specifically, an environment is used in which certain objects in the environment are known as landmarks by all agents and a route between different places can then be described by an ordered list of the landmarks that one sees as that path is travelled. The names of landmarks that the agents use in order to describe paths to each other are assumed to be fixed and common to all agents throughout the simulation. Informing another agent of a resource through the exchange of a path is an altruistic act for the reasons discussed in previous sections.

Agents can acquire knowledge of new paths in 2 ways. Agents may obtain paths through linguistic methods as noted above or they may find resources through exploration, in which case they will be able to construct a path linking this new resource to the previous location they visited by recalling the landmarks they have seen on their journey. In either case, the agent will store the new path internally in the same data structure in a form equivalent to

$$goto(resource) \rightarrow goto(locX), l_1, l_2, l_3, \ldots, l_i$$

in the case of a rule acquired through communication, where $l_1, \ldots, l_i$ are the landmark names received and $locX$ is the location the agent gained the knowledge. For rules acquired through exploration knowledge is stored in a form similar to the following.

$$goto(resource) \rightarrow goto(locY)$$

$$goto(locY) \rightarrow goto(locX), l_1, l_2, l_3, \ldots, l_i$$

where $l_1, \ldots, l_i$ are the landmarks seen during the journey, $locX$ is the previous location visited, and $locY$ is the location of the resource itself. $locX$ and $locY$ are stored as a list of landmarks visible from the location in question (range of sight is limited to 2 squares in all directions). The first rule given above can be understood as stating that to go to the resource is equivalent to first going to $locX$ and then passing the given landmarks in order. The second rule set can similarly be understood as stating that to go to the resource it is sufficient to go to $locY$ which can be achieved by going to $locX$ and then passing the landmarks in the stated order. Note that the path that can be generated to take an agent from $locX$ to the resource is the same using the either first rule or the rule set given above, the only difference being that in the latter case the agent has already visited the actual resource and thus can store a description of the environment at that point. A further rule of similar form is added to an agent's knowledge base when new paths are acquired through exploration that enables paths to be traversed in reverse direction. It should be noted that this description is very impoverished, containing no information on factors such as direction, absolute position or distance (aside from that which can be inferred from the number of landmarks mentioned in the rule).

These rules can be viewed in two ways, and are used as such by the agents. Firstly, they can be seen as procedural rules which capture the spatial relationship between locations and can be used for navigation by agents to resources and, secondly, as grammar rules forming a regular language which can be used by the agent to share knowledge with others. When viewed as a grammar, the rules form a proto-language whose structure mirrors that of the landscape.

To access the data stored in the grammar to reach a resource, the agent will need to generate a sequence of landmarks from the grammar which will form a path that the agent can follow. This is done by using the grammar to generate a list consisting of only landmark names. The starting rule for this expansion is a grammar rule in which the left-hand side is $goto(resource)$, where $resource$ is the type of resource the agent wishes to locate. The rule used is the one that leads to the resource which the agent most recently visited, which implies that rules the agent has acquired through exploration are used in preference to those gained linguistically. Symbols of the form *locX* are used as non-terminals in the parsing and landmark names as terminals. Expansion takes place using an A* search with a metric based on the length of the path (as measured by the number of landmarks).

Agents utilise the grammar in the same way when they are called upon to share their knowledge linguistically with others, but instead of following the path generated, it is passed to the other agent, who will store it in the same form as the first rule given above. Whether the route generated leads to food or water is decided before the interaction occurs based on the needs of the agents concerned. This ensures that the agent receiving the route knows whether to follow the route when it is hungry or when it is thirsty. There are a few minor but important changes to how the agents use the grammar when generating a path for another agent which ensure that hearsay and misinformation are not passed onto other agents. These changes involve only using rules which have been formed through exploration when communicating information to another agent and then only the subset of these rules that refer to resources that have been recently visited. These changes, which maximise the chances that a resource to which an agent is directed is actually there, were found to significantly improve the performance of communicating agents in our earlier research [16].

The deliberately impoverished representation of geographical knowledge that is used here might be found to be of use in other agent applications where navigation is needed. A particular strength of the representation is that it allows for a certain amount of generalisation to occur. As locations are not precisely specified as coordinates, but rather they are defined in terms of the landmarks visible from that position, positions close to each other may be viewed as the same location by the algorithm, which allows a degree of abstraction about an agent's position. For example, in a domain involving robots navigating a building, it may not be important exactly where in a room a robot is for a navigational planner, rather which room the agent is in may be much more significant at this level. Landmarks too can provide for a form of generalisation. In the current work, landmarks have unique names, but there is no reason why this must be the case. If different landmarks had the same name, generalisation of any structural regularity of the environment would be possible, indeed inevitable, without an exhaustive search. Returning to the robot example, an identical series of visual or radio beacons leading to each door of a given room could be used, allowing a generalised concept of a path heading into that room to be formed. It should be noted that the representation also includes some ambiguity about the routes it contains. This occurs as there are a vast number of routes which are described by the same sequence of landmarks but which involve visiting slightly different sequences of squares in the environment. This ambiguity leads to some useful abstraction: unimportant aspects of an agent's journey such as whether it should go one square north then one east or whether it should go east then north are removed as the paucity of the route description fails to encode this behaviour fully. This could prove useful in other domains by forming the basis of hierarchical route planning, such as robot navigation around a building; a higher level route planner such as the one used here could be used to plan the journey at the level of deciding the order in which rooms must be visited to reach the destination, while a low level planner could plan routes that avoided obstacles in those rooms. Planning in two stages like this reduces the complexity of the initial plan and allows detailed decisions to be delayed until needed. Other features, such as the minimum amount of information required to build up a series of routes, and the ability to associate scores rating the usefulness of particular rules, may also make this representation potential useful in other domains.

5   Study of the Role of Environment

Intuitively, the benefits to a community of the ability to use language in this scenario might seem obvious. However it is not inevitable that the capacity to share resource locations should lead to an increase in a population's ability to survive. It is conceivable that spreading knowledge of resources could lead to much faster depletion of those resources and hence starvation, or that a population could be created in which all individuals had sufficient resources to survive but insufficient to reproduce.

The benefits of a particular altruistic policy to a community of agents can be measured through conducting experimentation in which a population of agents is placed within an environment and the simulation is allowed to run for a period equivalent to several generations. The simulation is performed three times with different populations of agents, one of which is able to communicate, one of which is able to share resources and a final population which is entirely selfish. Agents in populations in which language use is not allowed still use the information gathered about the environment for personal navigation to make for fairer comparisons between the populations. Any survival or reproductive benefit associated with the use of a strategy should be manifested in the population size, in this way we study language evolution as a form of multi-agent learning which improves a population's performance as measured by its ability to utilise resources. An alternative experimental scheme in which different populations of agents were placed in the environment at the same time, with the most successful strategy being judged as the one most represented in the final population, was considered but rejected, as the interference between populations would make the results harder to analyse quantitatively and may have been more sensitive to initial fluctuations in the population.

In the present work, the environments in which agents were placed had two of their structural properties changed in order to evaluate the effect that these had on the various altruistic policies. A basic environment shape was defined, with four food resources equally spaced across the top of the environment and four water resources across the bottom as shown in figure 1. This map was then resized by different amounts in both the horizontal and vertical dimensions to produce a series of maps. The distance between resources of the same kind was one factor that was thus altered between experiments with the other factor be-

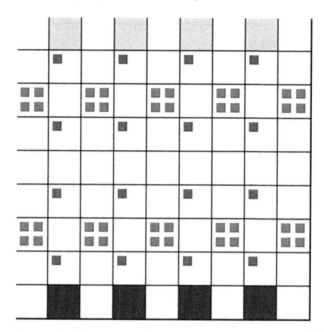

Fig. 1. An environment with a space of one square between resources of the same type and seven squares between resources of different kinds. The large shaded environment squares show where resources are located (food at the top, water at the bottom), and the smaller squares show the agents (in groups of four) and landmarks (uniformly spaced)

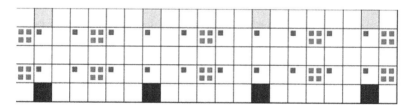

Fig. 2. An environment with spacing of 5 squares between like resources and 3 between differing ones. The same rendering as figure 1 is used

ing the distance between the different types of resource. Three values of each distance were chosen based on indications from preliminary experiments, 1, 3 and 5 squares for the distance between resources of the same kind and 3, 5 and 7 squares for the distance between resources of differing types. Each pair of distances were used in a map leading to a total of 9 environments. Figures 1 and 2 are two examples of the maps formed. Note that the number of resources in each environment is kept as a constant, as is their relative positioning, and that the different distances are thus achieved by altering the size of the environment.

To ensure valid comparisons between experiments, the same number of agents were used in each environment.

6   Results and Discussion

The results, as shown in figure 3, demonstrate that the population in which language is used performs significantly better then the other populations in most cases studied. As would intuitively be expected, the greater the distance between food and water the fewer agents manage to survive regardless of strategy. However, though the resulting size of the language-using population decreases as this distance increases, the relative benefits of language increase, as can be seen by the ratio of the size of the language-using population to the selfish population (which can be viewed as a baseline for comparison).

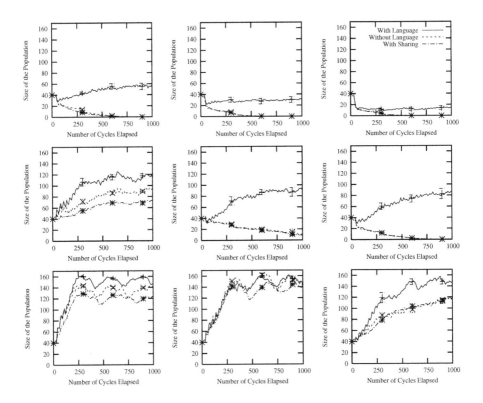

Fig. 3. Comparison of sharing information, sharing resources and selfish behaviour. The distance between resources of different kinds increases from bottom to top, from 3 to 5 to 7 squares. The distance between resources of the same kind increases from left to right, from 1 to 3 to 5 squares. All results are averaged over 10 runs

The size of the final population also appears to be dependant on the spacing between resources of the same kind. Again the general rule appears to be that the greater the distance, the lower the population which manages to survive though the effect is not as pronounced as changing the distance between food and water. Language use also appears to increase in effectiveness with increasing distance for this variable.

The reason for the decrease in the size of population as the food-water distance increases is quite obvious, and is simply due to the greater difficulty in an agent managing to find both resources before dying of hunger or thirst. This reveals why language use is more beneficial in situations where the distance is greater. By using language, the complexity of the search for resources is simplified, as agents are able to gain information on resource location without having to go through the process of exploration. In effect, the use of language manages to parallelise the searching for resources. The effect of language is likely to be particularly pronounced in later generations when agents born into non-communicating populations have to locate resources through exploration as their parents did, but communicating agents will most likely be able to gain this knowledge linguistically almost immediately from their parents.

It is less immediately obvious that the distance between resources of the same type should influence the population dynamics though there are actually two ways in which the spacing between resources is likely to do so. Firstly, as stated earlier in this paper, resources are exhaustible with use. This means that occasionally agents will need to migrate from one source of food to another (similarly with water). At this point the distance between food sources becomes relevant. When the resources are separated by one square, it is almost inevitable that a move from an exhausted food source will lead to a position in which a new resource can be seen, whereas the task of locating a new resource becomes a matter of quite extensive exploration when the next closest resource is 5 squares away. Secondly, the difficulty of locating a resource initially in the environment increases in complexity as the distance between resources of the same kind increases. To see why this is so, consider two environments with the same distance between food and water but different distances between food and food (and therefore water and water). The number of squares from which food is visible in both environments is constant, being one square in each direction away from the food. However the number of squares in the environments are different and hence the environment in which food is more spaced out will need a greater proportion of the squares to be searched in order for resources to be found. Again, the reason that language performs better is due to the fact that it manages to reduce the amount of searching that must be done to locate resources.

There are two other effects that may also explain some of the benefits that language use brings. Firstly, populations using language have a tendency to cluster into a smaller part of the environment: the majority of agents tend to become reliant on a subset of the resources available. This occurs as the process of agents informing others of the resources of which they know results in most agents becoming aware of the same resources and routes between them. By clustering themselves into a reduced part of the environment, the probability of a pair of agents who are able to mate meeting each other is increased and hence the expected birthrate will also be increased. Secondly, the process of being able to learn routes through language produces an effect that results in shorter, more efficient routes becoming used. As communicating agents are able to gain information through both exploration and language, they are able to learn of several different routes to the same location. The details of the navigational planning algorithm ensure that agents will tend to take the shortest route which they are able to, and hence agents in communicating populations will tend to travel shorter routes than those agents in other populations, which reduces their chances of dying while travelling between resources and increases the amount of time they are able to mate.

In all the experiments conducted, populations which shared resources performed no better than the baseline behaviour of not sharing at all, and in some cases did significantly worse. This serves to illustrate that the improved performance of the language-using community is not just down to the altruism of the communicating agents. The poor performance of the population who share resources can probably be best explained through the fact that sharing resources can lead to a population in which resources tend to become more evenly spread throughout the population. This creates a population in which fewer agents are able to reproduce, and those agents that are created through mating begin life with lower resource levels and thus a worse chance of surviving. One conclusion that might be drawn from the evidence produced is that agent populations would perform better if they concentrated on gathering more resources and were less concerned about how those resources were distributed between them.

A further point that should be mentioned with respect to the performance of agents who share resources is that they take noticeably longer to recover from the depletion of a resource than do agents who are not sharing resources. This can be seen in the graphs towards the bottom left-hand corner of figure 3. The periodic increase and decrease in population size seen in these graphs is characteristic of resources becoming depleted [16]. It can be seen that in these experiments, the population size of the agents who share resources falls for longer than the other populations. This is caused by exploration to locate new resources being delayed by agents, who are content to draw energy from others rather than find a new permanent source of resources. When agents do eventually begin to explore, their collective resource levels are much reduced by this period of inactivity and it takes agents longer to regain a state conducive to procreation.

In passing, it can perhaps be noted that the fact that the periodic increases and decreases in population size are not seen in some graphs is due to the fact that in the experiments in which this is the case the population size is much smaller in relation to the environment size. This means resources are not being used to their full potential and thus the time at which they become depleted varies from resource to resource and from trial to trial, blurring the cyclic behaviour to the point where it cannot be seen in the graphs.

7   Conclusion and Future Work

This paper has outlined a multi-agent system built specifically to study the phenomenon of language evolution and has presented a range of experiments that have been carried out in order to study the influence of certain features of the environment upon the usefulness of language to a community of speakers. Specifically, we have carried out investigations in which two different types of the distance between resources was varied. Our results show that in all the cases considered, language use was never detrimental to a population and became increasingly advantageous compared with other policies as distances between resources increased. Sharing resources, on the contrary, never offered any benefit over selfish behaviour and actually proved to be a disadvantage when resources were most easily discovered.

While the results presented here show clear advantages to the populations of using a particular altruistic policy, the evolutionary viability of this strategy has not been proven: we have not tested that any policy forms an evolutionary stable strategy. This is due to the fact that populations were formed of clones of a single agent, and thus the effects of such factors as agents with differing policies invading a population could not be modelled. Additionally, as the agents were all identical, altruism occurred in an effectively group selection framework rather than the model based on fully formed kin selection that is our eventual aim.

It is our future intent to assess the effect that other features of the environment may have upon the usefulness of language to a population, for example varying the spacing of landmarks or introducing impassible terrain. Through experimentation we hope to assess the way in which features of the landscape such as these affect the size of the population and the segmentation of the linguistic community, and draw parallels between this and speciation and cultural division in the natural world.

When completed, this research should shed light on when exactly language evolution of this type should be expected to provide some benefit and hence its use be selected for by natural selection. Our intuition is that we will find the conditions in which language use is encouraged to be similar to those found at the time when primitive language use is believed to have begun in humans.

References

1. Briscoe, E.J., ed.: Linguistic Evolution through Language Acquisition: Formal and Computational Models. Cambridge University Press (2002)
2. Kirby, S.: Learning, Bottlenecks and the Evolution of Recursive Syntax. In: Linguistic Evolution through Language Acquisition: Formal and Computational Models. Cambridge University Press (2002)
3. Steels, L.: The spontaneous self-organization of an adaptive language. In Furukawa, K., Michie, D., Muggleton, S., eds.: Machine Intelligence 15, St. Catherine's College, Oxford, Oxford University Press (1999) 205–224 Machine Intelligence Workshop: July 1995.

4. Kazakov, D., Bartlett, M.: A multi-agent simulation of the evolution of language. In Grobelnik, M., Bohanec, M., Mladenic, D., Gams, M., eds.: Proceedings of Information Society Conference IS'2002, Ljubljana, Slovenia, Morgan Kaufmann (2002) 39–41

5. Hauser, M.D., Chomsky, N., Fitch, W.T.: The faculty of language: What is it, who has it, and how did it evolve? Science **298** (2002) 1569–1579

6. Herner-Vazquez, L., Spelke, E.S., Katsnelson, A.S.: Sources of flexibilit in human cognition: Dual-task studies of space and language. Cognitive Psychology **39** (1999) 3–36

7. O'Keefe, J., Nadel, L.: The Hippocampus as a Cognitive Map. Oxford University Press (1978)

8. Oliphant, M.: Formal Approaches to Innate and Learned Communication: Laying the Foundation for Language. PhD thesis, Department of Cognitive Science, University of California, San Diego (1997)

9. Zuidema, W.H., Hogeweg, P.: Selective advantages of syntactic language - a model study. In: Proceedings of the Twenty-second Annual Conference of the Cognitive Science Society, Hillsdale, USA, Lawrence Erlbaum Associates (2000) 577–582

10. Turner, H., Kazakov, D.: Stochastic simulation of inherited kinship-driven altruism. Journal of Artificial Intelligence and Simulation of Behaviour **1** (2002) 183–196

11. Dawkins, R.: The Extended Phenotype. Oxford University Press (1982)

12. Hamilton, W.D.: The genetic evolution of social behaviour I. Journal of Theoretical Biology **7** (1964) 1–16

13. Ventana Wilderness Society: (2004) http://www.ventanaws.org/condhist.htm, visited Jan 2004.

14. Kazakov, D., Kudenko, D.: Machine Learning and Inductive Logic Programming for Multi-agent Systems. In: Multi-Agent Systems and Applications. Springer (2001) 246–270

15. Barwick, L., Marrett, A.: Aboriginal Traditions. In: Currency Companion to Dance and Music in Australia. Currency Press (2003) 26–28

16. Kazakov, D., Bartlett, M.: Benefits of sharing navigational information in a dynamic alife environment (Unpublished)

Baselines for Joint-Action Reinforcement Learning of Coordination in Cooperative Multi-agent Systems

Martin Carpenter[1] and Daniel Kudenko[2]

[1] School of Informatics,
University of Manchester,
** Manchester
M.Carpenter@umist.ac.uk
[2] Department of Computer Science,
University of York,
United Kingdom
kudenko@cs.york.ac.uk***

Abstract. A common assumption for the study of reinforcement learning of coordination is that agents can observe each other's actions (so-called *joint-action* learning). We present in this paper a number of simple joint-action learning algorithms and show that they perform very well when compared against more complex approaches such as OAL [1], while still maintaining convergence guarantees. Based on the empirical results, we argue that these simple algorithms should be used as baselines for any future research on joint-action learning of coordination.

1 Introduction

Coordination is a central issue in multi-agent system (MAS) development, and reinforcement learning of coordination has been intensively studied in recent years. In this paper we focus on coordination in cooperative MAS, i.e., where all agents share the same objective.

Coordination learning algorithms that have been developed for this task can be classified in two categories. The first category comprises those learning algorithms that make no assumption on whether agents can communicate, observe each other's action, or even be aware of each other's existence (so-called *independent* learning techniques, see e.g. [2]). In the second category there are those algorithms that assume that agents can observe each other's actions and use these observations to improve coordination (so-called *joint-action* learning techniques [3]). The latter case being considerably easier to handle, most research to date has been focused on joint-action learners.

** On October 1st 2004 UMIST merged into the University of Manchester.
*** We thank Spiros Kapetanakis for many useful discussions on this research.

D. Kudenko et al. (Eds.): Adaptive Agents and MAS II, LNAI 3394, pp. 55–72, 2005.
© Springer-Verlag Berlin Heidelberg 2005

However, we argue that there exist very simple coordination learning techniques for agents that can observe each other's actions, and that these algorithms perform comparably well while being guaranteed to converge towards the optimum. We strongly suggest that the techniques presented in this paper should serve as baselines in any further research on joint-action learning of coordination in cooperative MAS.

The paper is structured as follows. We first describe two formalisms that are commonly used to represent coordination problems: single-stage games and multi-stage Markov games. We then present simple algorithms for the learning of coordination in such games and evaluate them empirically on a number of difficult coordination games from the literature. We also compare the performance of these simple learning techniques to the OAL algorithm [1], that has been widely cited in recent research. In addition to the simple learning algorithms, we also present an improvement based on statistical confidence measurements, and discuss its applicability. We conclude the paper with a summary and an outlook to the future of joint-action learning of coordination.

2   Cooperative Games

Games are a common and highly suitable way to represent cooperative coordination problems. Depending on the problem to be modelled, there are two main representation options: single-stage games and multi-stage (or *Markov*) games. In this section we briefly introduce both.

2.1   Single Stage Games

Single stage games are relatively simple models of interaction, and have been mainly used in the context of game theory. A number of players simultaneously perform an action each from a set of possible actions, after which the game is over and each player receives a reward. In the co-operative case all players receive the same reward. More formally:

Definition 1. *An n-player single-stage co-operative game Γ is a tuple $(A^1, \ldots, A^n, r)$ for $k \in \{1 \ldots n\}$ where A^i is the discrete action space of player i, and $r : A^1 \times \ldots \times A^n \to \mathrm{R}$ is the payoff function mapping actions to numerical reward values. Each player shares identical payoff functions.*

Single stage games with only two players can be represented as a rectangular matrix of numbers. An example of a game represented in such fashion is given in Figure 1: each of the two players can choose between two actions (a1 and a2 for one player, b1 and b2 for the other). The matrix entries determine the payoff. For example if one player plays a1 and the other plays b2, then they both receive a payoff of 3.

A number of single-stage games have been defined in the research literature that pose specific challenges to learning of coordination, and we have used these to evaluate our approaches. These games are described below.

Player 1

		a	b
Player 2	a	3	5
	b	0	10

Fig. 1. A simple game matrix

Player 1

		a	b	c
	a	80	-60	0
Player 2	b	-60	40	30
	c	0	0	20

Fig. 2. Climbing Game

Player 1

		a	b	c
	a	40	0	-40
Player 2	b	0	20	0
	c	-40	0	40

Fig. 3. Penalty Game

Player 1

		a	b	c
	a	80/120	-30/30	-80/-120
Player 2	b	-30/30	0/40	-30/30
	c	-80/120	-30/30	80/120

Fig. 4. Stochastic Penalty Game

The Climbing Game. A variant of this single-stage game (shown in Figure 2) has been introduced in [3]. It poses a difficulty because the optimal joint action $((a, a)$ with a payoff of 80) has an associated high miscoordination penalty, and therefore a regular independent Q learning approach does not converge to the optimum [2].

The Penalty Game. This game (shown in Figure 3), also introduced in [3], has two optimal joint actions. The major difficulty is that a mis-coordination in the choice of the optimum leads to a penalty.

The Stochastic Penalty Game. This game (shown in Figure 4),is equivalent to the penalty game above. However, the payoffs are stochastic. Each joint action may lead to one of two payoffs with probability 0.5 each.

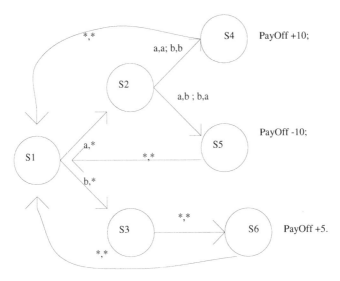

Fig. 5. C&B Game

2.2   Markov Games

In contrast to single-stage games, multi-stage (or Markov) games do not have to end after just one round. Players simultaneously perform actions, and after each round, a new state is reached. The new state is determined probabilistically based on the actions of the players. In each state the players receive a payoff.

Definition 2. *An n-player Markov game is a tuple (S, G, p, r) where S is the discrete state space of the game, G is a set of single stage games, one for each state in S, and $p: S \times A^1 \times A^n \to \Delta$ is the transition probability map, where Δ is the set of probability distributions over the state space S. $r : S \to \mathrm{R}$ is the payoff function that maps states to numerical reward functions.*

A Markov game can be considered as a collection of single state games linked by a function governing transitions between the games. They can be drawn as a set of matrices linked by arrows with the transition probabilities marked on them.

As in the case of single-stage games, a number of multi-stage can be defined that pose specific coordination challenges. Two representative games that we used for evaluation are presented below.

C&B Game. This game was introduced in [4] and is shown in Figure 5. At each state each player has a choice of two actions. The transitions on the diagram are marked by a pair of corresponding actions, denoting player 1's move and player 2's move respectively. "*" is a wild card, representing any action. States that yield a reward are marked with the respective value. All other states yield a reward of 0.

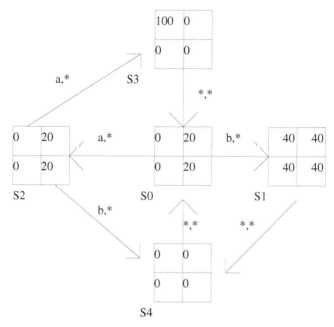

Fig. 6. Misleading Game

Misleading Game. The difficulty of the game shown in Figure 6 is that actions that lead to early high payoffs are not part of the best policy, and are thus misleading.

3   Simple Learning of Coordination

There are many approaches to learning coordination [5] in cooperative games. In this section we present simple joint-action learning techniques that will then be evaluated.

3.1   Simple Coordination Learning for Single Stage Games

Basic Approach. Our proposed learning algorithm for single stage games has a very simple form:

1. Choose between the possible actions at random
2. Observe the joint action played and reward recieved
3. Update the average reward obtained for the joint action just played
4. Repeat until stopped, or some preset number of repeated plays has completed.

The algorithm then outputs the agent's action that is part of the joint action with the highest average payoff. If two joint actions have the same average payoff then it chooses the action which was played first.

For a game with constant payoffs this algorithm is guaranteed to find the optimal joint action if given enough time. Formally, if the game matrix has size $n \times m$ with o optimal actions, the algorithm has a $1 - (\frac{nm-o}{nm})^k$ chance of converging to a optimal joint action in k moves. Note that this convergence speed is independent of any structural characteristic of the game besides the number of possible joint actions. For example in the climbing game presented below it will take an average of 25 moves to achieve 95% convergence and in the penalty game (which has two optima) it will take an average of 12 moves to achieve this. For games with stochastic payoff functions the time taken to find an optimal answer will scale linearly with the difficulty of finding the true averages of the payoff functions. For example in the stochastic penalty game either result from the optimal joint actions is optimal and so it solves it as fast as it does the penalty game. The simple stochastic game is harder to give exact figures for. In 45 moves it will on average have visited the optimal result 5 times with a bit over 50% chance of having found the right answer.

Performance Enhancement. While the basic learning algorithm already shows very good performance, there is a simple way to further improve it's performance by modifying the action selection technique employed during learning. Whilst purely random exploration is guaranteed to visit every joint action arbitrarily often as the number of moves tends to infinity, it is rather inefficient.

In order to improve performance we use the following action selection algorithm instead of purely random action choice: At each step choose the action for which the smallest number of joint actions has been observed at least once. If there is more than one action with this property then the choice is random.

The idea behind this algorithm can be visualized on a 2 x 2 game matrix: After the first move has been played, both agents will switch action forcing them to play in the diagonally opposite corner. Then once they randomly choose one the previously unplayed joint actions they are forced to choose the remaining unplayed joint action.

On average this will take 5 moves to visit every square in a 2 x 2 grid, and thus solve a single state 2 x 2 game with deterministic payoffs. This is significantly faster than using purely random move selection.

There is however the potential for this algorithm to deadlock on larger grids, as shown in the following example. Visited joint actions are marked as X's, previously unvisited joint actions as O's.

After 3 moves without loss of generality the agents reach the following position:

$$\begin{bmatrix} X & O & O \\ O & X & O \\ O & O & X \end{bmatrix}$$

The agents then choose a random move and might reach the following state:

$$\begin{bmatrix} X & X & O \\ X & X & O \\ O & O & X \end{bmatrix}$$

From that state they could end up in:

$$\begin{bmatrix} X & X & O \\ X & X & O \\ O & O & Z \end{bmatrix}$$

when the agents are stuck playing joint action Z forever.

No doubt more complicated deadlocks are possible on larger grids. Hence we need a mechanism to avoid these situations: if the algorithm generates the same action twice in a row without having invoked a random move, then it has to play a random action instead.

Whilst these problems mean that performance isn't as good as in the 2 x 2 case, the enhanced action selection is still an improvement over the basic technique. Since it also involves little extra complexity it was used in the experiments below.

The advantages of the modified action selection algorithm over random action choice are not as big in games with stochastic pay offs. In such games each joint action has to be visited multiple times, rather than just once, in order to solve the game. Random action choice leads to a more uniform distribution of actions.

3.2 Simple Coordination Learning for Multi Stage Games

For the multi-stage case, our proposed algorithm is based on Q learning [6], and uses random action selection during the learning phase. More formally, on observing the current joint action A, its payoff, and the current state s, an agent first updates the Q value for A and s:

$$Q(s, A) = R(s, A) + \gamma \sum_{s \in S} T(s, A, s') \max_{a' \in A} Q(s', a') \tag{1}$$

Here n is the number of times the joint action A has been seen, $R(s, a)$ its average payoff for action a in state s so far, γ is the discount factor (we chose 0.9), and T holds the transition probabilities so far observed. When learning is finished (after a fixed number of iterations), each agent returns the action that is part of the joint action with the highest Q value.

Because the Q values are calculated over the joint actions, with each agent calculating identical Q value tables, this is exactly analogous to the case of single agent Q learning and convergence to an optimal action choice is therefore guaranteed [6].

While it is difficult to generally compute the time required for the agents to converge to the optimal joint action, we present this computation for the C&B game from Figure 5.

Each choice of moves in a three state cycle can be viewed as single choice between $2^3 = 8$ different possible moves. The choice of move in the final state is however for this game irrelevant as you always return to the start state, so there are only four different actions to consider: aa, ab, ba, and bb. Since action choice at each state is independent of the choices made at previous states for this algorithm then this equivalence is clear. The factor of three is simply because you've treating three seperate moves as single ones. This could take quite a long time except that such games typically have numerous identical pay offs if considered in this way. For instance the game mentioned above in Figure 5 is equivalent to the following 4 by 4 game (with the actions being considered as aa, ab, ba, and bb).

	Player 1			
	aa	*ab*	*ba*	*bb*
aa	10	-10	-10	10
ab	10	-10	-10	10
ba	5	5	5	5
bb	5	5	5	5

Player 2 labels the rows *aa*, *ab*, *ba*, *bb*.

Fig. 7. single-state reduction of the C&B game

Thus the multi-state learning algorithm will have a $\left(1 - \left(\frac{12}{16}\right)^{\left(\frac{k}{3}\right)}\right)$ chance of converging in k moves. For example, it will reach 94.4% convergence in 30 moves.

4   Empirical Evaluation

In this section we show that the algorithms proposed in the previous section perform very well on a wide range of problems from the research literature. For further evidence, we compare the performance of the algorithms to the OAL algorithm [1], a widely cited learning technique that is applicable to both single-stage and multi-stage games. We do not present details of the algorithm here, but rather refer the reader to the original paper. Note however, that OAL is much more complex than the simple approaches presented in Section 3.

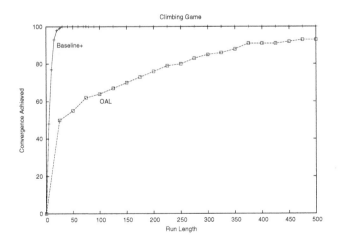

Fig. 8. Evaluation on the Climbing Game

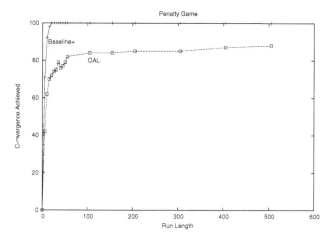

Fig. 9. Evaluation on the Penalty Game

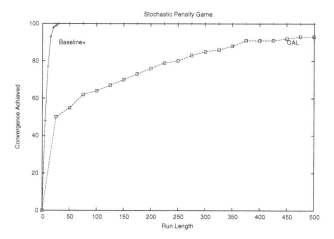

Fig. 10. Evaluation on the Stochastic Penalty Game

For our experiments OAL's results were averaged over 1000 runs, the simple algorithms, which run a lot faster, over 10,000 runs.

In the result graphs below, the single-stage game learning technique is denoted by `Baseline+` and the multi-stage game algorithm by `MSBaseline`.

4.1   Evaluationon Single-Stage Games

We evaluated the single stage game learning algorithm on the Climbing Game, the Penalty Game, and the Stochastic Climbing Game (described in Section 2.1. Figures 8, 9, and 10 show the probabilities of convergence to the optimal joint action as a function of the number of learning steps. The results show that the simple learning technique clearly outperforms OAL.

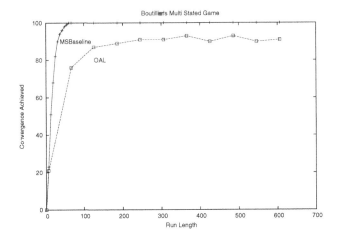

Fig. 11. Evaluation on the C&B Game

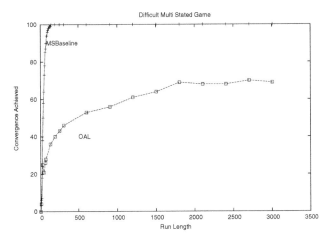

Fig. 12. Evaluation on the Misleading Game

4.2   Evaluation on Multi-stage Games

The multi-stage game algorithm has been evaluated on the C&B game and the Misleading Game from Section 2.2. The simple learning technique performs very well on both games, as shown in Figures 11 and 12.

5   Another Improvement

For reasons explained later, the `baseline+` algorithm currently only works for single state games (or multi state games with non stochastic state transition functions) and so these are the type of game referred to in it's description.

While the algorithms presented above are extremely fast joint action learners for games with constant pay offs there is still a lot of room for improvement in games with stochastic payoffs. This can be seen by considering a 3 x 3 game with one payoff which gives 100, -20 and -20 with equal probability and where the other payoffs give 0. An ideal learner would concentrate on observing the 100/-20/-20 payoff until it was fairly sure whether it was bigger or smaller than the 0 payoffs and spend little time on the constant payoffs.

The first possibility is biasing action selection in favour of those joint actions whose payoffs were displaying the highest standard deviations and of which we were thus least sure about the true value. However this would perform badly in games where there was a payoff with very low expectation but high standard deviation. Clearly some measure of how good an observed payoff is should also be taken into consideration.

Parametric statistics are a useful tool to achieve this. The observed expected payoffs for each joint action will be distributed approximately normally, in a distribution which tends towards the normal distribution as the number of observations tends toward infinity, and the standard deviations of these distributions are easy to calculate. This involves several approximations but they can be generally be expected to be within reasonable range to the true value.

Since agents know both the means and standard deviations for these normal distributions, they can compare their means and say how likely it is that one payoff might have a true mean bigger than another's. This idea (hypothesis testing) is very common in statistics and is central to our algorithm.

The second inspiration for our algorithm was a desire to have a self terminating algorithm. Our aim was to allow the user to set a confidence limit, after which the algorithm will take as long as it needs to get that accurate an answer given the game it is learning. This idea contrasts with many current algorithms where the designer explicitly specifies in advance when the algorithm should stop learning, whether directly as in the case of the algorithms above, or indirectly via a decaying temperature setting as in many Q learning implementations.

If the structure of a game is unknown, it is hard to predict how long it will take a given algorithm to reliably solve it.

5.1   The Statted Learning Algorithm

Ideally, a user would choose a percentage indicating a degree of confidence that the joint action that the agents choose is the true optimum. Unfortunately this is not completely possible due to the approximations involved.

Our proposed algorithm works in two distinct stages and requires initialisation of the following variables:

- SDTolerance : how many standard deviations the user wants to test against to see whether an action could possibly be the optimal action or not. This defines the desired confidence in the optimality of the resulting joint action.
- ExplorationCutOff: An integer constant that is explained below. This setting also effects the accuracy of the results obtained.

- ToleranceLevel : Explained below. This defines how close agents would let the expected values for a pair of joint actions be before they ceased to care about which joint action is selected from them.
- σ_0: A number used to try and increase the accuracy of the estimates of the sample standard deviations. This is useful as otherwise one can get quite misleading sample standard deviations when trying to approximate distributions far from the normal.

Having received these inputs, the algorithm then performs an exploration phase followed by a phase of continuous exploitation which is ended when it outputs a joint action which it considers to be likely to be optimal.

Exploration. This stage is designed to achieve two things: that all joint actions have been observed and that the observed payoffs from the joint actions are in some way representative of the actual expected pay off from playing those joint actions.

This phase consists of playing random moves whilst tracking both the mean and the sample variance of the joint actions observed, which is given by $\hat{\sigma}_\mu^2 = \frac{S+\sigma_0^2}{n^2-m^2}$. Here S is the sum of squared received rewards ,σ_0 is defined above and n is the number of times this joint action has been played.

Basically σ_0 is used as a safety net: if a joint action has turned up the same value multiple times, then we still want it to have some standard deviation in case it has a second value that it can also take. This is only an issue with stochastic payoffs of the form $p/-p$, where each of the payoffs has probability 0.5. The means observed from more continuously distributed payoff functions will approximate much faster to normal distributions.

When every joint action which has been observed at least once, has been seen at least `ExplorationCutOff` times, exploration ends and the algorithm moves into exploitation.

Exploitation. First, the joint action with the highest currently observed reward is identified.

Then form a set of all possibly optimal joint actions OA is formed by including joint action j_i if $\frac{m_1-m_j}{\sqrt{\sigma_1^2+\sigma_i^2}} \leq$ SDTolerance. This is a simple one tail hypothesis test on the sample means of the payoff distributions.

If OA has only one member then the action that is part of that joint action is returned as the proposed optimum.

The algorithm above has the problem that it does not terminate when there are two joint actions with identical long term payoffs. Also, it could take a very long time if there were two joint actions with very similar pay offs. In order to overcome these problems we introduced a test for whether all the means for the possibly optimal actions were within a given tolerance limit of each other.

This test is passed if for every $m_j \in$ OA:

$$(m_1 - m_j) + \text{SDTolerance} \times \sqrt{\sigma_1^2 + \sigma_j^2} \leq \text{TL} \tag{2}$$

Here m_1 is again the action currently believed to be optimal and TL is the tolerance level as provided as input into the algorithm. If this test is passed then the differences between the expected payoffs of the joint actions in OA are considered to be insignificant and you can output a member of OA as the optimal action. Various techniques for this choice are possible, going for the one with the lowest standard deviation seems a good idea.

If both tests of these tests fail, then the algorithm continues by playing the joint action in OA which has the highest standard deviation. The results for that joint action are then updated in line with the observed result, and the exploitation phase continues until one of these tests is passed and an answer is produced.

5.2   Statted Baseline Evaluation

The statted algorithm by it's very nature doesn't produce a graph of convergence achieved against time, but rather indvidual points which correspond to a fixed choice of settings. Each point has an average convergence and a average speed taken to achieve this level of convergence. Hence tables rather than graphs are used to present the results.

The statted Baseline is tested separately as it's use in game which don't feature large stochastic elements in their pay off functions is pointless.

The 'Simple' Stochastic Game. This game (shown in Figure 13) is designed to test the algorithm's ability to cope with having to pick out an optimal action from among some discouraging payoffs. The issue is how long it takes for the agents to play the 160/-40/-40 enough times in order to realise that it is the optimal action. The statted learning algorithm was inspired by this game and one would expect it to perform well on it.

Player 1

		a	b	c
	a	160/-40/-40	0	0
Player 2	b	0	0	0
	c	0	0	0

Fig. 13. Simple Stochastic Game

The evaluation results are shown in Figure 14 and in tables 1,2 and 3. The table are given to illustrate the effects of varying the values of the settings upon the algorithms performance.

The fastest settings tested were: ToleranceLevel = 1, MinSD = 0; SDTol = 2, ExpCutOff = 7 giving 95% Convergence in an average of 126 moves. If everything is kept the same except for setting ECOff = 10, the algorithm yields 98% convergence in 159 moves. Setting ECOff = 15 results 99% convergence in 212 moves. Many of the failures here are due to the joint action (a,a) coming out of the exploration phase with a large negative expectation and then being ignored subsequently.

Table 1. SD = 1, Min SD = 1, Sens = 0.1, Varying Exp Cut Off

Exploration Cut Off	Time Taken	Convergence
3	54	57
4	69	78
5	80	84
6	90	87
7	101	89
8	111	90
9	122	92
10	133	92
11	144	93
12	155	96

Table 2. Exp Cut off = 10, varying SDTol

SDTol	Time	Convergence
0	126	86
0.2	126	84
0.4	127	86
0.6	128	88
0.8	130	91
1	133	93
1.2	137	94
1.4	142	96
1.6	148	96
1.8	154	97
2	163	98
2.2	171	98
2.4	181	99

Table 3. as above but Exp Cut Off = 5

SDTol	Time	Convergence
0	67	75
0.5	69	78
1	80	85
1.5	94	89
2	116	90
2.5	142	91
3	178	91
3.5	220	91
4	267	91
4.5	318	93
5	379	93

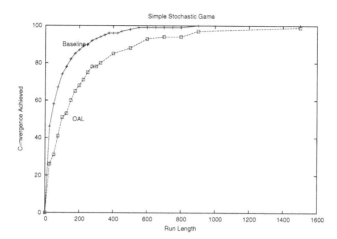

Fig. 14. 'Simple' Stochastic Game

The Stochastic Penalty Game. This game was defined in Section 2.1. It is not that interesting as an evaluation of the statted algorithm since either payoff from the optimal joint actions is higher than any other achievable pay off. Thus once the agents have played the optimal joint action once they know that it is optimal.

This game does however illustrate one big performance issue with the statted learning algorithm. If the tolerance level is set too low it can take a very long time to decide that two joint actions give equivalent pay offs.

For example, if ExpCutoff = 6, SDTolerance = 2, MinSD = 5, and ToleranceLevel = 1, 100% convergence is reached in 6300 steps. If the tolerance level is increased to 10 the required number of steps to guarantee convergence drops to 191. When set to 15 this further drops to 129 steps.

And with the settings of ExpCutoff = 20, increasing SDTolerance to 4 gives a success rate of 99% in 85 moves.

This is typical of games where there are several optimal joint actions with equal payoff. A lot of the average time taken in the simple stochastic game was due to the agents having decided that the optimal pay off was bad and then having to decide that the eight payoffs yielding zero were equal.

A large factor in causing this problem is the decision to have a minimum standard deviation in the algorithm. If this wasn't used then constant payoffs would have 0 standard deviation and the algorithm wouldn't take any time at all to solve these problems. In some cases the MinSD factor should therefore be removed from the algorithm entirely.

Two Difficult Tests. The game in Figure 15 has been designed as a tough test of an algorithm's ability to tell quite similar stochastic payoffs apart. In this setup the `Baseline+` algorithm achieves about 95% convergence after 5500 runs; whereas the statted algorithm only takes about 2700 moves to reach that level.

Player 1

	a	b	c
a	6/-4	3/-3	-6/4
Player 2 b	3/-3	5/-4	3/-3
c	-6/4	3/-3	5/-4

Fig. 15. Difficult Stochastic Game

One would expect this, as the statted baseline concentrates its action choice on distinguishing the 3 close payoffs (6/-4 and the 5/-4's).

Replacing one or two of the 5/-4 payoffs with 6/-4 payoffs should favour the baseline over the statted baseline as the statted baseline will worry about checking to see if they are the same, whereas the baseline will just have two or more targets instead of only one.

And indeed if one of the 5/-4's is replaced with a 6/-4 then the `Baseline+` algorithm reaches 95% convergence in about 2000 moves, and the statted algorithm performance is very similar.

If the final 5/-4 is replaced with another 6/-4 then, one would expect the baseline to dominate and it does: it reaches 95% convergence in only 400 moves. The reason for this is that there aren't any payoffs remaining close to the 6/-4's to distract it. The statted algorithm becomes very dependent on its sensitivity setting: if you set it to 0.5, then it achieves 94% in 2872; if you set it to 1 then it achieves 93.5% in 1032 moves. Clearly it is spending most of its time deciding whether or not the three 6/-4 pay offs are equal.

5.3   Comments

One observation about the statted algorithm is that if it sometimes played random moves during its exploitation phase and never terminated, then it would eventually find the truly optimal action. This would happen as the observed averages tend to the true averages with probability one over time. Also since the sample standard deviations tend towards zero over time then the algorithm as presented is guaranteed to eventually terminate at some stage.

Because this algorithm performs the exploitation deterministically based on information which is shared between all of the agents, it is guaranteed to achieve coordination at every stage and in particular in the choice of optimal action.

A question is whether it will output an optimal action when it terminates. There are several ways that it can fail to do this:

 - It can simply never observe the optimal joint action during the exploration phase.
 - It can omit the optimal joint action from the set of potential optimal joint actions, either upon formation of this set or later during exploitation, due to misleading results in the expected payoff.

The first problem is difficult to avoid and the chance of it occurring tends to zero as ExplorationCutOff tends to infinity. In practice for a 3 x 3 grid an exploration cut off of 4 gives a $1 - (8/9)^{32} \approx 98\%$ chance of seeing a single optimal action. An exploration cut off of 6 suffices to make it very unlikely that the optimal action is missed during exploration.

It is unfortunate that larger grids require larger values of ExplorationCutOff than smaller ones to reach the same degrees of confidence as this goes against the overall design philosophy by requiring (very basic) knowledge of the games structure to decide on the inputs to use. However this seems unavoidable.

The second problem is also unavoidable, although a large value of any of ExplorationCutOff, SDTolerance or MinSD will make this a rare occurrence.

If ExplorationCutOff is high then the observed averages will be very likely to be close to the true averages and so the optimal action is unlikely to be omitted due to having a low observed payoff. If MinSD or SDTolerance are very high then the set of possibly optimal actions is likely to be very large and include the optimal action.

The statted algorithm does struggle with joint actions which produce bad payoffs most of the time but very rarely produce a hugely positive action. In general such problems are fundamentally difficult for any reinforcement learner.

There curerntly is no version of this algorithm for games with multiple states. In principle the main ideas are still valid in this case: just track the Q values and their sample standard deviations instead of the raw means. A problem arises when calculating the standard deviations of the Q values.

As the transition probabilities are also sample means they are approximately normally distributed and need their standard deviations taken into account. One then ends up with a distribution for the observed mean of each Q value formed by summing the results of taking the products of various normal distributions. This distribution is rather difficult to work with. Having said that, this would probably be possible and would probably produce produce useful results for multi-stage games.

6   Conclusions

We have shown on a wide range of difficult coordination games from the research literature that learning of coordination can be effectively achieved with very simple and efficient approaches, where agents can observe each other's actions. We thus strongly argue for the use of the simple techniques as baselines in any future research on joint-action learning of coordination.

That such approaches are effective, and indeed close to optimal in terms of speed, in coordination games should not be surprising.

For a single stage game with constant payoffs the only thing a joint action learner has to worry about is viewing each possible joint action as quickly as possible. Since there is also in general in these games no coloration between the values of joint actions using most of the same actions, there is no way to predict good joint actions from the past results of observing other joint actions and random play is the best policy. Also the games under consideration are small enough to render observing the entire state/action space feasible. Multi-stage games with stochastic pay offs are a little more difficult but not at a fundamental level.

However in typical real world problems, you may only have time to observe a small fraction of the total state/action space and solutions which are at least locally optimal may well be clustered closely together. For such problems the simple learners presented in this paper will tend not to perform very well.

References

Wang, X., Sandholm, T.: Reinforcement learning to play an optimal nash equilibrium in team markov games. In: Proceedings of the Sixteenth Conference on Neural Information Processing Systems. (2002)

Kapetanakis, S., Kudenko, D.: Reinforcement learning of coordination in cooperative multiagent systems. In: Proceedings of the Eighteenth National Conference on Artifical Intelligence. (2002)

Claus, C., Boutilier, C.: Dynamics of reinforcement learning in cooperative multiagent systems. In: Proceedings of the Fifteenth National Conference on Artifical Intelligence, 1998. (1998)

Chalkiadakis, G., Boutilier, C.: Coordination in multiagent reinforcement learning: A bayesian approach. In: Proceedings of the Second international conference on Automonous Agents and Multiagent Systems. (2003)

Littman, M.L.: Markov games as a framework for multi - agent reinforcement learning. In: Proceedings of the Eleventh International Conference on machine Learning. (1994)

Watkins, C.: Learning from Delayed Rewards. PhD thesis, King's College, Cambridge University (1989)

SMART (Stochastic Model Acquisition with ReinforcemenT) Learning Agents: A Preliminary Report

Christopher Child[*] and Kostas Stathis

Department of Computing,
School of Informatics,
City University, London
{c.child,k.stathis}@city.ac.uk

Abstract. We present a framework for building agents that learn using SMART, a system that combines stochastic model acquisition with reinforcement learning to enable an agent to model its environment through experience and subsequently form action selection policies using the acquired model. We extend an existing algorithm for automatic creation of stochastic strips operators [9] as a preliminary method of environment modelling. We then define the process of generation of future states using these operators and an initial state and finally show the process by which the agent can use the generated states to form a policy with a standard reinforcement learning algorithm. The potential of SMART is exemplified using the well-known predator prey scenario. Results of applying SMART to this environment and directions for future work are discussed.

1 Introduction

Reinforcement learning has been shown to be a powerful tool in the automatic formation of action policies for agents [7]. There are two main approaches: Value learning (V-Learning) which assigns a value to each state in the system and Q-Learning, which assigns a value to each state action pair [11]. V-learning assigns state values by propagating back rewards received in future states after taking an *action* according to a *policy*. V-learning is limited in application because it requires a model of the world in order to predict which state will occur after each action. Q-Learning is more widely applicable because it assigns rewards to a state action pair. The agent is therefore not required to predict the future state and does not require a model. Often it is impossible for the designer of an agent to provide a model of the environment. Even if the environment has been designed in software, the transition from state to state may be impossible for the designer to predict due to factors such as the action of other agents.

In this paper we investigate "stochastic model acquisition". We define this to be any system which enables an agent to acquire a model of its environment from the environment. To be more precise we are modelling the agent's perception of the environment because this is all the information which it has access to. Initially the agent has knowledge of the actions it can perform, but not the effects, and has a perceive

---

[*] Corresponding author.

D. Kudenko et al. (Eds.): Adaptive Agents and MAS II, LNAI 3394, pp. 73 – 87, 2005.
© Springer-Verlag Berlin Heidelberg 2005

function that maps a world state to a set of percep variables. The agent's task is to discover which variables are effected by its actions, the conditions under which these effects will occur, and an associated probability. Using this model the agent can develop an action policy to achieve a goal using reinforcement learning. Similar work on modelling in deterministic environments has been called "discovery" [12] and "constructivist AI" [4].

A well-studied model based reinforcement learning architecture is Dyna-Q [11]. The algorithm suffers from the disadvantage that it relies on statistical measures of entire state transitions rather than state variable transitions. These require multiple visits to each state in a stochastic environment before an accurate model can be built. As the number of states increases exponentially with the number of state variables in the system, the method quickly becomes impractical.

Our approach is motivated by a number of observations:

1. V-learning reduces the state space for the reward function as compared to Q-learning by an order of magnitude;
2. Construction of a model allows us to make predictions about state action pairs that have previously not been visited;
3. Learning in the model, rather than through environment interaction can reduce the learning time of reinforcement learning algorithms.
4. Changes in the agents goals (reward function) result in re-learning a state-value map from the model, rather than re-learning in the environment. A new policy can therefore be formed with no environment interaction.

Several methods have been evaluated for representing a stochastic environment using a factored state model [1]. The most compact representation is identified as the use of probabilistic STRIPS operators [6]. Other methods they describe are generally based on two-tier Bayesian networks. These require exponentially large storage for the probability matrix as the number of state variables increases, unless the structure of variable dependencies is known. This structure can be learned but is a research area in itself. The MSDD algorithm [9] has been shown to be an effective method of learning stochastic STRIPS operators and will therefore be used in this work.

Having generated a set of stochastic STRIPS operators, the next stage is to generate expected world states using these STRIPS operators. Finally we use a standard reinforcement learning algorithm to create a value map and therefore an action policy for the agent. This results in a fully functional agent mind, generated with no human intervention.

2 Motivating Example

The broad motivation for this research is towards automatic action selection mechanisms for robotics, software agent and computer game applications. For the purposes of this extended abstract we have selected the well known predator prey scenario, which is a very simple example of an agent which has a limited number of actions and a restricted perceptual system.

We will be using a simple predator prey scenario (figure 1). There is a four by four grid surrounded by a "wall". There is *one* predator and *one* prey. The predator will be

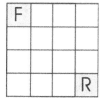

Fig. 1. Simple predator prey scenario. F indicates the predator (fox) and R the prey (rabbit)

assumed to have caught the prey when it lands on the same square. In this instance the prey will simply select a random action. Both predator and prey have four ac-tions:move north, east, south and west. An action has the effect of moving the agent one square in the selected direction, unless there is a wall, in which instance there is no effect. The predator and prey move in alternate turns. The agent's percep gives the contents of the four squares around it and the square it is on. Each square can be in one of three states: empty, wall or agent. For example a predator agent which is situ-ated in the north west corner of the grid with a prey to the east would have the percep <WALL, AGENT, EMPTY, WALL, EMPTY> corresponding to the squares to the north, east, south, west and under respectively, as shown in figure 2.

Fig. 2. The predator agent percep

3 Framework

The stages of the agent system are as follows: stochastic model acquisition, state generation and policy generation.

3.1 Stochastic Model Acquisition

3.1.1 Stochastic STRIPS Operators
The STRIPS planning operator representation has, for each action, a set of precondi-tions, an "add" list, and a "delete" list [5]. The STRIPS planner was designed for deterministic environments, with the assumption that actions taken in a state matching the operator's preconditions would consistently result in the state changes indicated by the operators add and delete lists. In a non-deterministic environment a less restric-tive view is taken, allowing actions to be attempted in any state. The effects of the action then depend on the state in which it was taken and are influenced by some properties external to the agents perception which appear random from the agent's perspective.

We follow the format for stochastic STRIPS operators used by Oates & Cohen [10]. A stochastic STRIPS operator takes the form:

$$O = < a, c, e, p >$$

where a specifies an action, c specifies a context, e the effects and p the probability. If the agent is in a state matching the context c, and takes the action a, then the agent will observe a state matching the effects e with probability p.

Contexts and effects of operators are specified as a list of tokens representing the percep and the action of the agent in the order described in section 2, with the addition of a wildcard symbol (*) denoting irrelevance, which matches any token.

As an example of the use of wildcards, consider the following operator:

<MOVE EAST, (* WALL * * *), (* WALL * * *)> *Prob:*1.0

In this example: a is MOVE EAST, c is (* WALL * * *), e is (* WALL * * *) and p is 1.0.

This operator specifies that if the agent chooses to move north and the contents of the square to the north is detected as WALL then the contents of the square to the north of the agent on the next time step will still be a wall, with probability 1.0. The wildcards specify that this condition is irrelevant of anything else that the agent observes. The percep order is as specified in section 2. Note that the agent's percep does not include the agent itself.

3.2   Learning STRIPS Operators

We have chosen to use Multi-Stream Dependency Detection (MSDD) [9] to learn the STRIPS operators in this context. Although inductive logic programming (ILP) [8] is powerful in its domain area of learning predicate logic rules, it is still an open research area to generate reliable stochastic logic rules with the system. MACCENT is another inductive logic system specifically designed for learning stochastic rules [2], but is not well suited to large rule sets. MSDD has been chosen for its suitability to deal with the domain area, and has previously been shown to be able to generate stochastic STRIPS operators from data [10].

3.2.1 MSDD

Formal statements of both the MSDD algorithm and its node expansion routine are given in the algorithms below. MSDD is a batch algorithm and uses H, the precep data observed by the agent in the preconditions-effects format shown in section 3.1.1. The function f evaluates the best node to expand next and typically counts the co-occurrence of the node's preconditions and effects. This requires a complete pass over the data set H.

```
MSDD (H, f, maxnodes)
1. expanded = 0
2. nodes   = ROOT-NODE()
3. while NOT-EMPTY(nodes) and expanded < maxnodes do
     a. remove from nodes the node n maximising f(H,n)
     b. EXPAND(n), adding its children to nodes
     c. increment expanded by the number of
        children generated in (b)
```

```
EXPAND (n)
1. for i from m down to 1 do
   a. if n.preconditions[i] ≠ '*' then
      return children
   b. for t ∈ Tᵢ do
      i.   child = COPY-NODE(n)
      ii.  child.preconditions[i] = t
      iii. push child onto children
2. repeat (1) for the effects of n
3. return children
```

This algorithm does not specify which children should be generated before others, but does ensure that each dependency is explored only once, and facilitates pruning of the search. For example, all descendants of the node

```
<*, (WALL * * * *), (WALL * * * *)>
```

can be pruned because there is no need to explore rules with a wildcard in the action position, and all descendants of this node will be expanded from the rightmost wild-card resulting in children with no action.

We have made two changes to standard MSDD. The first is in EXPAND (b.iii). We check that the generated child matches at least one observation in the database before adding it to children. For example, MSDD can generate the rule <*, (WALL WALL WALL * *), (* * * * *)>, but in our environment the agent can only observe a maximum of two walls (when it is positioned in the corner of the map). A check against the data set will reveal that the generated rule has no matches and can be eliminated from the node list, along with it's children as a consequence. This prevents the generation of a large number of incorrect rules, which would have been eliminated in the "filter" stage of MSDD.

The second change is that the effect part of the rule is allowed to have only one non-wildcard element. We have made this change because a very large number of rules are generated by standard MSDD. Combining individual effect fluents can generate complete successor states. This has the disadvantage that illegal states can be created, such as <WALL WALL WALL * *>. These can, however, be eliminated using constraints (section 3.3).

3.2.2 Filter

The second stage of MSDD is the "filter" process, which removes specific rules already covered by more general ones. For example, $<c_1 c_2 * * *>$ is a more specific version of $<c_1 * * * *>$. If the condition c_2 has no significant effect on the probability of the rule then it is unnecessary. For example, MSDD could generate two rules as follows:

```
<MOVE NORTH, (WALL WALL * * *), (* WALL * * *)> Prob: 1.0
<MOVE NORTH, (* WALL * * *),    (* WALL * * *)> Prob: 1.0
```

Both of these rules tell us that, if the agent moves north and there was a wall to the east, it will observe a wall to the east on the next move. The extra information that there was a wall to the north does not affect the agent's subsequent observation. More general operators are preferred because a reduced number of rules can cover the same information. For operators which do not have a probability of 1 we are testing, for an operator $O = <a, c, e, p>$, whether $Prob\ (e \mid c_1, c_2, a)$ and $Prob\ (e \mid c_1, a)$ are significantly different. If not, the general operator is kept and the specific one discarded.

```
FILTER (D, H, g)
1. sort D in non-increasing order of generality
2. S = {}
3. while NOT_EMPTY(D)
   a. s = POP(D)
   b. PUSH (s, S)
   c. for d ∈ D do
      if SUBSUMES(s, d) and G(s, d, H) < g then
         remove d from D
4. Return S
```

Where D is the set of dependency operators generated by MSDD. H is the history of observations made by the agent. SUBSUMES(d_1, d_2) is a Boolean function defined to return true if dependency operator d_1 is a generalisation of d_2. G(d_1, d_2, H) returns the G statistic to determine whether the conditional probability of d_1's effects given its conditions is significantly different from d_2's effects given its conditions. The parameter g is used as a threshold, which the G statistic must exceed before d_1 and d_2 are considered different (a value of 3.84 for g tests for statistical significance at the 5% level).

For example, dependency d_1 below returns a very low G statistic when compared with d_2:

```
d₁:<MOVE NORTH, (WALL * EMPTY * AGENT), (* * * * AGENT) >
d₂:<MOVE NORTH, (WALL * * * AGENT),     (* * * * AGENT) >
```

The additional condition that there is an EMPTY square to the south does not effect the probability of an agent being present on the square it inhabits after a move north (which will be the same square because there is a wall to the north). The predator agent already has the information that the prey is in the same square and that there is a WALL to the north, so the square to the south will either be the prey or be empty irrelevant of the empty square to the south. For an explanation of calculation of the G statistic see [9].

3.2.3 Rule Complements

When running MSDD on data collected from the predator prey scenario, we observed that the "filter" process occasionally filters rules and not their complements. For example the filter process could filter d_2 below, but leave d_1:

```
d₁: <MOVE NORTH, (WALL WALL * * AGENT), (* * * * AGENT) >
d₂: <MOVE NORTH, (WALL WALL * * AGENT), (* * * * EMPTY) >
```

This would cause a problem in state generation (section 3.3), because the rule generates only states with agents present. To avoid this we have added a further step to the algorithm in order to search through all generated rules checking that their complement rules are present. This process is less problematic in our system because rules only have effects in one fluent.

```
AddRuleComplements(D, H)
for d ∈ D do
  f = d.effect
  for fValue ∈ possibleValues(f)
  if fValue not equal to f.value
    newRule = copy of d with d.effect set to
              fValue
    if newRule is not present in D
       if newRule has match in H
          add newRule to D
```

The above algorithm goes through all rules in the learned dependencies, *D*, checking that all possible values of its effect fluent are either present in *D* already or do not match any observations in the history *H*. If a missing rule is found it is added to *D*.

3.3   Generating States from Learned Rules

The state generator function of the SMART learning process generates all possible next states, with associated probabilities, for an action that the agent could take in a given state. These states are generated using the rules learned by MSDD from the history of observations. This state generation process is necessary for the agent to generate a state value map using reinforcement learning (section 3.3.5).

Our modified implementation of the MSDD algorithm generates a set of rules with only one fluent in the effects part in order to reduce substantially the number of rules that must be evaluated. When we match these against some initial conditions, such as:

```
<MOVE EAST, (EMPTY WALL WALL EMPTY EMPTY)>
```

The subset of the generated rules matching these conditions is shown in table 1.

Table 1. Subset of the generated dependency rules matching the condition <MOVE EAST, (EMPTY WALL WALL EMPTY EMPTY)>. E = EMPTY, W = WALL and A = AGENT. The table shows the rule set after removing general rules (section 3.3.1)

Conditions						*Effects*					*Pr*
Action	N	E	S	W	U	N	E	S	W	U	
EAST	*	W	*	*	*	*	W	*	*	*	1.0
EAST	*	*	W	*	*	*	*	W	*	*	1.0
EAST	E	W	*	E	*	*	*	*	A	*	0.07
EAST	E	W	*	E	*	*	*	*	E	*	0.93
EAST	E	W	*	*	E	A	*	*	*	*	0.03
EAST	E	W	*	*	E	E	*	*	*	*	0.97
EAST	*E*	*	*W*	*E*	*	*A*	*	*	*	*	*0.06*
EAST	*E*	*	*W*	*E*	*	*E*	*	*	*	*	*0.94*
EAST	E	W	*	E	E	*	*	*	*	E	1.0

Notice that the rule set correctly tells us that moving east when there is a wall to the east results in us still observing a wall to the east. Also moving east with a wall to the south results in a wall to the south irrespective of any other contextual information. The rule set captures all the information we require for the given state and action and has the advantage that rules are also applicable to many other states.

The generated rule set for a given situation can provide several rules for each output fluent. To generate individual states from these rules we have to decide which rules are more relevant in the given situation. The following sections describe the process by which we choose rules, and why the decision was made to process the rules in this way.

The stages of the state generator are:

1. Remove general rules covered by specific.
2. Remove rules with less specific effects.
3. Generate possible states and probabilities.
4. Remove impossible states using constraints and normalise the state probabilities.

The output of the state generator is a table of states and associated probabilities.

3.3.1 Remove General Rules Covered by Specific

The subset of the generated rules that apply to a specific state action pair may contain rules with different conditions applicable to the same effect fluent. If the environment has not been well explored by the agent, a general rule may be more reliable because a specific rule will not have been encountered as often in the history of observations made by the agent. If, however, the agent has been allowed to explore the environment extensively, as was the case in our experiments, we can assume that a specific rule is likely to contain more relevant information than a general one. An expansion to the system would be to choose less specific rules depending on the statistical confidence measure of each rule. This is a subject for further research.

General rules are removed by searching through the rest of the dependencies for other nodes with an effect for the same fluent. If another rule is found which is more specific the general rule is removed. Rules with equal specificity are not removed.

```
RemoveRulesCoveredBySpecific(rules)
sort rules in non-increasing order of generality
for rule ∈ rules
  for testRule ∈ rules after rule
    if effectFluent of rule is same
        position as effectFluent of testRule
      if rule.wildcards > testRule.wildcards
    remove rule from rules
```

Table 2 gives an example of rules that were removed to give the rule set in table 1. The rules were removed because a more specific rule was available for the same effect fluent.

3.3.2 Remove Rules with Less Specific Effects

MSDD generates rules with equally specific conditions but less specific results. Rules which are more specific in the effects part are providing us with the information that the given effect cannot arise in this context. We can therefore eliminate the less specific effects. The rules shown in Italics in table 1 are removed by this part of the state generation process, because other rules exist with equal specificity of effect.

Table 2. The first two rules in the above table were removed because the specific rule (in bold) covered them

Conditions						Effects					Pr
Action	N	E	S	W	U	N	E	S	W	U	
EAST	*	*	*	E	*	*	*	*	*	A	0.04
EAST	*	*	*	E	*	*	*	*	*	E	0.96
EAST	**E**	**W**	*****	**E**	**E**	*****	*****	*****	*****	**E**	**1.0**

```
removeLessSpecificOutcome(rules)
for rule ∈ rules do
  effectP = position of effect in testRule
  NumEffects = countRules(rule.conditions,
                          effectP)
  for other ∈ matchingNodes do
    if other has same effectP and same
            conditions
        otherNumEffects
            = countRules(other.conditions,
                         effectP)
    if otherNumEffects >= NumEffects
       removeRules(other.conditions, effectP)
     else if otherNumbOfEffects > 0
         removeRules(rule.conditions, effectP)
```

If we do not remove rules with less specific effect in this way the state generator can produce states which could not occur in the real environment. Consider, for example, the rules in table 3.

Table 3. Removing rules with less specific outcomes. Rules in Italics are removed because their outcome is less specific than the other rules with the same effect fluent

Conditions						Effects					Pr
Action	N	E	S	W	U	N	E	S	W	U	
NOR	E	E	W	*	E	E	*	*	*	*	0.94
NOR	E	E	W	*	E	A	*	*	*	*	0.06
NOR	*E*	*E*	***	*E*	*E*	*E*	***	***	***	***	*0.07*
NOR	*E*	*E*	***	*E*	*E*	*A*	***	***	***	***	*0.05*
NOR	*E*	*E*	***	*E*	*E*	*W*	***	***	***	***	*0.88*

The rules removed by this process, shown in Italics, state that a move north could result in a wall to the north. In fact there is a wall to the south in the original state. A move north could, therefore, only result in an empty square or an agent, as there is no situation in which the agent can move from one wall to another opposite in a single move in the environment.

3.3.3 Generate Possible States

The possible states are generated by:

1. Creating a new state from each combination of effect fluent values in the remaining rules.
2. Multiply the probability of each effect rule to generate the probability of each state.

The states generated from the rules in table 1 are as follows:

Table 4. Possible after states for the given state and action generated from the rules in table 1

NORTH	EAST	SOUTH	WEST	UNDER	Pr:
EMPTY	WALL	WALL	EMPTY	EMPTY	~0.91
EMPTY	WALL	WALL	AGENT	EMPTY	~0.07
AGENT	WALL	WALL	EMPTY	EMPTY	~0.02
AGENT	*WALL*	*WALL*	*AGENT*	*EMPTY*	*~0.001*

There were two rules for the "north" fluent with results EMPTY and AGENT, and two rules for the "west" fluent with results EMPTY and AGENT. The other rules had one result each resulting in a total of: 2 * 1 * 1* 2 * 1 = 4 possible states. The probabilities are found by multiplying together the probabilities of the rules that resulted in these fluents.

3.3.4 Remove Impossible States with Constraints

Some of the states generated could not occur in the domain area. For example in the predator prey scenario the operators may generate a percep with two agents, when there is only one agent in the world. We would ultimately like our agent to generate its own constraints that tell it which world states are impossible. A rule such as IMPOSSIBLE (* * AGENT AGENT *) would allow elimination of the impossible world states generated. For the purposes of this paper, we will be using a user-defined set of constraints. If we do not use these constraints the erroneous generated states can propagate to create world states where there are five prey agents, or walls surround the predator agent, and the model becomes meaningless as it is too far detached from the real world states. Currently the system simply removes impossible states by checking that each generated state does not contain more than one agent, or walls opposite each other. This method breaks the principle of an autonomous learning agent that learns a model of its environment without human intervention. A constraint generator will therefore be the subject of future research.

After elimination of illegal states the probabilities of remaining states are normalised by dividing the probability of each state by the total probability of all generated states to give the final states. This process removes the state in Italics in table 4 because it contains two agents.

3.3.5   Removing Unused Rules

In the present system the state generator has to continually search through the dependency list and remove general rules which are covered by specific ones. We could reduce both the size of the rule set, and the time taken to generate states by removing general rules which are never used to generate states from the rule set as follows:

Starting from the most general rule, in order of increasing specificity, we check to see if there is a set of more specific rules entirely covering the possible observed values of each wildcard fluent. If, for example, the rule set below exists:

```
d₁: <MOVE NORTH, (* * * * AGENT), (* * * * AGENT) >
d₂: <MOVE NORTH, (* * * * AGENT), (* * * * EMPTY) >
```

The following more specific rule set would cover the above rules and cause them to be unused:

```
d₁: <MOVE NORTH, (WALL * * * AGENT), (* * * * AGENT) >
d₂: <MOVE NORTH, (WALL * * * AGENT), (* * * * EMPTY) >
d₃: <MOVE NORTH, (EMPTY * * * AGENT), (* * * * AGENT) >
d₄: <MOVE NORTH, (EMPTY * * * AGENT), (* * * * EMPTY) >
```

Notice that the more specific rule set covers WALL and EMPTY, but does not have an AGENT value. In our predator prey scenario it is not possible to have two agents in one percep. These rules therefore cover all fluent values with the remaining value finding no matches in the database. This feature has not been implemented in the current system.

3.4   Generating Policies

We use standard reinforcement learning techniques to generate a policy for the agent. The acquired model allows us to use value iteration, which is a simple and efficient method of generating a value map for the agent [11]. The update equation for value iteration is given by:

$$V_{k+1}(s) = \max_a \sum_{s'} P_{ss'}^a [R_{ss'}^a + \gamma V_k(s')]$$
(1)

The value of state s on pass k +1 of the value iteration is calculated by taking the maximum valued action. The value of the action is equal to the sum for s' of the probability of action leading from state s to s' multiplied by the reward plus the discounted value of state s' on pass k. In order to generate a value map, we start with a state generated by a random initial position of the predator prey scenario and add this to the value map. A single entry in the value map is as follows:

State, Value, Reward

State is a percep (e.g. <WALL, WALL, EMPTY, EMPTY, EMPTY>). *Reward* is set to a positive value if there is an AGENT in the last position of the percep (corresponding to the predator catching the prey) and zero or a negative value otherwise. *Value*, for each state is then generated by repeated application of the following algorithm, with the next state to refine picked at random from those generated in the getCreateState-Value step of the algorithm below.

```
refineValue(state, actions, valueMap)
maxUtility = 0
for action ∈ actions do
  nextStatesAndProb = generateStates(state,
                                     action)
```

```
actionUtility = 0
for afterState ∈ nextStatesAndProb
  getCreateStateValue(afterState)
  actionUtility += afterState.probability *
     (afterState.value * γ + afterState.reward)
  if (actionUtility > maxUtility)
    maxUtility = actionUtility
setStateValue(valueMap, state, maxUtility)
```

4 Empirical Results

Performance of the policy generated by SMART learning was assessed by tested against a standard Dyna-Q algorithm [11]. Dyna-Q is a model based learning system, which uses a state map generated by recording the frequency with which each action in each state leads to the next state. Dyna-Q has previously been applied to the predator prey scenario presented in this paper [14]. We therefore repeat the test conditions used for this work using the SMART framework, for the purposes of comparison.

4.1 Test Conditions

An experimental run consisted of a sequence of trials or episodes that end after the prey has been captured. In the first trial of each run, the predator and prey are given the start position as indicated by figure 1. The result of an experiment was the number of steps required for the predator to catch the prey averaged over 30 runs. Each run was 2000 steps, giving 1000 moves for both the predator and prey agents.

Table 5. Average life-span of prey under test conditions

Action Method	Prey life-span
Random moves	16.37
Dyna-Q	7.04
SMART learning	9.72

In our test environment we allowed the agent to gather a perceptual history (H) from 10,000 iterations of the environment. Our extended MSDD algorithm was subsequently run on the observation history to generate stochastic STRIPS operators. The state generator and reinforcement learning algorithm were then applied for 2,000 iterations to generate a value map. *Reward* was set to 1.0 for a state where the prey agent is "under" the predator, and –0.1 otherwise. The discount factor ($γ$) was 0.9. The environment was then run according to the test conditions. On each environment update the predator agent picked the highest utility action. This was achieved using a similar process to the selection of highest utility action in the "refineValue" algorithm (section 3.4).

Both predator and prey taking random moves resulted in the predator being on the same square as the prey every 16.37 moves. This result is expected. There are 16 squares in the grid and the predator will randomly occupy the same square roughly once every 16 moves. The extra fraction is probably due to the start positions being at opposite ends of the grid.

Using Dyna-Q the predator caught the prey in an average of 7.04 moves. Dyna-Q was required to learn a policy during the run, and, as the predator and prey take alternate turns, half the moves are taken by the prey and although random, are likely to result in the prey evading the predator.

SMART learning resulted in the predator catching the prey in an average of 9.72 moves. Initially this might appear to be a low score when compared to Dyna-Q, because the agent enters the world with a fully formed policy. An ideal state action policy should result in the predator being able to move onto the prey's square every time it moves once it has caught it the initial time. This would result in a prey life-span of approximately 2 moves. The SMART learner, however, is a state-value method, and does not have access to the immediate effect of its action as it perceives just before it moves and not just after. The prey takes a move between these two perceptions, so the predator is only able to learn by an approximate method.

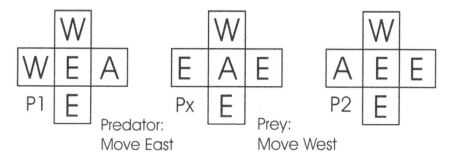

Fig. 3. Order of perceptions in predator-prey scenario

Figure 3 shows order of perceptions from the perspective of the predator. The predator initially has the percep P1. The move east action takes the predator onto the agent's square. The predator, however, does not observe the percep Px, because it is the prey's turn to move. When the predator observes again at P2 the prey has moved out of the "capture square". Methods such as Dyna-Q suffer less from this problem, because reward is associated with the state, action pair (e.g. <P1, Move East>) and the predator is therefore able to associate rewards with the actions which produced them.

Despite this problem, SMART learning enabled the agent to form a good policy in the predator prey environment and the failure to form an optimum policy owes more to the experimental conditions than a problem with the learning technique itself.

5 Conclusions and Future Work

We have presented a framework for stochastic model acquisition, which promises to be a powerful extension to the reinforcement learning paradigm. We have shown how to overcome some of the problems encountered when attempting to generate next states from automatically acquired STRIPS operators and demonstrated that action policies can be developed using a model represented by these operators.

The ability to learn a model of the environment through experience automates an otherwise difficult or impossible process for an agent designer. Future experiments aim to demonstrate that the agent can keep important experience when its goals are changed and the designer is able to change the reward structure and learn a new policy without the need for expensive interaction with the environment.

The use of a rule learning method to acquire a model provides an accessible format for a human designer. If the system is not performing as the designer wishes the rules can be investigated and anomalies spotted more easily than with a black box learning system such as a neural network.

Subjects of further research will include:

1. Testing the system in an environment more suited to model based learning, in which the results of action are immediately perceivable by the agent.
2. Evaluation of rule learning methods in environments with greater independence between state variables, where stochastic STRIPS operators are likely to more efficiently compress the environment model.
3. The addition of a parameterised value learning system to estimate state values, allowing compression of the state value map [13].
4. Investigation of stochastic predicate logic rule learning methods to learn stochastic situation calculus rules [8]. This would also require the use of a relational reinforcement learning method [3] to learn state values.

Acknowledgements

Chris Child would like to acknowledge the support of EPSRC, grant number 00318484.

References

1. Boutilier, C. Dean, T.Hanks, S. 1999. Decision-Theoretic Planning: Structural Assumptions and Computational Leverage. *Journal of Artificial Intelligence Research* 11: 1-94.
2. Dehaspe, L. 1997. Maximum Entropy Modeling with Clausal Constraints, In *Proceedings of the 7th International Workshop on Inductive Logic Programming*, volume 1297 of *Lecture Notes in Artificial Intelligence*, pages 109-125. Springer-Verlag.
3. Dzeroski, S. and De Raedt, L. and Blockeel, H. 1998. Relational Reinforcement Learning. *International Workshop on Inductive Logic Programming*.
4. Drescher, G.L. 1991. *Made-Up Minds, A Constructivist Approach to Artificial Intelligence*. The MIT Press.
5. Fikes, R.E. and Nilsson, N.J. 1971. STRIPS: a new approach to the application of theorem proving to problem-solving. *Artificial Intelligence* 2(3-4): 189-208.

6. Hanks, S. 1990. Projecting plans for uncertain worlds. Ph.D. thesis, Yale University, Department of Computer Science.

7. Kaelbling, L. P. and Littman, H.L. and Moore, A.P. 1996. Reinforcement Learning: A Survey. *Journal of Artificial Intelligence Research* 4: 237-285.

8. Muggleton, S.H. 2000. Learning Stochastic Logic Programs. *Proceedings of the AAAI2000 Workshop on Learning Statistical Models from Relational Data*, L. Getoor and D. Jensen, AAAI

9. Oates T., Schmill, M.D., Gregory, D.E. and Cohen P.R. 1995. Detecting complex dependencies in categorical data. Chap. in *Finding Structure in Data: Artificial Intelligence and Statistics V. Springer Verlag.*

10. Oates, T. and Cohen, P. R. 1996. Learning Planning Operators with Conditional and Probabilistic Effects. *AAAI-96 Spring Symposium on Planning with Incomplete Information for Robot Problems*, AAAI.

11. Sutton, R.S., and A.G. Barto. 1998. *Reinforcement Learning: An Introduction*. A Bradford Book, MIT Press.

12. Shen, W. 1993. Discovery as Autonomous Learning from the Environment. *Machine Learning* 12: 143-165.

13. Tesauro, G.J. 1994. TD-Gammon, a self-teaching backgammon program, achieves master-level play. *Neural Computation* 6, 2: 215-219.

14. Varsy, R. 2002. Extending Planning and Learning Through Reinterpretation of World Model. M.Sc. thesis, City Univesity.

Towards Time Management Adaptability in Multi-agent Systems

Alexander Helleboogh, Tom Holvoet, Danny Weyns, and Yolande Berbers

AgentWise, DistriNet,
Department of Computer Science K.U.Leuven, Belgium
Alexander.Helleboogh@cs.kuleuven.ac.be
Tom.Holvoet@cs.kuleuven.ac.be
Danny.Weyns@cs.kuleuven.ac.be
Yolande.Berbers@cs.kuleuven.ac.be

Abstract. So far, the main focus of research on adaptability in multi-agent systems (MASs) has been on the agents' behavior, for example on developing new learning techniques and more flexible action selection mechanisms. In this paper, we introduce a different type of adaptability in MASs, called *time management adaptability*. Time management adaptability focuses on adaptability in MASs with respect to execution control. First, time management adaptability allows a MAS to be adaptive with respect to its execution platform, anticipating arbitrary and varying timing delays which can violate correctness. Second, time management adaptability allows the execution policy of a MAS to be customized at will to suit the needs of a particular application. We discuss the essential parts of time management adaptability: (1) we employ *time models* as a means to explicitly capture the execution policy derived from the application's execution requirements, (2) we classify and evaluate *time management mechanisms* which can be used to enforce time models, and (3) we introduce a *MAS execution control platform* which combines both previous parts to offer high-level execution control.

1 Introduction and Motivation

Traditionally, the scope of research on adaptability in multi-agent systems (MASs) has been focused on trying to improve adaptability with respect to the behavior of individual agents and agent aggregations. As a consequence, the progress made by improving learning techniques and developing more flexible action selection mechanisms and interaction strategies over time is remarkable. This, however, may not prevent us from opening up our perspective and investigating other issues requiring adaptability in MASs. This paper is a report on ongoing work and introduces *time management adaptability* as an important form of adaptability with respect to the execution control of MAS applications.

1.1 The Packet-World

We introduce the Packet-World application we have developed [1], since this is used as an example MAS throughout the text.

D. Kudenko et al. (Eds.): Adaptive Agents and MAS II, LNAI 3394, pp. 88–105, 2005.

The Packet-World consists of a number of differently colored packets that are scattered over a rectangular grid. Agents that live in this virtual world have to collect those packets and bring them to their correspondingly colored destination. The grid contains one destination for each color. Fig.1 shows an example of a Packet-World of size 10x10 wherein 5 agents are situated. Colored squares symbolize packets and colored circles are delivery points. The colored rings symbolize pheromone trails discussed below.

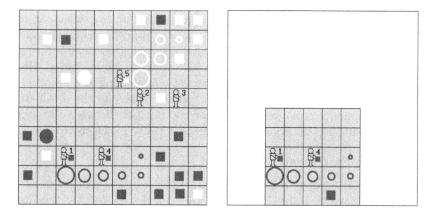

Fig. 1. The Packet-World: global screenshot (left) and view range of agent 4 (right)

In the Packet-World, agents can interact with the environment in a number of ways. We allow agents to perform a number of basic actions. First, an agent can make a step to one of the free neighbor fields around it. Second, if an agent is not carrying any packet, it can pick one up from one of its neighboring fields. Third, an agent can put down the packet it carries on one of the free neighboring fields around it, which could of course be the destination field of that particular packet.

It is important to notice that each agent of the Packet-World has only a limited view on the world. This view only covers a small part of the environment around the agent (see agent 4 in Fig.1).

Furthermore, agents can interact with other agents too. We allow agents to communicate indirectly based on stygmergy [2, 3, 4]: agents can deposit pheromone-like objects at the field they are located on. These pheromones can be perceived by other agents. Typical characteristics of pheromones are evaporation, aggregation and diffusion. Evaporation means that the strength of pheromones diminishes over time. Aggregation on the other hand means that different pheromone deposits at the same location are combined into a single pheromone with increased strength. Finally, diffusion means that pheromones deposited at a particular location are spread to neighboring locations over time, making it more likely that agents further away can perceive them.

In the Packet-World, only pheromone evaporation and aggregation are currently supported. This allows the impact of information that is not regularly reinforced to gradually decrease over time and to disappear eventually. In Fig.1, pheromones are symbolized by colored rings. The color of the ring corresponds to the packet color. The radius of the ring is a measure for the strength of the pheromone and decreases as the pheromone evaporates. In the Packet-World, agents use stygmergy to construct pheromone trails only when they move from clusters of packets towards the corresponding destinations [5]. Other agents noticing such a pheromone trail can decide to follow it in the direction of increasing pheromone strength to get to a specific destination (e.g. when they are already carrying a packet of corresponding color). On the other hand, agents can also decide to follow the trail in the direction of decreasing pheromone strength leading to the packet cluster (e.g. when they are not carrying anything). Hence they can help transporting the clustered packets, reinforcing the evaporating pheromone trail on their way back from the packet cluster to the destination. In this way, stygmergy provides a means for coordination between the agents which goes beyond the limitations of the agents' locality in the environment.

1.2   Problem Statement

So far, time in MASs is generally dealt with in an *implicit* and *ad hoc* way: once the agents have been developed, they are typically hooked together using a particular activation regime or scheduling algorithm, without an appropriate time management (see Fig.2). MASs with an implicit notion of time are generally not adapted at all to run-time variations of timing delays introduced by the underlying execution platform, e.g. network delays, delays due to scheduling policies, etc. Moreover, variations with respect to the execution of the agents can have a severe impact on the behavior of the MAS as a whole [6, 7, 8]. The main reason for this is that the temporal relations existing in the problem domain differ significantly from the arbitrary and variable time relations in an execution platform [9]. In other words, delays in an execution platform are based on quantities which have nothing to do with the problem domain. This emphasizes the need for an *explicit* time management. To illustrate this, consider the following examples from the Packet-World application:

1. In the Packet-World, agents with simpler internal logic can react faster than agents with more complex internal logic. Consider a packet lying in between a cognitive agent and a significantly faster reactive agent, for instance the

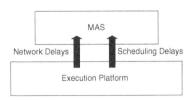

Fig. 2. MAS directly built upon an execution platform

white packet between agents 2 and 3 in Fig.1. In case both agents start
reasoning at the same time, it is required that the reactive agent can pick up
the packet before the cognitive one can. However, in practice, the response
order of both agents is arbitrary, because the underlying execution platform
could cause the cognitive agent's process to be scheduled first, allowing it to
start thinking earlier and pick up the packet before the faster reactive agent
even got a chance.

2. The agents can deposit pheromones in the environment to coordinate their
   activity. These pheromones evaporate over time. Because the effectiveness
   of pheromone-based communication is strongly dependent upon this evaporation rate, the latter is tuned to suit the needs of a particular application.
   However, fluctuations in the load of the underlying execution platform can
   cause agents to speed up or slow down accordingly, leading to a significant
   loss of pheromone effectiveness which affects the overall behavior of the MAS.

3. Problems can also arise with respect to the actions agents can perform. In the
   Packet-World application, the time period it takes to perform a particular
   action is required to be the same for all agents. However, fluctuations in
   processor load can introduce variations with respect to the execution time of
   actions. As a consequence a particular action of an agent can take longer than
   the same action performed by other agents. This leads to agents arbitrarily
   obtaining privileges compared to other agents due to the execution platform
   delays, a property which is undesirable in our problem domain.

The examples above show that a MAS without time management support
is not adapted to varying delays introduced by the execution platform, which
can be the cause of unforeseen or undesired effects. The execution of all entities
within a MAS has to be controlled according to the execution requirements of
the MAS, irrespective of execution platform delays. Currently the only option
for the developer is to hardcode these requirements from scratch into the MAS
application. However, this is a complex and error-prone task which has to be
tackled by the developer without any support. In this paper, we introduce *time
management adaptability* as a generic solution to this problem and a structured
way to control the execution of a MAS.

1.3   Time Management Adaptability

Time management adaptability allows the execution of a MAS to be controlled
according to an execution policy that can be adapted to suit the needs of a
particular MAS application. An execution policy specifies the desired timing
behavior for a MAS application in a platform-independent way. By enforcing
a particular execution policy, even in the presence of variable execution platform delays, time management adaptability allows all temporal relations that
are essential for the application to be correctly reproduced in the software system. In this way, a MAS application is adapted to varying delays introduced
by the execution platform. Moreover, time management adaptability allows easy

adaptation of a MAS's timing behavior, because it deals with time in an explicit manner and introduces execution control into a MAS as a separate concern. In order to achieve this, time management adaptability consists of three main parts (see Fig.3):

1. **Time models** are necessary to explicitly model the MAS's required timing behavior, irrespective of the underlying execution platform. As such, time models capture an execution policy according to which the MAS's execution has to be controlled. Time models are explicit which allows them to be adapted to reflect the customized needs of a particular MAS application.
2. **Time management mechanisms** are a means to enforce a MAS's customized time model, even in the presence of arbitrary delays introduced by the execution platform.
3. A **MAS execution control platform** combines both time models and time management mechanisms to control the execution of a MAS. In a MAS execution control platform, time models capture the execution requirements, and time management mechanisms are employed to prevent time models from being violated during execution. In this way, time as experienced from the point of view of the MAS application can be decoupled from the timing delays of the platform on which the MAS executes.

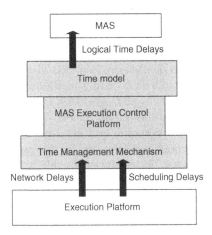

Fig. 3. Time management adaptability in MASs

Outline of the paper. We first clarify the concept of time in MASs in Sect.2. Then we discuss the various parts of time management adaptability: in Sect.3 we elaborate on *time models*. In Sect.4, we give an overview of the main *time management mechanisms* existing today, and Sect.5 discusses *MAS execution control platforms* in more detail. Finally, we look forward to future work in Sect.6 and draw conclusions in Sect.7.

2   Time in MAS

2.1   Time and Execution Requirements

MASs are characterized by a high degree of parallelism. A MAS consists of a (large) number of active, autonomous agents which coexist in a shared, active environment. A MAS does not have a global control flow, but instead each agent has its own, local flow of control [10] which allows the agent to have control over its own behavior. Because a MAS consists of several agents, the execution of all agents relative to each other has to be organized appropriately. More precisely, the execution of all agent activities within a MAS needs to be managed in a way that reflects the requirements of that particular MAS application. Because all agents run in parallel, each activity an agent can perform is related in time to the activities of other agents within the MAS. Moreover, also the environment of the MAS can contain activity, such as evaporating pheromones used for indirect communication [11]. The temporal relations between all activities (originating from the agents as well as from the environment) determine the relative timing and order in which these activities are executed. In MASs, these temporal relations between activities generally depend upon the semantic properties of the activities within the MAS application, and are independent of the time it takes to execute the corresponding code instructions. As such, the temporal relations determine execution requirements for the MAS application. These execution requirements of a MAS need to be enforced at run-time, irrespective of arbitrary delays in the execution platform.

2.2   Different Concepts of Time

One of the most common points of confusion with respect to time management is what is actually meant by time in software systems. In order to use time to express execution requirements of a MAS application, which are dependent upon semantic properties of the MAS, we need to make a clear distinction between two sorts of time [9] which are of relevance for the rest of the paper:

- **Wallclock time** is the (execution) time as measured on a physical clock while running the software system. For example, in the Packet-World the execution of a particular agent performing a move action might take 78 milliseconds on a specific processor, while a pick up packet action takes 140 milliseconds on the same processor.
- **Logical time** (also called virtual time) is a software representation of time. Logical time could for instance be represented by an integer number. From the viewpoint of the MAS application, only logical time is experienced. As such, temporal relations between activities in the MAS application can be expressed by means of logical time. For example, in the Packet-World a move action for an agent could take 2 units of logical time, while a pick up packet action semantically only takes 1 unit of logical time, and after executing the program for 3 minutes of wallclock time, 634 units of logical time may have passed in the Packet-World.

According to the way logical time advances in a system, a number of execution modes can be distinguished [9]. In a *real-time execution*, logical time advances in synchrony with wallclock time. In *as-fast-as-possible executions*, logical time is advanced as quickly as possible, without direct relationship to wallclock time. An example: suppose that in a software system 100 units of logical time are processed after 5 minutes of wallclock time. As a consequence, the total number of logical time units processed after another 5 minutes of wallclock time must be 200 in case of a real-time execution, and can be any number greater than 100 in case of an as-fast-as-possible execution.

3   Time Models

Time models are inspired by research in the distributed simulation community, where they are used implicitly to assign logical time stamps to all events occurring in the simulation [12][13]. In software simulations, the logical time stamp of an event corresponds to the physical time the event was observed in the real world which is being simulated.

However, we extend the use of time models from pure simulation contexts to execution control for MAS applications in general. Here, logical time is not used to obtain correspondence to physical time, which has no meaning outside the scope of simulation, but as a means to express the semantic time relations that reflect the execution requirements of a MAS (see Sect.2.1). Also in contrast to software simulations, time models are now explicitly represented, which has the advantages that all execution requirements are made explicit on the one hand and can be adapted on the other hand.

A time model captures the execution requirements in terms of logical time, according to the semantic properties of the MAS application. More precisely, a time model defines how the *duration* of various activities in a MAS is related to logical time [14], and these logical durations of activities are used as a means to determine the relative execution order of all activities within a MAS. In this way a time model allows the developer to describe the required execution of the MAS in a platform-independent way. The execution of a MAS application on a particular execution platform must be controlled according to the defined time model.

Because time models capture time relations that reflect the semantic properties of activities within the MAS application, we first investigate the structure of a MAS in order to identify the relevant activities that need to be time modeled.

3.1   Agent Activities

Agents within a MAS are generally able to perform several agent activities[1], and each agent can autonomously decide which activity to perform. As a conse-

---

[1] With the general term *agent activities*, we refer to all internal deliberations, as well as all actions in the environment and all perceptions of the environment, insofar they (1) can be performed by an agent and (2) are considered semantically relevant.

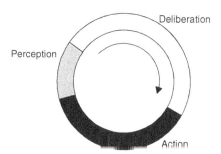

Fig. 4. A typical agent control flow cycle

quence, time modeling requires assigning logical durations to all of the agent's activities. Each time an agent decides to perform a particular activity, the agent's logical clock is advanced with a logical time period equal to the duration of that activity. For our discussion, we assume that an agent has a control flow cycle as the one depicted in Fig.4.

Agent Deliberation. A first important activity an agent can perform, is internal deliberation. The purpose of this deliberation is determining the next action the agent is going to perform. As such, agent deliberation is an activity that does not cross the agent's boundaries. Depending on the context, agent's deliberation can be very simple (e.g. stimulus-response behavior in reactive agents) or immensely complex (e.g. sophisticated learning and planning algorithms used in cognitive agents).

In the context of agent-based simulation, modeling the duration of an agent's deliberation activity has received a lot of interest. We describe various models which have been proposed to model how much logical time the deliberation of the agents takes, and discuss their relevance for specifying execution requirements.

- A constant time model for the agents' deliberation [15] implies that the deliberation of all agents is performed in a constant logical time, irrespective of the actual wallclock time that is needed to execute the deliberation. As a consequence, constant time models are independent of the underlying execution platform, which makes them suitable for specifying execution requirements. The advantage of a constant deliberation time model is the fact that it is simple and easy to understand and use. By assigning constant logical time durations to the deliberation activity of each agent, one can for instance specify the relative reaction speed of all agents within a MAS, irrespective of their implementation or execution efficiency. However, constant time models suffer from a lack of expressiveness since the agent's deliberation is considered as a single, course-grained, and black box activity.
- The deliberation activity of an agent can also be time modeled in a more fine-grained way. The time model has to take into account what the agent is actually deliberating about. In this case, a number of *deliberation primitives* [16] that are semantically relevant are distinguished within the deliberation activity of an agent, e.g. evaluating a board position for a chess playing

agent, or calculating the shortest path to reach a particular destination, etc. A logical duration is assigned to each of the deliberation primitives, and only the deliberation primitives the agent actually uses are taken into account to determine the logical duration of its deliberation activity. This kind of time model is also suitable for specifying execution requirements since it is independent of the actual implementation or underlying execution platform.

- A popular approach counts the actual computer instructions as a basis for determining the logical deliberation time [16]. Modeling the logical deliberation time of an agent as a function of the number of code instructions executed during deliberation is then considered as an extreme example of the previous approach in which each computer instruction is treated as a deliberation primitive. However counting computer instructions is dependent on the programming language of the underlying execution platform. As a consequence, this way of time modeling cannot be used for specifying execution requirements, since it is not platform-independent. Moreover, changes in the implementation and the presence of GUI or debug code can have a significant influence on the logical deliberation time, although these issues have no semantic value.

- The logical deliberation time can be modeled as a function of the wallclock time used for executing the deliberation [17]. This approach is also not feasible for specifying execution requirements, since the logical duration is now susceptible to the load and performance of the underlying computer system.

Agent Action. Another important activity of an agent is performing actions (see Fig.4). In contrast to agent deliberation, agent actions are activities that cross the agent's boundaries: actions typically change the state of the environment. Compared to agent deliberation, time modeling agents' actions in the environment has received little interest. However, in the context of defining execution requirements, imposing time models on the actions agents perform is indispensable. Depending on the semantic context, actions can be assigned a period of logical time. This period can be considered as the time it takes until the effects of the action are noticeable in the environment. In our initial time model, we assume that the agent is not allowed to perform anything else until the action has completed. However, we are currently investigating an extension which allows overlap of the activities of one agent. This could for example allow us to model an agent that can think while it is moving, something that is not possible in the current time model.

Agent Perception. Another important agent activity is perception, which allows an agent to observe its environment. Agent perception is also an activity that crosses the agent's boundaries, but it differs from agent actions as perception does not alter the state of the environment. Time modeling agent perception is often neglected, but its duration could be significant. Assigning a logical duration to agent's perceptions is analogous to time modeling the agent's actions, and allows a developer to specify the time it takes for an agent to perceive its neighborhood.

3.2   Ongoing Activities

Besides activities originating from the agents, there can be other activities within a MAS which require time modeling. In the MAS research community, there is an increased environmental awareness. The environment itself is often dynamic and evolves over time [11]. As a consequence the environment itself can contain a number of *ongoing activities* [18] which are essential for the correct working of the MAS as a whole. An example of ongoing activities in the Packet-World application are the pheromone trails which evaporate continuously. Ongoing activities are characterized by a state which evolves over time, even without agents affecting it. Agents can often initiate ongoing activities and influence their evolution. As a consequence the environment is not passive, but active, and responsible for managing all ongoing activities.

In many MAS applications however, the dynamics of ongoing activities are dealt with in an ad hoc way. Typically the evaporation rate of pheromones is modeled in wallclock time and the correlation between agent activity on the one hand and pheromone activity on the other hand is not specified. As a consequence optimal coordination efficiency can hardly be maintained: varying loads on the execution platform cause agent activity to slow down or speed up accordingly. Because pheromone evaporation is determined upon wallclock time, it does not adapt itself to the changes in the execution speed of the agents, and coordination efficiency drops. Therefore, to guarantee the correct execution behavior, it is essential to specify the logical duration of ongoing activities in the environment, because this allows us to relate their execution to other activities within a MAS application.

3.3   Execution Requirements for the Packet-World

We now return to the Packet-World application, and illustrate the use of time models to capture the execution requirements that are necessary for the correct working of the MAS.

In the Packet-World, the following activities can be distinguished for each agent: the deliberation activity of deciding upon its next action, the perception activity of perceiving its neighborhood, and a number of activities corresponding to the actions an agent can perform in the environment: move to a neighboring field, pick up a packet, put down a packet and drop pheromone. Stated formally:

$E = \{think, look, move, pick, put, drop\}$
with *think*: deliberate upon next action
    look: perceive neighborhood
    move: move to neighboring field
    pick: pick up packet
    put: put down packet
    drop: drop pheromone
$S = \{move, pick, put, drop\} \subset E$
$P = \{look\} \subset E$
$D = \{think\} \subset E$

E is the set of all possible activities of an agent, S the set of agent actions, P the set of agent perception activities, D the set of agent deliberation activities, and S, P and D are subsets of E.

We further distinguish between two types of agents in the Packet-World: reactive agents and cognitive agents. Each agent is either reactive or cognitive. Stated formally:

$$A^R = \{a_1^r, a_2^r, ..., a_n^r\}$$

$$A^C = \{a_1^c, a_2^c, ..., a_m^c\}$$

$$A = A^R \cup A^C = \{a_1, a_2, ..., a_{m+n}\}$$

A^R is the set of all reactive agents in the Packet-World application, A^C the set of all cognitive agents, and A the set of all agents, reactive and cognitive.

The problem statement (see Sect.1.2) mentions a number of typical problems which arise in the Packet-World application. We now elaborate on these problems to derive execution requirements in terms of logical time models.

Action Requirements. We take a closer look at the third problem mentioned in Sect.1.2. In the Packet-World application it was observed that the underlying execution platform can have an arbitrary influence on the time it takes to perform an action. However, in the problem domain it is required the same amount of time is needed for all agents to perform a particular action. Stated formally:

$$\forall a_i \in A; move, pick, put, drop \in S :$$
$$\Delta T_{move}(a_i) = cst_{move}$$
$$\Delta T_{pick}(a_i) = cst_{pick}$$
$$\Delta T_{put}(a_i) = cst_{put}$$
$$\Delta T_{drop}(a_i) = cst_{drop}$$
$$cst_{move}, cst_{pick}, cst_{put}, cst_{drop} \in I\!N$$

A is the set of all agents, S the set of all agent actions, $\Delta T_s(a_i)$ the logical duration of action $s \in S$ performed by agent $a_i \in A$, and $I\!N$ the set of natural numbers.

Since perception is considered as a kind of action in our application, we obtain the following expression:

$$\forall a_i \in A; look \in P :$$
$$\Delta T_{look}(a_i) = cst_{look}$$
$$cst_{look} \in I\!N$$

A is the set of all agents, P the set of all agent perception activities, $\Delta T_p(a_i)$ the logical duration of perception activity $p \in P$ performed by agent $a_i \in A$, and $I\!N$ the set of natural numbers.

Both expressions above can be combined in a more compact notation:

$$\forall a_i \in A; \forall e \in S \cup P:$$
$$\Delta T_e(a_i) = cst_e$$
$$cst_e \in I\!N$$

Deliberation Requirements. We now return to the first example of the Packet-World application (see Sect.1.2). The problem was the fact that the underlying execution platform can influence the reaction speed of the agents, leading to a response order which is arbitrary. However, this is not desired in the Packet-World, where it is required that a reactive agent always reacts faster than a cognitive agent, in case both start deliberating at the same moment in time. Based on the agent's control flow cycle as depicted in Fig.4, the duration in logical time it takes an agent to complete a control flow cycle can be stated formally as:

$$\forall a_i \in A; \forall s \in S; \forall p \in P; \forall d \in D:$$
$$\Delta T^{cycle}(p, d, s, a_i) = \Delta T_p(a_i) + \Delta T_d(a_i) + \Delta T_s(a_i)$$

$\Delta T^{cycle}(p, d, s, a_i)$ is the duration in logical time it takes agent $a_i \in A$ to complete a control flow cycle consisting of perception activity $p \in P$, followed by deliberation activity $d \in D$ and by action $s \in S$. $\Delta T_p(a_i)$ is the logical duration of perception activity $p \in P$ performed by agent $a_i \in A$, $\Delta T_d(a_i)$ the logical duration of deliberation activity $d \in D$ performed by agent $a_i \in A$ and $\Delta T_s(a_i)$ the logical duration of action $s \in S$ performed by agent $a_i \in A$.

In the Packet-World, $P = \{look\}$ and $D = \{think\}$ are singletons. As a consequence, the moment in logical time an agent completes an action can be defined as:

$$\forall a_i \in A; \forall s \in S:$$
$$T_{end}(s, a_i) = T_0 + \Delta T^{cycle}(look, think, s, a_i)$$

$T_{end}(s, a_i)$ is the moment in logical time agent a_i completes action s. T_0 is the moment in logical time that a new cycle in the control flow of agent a_i starts (which corresponds to the moment in logical time the previous action of agent a_i was completed).

The requirement that a reactive agent can always pick up the packet before a cognitive agent in case both start deliberating at the same moment time, is hence formalized as follows:

$$\forall a_i^r \in A^R; \forall a_j^c \in A^C; pick \in S:$$
$$T_{end}(pick, a_i^r) < T_{end}(pick, a_j^c)$$

A^R is the set of reactive agents, A^C the set of cognitive agents, and S the set of all agent actions in the environment.

By substitution we obtain:

$$T_0 + \Delta T^{cycle}(look, think, pick, a_i^r) < T_0 + \Delta T^{cycle}(look, think, pick, a_i^c)$$

or

$$T_0 + cst_{look} + \Delta T_{think}(a_i^r) + cst_{pick} < T_0 + cst_{look} + \Delta T_{think}(a_j^c) + cst_{pick}$$

Simplifying both sides of the equation gives us:

$$\Delta T_{think}(a_i^r) < \Delta T_{think}(a_j^c)$$

With $a_i^r \in A^R$ a reactive agent, and $a_j^c \in A^C$ a cognitive agent.

Hence to assure that the reactive agent always acts faster than the cognitive one, the logical duration of the agents' deliberation needs to be modeled such that the reactive agent's deliberation duration is smaller than the cognitive agent's deliberation time. This also corresponds to our intuition.

Pheromone Requirements. Finally, we take a closer look at the second problem of Sect.1.2. The load on the underlying execution platform causes the agents' execution speed to change accordingly. However, if we want to maintain pheromone effectiveness, we need a continuous adaptation of the pheromone evaporation rate to the agents' execution speed. Hence we want the duration of pheromone activity to be semantically related to the duration of agent activities. As a first step, we use a simple model for pheromone activity. For the pheromone evaporation rate in the Packet-World application we can state more formally:

$$\Delta T_{evap} = cst_{evap}$$
$$cst_{evap} \in I\!N$$

with ΔT_{evap} the logical duration it takes for a pheromone to evaporate until only half of its initial strength is remaining. Agent activity is related to logical time. Relating pheromone activity to the same logical clock, instead of the wallclock, allows the dynamics of both agents and pheromones to be coupled.

3.4   A Time Model for the Packet World

In Sect.3.3 we formulated a number of execution requirements which have to be met to allow the execution of our MAS to evolve according to the semantic properties of all activities within the Packet-World application. To formulate a simple time model, specific values to the various activities have to be assigned, expressing the logical durations. These values are expressed in *logical time units* (LTU). The execution requirements derived above give rise to an array of constraints which all have to be satisfied in a time model for the application.

An example time model which satisfies all requirements of the Packet-World application is given:

$\forall a_i \in A :$
$\Delta T_{move}(a_i) = 3 \ LTU$
$\Delta T_{pick}(a_i) = 2 \ LTU$
$\Delta T_{put}(a_i) = 2 \ LTU$
$\Delta T_{drop}(a_i) = 1 \ LTU$
$\Delta T_{look}(a_i) = 1 \ LTU$

$\forall a_i^r \in A^R :$
$\Delta T_{think}(a_i^r) = 4 \ LTU$

$\forall a_j^c \in A^C :$
$\Delta T_{think}(a_j^c) = 12 \ LTU$

$\Delta T_{evap} = 100 \ LTU$

Note that this time model is only one example which satisfies all requirements of the Packet-World application. Alternative time models that also satisfy the requirements can be modeled. As such, there exists a degree of freedom for the developer, enabling her/him to further tune and refine the working of the application within the boundaries defined by the execution requirements.

4   Time Management Mechanisms

By specifying time models, the developer can define execution requirements for a MAS. By relating MAS activities to logical time, time models impose an order on all MAS activities, dictated by logical time. However, as illustrated in the introduction, the temporal characteristics of the execution platform are not necessarily the same as those described in the logical time model. As a consequence, we additionally need *time management mechanisms* to ensure that all activities are executed according to the time model specification. These mechanisms avoid that any event with a logical time in the future can have influence on things with a logical time in the past, even in the presence of arbitrary network delays or computer loads. In other words, time management mechanisms preserve causality dictated by logical time.

Distributed simulation communities have been investigating the consistency of logical time in simulations for a long time. All events happening are ordered and hence causally related by means of the global notion of logical time. Therefore various time management mechanisms have been developed to prevent causality errors:

- **Execution directed by clock**. In this approach the logical time of the system is discretized in a number of intervals of equal size. The interval size is called *time-step*. Global synchronization schemes force all entities to advance together in a lock-step mode, and hence the execution of the system proceeds synchronously. In the case of MASs, a drawback is that synchronous execution forces all agents to act at the pace of the slowest one, which severely limits execution speed [19][20]. Moreover, since a central authority must control and keep track of the execution of all agents in the system, the cost of synchronous approaches increases rapidly as the number of agents grows.
- **Execution directed by events**. In this case, events are generated by all entities [12], and each event has a precise logical time stamp which allows sorting them. During execution, the next event to be processed is the one

with the smallest logical timestamp, ensuring causality and thereby skipping periods of inactivity. However in a distributed context (distributed discrete event simulation [13]), a system is modeled as a group of communicating entities, referred to as logical processes (or LPs). Each LP contains its own logical clock (indicating its local logical time) and all LPs process events asynchronously and advance at different rates, which allow a significant speedup, but may cause causality errors. Hence, for asynchronous execution additional synchronization is needed to ensure that each LP processes messages in increasing logical time order:

- **Conservative synchronization.** In conservative synchronization [21] each LP only processes events when it can guarantee that no causality errors (out of (logical) time order messages) will occur. This causes some LPs to block, possibly leading to deadlock. The performance of conservative synchronization techniques relies heavily on the concept of lookahead, but the autonomous, proactive behavior of agents could severely restrict the ability to predict events [22]. Moreover, to determine whether it is safe for an agent to process an event, information about all other agents must be taken into account, limiting the scalability of this approach.
- **Optimistic synchronization.** In optimistic approaches, causality errors are allowed, but some roll-back mechanism to recover from causality violations is defined (e.g. time warp [23]). While this approach is feasible for simulations, providing roll-back for MAS applications in general (outside the scope of simulation) is not feasible at all. Moreover, the cost imposed by the roll-back mechanisms can easily outweigh the benefits [22], and increases rapidly as the number of agents grows.

5   MAS Execution Control Platform

To control the execution of a MAS in an appropriate way, a *MAS execution control platform* must provide support for both explicit time models on the one hand and time management mechanisms on the other hand.

First, logical time models are needed as a means for the developer to explicitly express the execution policy for all MAS activities. However, the execution policy expressed in the time model has to be enforced in the MAS application, irrespective of delays in the underlying execution platform. For this reason, time management mechanisms are needed. They prevent time models from being violated, and ensure the execution of the MAS behaves according to the execution policy which is described.

We refer to our previous work [24] for a more technical description of the structure of a MAS execution control platform, and limit our discussion to its most important characteristics:

- **Higher level of abstraction**. The execution policy is described by means of an explicit model. This model focuses on *what* the execution policy of a particular MAS application is, while hiding the developer from *how* this execution policy is enforced. The model provides a higher level of abstraction to MAS developers: from a developer's point of view, only the logical durations described in the time model apply and determine the execution. As a consequence, abstraction can be made of the unreliable execution platform delays. By means of a time model as execution policy description, all activities within the MAS can be identified and can be assigned logical durations.

– **Separation of concerns**. A MAS's functionality can be developed without taking into account the execution policy. Controlling the execution of a MAS is considered as a separate concern. This relieves the developer from tackling execution control from scratch and from hard-coding it into the agents' functional behavior. Based on an explicit execution policy description provided by the developer, all time management mechanisms are integrated automatically into the MAS's functionality using aspect-oriented programming, without requiring the developer to change the design of the MAS. In this way, the complexity of time management mechanisms that enforce the execution policy can be hidden from the developer.

– **Independence with respect to the execution platform**. By combining a logical time model and a time management mechanism to enforce it, a MAS can be developed without taking into account the specific timing characteristics of the execution platform. A MAS application is subjected to logical delays defined in the time model, and execution platform delays can no longer introduce unforeseen effects. This results in MASs being unconstrained with respect to the timing characteristics of their execution platforms.

– **Adaptability of the execution policy**. The explicit representation of the execution requirements of a MAS in a time model has the advantage that execution requirements can be adapted. This enables fine-tuning of the existing execution policy and allows the integration of new execution requirements.

6   Future Work

This paper reports on ongoing work investigating a generic and structured way to deal with execution control in the context of MASs. The approach was described in general, and a lot of work still needs to be done on various issues described in this paper:

– We are currently working to improve the formalism for describing logical time models, to come to an approach which is generally applicable and more theoretically founded. It should for instance be possible to specify potential overlap of activities (see Sect.1). Also the dynamics of ongoing activities in the environment, such as pheromone evaporation, still needs to be investigated more in depth.

– As shown in Sect.4, mechanisms enforcing time models and ensuring global causality are limited in scalability, making these approaches inefficient for use in a large-scale distributed MASs. A possible alternative presumes we abandon the notion of a global (logical) clock to determine causal relationships. Hence not all parts of the MAS are related in time, and there is only a locally shared notion of time. This follows from the observation that agents within a MAS typically perceive and act locally. Based on this, it makes sense only to ensure temporal relationships between agents residing in each other's neighborhood, without modeling causality between agents far away from each other, at the benefit of increased scalability. Regional synchronization [20] provides a flexible mechanism to dynamically detect clusters of agents, based on the overlap of so called *spheres of influence*. Within such clusters of agents, the mechanisms discussed in Sect.4 could be applied locally, hence avoiding scalability limitations at the cost of a loss of a global notion of logical time.

7   Conclusion

In this paper, we emphasized time management adaptability as a type of adaptability which has significant importance, although this type of adaptability is not often considered in the context of adaptive MASs. Time management adaptability allows the execution requirements for a MAS application to be described explicitly and enforced transparently, irrespective of the unpredictable execution platform delays. A *time model* is employed to explicitly capture the execution policy and relate all MAS activities to logical time. *Time management mechanisms* form a second important part of time management adaptability: they are needed to enforce time models. Time models and time management mechanisms are combined in *MAS execution control platforms*.

The advantage of time management adaptability it twofold. First, time management adaptability allows a MAS to be independent of the underlying execution platform: the combination of time models and time management mechanisms prevents the MAS's behavior from being affected by timing issues introduced by the execution platform. More precisely, the relative execution order of all MAS activities remains invariant under various execution conditions. Second, time management adaptability allows the execution policy to be adapted to suit the needs of the MAS application, providing a higher level of abstraction to organize the execution of a MAS, and a means to introduce execution control as a separate concern.

References

1. Weyns, D., Holvoet, T.: The packet-world as a case to study sociality in multi-agent systems. In: Autonomous Agents and Multi-Agent Systems, AAMAS 2002. (2002)
2. Sauter, J.A., Matthews, R., Dyke, H.V.: Evolving adaptive pheromone path planning mechanisms. Autonomous Agents and Multiagent Systems, AAMAS 2002 (2002)
3. Parunak, H.V.D., Brueckner, S.: Ant-like missionaries and cannibals: Synthetic pheromones for distributed motion control. In Sierra, C., Gini, M., Rosenschein, J.S., eds.: Proceedings of the Fourth International Conference on Autonomous Agents, Barcelona, Catalonia, Spain, ACM Press (2000) 467–474

4. Brueckner, S.A.: Return From The Ant – Synthetic Ecosystems For Manufacturing Control. PhD thesis, Humboldt University Berlin, Department of Computer Science (2000)
5. Steels, L.: Cooperation between distributed agents through self-organization. Decentralized A.I. (1990)
6. Axtell, R.: Effects of interaction topology and activation regime in several multi-agent systems. Lecture Notes in Computer Science **1979** (2000) 33–48
7. Page, S.: On incentives and updating in agent based models. Journal of Computational Economics **10** (1997) 67–87
8. Cornforth, D., Green, D.G., Newth, D., Kirley, M.: Do artificial ants march in step? ordered asynchronous processes and modularity in biological systems. In: Proceedings of the Eighth International Conference on Artificial Life, MIT Press (2003) 28–32
9. Fujimoto, R.: Time management in the high level architecture. Simulation, Special Issue on High Level Architecture **71** (1998) 388–400
10. Wooldridge, M.J.: Multi-agent systems : an introduction. Wiley, Chichester (2001)
11. Parunak, H.V.D., Brueckner, S., Sauter, J., Matthews, R.S.: Distinguishing environmental and agent dynamics: A case study in abstraction and alternate modeling technologies. Lecture Notes in Computer Science **1972** (2001)
12. Lamport, L.: Time, clocks, and the ordering of events in a distributed system. Communications of the ACM **21** (1978) 558–565
13. Misra, J.: Distributed discrete-event simulation. Computing Surveys **18** (1986) 39–65
14. Anderson, S.D., Cohen, P.R.: Timed common lisp: the duration of deliberation. SIGART Bull. **7** (1996) 11–15
15. Uhrmacher, A., Kullick, B.: Plug and test software agents in virtual environments. In: Winter Simulation Conference, WSC'2000. (2000)
16. Anderson, S.D.: Simulation of multiple time-pressured agents. In: Winter Simulation Conference, WSC'97. (1997) 397–404
17. Anderson, S.: A Simulation Substrate for Real-Time Planning. PhD thesis, University of Massachusetts at Amherst (1995)
18. Weyns, D., Holvoet, T.: Formal model for situated multi-agent systems. Formal Approaches for Multi-agent Systems, Special Issue of Fundamenta Informaticae (2004)
19. Ferber, J., Muller, J.: Influences and reaction: a model for situated multiagent systems. In: Proceedings of the 2th International Conference on Multi-Agent Systems, AAAI Press (1996)
20. Weyns, D., Holvoet, T.: Regional synchronization for simultaneous actions in situated multiagent systems. Multi-Agent Systems and Applications III, Lecture Notes in Computer Science **LNAI 2691** (2003) 497–511
21. Chandy, K.M., Misra, J.: Asynchronous distributed simulation via a sequence of parallel computations. Communications of the ACM **24** (1981) 198–205
22. Uhrmacher, A., Gugler, K.: Distributed, parallel simulation of multiple, deliberative agents. In: Proceedings of the 14th Workshop on Parallel and Distributed Simulation, PADS'2000, Bologna, Italy, IEEE (2000) 101–110
23. Jefferson, D., Sowizral, H.: Fast concurrent simulation using the time warp mechanism. In: Proceedings of the SCS Multiconference on Distributed Simulation. (1985) 63–69
24. Helleboogh, A., Holvoet, T., Weyns, D.: Time management support for simulating multi-agent systems. In: Joint Workshop on Multi-Agent and Multi-Agent Based Simulation, MAMABS. (2004)

Learning to Coordinate Using Commitment Sequences in Cooperative Multi-agent Systems

Spiros Kapetanakis[1], Daniel Kudenko[1], and Malcolm J. A. Strens[2]

[1] Department of Computer Science, University of York,
Heslington, York, YO10 5DD, UK
spiros@cs.york.ac.uk
kudenko@cs.york.ac.uk
[2] Guidance and Imaging Solutions, QinetiQ,
Ively Road, Farnborough, Hampshire GU14 OLX, UK
mjstrens@qinetiq.com

Abstract. We report on an investigation of the learning of coordination in cooperative multi-agent systems. Specifically, we study solutions that are applicable to *independent* agents i.e. agents that do not observe one another's actions. In previous research [5] we have presented a reinforcement learning approach that converges to the optimal joint action even in scenarios with high miscoordination costs. However, this approach failed in fully stochastic environments. In this paper, we present a novel approach based on reward estimation with a shared action-selection protocol. The new technique is applicable in fully stochastic environments where mutual observation of actions is not possible. We demonstrate empirically that our approach causes the agents to converge almost always to the optimal joint action even in difficult stochastic scenarios with high miscoordination penalties.

1   Introduction

Learning to coordinate in cooperative multi-agent systems is a central and widely studied problem, see, for example [6, 1, 2, 9, 11]. In this context, coordination is defined as *the ability of two or more agents to jointly reach a consensus over which actions to perform in an environment*. We investigate the case of *independent* agents that cannot observe one another's actions, which often is a more realistic assumption. This generality distinguishes our approach from alternatives (e.g., [10]) that require complete mutual observation of actions.

In this investigation, we focus on scenarios where the agents must learn to coordinate their actions through environmental feedback. In previous research [5] we have presented a reinforcement learning technique (called FMQ) for independent agents, that converged to the *optimal* joint action in scenarios where miscoordination is associated with high penalties. Previous Q-learning approaches failed to solve such scenarios with independent agents, and the FMQ technique was the first to do so. However, the FMQ approach failed in fully stochastic environments, where the rewards associated with joint actions are randomised.

D. Kudenko et al. (Eds.): Adaptive Agents and MAS II, LNAI 3394, pp. 106–118, 2005.

In this paper, we present a novel technique that is based on a shared action-selection protocol (called *commitment sequence*) that enables the agents to estimate the rewards for specific joint actions. We evaluate this approach experimentally on a number of stochastic versions of two especially difficult coordination problems that were first introduced in [2]: the *climbing game* and the *penalty game*. The empirical results show that the convergence probability to the optimal joint action is very high, in fact reaching almost 100%.

Our paper is structured as follows: we first introduce a common testbed for the study of learning coordination in cooperative multi-agent systems: stochastic cooperative games. We then introduce a basic version of the novel commitment sequence technique that uses simple averaging and discuss the experimental results. Finally, we present an extension using Gaussian estimation that improves both the probability of convergence to the optimal joint action and the convergence speed. We finish with an outlook on future work.

2   Stochastic Cooperative Games

A common testbed for studying the problem of multi-agent coordination is that of stochastic cooperative games [3]. In these games, the agents may have common, conflicting or complimentary interests. In this work, we have concentrated only on cooperative games i.e. games where the agents are rewarded based on their joint action and all agents receive the same reward. At present, we only consider single-stage stochastic games. In these games, every agent chooses an action from its action space for every round of the game. These actions are executed simultaneously and the reward that corresponds to the joint action is broadcast to all agents. In multi-stage stochastic games, the execution of a joint action yields not only a common reward but also the transition of the agents to a new state.

Table 1 describes the reward function for a simple cooperative single-stage game. For example, if agent 1 executes action b and agent 2 executes action a, the reward they receive is 5. Obviously, the optimal joint-action in this simple game is (b, b) as it is associated with the highest reward of 10.

Table 1. A simple cooperative game reward function

	Agent 1	
	a	b
Agent 2 a	3	5
b	0	10

Our goal is to enable the agents to learn optimal coordination from repeated trials in cases where the game matrix is not known to the agents. To achieve this goal, one can use either *independent* or *joint-action* learners. The difference between the two types lies in the amount of information they can perceive in the game. Although both types of learners can perceive the reward that is associated with each joint action, the former are unaware of the existence of other agents whereas the latter can also perceive the actions of others.

Table 2. The climbing game

Agent 1

		a	b	c
	a	11	-30	0
Agent 2	b	-30	7	6
	c	0	0	5

Table 3. The penalty game

Agent 1

		a	b	c
	a	10	0	-10
Agent 2	b	0	2	0
	c	-10	0	10

In this way, joint-action learners can maintain a model of the strategy of other agents and choose their actions based on the other participants' perceived strategy. In contrast, independent learners must estimate the value of their individual actions based solely on the rewards that they receive for their actions. In this paper, we focus on individual learners, these being more universally applicable.

In the present study, we analyse a number of coordination problems, all of which are descendants of the *climbing game* and the *penalty game*. We show why these problems are of interest to us and why they are hard problems. The climbing game is representative of problems with high miscoordination penalties and a single optimal joint action, whereas the penalty game is representative of problems with miscoordination penalties and multiple optimal joint actions. Both games are played between two agents and their reward functions are shown in Tables 2 and 3:

In the climbing game, it is difficult for the agents to converge to the optimal joint action (a, a) because of the negative reward in the case of miscoordination. For example, if agent 1 plays a and agent 2 plays b, then both will receive a negative reward of -30. Incorporating this reward into the learning process can be so detrimental that both agents tend to avoid playing the same action again. In contrast, when choosing action c, miscoordination is not punished so severely. Therefore, in most cases, both agents are easily tempted by action c. The reason is as follows: if agent 1 plays c, then agent 2 can play either b or c to get a positive reward (6 and 5 respectively). Even if agent 2 plays a, the result is not catastrophic since the reward is 0. Similarly, if agent 2 plays c, whatever agent 1 plays, the resulting reward will be at least 0. From this analysis, we can see that the climbing game is a challenging problem for the study of learning coordination. It includes heavy miscoordination penalties and "safe" actions that are likely to tempt the agents away from the optimal joint action.

Similarly, the penalty game is a hard problem as it not only has heavy penalties for miscoordination but also includes multiple optimal joint actions. If agent 1 plays a expecting agent 2 to also play a so they can receive the maximum reward of 10 but agent 2 plays c (perhaps expecting agent 1 to play c so that, again, they receive the maximum reward of 10) then the resulting penalty can be very detrimental to both agents' learning

Table 4. The stochastic climbing game table (50%)

Agent 1

		a	b	c
	a	10/12	5/-65	8/-8
Agent 2	b	5/-65	14/0	12/0
	c	5/-5	5/-5	10/0

process. In this game, b is the "safe" action for both agents since playing b is guaranteed to result in a reward of 0 or 2, regardless of what the other agent plays.

Because of the difficulties discussed above, regular Q-learning agents failed to converge to the optimal joint action in both the climbing game and the penalty game. A Q-learning variant that solves these games for independent agents has been presented in [5] using an approach known as the FMQ heuristic. This heuristic works in a reinforcement learning setting and it allows two agents that have no communication capabilities or shared knowledge to jointly reach the optimal joint action in single-stage games.

However, the FMQ heuristic cannot distinguish adequately between miscoordination penalties and reward variance in stochastic games. Therefore, it fails to solve more complex games such as the *stochastic climbing game* which is shown in Table 4. The stochastic version of the climbing game differs from the original in that each joint action now corresponds to two rewards instead of just one. These two rewards are received with probability $1/2$. If the two agents were to commit to playing a specific joint action indefinitely, the reward they would accumulate over time would converge to the same value as in the original game. In this respect, the stochastic climbing game is equivalent to the original. This equivalence is maintained across all variations of the climbing and penalty game that we introduce in this work.

The difficulty in solving the stochastic climbing game with the FMQ heuristic stems from the fact that the heuristic is designed to deal with one type of uncertainty, namely that which arises from sampling heavily penalised actions. This uncertainty is due to the inability of one agent to observe the other agent's actions. The FMQ heuristic filters out the noise from failed coordination attempts to help the agents reach the optimal joint action. The difference in the stochastic version of the climbing game is that there are now two sources of uncertainty in the game, the other agent's actions (as before) and the multiple rewards per joint action.

We will show two ways to tackle the fully stochastic climbing game using the idea of commitment sequences. We also presently introduce two new variants of the game so as to show the full potential of our methods. The first variant is the *three-valued climbing game* in which that there are three rewards corresponding to any joint action. This game is shown in Table 5.

The probability of receiving any one of the three rewards that correspond to each joint action is $1/3$. If the two agents were to play the action profile (b, b) indefinitely, they would accrue an average reward of 7 as in the original game.

The next variant of the climbing game that we introduce is the *variable-probability climbing game*. There are again two rewards for each joint action. However, they are now received with non-uniform probabilities. Equivalence with the original game is again maintained. The variable-probability climbing game is included in Table 6. The notation

Table 5. The three-valued stochastic climbing game

		Agent 1		
		a	b	c
Agent 2	a	16/22/-5	4/6/-100	10/20/-30
	b	4/6/-100	25/0/-4	10/5/3
	c	8/12/-20	10/20/-30	4/5/6

Table 6. The variable-probability stochastic climbing game

		Agent 1		
		a	b	c
Agent 2	a	(0.4) 6.5	(0.25) -36	(0.6) 4
		(0.6) 14	(0.75) -28	(0.4) -6
	b	(0.25) -36	(0.8) 5	(0.8) 5
		(0.75) -28	(0.2) 15	(0.2) 10
	c	(0.7) 3	(0.6) 4	(0.8) 4
		(0.3) -7	(0.4) -6	(0.2) 9

Table 7. The stochastic penalty game (50%)

		Agent 1		
		a	b	c
Agent 2	a	8/12	-3/3	-8/12
	b	-3/3	0/4	-3/3
	c	-8/-12	-3/3	8/12

$(\pi)n$ signifies that the probability of getting a reward of n for playing that joint action is π. For example, the probability of getting a reward of 5 for joint action (c, b) is 0.8 whereas the probability of getting a reward of 10 for the same joint action is 0.2.

Finally, we introduce a stochastic variant of the penalty game. This game is called the *stochastic penalty game* and is shown in Table 7.

3   Reward Estimation

In games with stochastic rewards, such as all the climbing game variants and the stochastic penalty game, it is difficult to distinguish between the two sources of variation in the observed reward for some action. It would be useful to have a protocol that allows 2 or more agents to select the same joint action repeatedly in order to build up a model for the stochastic reward distribution. This section describes a novel approach for achieving this.

The basic principle is that agents follow a common action selection policy that enables them to estimate the potential reward for each joint action. The action selection policy is based on the following idea: if an agent chooses an action at time i, then the agent is required to choose the same action at specific future time points. The only assumption that this approach makes is that all agents share the same global clock and that they follow a common protocol for defining sequences of time-slots.

3.1   Commitment Sequences

A *commitment sequence* is some list of *time slots* $(t_1, t_2, \ldots)$ for which an agent is committed to taking the same action. If two or more agents have the same protocol for defining these sequences, then the ensemble of agents is committed to selecting a single joint-action for every time point in the sequence. Although each agent does not know the action choices of the other agents, it can be certain that the observed rewards will be statistically stationary and represent unbiased samples for the reward distribution of *some* joint action. In order to allow an arbitrarily high number of joint actions and consequently commitment sequences to be considered as the agent learns, it is necessary that the sequences are finite *or* have an exponentially increasing time interval $\delta_i \equiv t_{i+1} - t_i$ between successive time slots. A sufficient condition is that $\gamma \delta_{i+1} \geq \delta_i$ where $\gamma > 1$ for all $i > i_0$ (for some pre-defined constant i_0). In the results given here, sequences are infinite with $\gamma = 5/4$.

Here, the successive increments are generated by the function:

$$\delta_{i+1} = \left\lfloor \frac{c\delta_i + c - 2}{c - 1} \right\rfloor$$

where $c > 1$ is the increment factor and $\lfloor \cdot \rfloor$ indicates rounding down to an integer value. For example, if the increment factor is 5 (i.e. the increment ratio γ is $5/4$) the rule becomes: $\delta_{i+1} = \lfloor (5\delta_i + 3)/4 \rfloor$. The first such sequence starts with $(1, 3, 6, 10, 15, 22, \ldots)$. The second sequence therefore starts at time slot 2. To prevent any 2 sequences from selecting the same time slot, each sequence excludes the existing ones from counting. Hence the second sequence starts with $(2, 5, 9, 14, 20, 28, \ldots)$.

For time i suppose the agents chose actions $(a_1^i, a_2^i, \ldots, a_m^i)$ (where m is the number of agents). Then an estimate of the value of this joint action is available as the average reward received during the part of the sequence that has been completed so far. Longer sequences provide more reliable estimates. Initially, we evaluate the simplest approach possible where the agents maintain a running reward average for all the active commitment sequences. Later, we will explore a method that takes into account the stochasticity in the rewards and the length of sequences within the framework of Gaussian estimation.

3.2   Action Selection Policy

Each agent must choose an action at the start of each sequence. A new sequence starts whenever no existing sequence is active in the current time slot. There are two obvious ways to select the new action: either explore (select the action randomly and uniformly) or exploit (select the action currently considered optimal). The simple approach used here is to choose randomly between exploration and exploitation for each sequence. In order to prefer longer sequences (more reliable estimates), we maintain statistics about the commitment sequences that are active. One such statistic is the length of the sequence until the current time point. Agents only consider a commitment sequence to yield a reliable reward estimate if its length becomes greater than a threshold value, N_{min}. In these experiments, N_{min} was set to 10.

For a 2-agent system, we chose the exploration probability p to be 0.9. As an exception, the first N_{init} sequences (where $N_{init} \geq 1$) must be exploratory to ensure that an exploitative action can be calculated. The algorithm followed is shown in Figure 1. In the results below, $N_{init} = 10$.

if number of sequences $< N_{init}$ **then**
    explore randomly and uniformly
else
    with probability p : explore randomly and uniformly
    with probability $1 - p$: exploit
end if

Fig. 1. The average reward estimation algorithm

The exploit function simply returns the action that corresponds to the commitment sequence with the highest observed average reward among those whose current length is at least N_{min}.

3.3 Parameter Analysis

In this section, we analyse the influence of the algorithm's parameters on the learning. These parameters are:, the minimum number of commitment sequences that must have been started before the agents can exploit (N_{init}), the minimum length that a sequence must reach before it is considered for exploitation (N_{min}), the increment factor (c) and the exploration probability (p).

N_{init} was set to 10 in all our experiments. Since none of our experiments have less than 10 commitment sequences, N_{init} has no role in the learning other than to make sure

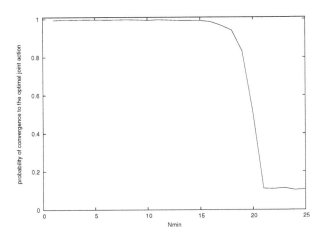

Fig. 2. Number of successful experiments out 1000 runs for $N_{min} \in [1, 25]$

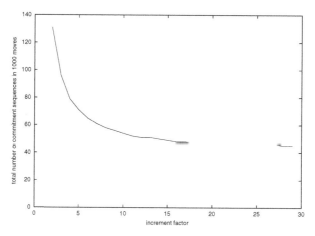

Fig. 3. The relationship between the increment factor and the total number of sequences

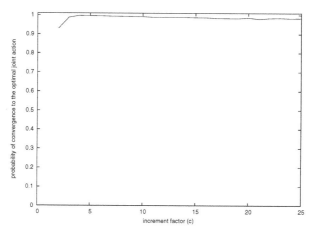

Fig. 4. The relationship between the increment factor and the probability of convergence to the optimal joint action

that, upon selection of an exploitative action, there are *some* sequences among which to choose.

N_{min} affects the learning as follows: In experiments where only short commitment sequences are created (either short experiments or long ones with a small increment factor), learning performance improves by setting N_{min} to a reasonably high value since our confidence is higher for longer commitment sequences. In longer experiments, N_{min} plays no part in the learning other than to decrease learning performance if set too high. This is because it is possible that an agent never explores as no commitment sequences reach the required length. Figure 2 illustrates this effect. We have plotted the convergence probability of the learners in the stochastic climbing game after 1000

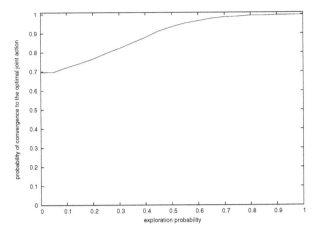

Fig. 5. The relationship between the exploration probability and the probability of convergence to the optimal joint action

moves. Since no commitment sequences of length greater than 20 have been created, the learning performance decreases for values of $N_{min} > 20$.

The increment factor c defines how quickly a commitment sequence is visited again. Informally, the higher the value of the increment factor, the greater the time between two successive updates of a commitment sequence. Consequently, the total number of commitment sequences reduces monotonically with the increment factor for any length of the experiment. To illustrate this relationship, Figure 3 shows the total number of sequences for an experiment of 1000 moves with increment factor $c \in [2, 29]$.

The performance of the learners for different increment factors is also plotted in Figure 4. This plot was generated for the stochastic climbing game with $N_{min} = 10$ and experiment length 1000.

Finally, in order to understand the influence of the exploration probability p on the learning, we have plotted its effect on the learning performance in Figure 5. The exploration probability has been varied from 0 (always exploit) to 1 (always explore), N_{min} and N_{init} were set to 10 and the experiment was 1000 moves long. This plot was created for the stochastic climbing game.

From Figure 5, we can see that 100% exploration is optimal in this case. However, we have identified some games where one agent's exploitative behaviour can help the other agent to learn. If performance during learning is an issue, a low exploration probability is also desirable. In our experimental evaluation, the exploration probability will be 0.9.

3.4   Experimental Results

This section contains the experimental results for the basic approach in all three versions of the climbing game and in the stochastic penalty game. As before, we repeated each experiment 1000 times to obtain high confidence in the results. The number of moves was varied from 500 to 3000 and the parameters N_{init} and N_{min} were both set to 10. In all experiments, we chose $\gamma = 5/4$. The results for the climbing game variants are plotted in Figure 6.

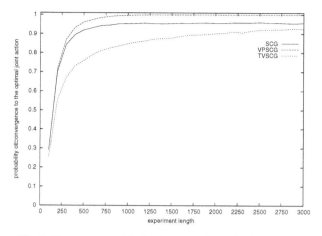

Fig. 6. Convergence of the basic approach on the three games

In Figure 6, SCG stands for Stochastic Climbing Game, TVSCG stands for Three-Valued Stochastic Climbing game and VPSCG stands for Variable-Probability Stochastic Climbing Game. From Figure 6, we can see that the probability of convergence to optimal eventually reaches over 90% for all cases, with some reaching over 95% even for relatively short experiments. The most difficult game is the three-valued climbing game as there is more variance in the rewards that correspond to each joint action.

The stochastic penalty game is solved much quicker by this approach. The probability of convergence to the optimal joint action reaches over 95% even for very short experiments (500 moves). This is because the variance in the rewards is small and the method is impervious to the existence of multiple optimal joint actions. Regardless of how many optimal joint actions there are in the game, one will always have a higher estimate than others[1] so that choosing an action for exploitation is not affected by the number of optimal joint actions.

4   Variance-Sensitive Approach

The basic approach using averaging performs fairly well. However, there are cases (e.g. the three-valued stochastic climbing game) where convergence only reaches above 90% for very long experiments. This section outlines an extended approach using a Gaussian estimator that improves both the convergence speed and the probability of convergence to the optimal joint action.

4.1   Finding the Exploitative Action

As in the basic approach, if the agents chose actions $(a_1^i, a_2^i, \ldots, a_m^i)$ (where m is the number of agents) at time i then an estimate of the value of this joint action is available

---

[1] If multiple estimates are equal, the agents will choose the one that corresponds to a longer commitment sequence.

as the average reward received so far for this sequence. For the extended approach, we attempt to reason about the *true* expected reward. To do this, we must make some assumptions about the possible form of the reward for each joint action, e.g. that it must have finite variance.

Here we use a Gaussian model and estimate its mean and variance from the observations. If n rewards are observed with empirical average m and sum of squares S, we obtain estimates for the population mean μ and *its* variance σ_μ (estimates of a quantity x are denoted by $\hat{x}$):

$$\hat{\mu} = m$$

$$\hat{\sigma}_\mu^2 = \frac{S + \sigma_0^2}{n^2} - \frac{m^2}{n}$$

σ_0 is a parameter to the algorithm and should be based on the expected variance of rewards in the game. In order to prefer longer sequences (more reliable estimates), a pessimistic estimate $\hat{\mu} - N_\sigma \hat{\sigma}$ is used to provide a lower bound on the expected return for each sequence. At any given time, the exploitative behaviour for an agent is to choose the action corresponding to the sequence with the greatest lower bound. Large values of N_σ reduce the risk that an optimistic bias in the reward estimate from a short sequence will affect the choice of action. However, smaller values may give faster initial learning. In the results below, $N_\sigma = 4$.

4.2   Exploration Policy

In the variance-sensitive approach, the agents choose randomly between exploration and exploitation for each sequence. For a 2-agent system, we chose the exploration probability to be 0.9 as before. We have maintained the N_{init} parameter ($N_{init} >= 1$) but have eliminated N_{min}. We simply allow N_{init} commitment sequences to start and then only use the variance-sensitive estimator to find the exploitative action. In the results below, $N_{init} = 10$.

4.3   Experimental Results

Figure 7 depicts the convergence performance of the variance-sensitive approach for the three variants of the climbing game. In these experiments, σ_0 was set to 50 for the three-valued stochastic climbing game and to 10 for the rest. In Figure 7, SCG, VPSCG and TVSCG stand for Stochastic Climbing Game and its Variable-Probability and Three-Valued variants.

As we can see from Figure 7, the variance-sensitive approach outperforms the averaging approach in all cases. In fact, the probability of convergence to the optimal joint action consistently reaches over 98%. For the three-valued game, we chose $\sigma_0 = 50$ because the variance in the stochastic rewards is higher. The probability of convergence to the optimal joint action in this game reached over 90% for longer experiments i.e. after 2000 moves.

Finally, the stochastic penalty game was once again much easier to solve. Here, the probability of convergence to the optimal joint action exceeded 95% for 200 moves and reached 100% after only 800 moves. This clearly illustrates the ability of the variance-sensitive approach to avoid the problem of choosing between multiple optimal joint actions.

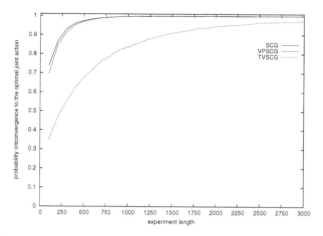

Fig. 7. Convergence of the variance-sensitive (Gaussian) approach on the three games

5   Related Work

There are two main paradigms for the learning of coordination, one using independent agents and another using joint-action learners. While joint-action learners are able to observe one another's actions, their independent counterparts can not. Therefore, approaches using independent learners (such as ours) are more general and more universally applicable.

[2] used joint-action learners and fictitious play in their approach to learning coordination in cooperative multi-agent systems but reported a failure to solve problems where miscoordination is heavily penalised. Later, [1] developed an extension to value iteration that allowed each agent to reason explicitly about the state of coordination, i.e. whether the group of agents are in a coordinated or non-coordinated state. [10] developed a learning algorithm for joint-action learners that provably converges towards the optimal Nash equilibrium.

[4] presented a Q-learning approach to 2-player general-sum games. However, their approach is only successful in games with one Nash equilibrium that is a global optimal point (unlike the penalty game presented and solved in this paper).

[9] argued convincingly that shared knowledge or the ability to communicate is not a necessary condition for multi-agent coordination. They implemented a system where two independent agents learnt to coordinate their actions so as to push a block to a specific location without even being aware of one another. However, their agents did only converge to suboptimal policies.

Similarly, [8] developed a gradient-descent policy-search algorithm for cooperative multi-agent domains that is guaranteed to find a local optimum in the space of factored policies but may not always find an optimal Nash equilibrium.

[7] used social agents that employ a periodical policy to tackle learning in single-stage 2-player games. In contrast to our approach, these agents rely on communication to achieve coordination.

6   Concluding Remarks and Outlook

We have presented a novel learning technique based on commitment sequences that enables independent agents to converge to the optimal joint action even in difficult scenarios with miscoordination penalties and stochastic rewards. Such scenarios were previously approached with Q-learning techniques but remained unsolved using independent agents.

To extend our system to multi-stage games will require a combination of the commitment sequence approach (applied separately in each state to evaluate the expected immediate reward) with state-action value functions that estimate expected discounted returns taking into account the state-transition function. Value functions of this kind may be associated with sequence-action pairs and/or state-action pairs. A hybrid method that makes use of the FMQ heuristic [5] will be considered first.

References

1. Craig Boutilier. Sequential optimality and coordination in multiagent systems. In *Proceedings of the Sixteenth International Joint Conference on Articial Intelligence (IJCAI-99)*, pages 478–485, 1999.
2. Caroline Claus and Craig Boutilier. The dynamics of reinforcement learning in cooperative multiagent systems. In *Proceedings of the Fifteenth National Conference on Articial Intelligence*, pages 746–752, 1998.
3. Drew Fudenberg and David K. Levine. *The Theory of Learning in Games*. MIT Press, Cambridge, MA, 1998.
4. Junling Hu and Michael P. Wellman. Multiagent q-learning. *Machine Learning Research*, 2002.
5. Spiros Kapetanakis and Daniel Kudenko. Reinforcement learning of coordination in cooperative multi-agent systems. In *Proceedings of the Eighteenth National Conference on Artificial Intelligence (AAAI'02)*, 2002.
6. Martin Lauer and Martin Riedmiller. An algorithm for distributed reinforcement learning in cooperative multi-agent systems. In *Proceedings of the Seventeenth International Conference in Machine Learning*, 2000.
7. Ann Nowé, Johan Parent, and Katja Verbeeck. Social agents playing a periodical policy. In *Proceedings of the 12th European Conference on Machine Learning*, Freiburg, Germany, 2001.
8. Leonid Peshkin, Kee-Eung Kim, Nicolas Meuleau, and Leslie Kaelbling. Learning to cooperate via policy search. In *Proceedings of the Sixteenth Conference on Uncertainty in Artificial Intelligence*, 2000.
9. Sandip Sen, Mahendra Sekaran, and John Hale. Learning to coordinate without sharing information. In *Proceedings of the Twelfth National Conference on Artificial Intelligence*, pages 426–431, Seattle, WA, 1994.
10. Xiaofeng Wang and Tuomas Sandholm. Reinforcement learning to play an optimal nash equilibrium in team markov games. In *Proceedings of the 16th Neural Information Processing Systems: Natural and Synthetic (NIPS) conference*, Vancouver, Canada, 2002.
11. Gerhard Weiss. Learning to coordinate actions in multi-agent systems. In *Proceedings of the Thirteenth International Joint Conference on Artificial Intelligence*, volume 1, pages 311–316. Morgan Kaufmann Publ., 1993.

Reinforcement Learning of Coordination in Heterogeneous Cooperative Multi-agent Systems

Spiros Kapetanakis and Daniel Kudenko

Department of Computer Science, University of York,
Heslington, York, YO10 5DD, UK
{spiros, kudenko}@cs.york.ac.uk

Abstract. Most approaches to the learning of coordination in multi-agent systems (MAS) to date require all agents to use the same learning algorithm with similar (or even the same) parameter settings. In today's open networks and high inter-connectivity such an assumption becomes increasingly unrealistic. Developers are starting to have less control over the agents that join the system and the learning algorithms they employ. This makes effective coordination and good learning performance extremely difficult to achieve, especially in the absence of learning agent standards. In this paper we investigate the problem of learning to coordinate with heterogeneous agents. We show that an agent employing the FMQ algorithm, a recently developed multi-agent learning method, has the ability to converge towards the optimal joint action when teamed-up with one or more simple Q-learners. Specifically, we show such convergence in scenarios where simple Q-learners alone are unable to converge towards an optimum. Our results show that system designers may improve learning and coordination performance by adding a "smart" agent to the MAS.

1 Introduction

Learning to coordinate in cooperative multi-agent systems is a central and widely studied problem, see, for example, any of the following works: [11], [8], [1], [3], [10]. In this context, coordination is defined as *the ability of two or more agents to jointly reach a consensus over which actions to perform in an environment.*

To date, learning techniques require the multi-agent system to be *homogeneous*, i.e. all agents need to employ the same learning algorithm and often use the same (or at least similar) parameter settings to achieve optimal coordination.

In today's open networking environment the assumption of agent homogeneity is becoming increasingly unrealistic. Agents are designed by different individuals with different preferences and learning agent standards are virtually non-existent. This poses a problem to designers of open multi-agent systems who don't have control over the algorithms that the agents acting in these systems actually use. How can the designers ensure optimal coordination in the multi-agent system under such conditions?

D. Kudenko et al. (Eds.): Adaptive Agents and MAS II, LNAI 3394, pp. 119–131, 2005.

In this paper we suggest that it may be possible to control learning performance in a heterogeneous multi-agent system by adding a specific agent to the population. More precisely, we investigate the applicability of the FMQ technique [6] for the reinforcement learning of coordination. We show that a team consisting of an FMQ agent and one or more simple Q-learners can achieve high probabilities of convergence to an optimal joint action in single-stage cooperative games, even in cases where Q-learners alone are unable to achieve any reasonable rates of convergence to the optimum. In other words, the FMQ-learner is able to "push" the simple Q-learner(s) to the optimum.

Note that the FMQ technique has been developed for *independent* agents that do not communicate or observe one another's actions, which is a more general and often more realistic assumption. This generality distinguishes our approach from alternatives such as the work by [12] and [2].

This paper is structured as follows: we first present a common testbed for the study of learning coordination in cooperative multi-agent systems, namely single-stage cooperative games. We then introduce three particularly difficult examples of such games that we will use in the experiments. Following this, we present the experimental setup and discuss the results. We finish the paper with an outlook on future work.

2   Single-Stage Cooperative Games

Markov games are a widely used testbed for studying reinforcement learning in multi-agent systems [4, 9]. One particular variation of them which is often used in the study of coordination in multi-agent systems is that of single-stage cooperative games. In these games, the agents have common interests i.e. they are rewarded based on their joint action and all agents receive the same reward. In each round of the game, every agent chooses an action. These actions are executed simultaneously and the reward that corresponds to the joint action is broadcast to all agents at the same time.

A more rigorous account of single-stage cooperative games was given by [3]. In brief, we assume a group of n agents $\alpha_1, \alpha_2, \ldots, \alpha_n$ each of which has a finite set of *individual actions* A_i which is known as the agent's *action space*. In each iteration of the game, each agent α_i chooses an individual action from its action space to perform. The action choices of all agents put together make up a *joint action*, upon execution of which, all agents receive the reward that corresponds to the chosen joint action.

An example of such a game is the *climbing game* which was introduced by [3]. This game, which is shown in Table 1, is played between 2 agents, each of which has 3 actions. If agent 1 executes action c and agent 2 executes action b, the reward they receive is 6. Obviously, the optimal joint action in this game is (a, a) as it is associated with the highest reward of 11.

Our goal is to enable the agents to learn optimal coordination from repeated trials. To achieve this goal, one can use either *independent* or *joint-action* learners. The difference between the two types lies in the amount of information

Table 1. The climbing game

	a	b	c
a	11	-30	0
b	-30	7	6
c	0	0	5

Table 2. The penalty game

	a	b	c
a	10	0	k
b	0	2	0
c	k	0	10

Table 3. The number-matching game

	a	b	c
a	1	-2	-3
b	-2	2	-3
c	-3	-3	3

they can perceive in the game. Although both types of learners can perceive the reward that they receive for the execution of a joint action, the former are unaware of the existence of other agents whereas the latter can also perceive the actions of others. In this way, joint-action learners can maintain a model of the strategy of other agents and choose their actions based on the other participants' perceived strategies. In contrast, independent learners must estimate the value of their individual actions based solely on the rewards that they receive for their actions. In this paper, we focus on individual learners, these being more universally applicable.

In our present study, we focus on three particularly difficult coordination problems, the *climbing game* (Table 1), the *penalty game* (Table 2) and the *number-matching game* (Table 3). All three games are played between two agents. We also introduce general versions of the penalty and number-matching game which any number of agents can take part in. We use these to evaluate the applicability of this work on teams of more than 2 agents.

In the climbing game, it is difficult for the agents to converge to the optimal joint action (a, a) because of the negative reward in the case of miscoordination. Incorporating this reward into the learning process can be so detrimental that both agents tend to avoid playing their respective components of the optimal joint action again. In contrast, when choosing action c, miscoordination is not punished so severely. Therefore, in most cases, both agents are easily tempted by action c.

Another way to make coordination more elusive is by including multiple optimal joint actions. This is precisely what happens in the penalty game. In this game, it is not only important to avoid the miscoordination penalties associated with actions (c, a) and (a, c) but it is equally important to agree on which optimal joint action to choose out of (a, a) and (c, c). If agent 1 plays a expecting agent 2 to also play a so they can receive the maximum reward of 10 but agent 2 plays c (perhaps expecting agent 1 to play c so that, again, they receive the maximum reward of 10) then the resulting penalty can be very detrimental to both agents' learning process. In this game, b is the "safe" action for both agents since playing b is guaranteed to result in a non-negative reward, regardless of what the other agent plays.

In the last testbed, the number-matching game, the two agents can only receive a positive reward for playing the *same* action. Any of (a, a), (b, b) or (c, c) will result in a positive reward with (c, c) being the optimal joint action. The difficulty, however, in solving this game stems from the fact that actions with a higher reward carry the risk of a higher penalty in the case of miscoordination. Every time the two agents play different actions, they are *both* punished with a penalty that matches the action of the more ambitious of the two. For example, if the agents play joint action (c, b) they will both receive a payoff of -3 because agent 1 tried its individual component of the optimal joint action.

3   Reinforcement Learning of Coordination

A popular technique for learning coordination in cooperative single-stage games is one-step Q-learning, a reinforcement learning technique. Since the agents in a single-stage game are stateless, we need a simple reformulation of the general Q-learning algorithm such as the one used by [3]. Each agent maintains a Q value for each of its actions. The value $Q(\text{action})$ provides an estimate of the usefulness of performing this action in the next iteration of the game and these values are updated after each step of the game according to the reward received for the action. We apply Q-learning with the following update function:

$$Q(\text{action}) \leftarrow Q(\text{action}) + \gamma(r - Q(\text{action}))$$

where γ is the learning rate $(0 < \gamma < 1)$ and r is the reward that corresponds to choosing this action.

In a single-agent learning scenario, Q-learning is guaranteed to converge to the optimal action independent of the action selection strategy. In other words, given the assumption of a stationary reward function, single-agent Q-learning will (eventually) converge to the optimal policy for the problem. However, in a multi-agent setting, the action selection strategy becomes crucial for convergence to *any* joint action. In fact, two regular Q-learners fail to converge to the optimal joint action in all games presented in the previous section.

In previous work [6], we developed a novel action selection heuristic, called FMQ. Using this technique, agents are able to converge to the optimal action in the three games from Section 2. FMQ is based on the Boltzmann strategy [5] which states that agent α_i chooses an action to perform in the next iteration of the game with a probability that is based on its current estimate of the usefulness of that action, denoted by EV(action)[1] :

$$P(\text{action}) = \frac{e^{\frac{\text{EV(action)}}{T}}}{\sum_{\text{action}' \in A_i} e^{\frac{\text{EV(action}')}{T}}}$$

In the case of Q-learning, the agent's estimate of the usefulness of an action may be given by the Q values themselves, an approach that has been usually taken to date. Instead, the FMQ approach uses the following formula to compute EV(α):

$$\text{EV}(\alpha) = Q(\alpha) + c * \text{freq}(\text{maxR}(\alpha)) * \text{maxR}(\alpha)$$

where:

1. maxR(α) denotes the maximum reward encountered *so far* for choosing action α.
2. freq(maxR(α)) is the fraction of times that maxR(α) has been received as a reward for action α over the times that action α has been executed.
3. c is a weight that controls the importance of the FMQ heuristic in the action selection.

Informally, the FMQ heuristic carries the information of how frequently an action produces its maximum corresponding reward. Note that, for an agent to receive the maximum reward corresponding to one of its actions, the other agent must be playing the game accordingly.

4   Experimental Results with 2 Learners

This section contains our experimental results with a pair of heterogeneous reinforcement learners. We show that one FMQ-learner is indeed sufficient to achieve a high probability of convergence towards an optimal joint action when paired with a simple Q-learner. The simple Q-learner uses one-step Q-learning with the same temperature function as the FMQ-learner. We vary the learning rate γ for the Q-learner to show the performance of the FMQ/Q pair with different degrees of heterogeneity. The evaluation of the two approaches is performed on the climbing game, the penalty game and the number-matching game.

In all sections, we compare the performance of the FMQ/Q pair of learners with the baseline experiment of two homogeneous Q-learners using Boltzmann exploration with the following temperature function:

$$T(x) = e^{-sx} * \text{max\_temp} + 1$$

where x is the number of iterations of the game so far, s is the parameter that controls the rate of exponential decay and max_temp is the value of the temperature at the beginning of the experiment. For a given length of the experiment

---

[1] [5] introduce the estimated value as *expected reward* (ER).

(max_moves) and initial temperature (max_temp), the appropriate rate of decay
(s) is automatically derived. Varying the parameters of the temperature function
allows a detailed specification of the temperature. The settings for the baseline
experiments are: max_temp $= 499, \gamma = 0.9$. All sets of experiments have been
run 1000 times to minimise the variance in the results.

4.1   Evaluation on the Climbing Game

The climbing game has one optimal joint action, (a, a), and two heavily penalised actions, (a, b) and (b, a). In the evaluation that follows, we use the setting
max_temp $= 499$ and set the learning rate for the FMQ-learner to 0.9 and the
confidence parameter of the FMQ-learner to $c = 10$. We show results for two
experiment lengths, namely 1000 and 2000 moves. For each experiment length,
we vary the learning rate for the standard Q-learner from 0.3 to 0.9. Figure 1
depicts the likelihood of convergence to the optimal joint action in the climbing
game.

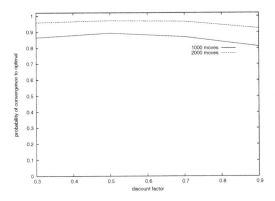

Fig. 1. Probability of convergence to the optimal joint action in the climbing game

The results shown in Figure 1 are significantly better than the baseline results.
The two Q-learners with the baseline settings as explained above, only manage
to converge to the optimal joint action with probability 0.168 in 1000 moves and
with probability 0.19 in 2000 moves. This represents a major change in behaviour
when one of the original Q-learners is substituted with an FMQ-learner.

4.2   Evaluation on the Penalty Game

The penalty game is harder to analyse than the climbing game because it has
two optimal joint actions (a, a) and (c, c) for all values of k. The extent to which
the optimal joint actions are reached by the agents is affected severely by the
size of the penalty. However, the performance of the agents depends not only
on the size of the penalty k but also on whether the agents manage to agree on
which optimal joint action to choose. Figure 2 depicts the performance of the

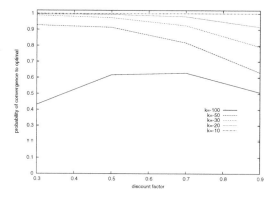

Fig. 2. Probability of convergence to the optimal joint action in the penalty game

Table 4. Probability of convergence to optimal in the penalty game for the baseline experiment

k	(a, a)	(c, c)	total
-10	0.373	0.359	0.732
-20	0.256	0.276	0.532
-30	0.242	0.230	0.472
-50	0.194	0.222	0.416
-100	0.176	0.211	0.387

FMQ/Q pair of learners in the penalty game. Again, we set max_temp $= 499$ and set the learning rate for the FMQ-learner to 0.9. The confidence parameter of the FMQ-learner was set to $c = 10$ and we varied the Q-learner's learning rate from 0.3 to 0.9. In the interest of clarity, we show results for only one experiment length, namely 1000 moves.

The performance of the two Q-learners in the baseline experiment is slightly better in the penalty game than in the climbing game. For 1000 moves and the default settings, the two Q-learners' probability of convergence to either optimal action is shown in Table 4.

From Figure 2, it is clear that in the pair of agents solving the penalty game, the substitution of a Q-learner by an FMQ-learner is always beneficial, for all values of γ for the remaining Q-learner. The benefit is most striking when k is low and the Q-learner's learning rate is also low.

4.3   Evaluation on the Number Matching Game

The number-matching game turned out to be much less difficult than originally expected. The reason for this is that the FMQ-learner is not easily convinced that its c action is not a component of the optimal joint action when confronted with the reward of -3 for miscoordination. When the FMQ-learner witnesses a successful coordination on (c, c) and the resulting reward of 3 for playing c, this reward becomes the maximum reward corresponding to action c. This event, a

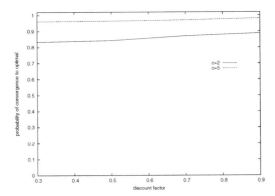

Fig. 3. Probability of convergence to the optimal joint action in the number-matching game

successful coordination on the optimal joint action, inevitably happens in the early part of the experiment when the temperature is still relatively high and the agents play actions almost randomly. Eventually, the FMQ-learner manages to convince the standard Q-learner that (c, c) is the optimal joint action as it persists in playing c.

The results for the number-matching game are included in Figure 3. The settings for these results are: max_temp = 499, the learning rate for the FMQ-learner is 0.9 and the confidence parameter of the FMQ-learner is set to two values, namely 2 and 5. Normally, a value of $c = 2$ for the confidence parameter is too low to help the learners to converge to the optimal joint action. However, for the number-matching game where the optimal joint action has very low corresponding reward and the maximum penalty is not significantly greater in absolute value than the reward for the optimal joint action, even a value of 2 is enough to solve the game adequately. For illustration, Figure 3 depicts the performance of the learners for an experiment that is 1000 moves long, for both $c = 2$ and $c = 5$ for the FMQ-learner.

Again, the baseline experiment using two regular Q-learners is heavily outperformed by the FMQ/Q pair's performance. In 1000 moves, the probability of convergence to the optimal action (c, c) in the baseline experiment is 0.32, which is significantly lower than the probability of success for the FMQ/Q pair, which is always above 0.833, for all tested values of γ and even for a low confidence value $c = 2$.

5   Evaluation with Greater Size Teams

In this section, we present our experimental results with one FMQ-learner that is teamed up with more than one Q-learner. The results show that the FMQ-learner is still able to increase the probability of convergence to the optimum but not as drastically as in the two-agent case.

Two of the games from the above experiments can be generalised to more than 2 agents while keeping the overall philosophy of the game, namely the number-matching game and the penalty game. Their definitions are as follows:

> The *general number-matching game*: if all agents play the same action, return the corresponding reward e.g. for action $(a, a, \ldots, a)$ return 1. If they play different actions, return the penalty corresponding to the agent that played the most ambitiously, e.g. for action $(a, a, \ldots, a, c)$ return -3

> The *general penalty game*: if all agents play a return 10, if all agents play c return 10, if all agents play b return 2. If any number of agents play a (or c) and at least one agent plays c (or a) return the penalty k as the group have just miscoordinated. For any other joint action, return a reward of 0.

In the sections that follow, we will use the short-hand notation $< \alpha >$ to denote the joint action that results from all agents playing their individual action components α. For example, in the 4 agent case, $(< b >)$ corresponds to the joint action (b, b, b, b).

From the definitions of the two general games, we can see that they correspond appropriately to their original counterparts. The climbing game cannot be generalised to more than 2 agents as there is no symmetry to exploit in doing so. For that reason, we will perform the evaluation on agent teams of greater size than 2 only on the general penalty game and number-matching game.

In the text that follows, we will illustrate the performance of agent teams that comprise a single FMQ-learner and 2, 3 or 4 Q-learners. In all experiments, the agents use the same temperature function as previously with max_temp = 499 and $\gamma = 0.9$, for all agents. The FMQ-learner's confidence parameter has been set to $c = 10$ throughout.

5.1   Evaluation with the Penalty Game

The general penalty game for teams of more than 2 agents is quite a challenging game. This is because even the FMQ heuristic that was so successful in two-agent experiments can be mislead by greater size teams. For the heuristic to be more useful, the participating agents should all base their action selection decisions on the same reasons, namely that the action they are most tempted by is the one that produces better reward more often. In fact, had this been the case, i.e. if we were interested in the performance of a homogeneous FMQ-learning team, the probability of convergence to the optimal joint action would be significantly higher. For example, a team of 4 FMQ-learners would solve the general penalty game with probability comfortably greater than 0.95 in 5000 moves.

However, when one teams up more than 1 Q-learner with an FMQ-learner, the performance of the learning team suffers as the Q-learners play too randomly. This means that the frequency of getting high reward for coordinated actions is too low and the FMQ-learner is misled into believing that its b action is better than either a or c. In effect, although the FMQ-learner is still "pushing" the group towards some joint action, that joint action is (b, b) and not one of the optimal joint actions.

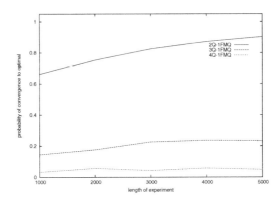

Fig. 4. Probability of convergence to the optimal joint action in the general penalty game (FMQ/Q-learners)

From Figure 4, we can see that although the experiments with 2 Q-learners and 1 FMQ-learner are still quite successful, those with greater size teams are not. This is attributed to the problem described above where the optimal joint action is simply not experienced often enough to be considered by the FMQ-learner. Note that the move from 2-agent to 3-agent experiments increases the size of the joint action space by a factor of 3, from a total of 9 joint actions to 27.

One observation that is important is that, despite the limited success of the experiments with the FMQ-learner, the learning team still performed better than the same size team of only Q-learners. More importantly, the team with the added FMQ-learner performed better overall than the team without the FMQ-learner even though the two problems differ greatly in the size of the joint action space.

To illustrate this point, we have included a plot of the probability of convergence to the optimal joint action in teams with only Q-learners in the general penalty game. This is shown in Figure 5.

5.2   Evaluation with the Number-Matching Game

The general number-matching game was again less challenging than its penalty game counterpart. The addition of the FMQ-learner proved positive in all experiments, as is shown in Figure 6.

The same efect as before was observed in these experiments too. The addition of one FMQ-learner, although it causes the joint action space to grow significantly, it still provides better learning performance. We hope this is a general enough result to be exploited further in our future work.

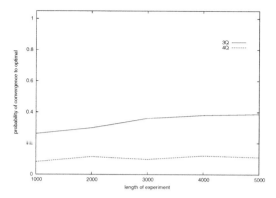

Fig. 5. Probability of convergence to the optimal joint action in the general penalty game (Q-learners)

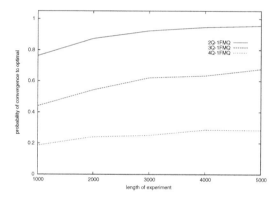

Fig. 6. Probability of convergence to the optimal joint action in the general number-matching game (FMQ/Q-learners)

5.3   Discussion

In the previous sections, we have investigated the effect that the addition of one or more FMQ-learning agents has to a group of Q-learners.

The rather surprising result is that adding an FMQ-learner is always beneficial. This is quite significant since the addition of another agent to the system makes the joint action space grow exponentially. When a 2-agent problem with 3 actions per agent had only 9 joint actions, a 3-agent problem with, again, 3 actions has 27 joint actions. The addition of an FMQ-learner to a group of agents means both that the agents converge more often to the optimal joint action and that they converge to better actions in general. This is a phenomenon that obtains in all games that we have tried.

However, another interesting phenomenon is that the agents need only polynomially more time to solve a problem that is exponentially bigger. Again, this is supported by our experimentation and will be evaluated further in our future work to show whether this observation obtains in general.

6   Limitations

Heterogeneity in agents is not merely a question of learning algorithm. Changing just one setting can turn a successful experiment into an unsuccessful one. For example, if we pair up a Q-learner and an FMQ-learner to solve the climbing game (see Table 1) and set the maximum temperature to 499, set the FMQ-learners confidence parameter to 5, set both learning rates to 0.9 and allow them to run for 1000 moves, they will converge to the optimal joint action (a, a) approximately 55% of the time. This may not be great but it is still better than if we allowed the Q-learner the use of a different temperature function. If the Q-learner was using a linear temperature function instead of the exponential one, the learners would not converge at all to the optimal joint action. The learners would, instead, consistently converge to a suboptimal action. This instability with respect to the degree of heterogeneity in the agents is an issue that has to be addressed in future research.

Finally, it is important to note that the addition of more than one FMQ-learner to the agent population does not improve results. In fact, it even tends to reduce performance a little for the same or slightly greater experiment length. The advantages of the addition of more "smart" agents seem to be outweighed by the exponential increase in the joint action space.

7   Conclusions and Outlook

We have presented an experimental study of the learning of coordination for heterogeneous multi-agent systems. Specifically, we have shown that a learning agent which employs the FMQ heuristic can achieve high levels of convergence towards an optimal joint action when teamed-up with one or more simple Q-learners. This has been shown on games where two or more simple Q-learners would not be able to achieve optimal coordination by themselves. In other words, the FMQ-learner "pushes" the simple Q-learners to the optimum. This result indicates that it is possible for a multi-agent system developer to achieve optimal coordination even when he/she does not have complete control over the nature of the agents that are going to be part of it.

While the results presented are very encouraging, there is still more work to be done in generalising our results. Specifically, we plan to study the performance of other heuristic learners when teamed-up with a wider range of other kinds of learning agents. Furthermore, we plan to investigate limitations, such as those mentioned in the previous section. We also intend to extend our studies to stochastic single-stage games [7], as well as multi-stage games.

References

1. Craig Boutilier. Sequential optimality and coordination in multiagent systems. In *Proceedings of the Sixteenth International Joint Conference on Articial Intelligence (IJCAI-99)*, pages 478–485, 1999.
2. Georgios Chalkiadakis and Craig Boutilier. Coordination in multiagent reinforcement learning: A bayesian approach. In *Proceedings of the Second International Joint Conference on Autonomous Agents and Multiagent Systems*, pages 709–716, Melbourne, Australia, 2003.
3. Caroline Claus and Craig Boutilier. The dynamics of reinforcement learning in cooperative multiagent systems. In *Proceedings of the Fifteenth National Conference on Articial Intelligence*, pages 746–752, 1998.
4. Drew Fudenberg and David K. Levine. *The Theory of Learning in Games*. MIT Press, Cambridge, MA, 1998.
5. Leslie Pack Kaelbling, Michael Littman, and Andrew W. Moore. Reinforcement learning: A survey. *Journal of Artificial Intelligence Research*, 4, 1996.
6. Spiros Kapetanakis and Daniel Kudenko. Reinforcement learning of coordination in cooperative multi-agent systems. In *Proceedings of the Nineteenth National Conference on Artificial Intelligence*, pages 326–331, Edmonton, Alberta, Canada, 2002.
7. Spiros Kapetanakis, Daniel Kudenko, and Malcolm Strens. Learning to coordinate using commitment sequences in cooperative multi-agent systems. In *Proceedings of the Third Symposium on Adaptive Agents and Multi-agent Systems (AAMAS03)*. Society for the study of Artificial Intelligence and Simulation of Behaviour, 2003.
8. Martin Lauer and Martin Riedmiller. An algorithm for distributed reinforcement learning in cooperative multi-agent systems. In *Proceedings of the Seventeenth International Conference in Machine Learning*, 2000.
9. Michael L. Littman. Markov games as a framework for multi-agent reinforcement learning. In Morgan Kaufman, editor, *Proceedings of the Eleventh International Conference on Machine Learning*, pages 157–163, San Mateo, CA, USA, 1994.
10. Sandip Sen and Mahendra Sekaran. Individual learning of coordination knowledge. *JETAI*, 10(3):333–356, 1998.
11. Katja Verbeeck, Ann Nowe, and Karl Tuyls. Coordinated exploration in stochastic common interest games. In *Proceedings of Third Symposium on Adaptive Agents and Multi-agent Systems*, pages 97–102, University of Wales, Aberystwyth, 2003.
12. Xiaofeng Wang and Tuomas Sandholm. Reinforcement learning to play an optimal nash equilibrium in team markov games. In *Proceedings of the 16th Neural Information Processing Systems: Natural and Synthetic conference*, Vancouver, Canada, 2002.

Evolving the Game of Life

Dimitar Kazakov and Matthew Sweet

Department of Computer Science, University of York,
Heslington, York YO10 5DD, UK
{kazakov, mts104}@cs.york.ac.uk
http://www.cs.york.ac.uk/~{kazakov,mts104}

Abstract. It is difficult to define a set of rules for a cellular automaton (CA) such that creatures with life-like properties (stability and dynamic behaviour, reproducton and self-repair) can be grown from a large number of initial configurations. This work describes an evolutionary framework for the search of a CA with these properties. Instead of encoding them directly into the fitness function, we propose one, which maximises the variance of entropy across the CA grid. This fitness function promotes the existence of areas on the verge of chaos, where life is expected to thrive. The results are reported for the case of CA in which cells are in one of four possible states. We also describe a mechanism for fitness sharing that successfully speeds up the genetic search, both in terms of number of generations and CPU time.

1   Introduction

The aim of this work is to evolve a set (table) of rules for a cellular automaton (CA) with a good potential for producing "interesting" life forms, e.g., such that grow, move, have a long life span, consist of differentiated types of tissue, are compact and/or preserve their shape or produce a copy of themselves as a by-product of their growth. Rather than focussing on each such property in isolation, and trying to find the combination of rules that promotes it, an attempt is made to study an entropy-based criterion that is used as an indicator of the likelihood of such desirable life-forms appearing in a given CA. The criterion is used as a fitness function of a genetic algorithm (GA) searching through the range of possible CA. Also, to improve the GA performance on a task in which, intuitively, good solutions are few and far apart, we employ two techniques to maintain the balance between population quality and diversity — crowding [1] and extended fitness — and show the substantial advantages that the latter brings in.

Cellular automata are dynamic systems consisting of a lattice of cells (in any number of dimensions) each of which has a number of associated discrete states k. The state of these cells is updated at discrete time steps, the resultant state dependent upon local state rules. Here we study two-dimensional automata with cells being in one of four possible states ($k = 4$, in other words, the cell belongs to one of three different types or is in a *quiescent* state, i.e., non-live). The range

D. Kudenko et al. (Eds.): Adaptive Agents and MAS II, LNAI 3394, pp. 132–146, 2005.
© Springer-Verlag Berlin Heidelberg 2005

of cells that influence the subsequent state of a cell is limited to immediate neighbours (sometimes denoted as $r = 1$ [2]). Each CA is defined by the table of rules that describe the subsequent state of the central cell for each 3×3 neighbourhood.

2   Genetic Algorithms and Extended Fitness

Genetic algorithms are search algorithms based on the mechanics of Darwinian evolution and genetics. GAs, despite their large variety, are all based on the same basic principles. They maintain a population of individuals representing candidate solutions to an optimisation problem. For each generation, a *fitness* reflecting estimated or actual quality is assigned to each solution (individual). A next generation of individuals is obtained by sampling the current so that individuals with higher fitness are favoured. Finally, the new generation is subjected to genetic operations such as crossover and mutation that aim at introducing a variety of new individuals. Then the cycle is repeated until some termination condition is fulfilled [3].

The fitness of an individual may measure the quality of the solution it proposes in absolute terms, say, as a scalar representing the value of a function that the GA is trying to maximise. In other cases, e.g., when it is normalised, fitness only represents the relative quality of an individual with respect to the rest. Fitness could be an even more abstract concept only reflecting the rank of the individual in the population.

Whether the goal of the GA is to provide a single best solution or a number of these, its principle remains the same: to store copies of the best one(s) aside from the main population, and wait until better ones are produced. For that ever to happen, it is essential that the GA should be capable of producing individuals that have not been seen in the previous generations. While the genetic operators, such as crossover and mutation, are the GA components that introduce new individuals in the population, their success depends on preserving sufficient genetic variety in it. Evolution, whether in nature or as implemented in GAs, can be seen as a dynamic process driven by two factors: (natural) *selection*, which favours the survival of the fittest, and *genetic variation*, which introduces new individuals, some of which could potentially outperform the best so far. Neither factor is sufficient on its own: without selection, the search for the best individual will become completely random; without genetic variation, there will be nothing that selection can act upon as a uniform population of identical individuals reaches a dead end.

GAs employ several techniques that study the individual's fitness in the context of the whole population and modify it to preserve the balance between the forces of selection and those increasing genetic variation. Fitness *scaling* is used to reduce the risk of clones of one 'superindividual' taking over the whole population in the early stages of the search when the individuals' fitness is very varied and generally low. Also, in a population with a minimum of variety in the fitness, scaling helps emphasise the existing differences and promote the best individuals more strongly. In either case, scaling aims at normalising the differences between the fitness of individuals with respect to the extremes present in the population. This could be done in a number of ways, from using a linear scaling function to ranking individuals according to their fitness and substituting rank for the original fitness.

Holland [4] has observed that for fitness functions with a rugged landscape two high fitness parents often generate 'lethals' (very low fitness offspring). De Jong [1] suggests that this effect can be combated using an algorithm with crowding factoring such that a new individual will replace an individual from the previous generation with a similar genetic make up. For each child, a subset of the population is selected at random that contains k individuals and the member of that set closest (by bitwise comparison) to the new offspring is replaced. In this model, k is known as the crowding factor, and was shown by De Jong to have an optimal value of 2 over the complex multimodal foxhole function. In this work, trials have shown that 10 is an optimal value for the crowding factor given an initial population size of 150.

Inbreeding with intermittent crossbreeding is a technique proposed by Hollstien [5] for search using genetic algorithms with multimodal fitness functions. The idea is that the individuals in each niche mate until the average niche fitness ceases to rise and then the individuals in that niche can mate with individuals in different niche. This allows the neighbourhood of each local maximum to be thoroughly searched before guiding the search for a global maximum to another unexplored part of the search space.

```
procedure evaluateExtendedFitness

for each chromosome C do
|extFitness(C) = 0
|  for each locus L do
|  |  extFitness(C,L) = 0
|  |  numberOfMatches=0
|  |  for each chromosome C' do
|  |  |  if locus L in C = locus L in C'
|  |  |  increment numberOfMatches
|  |  |_ extFitness(C,L) += fitness(C')
|  |  extFitness(C,L)/=(numberOfMatches *
|  |                     chromosomeLength )
|_ |_ extFitness(C) += extFitness(C,L)
```

Fig. 1. Procedure computing extended fitness

Although not used here, another technique worth mentioning is *niching*, which is used to modify fitness in order to avoid overpopulating parts of the search space in favour of others. In general, this technique is based on partitioning the range of all individuals into *niches* and then reducing the fitness of individuals in overpopulated niches [6].

```
procedure evaluateExtendedFitness2

for each locus L do
for each allele A in L do
|  fitness(L,A) = 0
|_ presence(L,A) = 0

for each chromosome C do
for each locus L in C do
for each allele A in L do
|  fitness(L,A) += standardfitness(C)
|_ presence(L,A)++

for each locus L do
for each allele A do
|_ fitness(L,A) = fitness(L,A) / ( presence(A) * chromosomeLength )


for each chromosome C do
|  extFitness(C) = 0
|  for each locus L in C do
|  for the allele A in L do
|_ |_ extFitness(C) += fitness(L,A)
```

Fig. 2. More efficient computation of extended fitness

Yet another alternative proposed here is the approach we call *extended fitness* (see Figure 1), in analogy to Dawkins's notion of extended genotype [7]. As in population genetics, the components of this fitness are defined to measure the relative advantage that a gene gives to its carrier with respect to all other genes that can appear in the same locus. The fitness of the whole genome then can be computed as the averaged contribution of all its loci [8]. Extended fitness favours individuals with good genetic material (building blocks) and relies on the assumption that these could potentially be useful in the evolutionary search. Figure 2 shows the actual implementation of the way extended fitness is computed, which is faster, but more difficult to follow than the one shown in Figure 1. The overhead $O(numberOfChromosomes*chromosomeLength)$ introduced by this latter implementation is very modest, and, as the experimental section of this article shows, it can be easily outweighed by the benefits it brings.

3   Evolving Cellular Automata

Using genetic algorithms for the search of CA with desired properties is a trend with a relatively short history. Previous research has often focussed on one-dimensional automata [9, 2] or ones with two cell states ($k = 2$) [9, 2, 10]. In all cases, the resulting cellular automata (sets of rules) fall into one of four classes as defined by Wolfram [11]. Class 1 automata evolve after a finite number of time steps from almost all initial configurations to a single unique homogenous configuration in which all cells in the automaton have the same value. Class 2 automata generate simple disjoint structures dependent upon their initial configuration. The evolution of class 3 automata produces chaotic patterns from almost all initial configurations; the statistical properties, after sufficient time steps, of the patterns produced by almost all initial configurations is the same. All other automata fall into a fourth class where for most initial configurations the automaton cells will become almost entirely unpopulated, however some stable live structures will develop which will persist indefinitely.

It would be unlikely that interesting creatures could exist in class 1 automata since after a finite time period all cells in the automaton would have the same value; therefore no interesting creatures could persist past this point. Class 2 automata merely generate simple disjoint structures (either periodic or static), which means that no reproducing or dynamic creatures could be created. Class 3 automata cannot support interesting creatures since the patterns produced are chaotic. Therefore the focus of this paper must be the fourth class of automata since they are most likely to be able to satisfy the criteria of supporting interesting creatures. The above speculations should be compared with Wolfram's suggestion that the fourth class of CA is of sufficient complexity to support universal computation [12].

When the fitness of a set of rules is to be determined then the cellular automaton that is represented by that set of rules needs to be run on some initial configuration of cells in the lattice. There are two techniques to consider that have been used in previous research to generate initial states — random generation and specific pattern generation. In random generation, some portion of the board is populated at random with live cells, and the density of live cells is dependent upon the probability of each cell being live. In specific pattern generation, a user defined pattern is created usually at the centre of an otherwise unpopulated lattice.

In their work, Basanta *et al.* [13] used a static initial state — only the central cell is live and all others are initially unoccupied. This reduces the amount of computation necessary for each fitness calculation. For an algorithm using randomised initial states, several runs are needed to attain an accurate fitness for the rule set, however with a single static initial state the fitness must only be calculated once.

The approach adopted here is based on two GAs. Each individual of the first GA encodes the rules of one CA. For each of these CA, another, nested, GA is used to search for an initial configuration of the given CA that has the highest possible fitness. The fitness of an initial configuration is computed by running the CA through a number of time steps, summing the fitness for each ot them. This fitness is then used as the fitness of the CA. The inner genetic algorithm uses the fitness function described in the next section to discover initial configurations which favour the evolution of interesting life. All this can be summarised as follows:

1. Use a GA to select the best CA (set of rules).
2. To evaluate each CA, use another GA to select the best initial configuration (IC) and use its fitness as the CA fitness.
3. To evaluate each pair (CA,IC), run CA with IC for a predefined number of steps, measuring fitness at each step, summing it up, and returning the total. In other words, a CA, as defined by its set of rules, is only as fit as the fittest initial configuration that has been found for it.

The fitness landscape for this problem is highly rugged and therefore one must consider techniques for improving the effectiveness of the genetic algorithm under these conditions, with a particular attention to fitness scaling. In this work, crowding and extended fitness have been employed and compared.

4   Entropy Based Fitness of Cellular Automata

In this section, we introduce the fitness criterion used by the inner of the two above mentioned GAs.

The entropy of a system is defined to be the level of orderliness or chaos in that system – the higher the level of chaos, the higher the entropy. Wolfram [11] defines the entropy of a CA to be:

$$S = -\sum_i p_i \, \log_2 p_i \tag{1}$$

where S is the entropy and p_i is the probability of state i. For two-dimensional automata an equation was developed by Wolfram and Packard [14] to express the *set entropy* of an automaton.

$$S = \lim_{X,Y \to \infty} \frac{1}{XY} \log_k N(X,Y) \tag{2}$$

where S is the entropy, X and Y are dimensions of the area for which the entropy is being calculated and k is the number of different states. When used to calculate the entropy of a particular state, $N(X,Y)$ is the number of possible different states by which the current configuration can be represented. E.g., a 3×3 area containing one live cell could be represented by 9 different states, so $N(X,Y) = 9$. The division by XY normalises the entropy values, so that entropies over different tile sizes can be compared.

To calculate an approximation of this set entropy is far cheaper than to calculate the entropy using the first equation, since this first option would require us to enumerate all possible states. Also we are not interested in the overall automaton entropy but rather in the entropy of *tiles* [10], a lattice of cells which is a component of the overall lattice of cells making up the automaton.

Another possible method of calculating the entropy would be to use the site entropy approach used by Langton. This is based on the entropy of a single cell of the lattice, and is defined to be 1 if the cell is in a different state to its state in the previous time step. The entropy of a tile therefore would be the sum of the entropies of all its constituent cells. To normalise the tile entropies, as with the set entropy calculation, it would be necessary to divide the tile entropy by the tile size, which gives the proportion of the cells that are in the same state as in the previous time state.

If we based the fitness function on the overall entropy then selecting for high entropy would result in a chaotic class 3 automaton which could not support interesting life. Conversely, selecting for a high degree of order (low entropy) would favour class 1 and class 2 automata which reach a stable state and never leave it. Interesting life is most likely to develop on the boundary between order and chaos; we need dynamic behaviour inherent in chaotic systems but we also need a degree of order to keep any developing life coherent. Therefore we wish to promote rule sets that contain both order and chaos — this can be achieved by assigning a *fitness based on the spread (standard deviation) of the entropies of (a sample of) the tiles making up the automaton.* We have also hoped that setting $k = 4$ would allow for specialisation among the types of cell, in a way specialised types of cells (tissue) have evolved in nature.

5   Results and Evaluation

A rule set was generated using a 100×100 board, and an initial population of 150 rule sets for the outer entropy based GA, which was run for 300 generations. The inner genetic algorithm, evolving for a given rule set inital configurations that create interesting creatures, had a population of 10 and was run for 20 generations — the population size and number of generations have to be kept low since they have a large effect on the run time of the algorithm. To evaluate each initial configuration, the CA was run with the given set of rules and initial

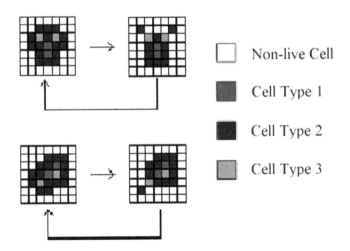

Fig. 3. Cyclic structures with period 2

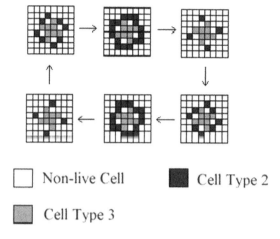

☐ Non-live Cell   ■ Cell Type 2

▨ Cell Type 3

Fig. 4. A cyclic structure with period 6

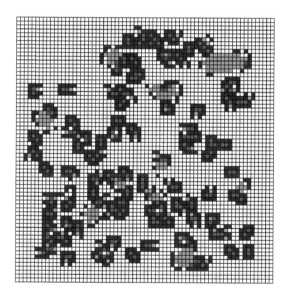

Fig. 5. A large structure evolved from a dense, random configuration

configuration for 200 steps. To compute the fitness of a configuration (CA board), only tiles of size 3×3 and 15×15 were considered.

The properties of the best rule set found have been empirically analysed and are as follows. No single cell of any type can survive, and neither can groups

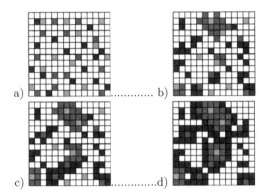

Fig. 6. (a) Randomly generated initial configuration of the cellular automaton (density 0.2); (b) state after 1 transition; (c) state after 2 transitions; (d) state after a large number of transitions

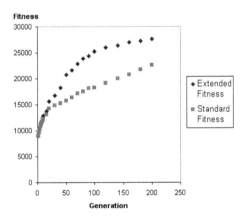

Fig. 7. Comparison of the average fitness of rule sets for extended fitness and standard fitness approaches by generation (averaged over 10 runs using a population size of 100)

of cells which are composed of only type 1 or 2 cells. Cells of type 3 survive, unchanged and unproductive in some compact formations of sufficient size. All other life seen so far under the rule set consists of more than one different type of cell (and this is observed, as a rule, whenever the experiment is repeated). We have produced a rule set which favours life consisting of different types of tissue, one of the aims of the work, without specifying this as part of the genetic algorithm.

Here are some examples of the ways different types of cell interact. Any cell of type 1 requires another cell of the same type, as well as a cell of type 3 in its neighbourhood in order to survive. Type 1 cells catalyse the growth of type 2 cells: any non-live cell adjacent to a type 1 cell and a type 2 cell will grow into a live type 2 cell. As a result, a cluster of type 1 and type 2 cells will gradually

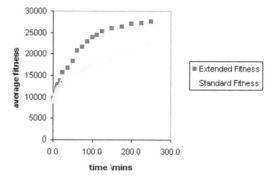

Fig. 8. Comparison of the average fitness of rule sets for extended fitness and standard fitness approaches by time (averaged over 10 runs using a population size of 100)

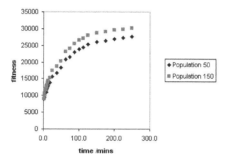

Fig. 9. Comparison of the average fitness of rule sets for extended fitness and standard fitness approaches by population size (averaged over 10 runs)

evolve into a connected core of type 1 cells completely enclosed by the type 2 cells. Cells of type 3 grow in the presence of other 4 cells of type 3, as well as when a combination of 1 type 3 and 1 type 1 is present. Certain combinations of type 2 and type 3 neighbour cells breed another type 2 cell, and often clusters of these two types of cell are stable or show periodic behaviour.

To summarise, one can see type 1 cells serving as an inert 'skeleton' which has to be protected by a layer of type 2 cells; type 3 cells promote periodic behaviour in combination with type 2, and can be grown themselves in the presence of type 1 cells. Figures 3–4 are examples of some of the small structures that survive in this CA. For configurations with sufficient density (e.g., 0.7) complex, connected structures such as the one in Figure 5 with stable and periodic components, spanning more than half the environment in each direction, emerge as a rule.

Here size is an important factor. A large structure will show a periodic behaviour equal to the least common multiple of the periods of all dynamic substuctures. For substructures of period 3,4 and 5 (all observed), the overall period will be 60, etc.

Figure 6 shows the type of life produced by another rule set selected by our algorithm after 200 generations. This rule set started from almost any initial configuration will generate a pattern resembling that of animal spots or organs made of layers of tissue. The automaton is resilient to damage and will regrow any killed cells so long as the core (green) cell is not removed.

Figures 7–8 show an interesting result related to the way GA is implemented: extended fitness produces faster improvements of the average population fitness despite the computational overhead it introduces. Moreover, extended fitness has a positive effect not only when the number of generations is compared, but also in terms of computational time, which is a very rewarding result. In a final observation on extended fitness (Figure 9), we have shown that the average population fitness can improve faster (again, in the stronger terms of time needed) with a larger population, which may seem counter-intuitive. This could be explained by the rugged fitness landscape which can be mapped more accurately by a larger population.

6   Identifying Moving, Reproducing Creatures in Cellular Automata

In order to identify rule sets that support interesting life forms, the population of the genetic algorithm with the entropy based fitness function at the final generation will be used as the initial population to a second genetic algorithm. This second algorithm evaluates CA with a fitness function that identifies individual creatures (connected groups of cells) and maintains a table of those which it has seen. Creatures are identified by the proportion of each type of cell of which they are made up. The creatures which have been seen are stored in a list, the members of which are compared with the board at regular intervals. If a creature is seen again, then its past and present positions are compared. If the creature has moved, then the CA fitness is increased by the number of cells making up that creature. As a result, the fitness promotes CA generating long-living creatures that move. Creatures can be composed a minimum of 5 and a maximum of 200 live cells to reduce computation costs.

The problem with this fitness function is that it is very expensive to compute taking nearly 600ms (on the 700 MHz test machine). If we were to substitute this fitness function for the entropy-based one, and run the experiment described at the beginning of Section 5, it would mean calling it around 8.10^6 times, which would take approximately 8 weeks. Instead, the genetic algorithm using this fitness function was used to further evolve a population of rule sets generated by the an initial genetic algorithm using the entropy based fitness function (see Figure 10). So, the process for identifying creatures is as follows:

Fig. 10. Generation of an interesting ruleset combining two different fitness measures

1. Initially create a new array the same size as the game board, called the creature search array, and initialise all cells to 'unchecked'.
2. Run through the game board sequentially checking each cell in the creature search array marked as 'unchecked'.
3. When a cell in the game board is discovered which contains life then check the surrounding unchecked cells to identify if any of those are live. As each cell is checked remember that, so that it is not looked at again.
4. Keep a count of each type of cell encountered in the creature stopping once no more live cells are found to be connected to the original live cell. Now check that the creature size is between the minimum and maximum size for an organism; if so, keep a record of it, in terms of the three different cell types.
5. Continue traversing the game board until each cell is recorded as 'checked'.
6. Now check to see if any of these creatures have been seen before since the start of this game: a creature with relative counts of each type of cell that fall within 5% of the counts of a previously seen creature, is seen as matching.

   Do this by dividing the number of cells containing each life type by the number of cells containing that type for the recorded creature. Then compare the three values produced which should also be within a set percentage (5% during testing) of each other.
7. If a creature has not been seen before then it must be added to the list of creatures.
8. Check the creature has moved from its previous position before incrementing the fitness by the number of live cells in that creature. If more than one copy of a single type of creature is seen in a turn then multiply the number of live cells in all organisms of that type by the number of the organism present. For instance, if there are three copies of an eight-celled creature then each creature has a fitness of 24 and so a total of 72 is added to the turn fitness for all three creatures.

Using this genetic algorithm to further evolve the rule sets from the final generation of the entropy based genetic algorithm several interesting creatures were discovered. One of the most interesting is a moving reproducing creature. The creature is resistant to damage and splits every 11 time steps. Another example of moving, reproducing creatures is shown in Figure 11.

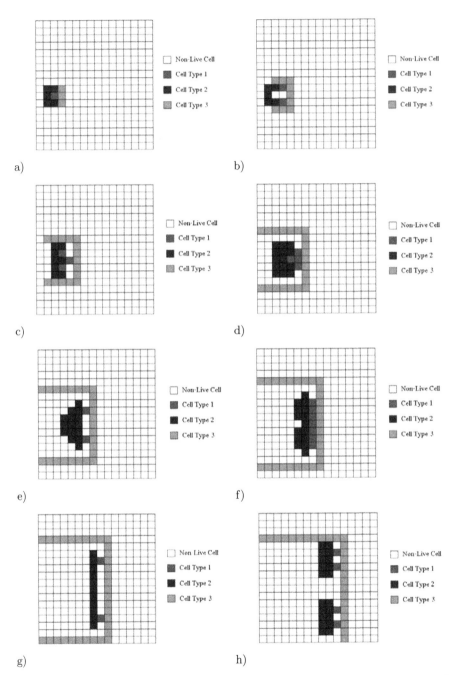

Fig. 11. A trace of a creature over 8 consecutive steps. The creature moves to the right, expanding, and eventually splitting into two. Two very similar copies of the initial structure reappear in frame (g). In frame (h) they separate and the protruding 'nucleus' of each splits into two

7   Discussion and Further Work

The experiments described above show that the fitness function based on entropy did, indeed, generate non-trivial cellular automata. The addition of another fitness function promoting moving and reproducing creatures has also achieved its goal. Future work should continue to concentrate on automatically isolating and following the development of life-forms in a given CA. The behaviour of these creatures should be compared with the CA rules they are based on, in an attempt to find analogies with the processes of autocatalysis, mutual catalysis and inhibition, characteristic of biological systems.

Another achievement of this work is that it demonstrates the substantial benefits of using extended fitness on a task with an apparently very complex fitness landscape.

For the chosen type of CA (two-dimensional, $k = 4$ and $r = 1$), there are hundreds of rules in each rule set. Such large number of rules means it is difficult to analyse all the pathways in which cells can interact. One way to deal with this issue is to use a machine learning technique to summarise all rules and represent them in a more expressive formalism, stating, for instance, "cell of type X will be created if 2 to 4 cells of type Y are present", rather than enumerating these cases separately. Inductive Logic Programming (ILP) is an excellent candidate for the task [15].

References

1. De Jong, K.: An Analysis of the Behaviour of a Class of Genetic Adaptive Systems. PhD thesis, University of Michigan (1975)
2. Mitchell, M., Hraber, P.T., Crutchfield, J.P.: Revisiting the edge of chaos: Evolving cellular automata to perform computations. Complex Systems **7** (1993) 89–130
3. Goldberg, D.: Genetic Algorithms in Search, Optimization and Machine Learning. Addison-Wesley (1989)
4. Holland, J.: Adaption in natural and artificial systems. University of Michigan Press (1975)
5. Hollstien, R.: Artificial Genetic Adaption in Computer Control Systems. PhD thesis, University of Michigan (1971)
6. Mahfoud, S.: Niching Methods for Genetic Algorithms. PhD thesis, University of Illinois, Urbana-Champaign (1995)
7. Dawkins, R.: The Extended Phenotype. Oxford University Press (1982)
8. Falconer, D.: Introduction to Quantitative Genetics. Second edn. Longman, London (1981)
9. Packard, N.H.: Adaptation towards the Edge of Chaos. In: Dynamic Patterns in Complex Systems. World Scientific (1988)
10. Sapin, E., Bailleux, O., Chabrier, J.: Research of complex forms in the cellular automata by evolutionary algorithms. In et al., P.L., ed.: Proc. of the 6th Intl. Conf. on Artificial Evolution, Marseille (2003)
11. Wolfram, S.: Statistical mechanics of cellular automata. Reviews of Modern Physics **55** (1983)
12. Wolfram, S.: Universality and complexity in cellular automata. Physica D **10** (1984) 1–35

13. Basanta, D.: Evolving automata to grow patterns. Symposium on Evolvability and Interaction (2003)
14. Wolfram, S., Packard, N.: Two-dimensional cellular automata. Statistical Physics **38** (1985) 901–946
15. Muggleton, S., Raedt, L.D.: Inductive logic programming: Theory and methods. Journal of Logic Programming **19,20** (1994) 629–679

The Strategic Control of an Ant-Based Routing System Using Neural Net Q-Learning Agents

David Legge

Centre for Telecommunication Networks,
School of Engineering,
University of Durham
d.n.legge@durham.ac.uk

Abstract. Agents have been employed to improve the performance of an Ant-Based Routing System on a communications network. The Agents use a Neural Net based Q-Learning approach to adapt their strategy according to conditions and learn autonomously. They are able to manipulate parameters that effect the behaviour of the Ant-System. The Ant-System is able to find the optimum routing configuration with static traffic conditions. However, under fast-changing dynamic conditions, such as congestion, the system is slow to react; due to the inertia built up by the best routes. The Agents reduce this inertia by changing the speed of response of the Ant-System. For an effective system, the Agents must cooperate - forming an implicit society across the network.

1 Introduction

Ant-Based Routing has some attractive properties for communication networks due to the distributed nature of the algorithm. Schoonderwoerd et al. [1996 & 1997] and Dorigo et al. [1997] described the first systems, which tackle slightly different problems (telephone networks and datagram networks). There have been numerous improvements described, but all have concentrated on the algorithms controlling the behaviour of the ants.

The drawback to Ant-Systems is that they are purely reactive in nature and the probabilistic advantage built up by the best route in good conditions becomes a disadvantage if that route becomes congested.

By using ideas from the area of Subsumption Architecture [Brooks 1986] – i.e. blending purely reactive agents with strategic proactive agents to create a more balanced society – this problem could be overcome.

The Ant-Colony on each node can be viewed as an agent - the ants being only messages, rather than each ant being viewed as an agent, which is an alternative model. It is then a logical step to place a second agent on a node to perform the more strategic role.

The Agent (as distinct from the Ant-Colony), can then monitor the operation of the Ant-Colony and adjust the parameters that effect the speed of response of the Ant-System. This should be done in a way that does not increase the level of Ant-traffic, since this will add to the congestion being tackled.

D. Kudenko et al. (Eds.): Adaptive Agents and MAS II, LNAI 3394, pp. 147 – 166, 2005.
© Springer-Verlag Berlin Heidelberg 2005

The Agents across the network must coordinate to some degree, since the effect of only one taking any action would be minimal. This would ideally be done without explicit coordination since the messages could also add to congestion; thus a parallel is drawn to independent game-playing agents studied in Reinforcement Learning, including [Kapetanakis et al. 2003].

2 Aim

The aim of this research is to show that an intelligent agent can be used to modify the parameters associated with the Ant-system to make both the convergence from start-up, and the response to changing conditions within the network, quicker, whilst retaining the stability in steady-state.

A society of Agents distributed across the network is required however, since the parameters are changed on a per-node basis for distributed control - an agent on each node is in control of the parameters used on that node. At this stage, the agents are acting independently from each other. Conversely, both the ant system and the agents use stigmergy – where the environment is the media for an implicit form of communication.

An agent could observe how other agents are acting by checking the parameters carried by ants originating from other nodes.

3 Current Work

A significant amount of research has investigated the self-organisational properties of Ant-Based systems within telecommunications – for both load-balancing and routing purposes.

Schoonderwoerd et al. [1996 & 1997] used ants to reinforce the return route so that the link just tested is rewarded, rather than rewarding a link that is *about* to be tested, this is termed *Backwards Reinforcement*.

Dorigo et al. [1997], and many others, use two types of ants, one to explore the network, and a second type to propagate the information back across the network.

Other techniques include [Vittori and Araújo 2001], in which the probabilities are interpreted as Q-values, and the Q-Learning reinforcement equation is used to update them.

However, both these papers use single-valued parameters, such as rate of production of ants, rate of deposition of pheromones etc., that are empirically obtained. These are not changed at runtime, or indeed off-line.

The Vittori paper utilises Q-learning to update the routing tables and found performance gains in doing so. In this paper, it is intended to use Q-learning to modify the parameters used by the ants.

[Kapetanakis et al 2002, 2004] discusses agents participating in games with other agents, where the reward gained at the end of the round is a function of the decisions made by all the agents. e.g. Agent 1 decides on action A, while Agent 2 opts for action B. The games are taken further by the addition of a probabilistic effect, so that the the reward is f (A, B, P).

Kapetanakis' agent's decisions are made without conferring with any other agent(s), indeed the agent is not aware of the presence of other agents. The agents use Q-learning, and are able to find successful joint strategies. This is analogous to the situation described in this paper.

Other research effort have concentrated on improving and fine-tuning the rules that govern the behaviour of the ants. This paper attempts to branch away from these efforts and strategically manipulate the Ant-System in a similar way to Subsumption Architecture.

4 Ant-System

This section describes the implementation of the Ant-System used. It is broadly based on the system discussed in Schoonderwoerd et al. [1996].

The basis for the ant system is many simple-acting entities displaying complex behaviour on the macro-scale. To this end the ants are small packets of data that are kept as simple as possible. Carried within the ant are: Source, Destination, Amount of Pheromone and Deposition rate. Rather than carrying code with every ant, the processing is performed by the node.

The Rate of Ant Production is a self explanatory parameter, and at generation the ant is given a uniformly-random destination, chosen from all the known nodes on the network. It is also branded with an *Initial Amount of Pheromone* (IPL) and a *Deposition Rate,* DR, (which describe its longevity and its potency). Once generated, and at each node along its journey it selects its next-hop by the generation of a uniformly random number and the consultation of the local probability table associated with the ants final destination.

On arrival at a node, and after ensuring the ant has not returned to its source, the ant deposits some pheromone. The amount of pheromone left by the ant is a simple percentage (defined by the Deposition Rate) of the current amount the ant has. If the ant has travelled in a loop, it is discarded.

Before this is added to the probability table (for pheromone table) it is multiplied by the (relative) available size of the traffic queue for the link just used by the ant.

The resultant amount of pheromone is added to the local table regarding the ant's source, i.e. The ant reinforces the return route, not the route it is currently taking. The tables are then normalised to sum to unity; this has the effect of rewarding the route just used, but also punishing all the routes not just used; a Minimum Probability is applied to ensure all routes are explored periodically. If the ant is at its destination it is then discarded.

The output of the ant-colony is the best next-hop for each known node. This is the highest probability link, except for when an extra threshold is applied – i.e. a link must exceed the probability of the current best route by some value for the recommendation to change.

The effect of the ant parameters on the probabilities have been investigated with and without traffic. It has been shown that it is possible to have a very quick response, but with a relatively noisy steady-state condition, or a smoother steady-state but a slower response. The Rate of Production also has an effect on the response.

An assumption is made that each and every link is bi-directional; a full discussion of the validity of this assumption is beyond the scope of this paper, but the current Internet routing protocol OSPF (Open Shortest Path First) makes the same assumption. In [Vittori 2001] routes are reinforced in both forward and backwards directions; although this may aid speed of convergence, the forward reinforcement has no logical basis, and so the feedback may be incorrect, leading to problems with incorrect routes.

The Ant-System is a separate entity, is reactive in nature and can operate with or without the Agent. The Agent provides a supervisory and proactive role and is described next.

5 The Agent

An agent sits on each node and monitors the ant colony on that node. The agent receives reports from the colony, both regular ones and ones triggered by any route changes that occur.

The Agent is informed of all the parameters associated with the ants (Rate of Production, and those carried by the ant), as well as the threshold value for route change.

The agent is also told the current probability of the preferred route, as well as its mean, standard deviation and gradient. Obviously, the windowing function for calculating the mean etc. is an important property, and this has been tuned to highlight important features - ignoring short-term *noise*, but highlighting long term trends.

The success or failure of the agent can be determined by a comparison between the performance of the Ant-system by itself, and the Ant-system when supervised by the agent.

The type of learning strategy employed by the agent is discussed in the next section.

6 Agent Learning Strategies

The agent is being asked to react to different states, and should be capable of learning the correct action from any state. The environment is also non-deterministic, so simple Temporal Difference Learning (TD-Learning) would not be suitable; therefore the preferred strategy would be Q-Learning - where an agent learns state-action values.

Although Q-Learning was originally based on tables of state-action pairs, this technique becomes unwieldy when there are more than a handful of states and/or actions. Other problems occur when the system is continuous and must be approximated to a specific state before an action is chosen.

This process of function approximation and the subsequent choice of action has been performed in a single step by Tesauro [1994, 1995, 1998, 2002] and applied to the game of Backgammon with remarkable success.

In the context of Backgammon, TD-Learning is sufficient, since the environment is predictable (the "after-position" of a move is deterministic). The extension of this approach to Q-Learning is a logical next step, and has been investigated by Tesauro [1999] himself.

Tesauro's approach uses an artificial Neural Network, NN, to approximate the Q-value for each action presented to the network for a particular state. Standard NNs are trained to perform known functions - e.g. the Exclusive-Or Function – where the correct inputs and outputs are defined. The error across the outputs can be calculated easily by taking the difference between the desired results and the actual results. The NN weights can then be adjusted accordingly.

Of course, with NN-based Q-Learning the correct outputs are the unknown; but if the Q-Learning update rule is applied instead of the simple error, then the effect is directly equivalent to incrementing table-entries.

The NN-Based Q-Learning system can therefore be trained in the same way as a table-based system. Results from [Tesauro 1999] show that although the Q-values are shown to be less accurate than the table-based equivalent, the actions selected tend to be sound.

7 Implementation

An NN-Based Q-Learning Agent which strategically adapts the performance of an Ant-Based Routing System has been built and tested.

In the current configuration the Agent is able to adjust the Initial Age of the ants. If the Rate of Production were to be adapted there is a danger that congestion would be caused by the control system attempting to reduce it.

The Agent therefore (usually) has three actions available to it – increase or decrease the Initial Age, or do nothing. The parameter is bounded as a precautionary "sanity-check", in which case an action that would break this constraint is not presented as an option.

The representation of the actions to the NN is of note. This can either be achieved by using a single input, and using arbitrary values to represent each value (e.g. -1 for decrease, 0 for stay the same, and +1 for increase) or, using three different inputs with a "1" input to show selection (0 otherwise).

The NN must have at least a single hidden layer to be able to approximate non-linear functions. Initially for speed of convergence and simplicity, only the single extra layer will be used. The output layer is a single node – the Q-value for the action considered – whilst the input layer is composed of the data inputs and the three action inputs. The hidden layer is composed of three nodes to match the action nodes of the input layer.

In order to achieve the objectives, the system must be allowed to train for a sufficiently long time; it is important to note that there is no distinction between training and runtime – the system will be constantly learning so that it is able to adapt to conditions. There could be a danger of "over-training"; however, given the noisy nature of the environment this is not anticipated to be a problem.

Different reward functions have been tested to find the most effective. Ideally, the reward function would be composed of a smooth function of one of the (non-action) inputs – this negates the requirement to introduce an arbitrary threshold that may be suitable for some situations but not for others. This will allow the agent to adapt to the maximum number of conditions; it must be noted however, the the cost of generalising solutions is often prohibitive – in this case in terms of research time.

The two main statistical descriptions of the system that could be used as the reward function are the *standard deviation of the highest ant-probability* and the *magnitude of the change in the maximum probability.* These will be maximal when the conditions on the network are changing, so can be used as the detection mechanism.

7.1 Reward Functions

As already discussed, a critical factor in the satisfactory operation of the system is the form of the function that decides the reward the agent receives for taking a particular action. In this case, a suitable reward function could be formed from the *standard deviation of the highest ant-probability.* With the correct manipulation this means that the network will be rewarded for the probability *not* changing, but punished when it does.

8 Experimentation

The aim of the experimentation is to show that there is an improvement in performance when the parameters governing the ants are changed dynamically at run-time - thus taking account of changing conditions on the network. The results presented here are a comparison of different solutions, although each based on the use of Ant-Based Routing.

The first solution uses the ordinary Ant-Based Routing Scheme, described in the previous Chapter. No adaptation of the parameters is involved. This is used as the control test, and it is expected that the other solutions will out-perform it.

In the second solution, the Ant-Based Routing Scheme is augmented by an *Ideal Agent.* This represents the bound on the best possible strategy that the proposed Agent would be able to achieve. Indeed, the Ideal Agent strategy is unrealisable, outside of these simulations, since the strategy is based on *a priori* knowledge of the traffic. This strategy should however provide evidence that it is desirable to be able to manipulate the parameters, in whatever method - it should show that improvements to the Ant Control are possible.

Thirdly, a *Simple Reactive* agent is implemented. This uses a simple thresholding mechanism that increases the IPL when the *Standard Deviation* exceeds a certain level, but decreases it when it is below the threshold.

This strategy should outperform the ordinary Ant-Based Routing System, but in a comparison with the proposed Q-Learning agent should not be as successful; the approach is included here to validate that the learning mechanism provides an advantage over such a simple threshold mechanism.

Finally the proposed Q-Learning agent is tested and is able to change the parameters as it sees fit at runtime, according to strategies it learns.

The results are presented in the form of graphs of the probabilities for each next-hop from the source node of user-traffic. Where applicable, they are presented in combination with graphs of the parameters being changed by the agent strategy.

Of interest in each test, is the reaction of the ant-system (both managed and unmanaged) to congestion; the speed of response is of importance, as is the amount of data-traffic lost (the ants, by their nature, are expendable as information is gained by them not arriving). A further concern is that the routing should not constantly change between two or more routes - *route-flapping*.

Because of the different complexity involved in testing a network, two relatively simple simulations are used. Firstly, a network where there is a number of equally long routes between the two nodes of interest and one of them becomes congested; while the second is where there is an obvious shortest route which then becomes congested (with at least one other alternative route).

For each scenario, the Managed Ants performance must be compared with that of the Unmanaged Ants. As an intermediate step, a predetermined strategy, with *a priori* knowledge of the traffic conditions, is implemented that will also improve the performance. This will give a further benchmark with which to contrast the performance of the full system.

8.1 The Simulator

The simulator being used is *ns* (Network Simulator). It is designed to model TCP/IP networks. These networks use a *connectionless* paradigm; that is to say packets of data are transmitted without setting up a definite route first. This means that at each hop, packets are routed according to the instantaneous best route. Packets from the same flow do not necessarily follow the same path. Consideration of Circuit-Switched and Connection-Oriented networks are left to later discussion.

8.2 The Traffic Scenario

Both network scenarios will be required to transmit some user-data, which we shall describe as real-time, loss-sensitive data. This shall be transported from Node 0 to Node 1, in all network topologies. The traffic shall be offered to the network intermittently over the whole simulation, causing congestion numerous times on an on-off basis for periods of 15s duration.

Problems would be caused by the network dropping the user-data, excessive delay or excessive jitter - variation in the inter-arrival time of packets, often caused by switching of routes.

The situation under which the network will be tested is as follows. The traffic causing congestion, shall represent other network load and will be set at a level that will not, by itself, cause packets to be dropped (other than ants).

The simulation will start with no data-traffic on the network. Two flows of traffic are involved. Firstly, a constant-bit-rate (CBR) flow, that uses the majority of the bandwidth available on the link between Node 0 and Node 2. Secondly, a smaller Variable-Bit-Rate (VBR) flow also uses the same link. Both flows stop after fifteen seconds.

This combination of traffic will result in intermittent congestion during the time when both flows are present on the network. Traffic will require storage in queues during congestion whilst it is waiting to be transmitted. Ant-packets will be dropped having been assigned a lower priority than traffic.

This pattern of traffic is repeated, at irregular intervals, to provide both the training and the testing of the Agent-Managed-Ant System.

8.3 Comparison Tests

The Agent-Managed Ants must be compared with the ordinary Ant-System to show that an improvement has been made. Therefore the basic Ant-System by itself is used a the control test.

Further comparisons could be made with both an *ideal* agent (that is not constrained by processing power/time) and a *simple reactive* agent (to confirm whether the overhead of the Learning mechanism is actually needed).

The simple reactive agent could just use a simple threshold mechanism, so when the standard deviation exceeds a level, the age is increased, and reduced when it falls below.

The expected shortcoming of this simple scheme is that it will undoubtedly cause excessive noise during steady state, and setting the threshold to the correct level is a non-trivial task, and it may not be the same for every network – for instance if there are numerous links from one particular node then the standard deviation will be higher on average than on a node with few links.

9 Initial Results

To aid the development of the system, two simple networks were used to test the system, and it is results of this investigation that are described in this section, before a more complex, but more realistic network is used to validate the system in the next section.

9.1 Test Networks

In the development of the system, two networks were used to test the Agent-Managed Ants. This ensures that the system can adapt to different scenarios, and does not merely provide a solution by chance. In each case the results concentrate on the routing decision between two (non-adjacent) nodes, labelled Node 0 and Node 1 in both cases. The first of these Network One, provides three different routes of equal length between the two nodes of interest. The second, Network Two, again provides three routes, but one is shorter than the other two routes.

Network One is shown in Fig. 1(a). It is a simple five node network. The important feature, as stated, is that there are three equally-long routes between Node 0 and Node 1, one of these routes will at times be congested. This Network has also been used in work on Braess' Paradox [Tumer et al. 1999].

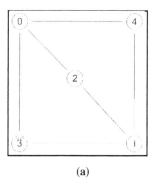
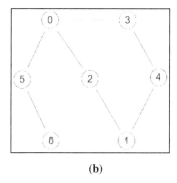

(a)   (b)

Fig. 1. Diagrams of Networks (a) One and (b) Two

Network Two is shown in Fig. 1(b). It is a seven node network with two equal-length routes and one shorter. It is the shorter route that will, at times, be congested.

When the shortest route becomes congested, the ants must react as quickly as possible to the congestion. They must overcome a large amount of inertia, represented by the high probability built-up by the shortest route - this inertia is greater than that of the previous scenario.

9.2 Ant-Based Routing

This set of results uses "standard" Ant-Based Routing and as such is the control test in these experiments. The details of the configuration is provided in the previous Chapter.

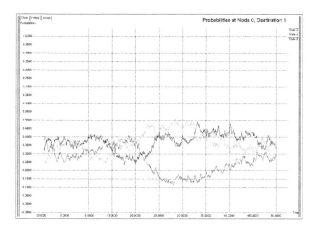

Fig. 2. Graph of probabilities for Ant-Based Routing on Network One

Figs 2 and 3 show the probability for each route from Node 1 to Node 0 for Network One and Network Two respectively. The vertical axis is probability, and ranges from zero to one, whilst the horizontal axis shows time from zero to 50s. The network stabilises almost immediately since there is nothing to choose between the three routes; in this scenario one route must be chosen, however arbitrarily, for the sake of network stability. When the traffic conditions change, at 20s, the ants take a little time to react but the control traffic is not using the congested route. However, it can be observed that the probability of the congested route falls sharply, from this time. After 35s, the route starts to recover, showing that the system implements constant exploration of the network, in search of the best route.

In the case of Network Two, Figure 3, there is a definite shortest route to begin with, and the probabilities reflect this from the start. The shortest route, via node 2, receives the majority of the reinforcements provided by the ant-packets moving around the network. This means that an advantage is built up by this "best" route, meaning that the user-traffic will be routed by this route, as it should be. However, after 20s when the congestion starts to occur on this shortest route, this "advantage" for the shortest route turns into a *dis*advantage in terms of the network and traffic as a whole. It can be seen that the other routes' probabilities take significant time or overcome this difference in probability. The route changeover occurs after 4.30s of congestion, during which time a significant amount of traffic is dropped.

Whilst the congestion occurs, the probability of the actual shortest route is suppressed as the link is overloaded. However, this does not prevent it being the selected route for a portion of this congestion – but this is during a period when the congestion has slightly abated.

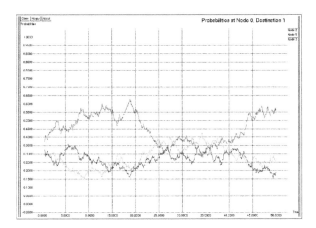

Fig. 3. Graph of probabilities for Ant-Based Routing on Network Two

At the end of the time of congestion, at 35s in Figure 3, it can be seen that the probability recovers to its previous level from before the time of congestion, but takes some time in doing so.

9.3 Ideal Agent Solution

This set of results utilises a pre-programmed attempt at the solution to the problem. It is a simple hypothesis of what a hypothetical *ideal agent* might do. However, through having knowledge of the traffic-levels beforehand, a certain advantage is evident. Although this strategy may be effective in this particular circumstance, it is likely to be a fragile solution, being unsuited to scenarios it was not specifically designed for – i.e. every other situation apart from than this one

In both scenarios, shown in Figures 4 (a) and (b), the to promote exploration of other routes, and to emphasise the congestion present on the network - since ants in excess of the capacity will be discarded.

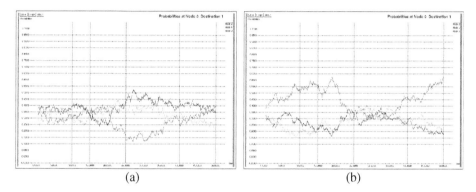

(a)   (b)

Fig. 4. Graph of probabilities for (a) Network One and (b) Network Two with Ideal Agent

Because the routes are equally-probable from the beginning, no settling time is required by the network, but the ants change the best route frequently to begin with.

Again on Network One, shown in Figure 4(a), the congested route is not being used by the user-traffic when the congestion starts, although it has only just fallen below another route. It can be seen however that the probability of the congested route drops off more sharply compared to the ordinary ant-based routing, and then recovers faster when the congestion is removed.

For Network Two, Figure 4(b), an improvement in the response is shown by the change of route occurring after only 3.60s. This is an improvement of more than a second to the ordinary ant system's response - almost a 20% reduction in time to decisively respond. When the congestion stops, the shortest route quickly recovers a large probability, and the system finds its equilibrium again.

In more detail, a dramatic drop in probabilities occurs after 20s. The route-change occurs and the probability is suppressed until the congestion finishes, at which point the probability recovers, but only slowly as the parameter has been reduced again.

9.4 Simple Reactive Agent Managed Ants

This solution uses an agent that simply changes the ant's parameters (the *Deposition Rate* in this case) when the *Standard Deviation*, *SD*, exceeds a threshold.

In manually setting a threshold on the SD a number of issues become apparent. The level of the threshold must be thoroughly researched, otherwise the level could be inappropriate. This level could also be overly sensitive to the topology; since a node with only two links is likely to have a lower SD than a node with four links, since fewer ants are likely to arrive (on a very generalised level). Therefore this solution is likely to be a little fragile, although not as fragile as the previous hard-coded solution.

The solution is considered in this paper to provide proof that an active learning mechanism is required, and actually provides an advantage over solutions such as this.

The results from the two networks are shown in Figure 5(a) and (b). These figures are made up with two graphs firstly the normal probability graph, but these overlaid on a graph that shows when the reactive agent reacts. The spikes on the lower portion of graph show that the parameters have been adapted.

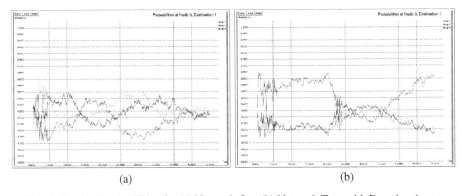

(a)   (b)

Fig. 5. Graph of probabilities for (a) Network One (b) Network Two with Reactive Agent

An obvious feature of both graphs is the noisy section at the beginning. This is due to a large SD caused by the initialisation of the system. This triggers the threshold mechanism, which increases the effect each ant has on the probabilities, making the probabilities more noisy.

Considering Network One, Figure 5(a), after the initial noisy period, the probabilities settle down until the congestion starts at 20s. Although there is a significant route change at approximately 14s, this is not unreasonable as the routes are of equal lengths. The probability then drops off sharply after 20s, and quickly changes the route – after 1.2s. After the congestion the system is sluggish to recover; however, the recovered route is only as good as the other two routes so no harm is done.

The result from Network Two, Figure 5(b), anomalously gives a time of 4.3s, compared with the 4.2s of the ordinary Ant-System. However it can be seen that the agent has an effect, increasing the speed of response when congestion is present on the system. For the duration of the congestion the probability of the shortest route is suppressed, but it quickly recovers without the need of the agents manipulation.

9.5   Q-Learning Agent Managed Ant Solution

The final solution presented here, the Agent-Managed Ant System should provide a realisable solution which responds in a time comparable to the solutions described so far. The ordinary Ant-System should be outperformed by the Agent, but the hard-coded solution is the ideal - which the Agents should not actually be able to achieve. The Simple Reactive agent may well in some circumstances be comparable to the more sophisticated Q-Learning Agent, but as it does not adapt its strategy (it has a set threshold) it will not perform as well over varying scenarios.

Figures 6 and 7 show the graphs for the Q-Learning Agent on Network One. Figure 6 is of a larger scale than those previously, hence it looks larger and more noisy; however this is necessary as the detail would be obscured if seen in the same scale. It can be seen that the agent reacts to congestion, and takes the appropriate action which is shown in the lower portion of graph, with the rising line showing the agent manipulating the IPL. It can also be seen by the increase in noise, and steeper gradient of the probability of the congested route.

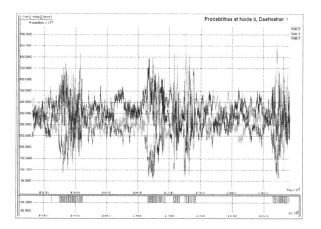

Fig. 6. Graphs to show the Agent reacting to congestion on Network One

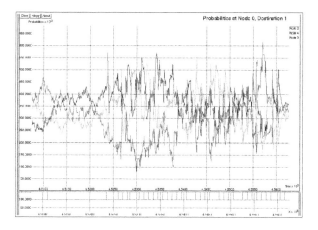

Fig. 7. Graphs to show the Agent on Network One in Detail

Figure 7 shows the agents action on Network One in more detail and it can be seen that the agent reacts to the fall in the probability of the congested route in reasonable time.

Figure 8 shows the response to congestion in the Ant-Managed system on Network Two. The route change occurs at 3.89s. This is an improvement over the 4.3s of the Ant-System, but does not improve on the hard-coded solution of 3.60s as was expected. It is noticeably more *noisy* than other graphs, not only because of the increased effect each ant has, but also because of the closeness of the probabilities and the fact that they are always similar.

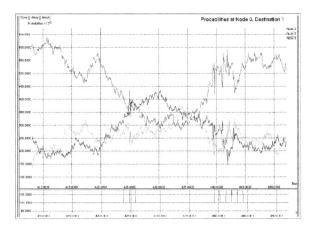

Fig. 8. Graphs to show the Agent reacting to congestion on Network Two

9.6 Summary of Results

This section has described the initial testing of the Agent-Managed Ant system. The next section goes on to test the system on a larger, more complex network, which is more realistic in its topology, it is a sparsely-connected network, which is more able to be generalised.

To summarise the results so far it has been shown that the four different solutions perform as expected over the two networks. Each is based on the use of the Ant-Based Routing System, as described in the previous chapter, and this basic system is used as the control test for comparison with the others. Whilst a simple threshold mechanism was found to produce satisfactory results it is also a fragile solution, needing to be tuned to its environment manually (by changing the threshold). The *Ideal* agent performs the best, but is unrealisable, since it requires prior knowledge of the traffic conditions. Finally, the learning agent performs satisfactorily, and demonstrates the potential for AI techniques to be applied to real-world, complex problem domains.

The next section takes the solutions described here and applies them to a larger network, to demonstrate that Q-Learning solution is not restricted to simple networks.

10 System Performance

Having performed initial tests on the Agent system that were used in the development of the techniques, it is now required to test the system on a more complex network. Rather than apply the techniques to a simulations of the topology of a national telephone network, which is the approach taken by [Schoonderwoerd et al. 1996, 1997] [Vittori 2001], the approach taken here is to apply them to a generalised network – i.e. a sparsely connected network.

10.1 Network Three

The network to be investigated is a configuration where every node is connected to at least two others, but the network is not fully connected (the number of links is less than n-factorial $(n!)$, where n is the number of nodes). This network is shown in Figure 9.

   The third network under test, Figure 9, is a more complex one – and is more realistic. It is a sparsely connected network, with a number of cross-links. The route between Nodes 0 and 1 still has a number of alternatives.

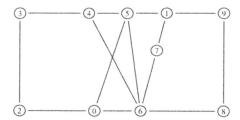

Fig. 9. Diagram of Sparsely Connected Network

10.2 Traffic Scenario

The traffic scenario used here will be based upon the scenario described in the previous section. The main feature is again congestion on the network, specifically between Nodes 1 and 0. This congestion is split into specific time periods of about 15s, but is still intermittent within those periods.

10.3 Ant-Based Routing System

The ordinary Ant Based Routing System does react to the congestion, but only changes the route after 9.1s, as can be seen in Figure 10. This is a significantly longer time in comparison to Networks One and Two, primarily due to the size of the network, but also due to the large difference in the probabilities when in the uncongested steady state. The probability starts to drop off at 20s, when the congestion starts, but due to the lack of adaptation of the ant parameters, the system must respond at a fixed rate which is unsuited to this situation.

10.4 Ideal Agent Solution

The Ant-System managed by the Ideal Agent shows significant improvement over the ordinary Ant-Routing. Figure 11. shows the Ideal Agent operating on Network Three.

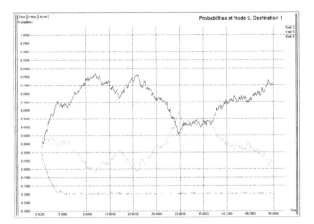

Fig. 10. Graph of Probabilities for Ant-Based Routing on Network Three

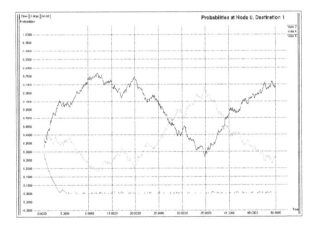

Fig. 11. Probabilities for Ideal-Agent Scheme on Network Three

The route change occurs after 7.1s, and in this time the probabilities have had to change by a large amount, but have been assisted by the ant parameters being manipulated to increase the speed of response.

10.5 Simple Reactive Agent

The Simple Reactive Agent takes some time before switching routes, only improving on the performance of the ordinary Ant-System by 0.1s, taking 9.0s to do so. It can be seen from the lower graph in Figure 12 that the manipulation of ant-parameters is triggered frequently and not just when it should be. This shows the fragility of the system which was designed for the characteristics of Network One and Two. Due to the size of the network, the SD tends to be larger, so the simple threshold is set too low in this instance.

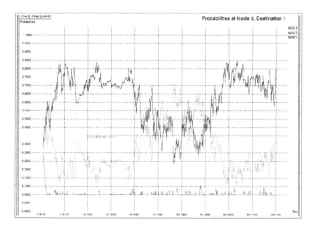

Fig. 12. Probabilities for Reactive Agent on Network Three

10.6   Agent-Managed Ant System

Figure 13 shows the response of the Q-Learning Agent to the problem described. It can be seen that the Agent responds to the large changes on the network caused by congestion by increasing the response speed of the network. It does this consistently, and then returns the Pheromone levels to their lower values, once the congestion has gone.

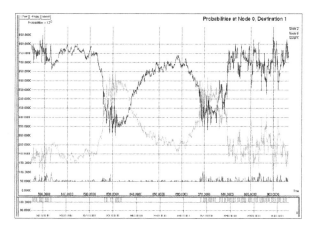

Fig. 13. Diagram to show Agent reacting to congestion on Network Three

It can be seen from Figure 13 that the parameter is manipulated (shown in the bottom graph) when a drop in the highest probability is encountered. This manipulation means that the route change will proceed faster than if unaided. This graph also shows that the system works consistently across time. There are two periods of congestion covered in this graphic, with the probabilities recovering in between time.

Although the the parameter is not returned immediately after the second period of congestion, it does at the end of the graphic.

Figure 14 shows a period of congestion in more detail, and from this it can be seen that the route change takes only 6.5s from the beginning of the period of congestion. This compares very favourably with the other schemes described – 7.1s and 9s. The difference in level of noise between when the parameter is increased and when it is not is obvious. In this instance the parameter is returned to its original level promptly which will help in terms of system stability.

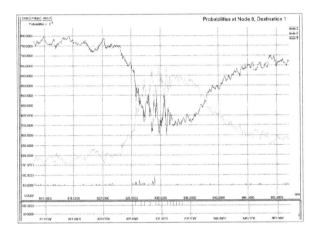

Fig. 14. Diagram to show Agent reacting to congestion on Network Three in more detail

11 Discussion of Results

The results presented in this paper have attempted to set out the case for the use of AI techniques, or more specifically Reinforcement Learning (and then Q-Learning), to improve the performance of telecommunications networks, and prove the concept that they are able to.

By the use of some simple networks, and then a more complex one that represents the generic, sparsely connected network, this has been proven. The first experiments were designed to be concerned with a single decision point, and so the networks represented different generic types of decision – i.e. many routes of equal lengths, and a number of routes with a *definite* shortest one. The system has then been run on the generic network and has been shown to improve the performance.

A comprehensive set of strategies were presented, the ordinary Ant-System, the ideal strategy, a simple threshold mechanism, and the proposed Q-Learning agent. These were used to show firstly that the adaptation of parameters by any sensible mechanism can improve the performance of the Ant-System, and secondly to show that the Q-Learning Agent outperforms that of a simple reactive mechanism – so justifying the use of the overhead and complexity of the learning system. Thirdly, an "ideal" strategy is presented to show the bound on the improvement in performance.

It is important to note that the Agent controls the Ant-System in a strategic manner, it does not interfere with the minutia of the ants, and the actions of individual ants, but monitors the performance of the system as a whole, and acts accordingly. This architecture is similar to that of Subsumption Architecture used by Brooks [1986] who used it to control robots in a robust and progressive manner.

The phenomena of noise in the context of the probabilities is the effect of individual ants arriving and the probabilities being updated. If each ant has a large effect on the probabilities, then they will be more "spiky" – or *noisy* in our terms. If each ant has only a small effect on the probabilities, then they will be updated in a much smoother matter. It is not however, merely a question of aesthetics in terms of wanting a nice smooth graph. The effect of the noise in certain circumstances would be to move the probability of one route above the probability of another. This may or may not be a desirable thing to occur. If this occurs *only* because of the presence of the noise, and not due to a longer term trend (i.e. because congestion means that a different route is now better) then this is undesirable. It is also likely to be reversed when an ant arrives on the other route and so that probability becomes larger again. The results of a constant change of best-route would mean that, potentially, packets from the same flow are spread over many routes and the reassembly at their destination becomes non-trivial.

The performance of the ordinary Ant-System provides the benchmark for this set of experiments. Since it is the parameters controlling the Ant-System that are being manipulated, this set of results describe what would happen to the system if no manipulation took place.

At the opposite end of the scale from the ordinary Ant-System is the use of an ideal strategy defined to be the perfect solution to the problem scenario. This strategy, although unrealisable, defines the bound of the improvement the agent would theoretically be able to make.

Thirdly, a simple reactive agent was devised that merely adapted the parameters effecting the Ant-System when a threshold on the SD was exceeded. The SD should increase when there is congestion as the probabilities will change. However it was shown that this was a fragile solution, only ideally suited to the conditions under which the threshold level was set. From this it can be concluded that the level of intelligence provided by the Q-Learning system is required if adaptation of the parameters is to be undertaken – and that the simple reactive agent was not sufficient.

The techniques described in this paper are used on a particular routing method (Ant-Based) and a particular implementation of that method. It is intended however that the conclusions of the paper have a broader scope than the specific application; it is intended that by using the principle of the subsumption style architecture within an agent society context, that the techniques could be applied to other problems of lesser, equal, and eventually greater complexity. This is especially true as the reinforcement learning techniques themselves become more comprehensive and mature. There are a number of learning techniques that could be applicable to the domain of telecommunicat ions, but also in developing these techniques, new methodologies are developed.

12   Further Work

The Agent is currently able to manipulate a single parameter strategically; this was for the sake of simplicity, but it could easily be envisaged that more parameters could also be adapted; such as the rate at which pheromone is dropped, and ultimately the rate at which ants are produced. This, as already noted is a double-edged sword, as the ants may start to contribute to the congestion itself.

Secondly, there is potential for a further agent to operate on the actual routing decision – note that the purpose of an Ant-System is to measure the performance of different routes, while the Agent described here changes it speed of response. The Ant-System in effect *recommends* a route and this further agent could apply reasoning to the process – to stop the route flapping and to provide coordination which would prevent routing-loops; this level of coopcration would represent a *"massive coordination step"* [Kapetanakis 2004].

13   Conclusions

The Ant-Based System has been shown to find optimal routing solutions to static conditions, but has been found to show undesirable characteristics when put under the strain of dynamic loading.

A solution has been sought that utilises software agents to adapt to these changing conditions by manipulating a parameter that controls the speed of response of the Ant-System.

The solution has been implemented, and utilises a Neural Network to perform Q-Learning and choose the optimum action for the state of the network.

References

Brooks R.A., "A Robust Layered Control System for a Mobile Agent", IEEE Journal of Robotics and Automation, 2(1), pp:14-21, March 1986

DorigoM. & Di Caro G., "AntNet: A Mobile Agents Approach to Adaptive Routing", Technical Report IRIDIA 97-12, 1997.

Kapetanakis S., Kudenko D., "Improving on the Reinforcement Learning of Coordination in Cooperative Multi-Agent Systems", Proc. AAMAS-II, AISB'02, pp 89-94, Imperial College, London, April 2002.

Kapetanakis S., Kudenko D., Strens M., "Learning to Coordinate using Commitment Sequences in Cooperative Multi-Agent Systems", "Adaptive Agents and Multi-Agent Systems II", Eds. D. Kudenko, D. Kazakov, E. Alonso, Springer-Verlag, 2004.

Schoonderwoerd, R., Holland, O., Bruten, J., "Ant-Like Agents for Load Balancing in Telecommunications Networks" Proc. 1st Int. Conf. on Autonomous Agents, Marina del Rey, pp 209-216, ACM Press, 1997.

Schoonderwoerd R., Holland O., Bruten J., Rothkrantz , "Ant-Based Load Balancing in Telecommunications Networks", Hewlett-Packard Laboratories Bristol, 1996.

Tesauro G., "Programming backgammon using self-teaching neural nets", Artificial Intelligence, 134 (1-2): 181-199 January 2002.

Tesauro, G., "Pricing in Agent Economies using Neural Networks and Multi-Agent Q-Lear ning", Proc. Workshop ABS-3 "Learning About, From and With other Agents", August 1999.

Tumer, K., Wolpert, D.H., "Avoiding Braess' Paradox through Collective Intelligence", AAAI/ IAAI, 2000.

Vittori K. & Araújo F.R., "Agent-Oriented Routing in Telecommunications Networks", IEICE Transactions on Communications, E84-B(11):3006-3013, November 2001.

Dynamic and Distributed Interaction Protocols

Jarred McGinnis and David Robertson

Centre for Intelligent Systems and their Applications,
University of Edinburgh,
Appleton Tower, Room 4.15,
Edinburgh EH8 9LE
j.p.mcginnis@sms.ed.ac.uk

Abstract. This paper describes a protocol language which can provide
agents with a flexible mechanism for coherent dialogues. The protocol
language does not rely on centralised control or bias toward a particular model of agent communication. Agents can adapt the protocol and
distribute it to dialogical partners during interactions.

1 Introduction

As the programming paradigm of agency evolves, more robust, diverse, and
complex agents are developed. The growing heterogeneity of agent societies will
increase even further as the research and development of deliberative and communicative models produce new and interesting approaches [18]. The need for an
equally adaptive means of communication between this heterogeneous multitude
also grows.

Electronic Institutions [4] and other state-based approaches are not feasible
for use in open multi-agent systems with dynamic or large conversation spaces.
The term conversation space is used to express every possible sequence and
combination of messages that can be passed between two or more agents participating in a given agent system. Protocols provide a useful framework for agent
conversations and the concern that they sacrifice agent autonomy is exaggerated.
In social interactions, humans and agents must willingly sacrifice autonomy to
gain utility. If I want my train tickets or cup of coffee, I must follow the implicit
protocol and join the queue. It is the same for software agents. If the agent
must gain a resource only available by participating in an English auction, it
behoves the agent to adopt the protocol necessary for participation in the auction. Whether this is done by an explicitly defined protocol or the agent learning
the protocol implicitly makes no difference to the agent's behaviour within the
system.

Electronic Institutions take a societal approach to agent communication. Control is top-down. Administrative agents perch above the system and keep an eye
on the agents as they interact inside the system. Agent-centric approaches build
systems bottom-up. These approaches attempt to pack individual agents with a
model of communication which can react to a multi-agent system. They have a

D. Kudenko et al. (Eds.): Adaptive Agents and MAS II, LNAI 3394, pp. 167–184, 2005.

communicative model that sits besides or is intertwined with its rational model. This is done in a number of ways. The most common is a BDI-model of communication as typified by the standardisation organisation, FIPA. There is a lot of dissatisfaction with FIPA ACL, and a variety of alternative models for agent communication have been proposed. All trying to address faults perceived with the FIPA approach.

The protocol language described in this paper seeks a balanced approach. It utilises the useful aspects of Electronic Institutions without relying on administrative agents or statically defined protocol specifications. Agents communicate not only individual messages but the protocol and dialogue state as well. The use of protocols provides structure and reliability to agent dialogues. Yet, by describing protocols as a process rather than a fixed state-based model, the conversation space can be defined as the agent interaction progresses rather than being statically defined during the engineering process. Distributing the protocol along with the message also allows agents to communicate the social conventions of the dialogue as well as coordinate it.

Section 2 will discuss some of the dominant agent communication paradigms. Section 3 describes the syntax and features of the protocol language. A discussion of adaptable protocols in section 4 is followed by an example illustrating an adaptable protocol using dialogue games in section 5. Section 6 concludes the paper enumerating the accomplishments and potential issues associated with the approach.

2   Approaches to Agent Communication

2.1   Electronic Institutions

Electronic Institutions(EI) provide structure to large and open multi-agent systems(MAS). By emulating human organizations, Electronic Institutions provide a framework which can increase interoperability. The EI framework formally defines several aspects of an agent society. The core of an EI is the formal definition of roles for agents, a shared dialogical framework, the division of the Institution into a number of scenes and a performative structure which dictates, via a set of normative rules, the relationships between the scenes. Agents interact with an Institution through the exchange of illocutions, i.e. messages with intentional force.

Participating agents are required to adopt a role within the Institution. This is similar to our entering a shop and assuming the role of a customer, and the employee adopting the role of salesperson. A role is defined as a finite set of dialogical actions. By the adoption of a role within an Institution, an agent's activities within the Institution can be anticipated. This abstraction of agents as a role allows the Institution to regulate and identify agent activities without analysing individual agents. Relationships between agents can be dealt with as generalizations. A role can be defined as subsuming or being mutually exclusive to another role.

The dialogical framework provides a standard for communication. Agents are guaranteed to have a shared vocabulary for communication as well as a common world-view with which to represent the world they are discussing. The dialogical framework is defined as a tuple consisting of an ontology, a representation language, a set of illocutions, and a communication language. The representation is an encoding of the knowledge represented by the ontology and makes up the inner language. This is contained with an individual illocution that is passed between agents. The illocution, as part of the outer language or communication language, expresses the intention of the agent by its communicating the message of the inner language. The dialogical framework, which contains the ontological elements, is necessary for the specification of scenes.

All interactions between agents occur within the context of scenes. Scenes are interaction protocols between agent roles. They are expressed as a well-defined protocol which maps out the conversation space between two agent roles. These scenes are represented as graphs. The nodes are conversation states and arcs representing the utterances of illocutions between the participants. Each scene will have a set of entrance and exit states with conditions that must be satisfied before the agent can begin or exit a scene. A set of roles and scene states are formally defined. An element of the set of states will be the initial state and a non-empty subset will be final states. Between the states there is a set of directed and labeled edges.

Scenes are individual agent conversations. In order for agents to participate in more interesting activities, it is necessary to formalize relationships between these individual conversations. The performative structure formalizes this network of scenes and their association with each other. The roles an agent adopts and the actions of the agents create obligations and restrictions upon the agent. These obligations restrict the further movement of agents. The performative structure is made of a finite non-empty set of scenes. There is a finite and non-empty set of transitions between these scenes. There is a root scene and an output scene. Arcs connect the scenes of the Institution. These arcs have different constraints placed upon them. For example, the constraints can synchronize the participating agents before the arc can be fully traversed, or there are constraints that provide an agent a choice point upon which scene to enter.

Within the scenes of an Electronic Institution, the actions an agent performs affect the future actions available to the agent. These consequences can extend beyond the current scene. These consequences could be the requirement for a agent to perform an action in some future scene or even which scenes or sequence of scenes an agent is now required to be a participant. These normative rules are categorized between two types. *Intra-scene* dictate actions for each agent role within a scene, and *inter-scene* are concerned with the commitments which extend beyond a particular scene and into the performative structure [5].

Tools [7] exist to aid in the creation of the various components and development of Electronic Institutions. This includes a tool to verify any specifications developed as well as tools to aid the synthesis of agents that can participate in the Electronic Institution [25].

2.2   Agent-Centric Design

FIPA ACL for better or for worse has made a large impact of agent communication research. A victim of its own success, most new approaches to agent communication are attempts to redress FIPA's ACL deficiencies. Conversation Policies [10] were an attempt to produce a more 'fine-grained' means of generating dialogues. More recently, researchers have developed communicative models to address the semantic verification problem of FIPA ACL [26]. There are other approaches which see the importance of separating the agent's internal states from the conversational model [12]. Two approaches of interest are theories based on social commitment or obligation and formal definitions of agent systems based on dialogue theory.

FIPA ACL. The Foundation for Intelligent Physical Agents develops software standards for agent communication. This is expressed in their official mission statement: *The promotion of technologies and interoperability specifications that facilitate the end-to-end interworking of intelligent agent systems in modern commercial and industrial settings.* In practice, this includes the publishing of standards concerning speech acts, predicate logic, and public ontologies. The individual communicative acts of FIPA's Agent Communication Language (ACL) is based on the speech act theory of [20]. The semantics of FIPA ACL are based on the Belief-Desire-Intention (BDI) model of agency and is formalised in a language SL[8].

Each communicative action by a FIPA compliant agent implies that agent is following the requirements specified for that action. This includes general properties for all communicative acts, the interaction protocol of which the act is a part, and the feasible preconditions and rational effects for that particular act [9]. For example, an agent i must believe a proposition p and believe that an agent j neither has any amount of belief about p or not p before it can send an **inform** FIPA ACL communicative act to agent j. Afterwards, agent i is entitled to believe that agent j believes p.

Social Commitment. Researchers have adopted the idea of social commitments to redress the semantic difficulties that arise when agents rely on mentalistic (e.g BDI) Agent Communication Languages (ACL). Social-based semantics consider the agent's relationship to its communicative partners. It is a recognition that an agent's communicative acts do not exist in a vacuum. It is the use of the intuitive idea that an agent's communication is an event which necessarily involves other agents.

In [21], the authors identify several criteria for the semantics of an Agent Communication Language. According to Singh, an ACL should be formal, declarative, verifiable, and meaningful. To this end, he has developed a *social semantics*. He defines three facets to every communicative act. The *objective claim* which commits an agent to another that some proposition p holds. The *subjective claim* is that an agent believes p, and the *practical claim* that the agent has some justification or reason for believing p. This is a novel approach, because most reactions to the semantic verification problem of the mentalistic approach is to completely throw it away. Singh has, instead, embraced the mentalistic approach but coupled it with the idea of social commitment. The purely mentalistic approach rests on the assumption that the agent is sincere about p, but Singh has added that the agent is also socially committed to being sincere about p. It is recognized that the use of social semantics does not replace the need for protocols, but the combination of social semantics and protocols would create a much more flexible ACL [12].

The approach described in [6] uses the commitment themselves to develop the conversation between two agents. Flores argues that our verbal utterances carry with them obligations dependent on the role of the agent within a society. The question 'What time is it?' carries with it the obligation (in polite society) to not only reply but make an attempt to actually find out the time. The use of social commitments in multi-agent communication is to provide a number of rules that dictate appropriate illocutions and actions performed based on the agent voluntarily obligating itself to commitments with other agents and eventually discharging those commitments. A protocol is defined for the negotiation of the adoption of social commitments. Agents propose to add and remove commitments for action from personal commitment stores. An agent will propose to add a commitment to perform some actions. Once this is accepted and the commitment is satisfied the protocol includes steps to propose the release of any further commitment to that action. It is through this simple protocol and the social commitment-based conversation policies an agent conversation can be developed.

Dialogue Theory and Games. The philosophers Doug Walton and Erik Krabbe have developed a typology of dialogues to detect fallacious reasoning [24]. This typology was adopted by Chris Reed [19] in a formalism for multi-agent systems and inter-agent communication. Of the six kinds of dialogue identified, five of these dialogue types are applicable to the domain of agent communication. The sixth, eristic, is a dialogue where reasoning has ceased and the participants use the dialogue for the airing of grievances and one-upmanship. This dialogue type is important for the study of human conversations, but it is ignored by the agent research community. Dialogues are classified into the different types by three criteria. The first criterion considers the initial situation. What information does each of the participants have? Are the agents cooperative or competitive with each other? The second criterion concerns the individual goals an agent has for the interaction, and the third criterion are the goals shared by the participating agents. In *Information-Seeking* dialogues, one agent seeks the answer to a question which it believes the other agent possesses. *Inquiry* dialogues occur when two agents work together to find the answer to a question whose solution eludes both agents. A *Persuasion* dialogue has one agent attempting to convince another to adopt some proposition which it currently does not believe.

Negotiation dialogues occur when the participants haggle over the division of a scarce resource. In *Deliberation* dialogues, the agents attempt to agree on a course of action for a particular situation. It is rare that any actual dialogue will be purely of one instance of one kind of dialogue. It is more likely that a dialogue will consist of an amalgamation of the different types. For example, during a negotiation, propositions may need clarification and an information-seeking dialogue would occur. This dialogue typology is fundamental to recent agent communicative models using dialogue games.

Dialogue games have existed for thousands of years, since Aristotle, as a tool for philosophers to formalise argumentation. It is an attempt to identify when an argument or its justification is weakened or undercut by an argument or refutation made be the other participant. By each player making 'moves' and following a set of rules, it was hoped that properties of good and bad arguments could be identified. This formalism for argumentation has been employed to increase the complexity and robustness of software agents conversations. The objective is to produce a meaningful interaction between dialogical partners by following the rules of an individual dialogue game.

There are several components to a dialogue game. Firstly, the participants must share a set of locutions. This is a common requirement for models of agent communication. The commencement and termination rules specify the conditions under which a dialogue can start or end. This is a set of performatives from an agent communication language that is shared between the agents. This language must include the ability to utter assertions as well as justifications and challenges to those assertions. Another component is the combination rules. These rules define when particular illocutions are permitted, required, or illegal. The last part necessary for a dialogue game is the rules for commitment. These rules create obligations on the agent with respect to the dialogical moves of the agent. These commitments can be divided into dialogical and semantic. Dialogical commitments are the obligation of an agent to make a particular move within the context of the dialogue game. Semantic commitments indenture the agent to an action beyond the dialogue game itself. A record of these commitments is publicly stored. For example, if you say you are willing to pay the highest price in an auction, it will be known that you are committed to actually pay that price.

Dialogue game frameworks [14, 13] attempt to construct more complex and robust agent conversations. This is achieved by combining different atomic dialogue types which have been identified by philosophers analysing human dialogues [24]. This approach avoids the semantic ambiguities inherent in mentalistic models and the rigidity of static protocol-based approaches [9]. The dialogue game approach depends on several assumptions about participating agents. Agents participating in the dialogue game framework must agree on all the rules of the framework. The number of requirements made on individual agents in order for them to play dialogue games makes the approach unsuited for open multi-agent systems.

3   The Protocol Language

The development of the protocol language is a reaction to Electronic Institutions [1]. Although the EI framework provides structure and stability to an agent system, it comes at a cost. Integral to EI is the notion of the administrative agents. Their task is to enforce the conventions of the Institution and shepherd the participating agents. Messages sent by agents are sent through the EI. This synchronises the conversation between the conversing agents, and keeps the administrative agent informed of the state of the interaction.

An unreliable keystone makes the whole of the arch defective, just as the system is now dependent on the reliability and robustness of its administrative agent. Also, this centralisation of control runs counter to the agent paradigm of distributed processing. Within the scenes of Electronic Institutions, interaction protocols are defined to guarantee that agents utter the proper illocutions and utter them at the appropriate time. This is defined formally by the specifications of the EI and left to the designers of individual agents to implement. It assumes that the agent's interaction protocol covers the entire conversation space before the conversation occurs. If the interaction needs of the institution change, this would require redefinition of the Institution and re-synthesis of the individual agents. Agents are also expected to know the global state of the system and their exact position within it. In EIs this is handled by an administrative agent whose job it is to synchronise the multitude of agents involved.

The protocol language addresses some of these shortcomings of EIs but retains the benefits of implementing the EI framework. Its goal is to lessen the reliance on centralised agents for synchronisation of individual participants in the system, provide a means for dissemination of the interaction protocol and the separate the interaction protocol from the agent's rationalisations to allow the dynamic construction of protocols during the interaction. By defining interaction protocols during run-time, agents are able to interact in systems where it is impossible or impractical to define the protocol beforehand. The protocol language defined in Figure 1 is similar to the protocol language described in [22] for which the formal semantics have been defined.

Figure 1 defines the syntax of the protocol language. An agent clause is composed of an agent definition and an operation. The agent definition individuates the agents participating in the conversation (id), and the role the agent is playing (r). Operations can be classified in three ways: actions, control flow, and conditionals. Actions are the sending or receiving of messages, a no op, or the adoption of a role. Control Flow operations temporally order the individual actions. Actions can be put in sequence (one action must occur before the other), in parallel (both action must occur before any further action), or given a choice point (one and only one action should occur before any further action). Conditionals are the preconditions and postconditions for operations. The message passed between two agents using the protocol consists of three parts. The first is the actual illocution (m) the agent is wishing to express. The second is the full protocol ($\mathcal{P}$) itself. This is the protocol for all agents and roles involved in the conversation. This will be necessary for the dissemination of the protocol as

$$
\begin{array}{lll}
\mathcal{P} & \in \text{Protocol} & :: \langle C, A^{\{n\}}, K \rangle \\
A & \in \text{Agent Clause} & :: \theta :: op. \\
\theta & \in \text{Agent Definition} & :: \mathbf{agent}(r, id) \\
op & \in \text{Operation} & :: \text{null} \\
& & \mid \theta
\end{array}
$$

	(Precedence)	$\mid (op)$
	(Send)	$\mid M \Rightarrow \theta$
	(Receive)	$\mid M \Leftarrow \theta$
	(Sequence)	$\mid op1 \textbf{ then } op2$
	(Choice)	$\mid op1 \textbf{ or } op2$
	(Parallelism)	$\mid op1 \textbf{ par } op2$
	(Consequence)	$\mid \psi \leftarrow M \Leftarrow \theta$
	(Prerequisite)	$\mid M \Rightarrow \theta \leftarrow \psi$

$$
\begin{array}{lll}
M & \in \text{message} & :: \langle m, \mathcal{P} \rangle \\
\psi & \in \text{state} & :: \text{a predicate}
\end{array}
$$

Fig. 1. The abstract syntax of the protocol

new agents enter the system. Other aspects of the protocol are the inclusion of constraints on the dialogue and the use of roles. An agent's activities within a multi-agent system are not determined solely by the agent, rather it is the relationship to other agents and the system itself that helps determine what message an agent will send. These can be codified as roles. This helps govern the activity of groups of agents rather than each agent individually. Constraints are marked by a '←'. These are requirements or consequences for an agent on the occurrence of messages or the adoption of roles. The constraints provide the agent with a shared semantics for the dialogue. These constraints communicate meaning and implication of the action to the agent's communicating partner. For example, an agent receiving a protocol with the constraint to believe a proposition s upon being informed of s can infer that the agent sending the protocol has a particular semantic interpretation of the act of informing other agents of propositions. The '⇒' and '⇐' mark messages being sent and received. On the left-hand side of the double arrow is the message and on the right-hand side is the other agent involved in the interaction.

An agent must be able to understand the protocol, the dialogue state, and its role within the protocol. Agents need to be able to identify the agent clause which pertains to its function within the protocol and establish what actions it must take to continue the dialogue or what roles to adopt.

3.1   Implementing the Protocol Framework

A message is defined as the tuple, $\langle m, \mathcal{P} \rangle$. Where m is the message an agent is currently communicating, and $\mathcal{P}$ is the protocol written using the language described in figure 1. The protocol, in turn, is a triple, $\langle C, A^{\{n\}}, K \rangle$. C is the dialogue state. This is a record of the path of the dialogue through the conversation space and the current state of the dialogue for the agents. The second part is a set of agent clauses, $A^{\{n\}}$, necessary for the dialogue. The protocol also includes a set of axioms, K, consisting of common knowledge to be publicly known between the participants. The sending of the protocol with the messages allows agents to represent the various aspects of Electronic Institutions described in section 2.1. In addition, agents themselves communicate the conventions of the dialogue. This is accomplished by the participating agents satisfying two simple engineering requirements. Agents are required to share a dialogical framework. The same is required of Electronic Institutions, and is an unavoidable necessity in any meaningful agent communication. This includes the requirements on the individual messages are expressed in a ontology understood by the agents. The issue of ontology mapping is still open, and its discussion extends beyond the scope of this paper. The second requirement obligates the agent to provide a means to interpret the received message and its protocol. The agent must be able to unpack a received protocol, find the appropriate actions it may take, and update the dialogue state to reflect any actions it chooses to perform.

Figure 2 describes rules for expanding the received protocols. Details can be found in [3]. A similar language for web services is described in [2]. An agent receives a message of the form specified in figure 1. The message is added to the set of messages, M_i, currently being considered by the agent. The agent takes the clause, C_i, from the set of agent clauses received as part of $\mathcal{P}$. This clause provides the agent with its role in the dialogue. The agent then expands C_i by the application of the rules in figure 2. The expansion is done with respect to the different operators encountered in the protocol and the response to M_i. The result is a new dialogue state, C_n; a set of output messages, O_n and a subset of M_i, which is the remaining messages to be considered, M_n. The result is arrived at by applying the rewrite rules. The sequence would be similar to figure 3. C_n is then sent as part of $\mathcal{P}$ which will accompany the sending of each message in O_n.

3.2   Features of the Protocol

Several features of the protocol language are useful for agents capable of learning and adapting to the multi-agent system in which they participate. Sending the dialogue state during the interaction provides agents with several advantages. It is no longer necessary for an administrative agent to shepherd the interaction. The sending of the protocol with the message uses the 'hot potato' approach to communication. The interaction is coordinated by which agent currently 'holds' the protocol. The reception of a message would cue an agent to action. The sending of the protocol provides a means for disseminating the social conventions for the dialogue. The most common approach is to use specifications to be interpreted by individual engineers. The protocol directly communicates the social conventions and expectations an agent has for the dialogue. Agents with the ability to learn could use the received protocol to plan ahead or modify its own social conventions to be able to communicate with other agents. The protocol language is strictly concerned with the interaction level of communication. The semantics of the language does not depend on any assumptions about the agent's internal deliberative model. All requirements for the interaction are pub-

$$A :: B \xrightarrow{M_i, M_o, \mathcal{P}, O} A :: E$$
$$\text{if} \quad B \xrightarrow{M_i, M_o, \mathcal{P}, O} E$$
$$A_1 \text{ or } A_2 \xrightarrow{M_i, M_o, \mathcal{P}, O} E$$
$$\text{if} \quad \neg closed(A_2) \wedge A_1 \xrightarrow{M_i, M_o, \mathcal{P}, O} E$$
$$A_1 \text{ or } A_2 \xrightarrow{M_i, M_o, \mathcal{P}, O} E$$
$$\text{if} \quad \neg closed(A_1) \wedge A_2 \xrightarrow{M_i, M_o, \mathcal{P}, O} E$$
$$A_1 \text{ then } A_2 \xrightarrow{M_i, M_o, \mathcal{P}, O} E \text{ then } A_2$$
$$\text{if} \quad A_1 \xrightarrow{M_i, M_o, \mathcal{P}, O} E$$
$$A_1 \text{ then } A_2 \xrightarrow{M_i, M_o, \mathcal{P}, O} A_1 \text{ then } E$$
$$\text{if} \quad closed(A_1) \wedge A_2 \xrightarrow{M_i, M_o, \mathcal{P}, O} E$$
$$A_1 \text{ par } A_2 \xrightarrow{M_i, M_o, \mathcal{P}, O_1 \cup O_2} E_1 \text{ par } E_2$$
$$\text{if} \quad A_1 \xrightarrow{M_i, M_n, \mathcal{P}, O_1} E_1 \wedge A_2 \xrightarrow{M_n, M_o, \mathcal{P}, O_2} E_2$$
$$C \leftarrow M \Leftarrow A \xrightarrow{M_i, M_i - \{M \Leftarrow A\}, \mathcal{P}, \emptyset} c(M \Leftarrow A)$$
$$\text{if} \quad (M \Leftarrow A) \in M_i \wedge satisfy(C)$$
$$M \Rightarrow A \leftarrow C \xrightarrow{M_i, M_o, \mathcal{P}, \{M \Rightarrow A\}} c(M \Rightarrow A)$$
$$\text{if} \quad satisfied(C)$$
$$null \leftarrow C \xrightarrow{M_i, M_o, \mathcal{P}, \emptyset} c(null)$$
$$\text{if} \quad satisfied(C)$$
$$agent(r, id) \leftarrow C \xrightarrow{M_i, M_o, \mathcal{P}, \emptyset} a(R, I) :: B$$
$$\text{if} \quad clause(\mathcal{P}, a(R, I) :: B) \wedge satisfied(C)$$

A protocol term is decided to be closed, meaning that it has been covered by the preceding interaction, as follows:

$$closed(c(X))$$
$$closed(A \text{ or } B) \leftarrow closed(A) \vee closed(B)$$
$$closed(A \text{ then } B) \leftarrow closed(A) \wedge closed(B)$$
$$closed(A \text{ par } B) \leftarrow closed(A) \wedge closed(B)$$
$$closed(X :: D) \leftarrow closed(D)$$

$satisfied(C)$ is true if C can be solved from the agent's current state of knowledge. $satisfy(C)$ is true if the agent's state of knowledge can be made such that C is satisfied. $clause(\mathcal{P}, X)$ is true if clause X appears in the dialogue framework of protocol $\mathcal{P}$, as defined in Figure 1.

Fig. 2. Rules for expanding an agent clause

$$\langle C_i \xrightarrow{M_i, M_{i+1}, \mathcal{P}, O_i} C_{i+1}, \ldots, C_{n-1} \xrightarrow{M_{n-1}, M_n, \mathcal{P}, O_n} C_n \rangle$$

Fig. 3. Sequence of rewrites

licly specified with the protocol. Agents with different models of deliberation are able to communicate [16].

4 Means of Adaptation

Protocols are traditionally seen as a rigid ordering of messages and processing to enable a reliable means of communication. Agent-centric approaches have tended to avoid their use, lest agents be reduced to nothing more than remote function calls for the multi-agent system. The control over agent interactions within an electronic institutions is indeed intrusive. As described in section 2.1, the administrative agents of electronic institutions have complete control. The sequence of messages are dictated but also the roles an agent may adopt and the actions an agent must take within and outside of the context of the dialogue.

The protocol language of this paper does not follow this tradition. It is designed to bridge the gap separating the two approaches to agent interaction. The language is capable of representing the scenes and performative structure of electronic institutions, but it is not limited to electronic institution's inflexible model of agent interaction. The protocol language and the process of sending the protocol during execution provides agents with a means of adaptation.

In the electronic institution model, the protocol does not exist within the participating agents. It is retained by the institution itself, and designers must engineer agents that will strictly conform to the protocol which will be dictated by the administrative agents. Our approach delivers the protocol to the participating agents. Individual agents are given providence over the protocol they receive. This returns the power of the interaction to the participating agents. For example, the protocol received is not required to be the protocol that is returned.

The protocol, as described so far, already allows for a spectrum of adaptability. At one extreme, the protocol can be fully constrained. Protocols at this end of the spectrum would be close to the traditional protocols and electronic institutions. By rigidly defining each step of the protocol, agents could be confined to little more than remote processing. This sacrifice allows the construction of reliable and verifiable agent systems. At the other extreme, the protocols would be nothing more than the ordering of messages or even just the statement of legal messages(without any ordering) to be sent and received. Protocols designed this way would be more akin to the way agent-centric designers envisage agent communication. Agents using these protocols would be required to reason about the interaction to determine the next appropriate step in the dialogue. Though the protocol language is expressive enough for both extremes of the spectrum, the bulk of interactions are going to be somewhere in the middle. A certain amount of the dialogue will need to be constrained to ensure a useful dialogue can occur. This allows agents to express dynamic and interesting dialogues.

The protocol language is flexible enough to be adapted during run-time. Yet, protocols modified indiscriminately would return us to the problem facing the agent-centric approach. We would have a model for flexible communication, but no structure or conventions to ensure a meaningful dialogue can take place. It is necessary to constrain any adaptation in a meaningful way. By the examination of patterns and standards of an agent-centric approach, protocols can be construct to have points of flexibility. Portions in the dialogue can be adapted without losing the benefits of a protocol-based approach. The example below employs the rules for playing a dialogue game, the protocol language, and an amendment to the rewrite rules to allow a more dynamically constructed protocol.

5 Example

Figure 4 shows an example of an Information-seeking dialogue game similar to the one defined in [17]. The dialogue game rules are simplified to clarify its implementation within the protocol. There are countless variations on the rules for any one type of dialogue game. This illustrates a continuing problem with agent-centric communication design. It is not a trivial requirement to ensure agents within a system are employing the same communicative model. This is the same with dialogue games. Subtle differences could break the dialogue. By the use of the protocol, agent can communicate their 'house' rules for the game. The rules for this particular game are as follows:

1. The game begins with one agent sending the message *question(p)* to another agent.
2. Upon receiving a *question(p)* message, an agent should evaluate p and if it is found to be true, the agent should reply with *assert(p)* else send an *assert(null)* which is a failure message.
3. Upon receiving an *assert(p)*, an agent should evaluate the assertion, then the agent can send an *accept(p)* or *challenge(p)* depending on whether the agent's acceptance attitude will allow.
4. Upon receiving a *challenge(p)*, an agent should send an *assert(S)*. S is a set of propositions in support of p.
5. For each proposition in S, repeat steps 3 and 4.
6. The game is over when all propositions have been accepted or no further support for a proposition can be offered.

Rule one is satisfied by an agent taking up the role of the 'seeker'. This provides the agent with the legal moves necessary to play that side of the information-seeking dialogue game. The other agent will receive the *question(p)* message along with the protocol of figure 4. The agent identifies the clause which it should use. In this example, the clause playing the 'provider' role. It is necessary to use constraints to fully satisfy the second rule. Part of the rule states an agent sending an *assert(p)* depends on its knowledge base and its assertion attitude, otherwise an *assert(null)* is sent. The constraint *verify(p)* is assumed to be satisfiable by the agent. The agent is free to satisfy the constraint how it prefers. This could range from a simple function call to a complex belief logic with identity evaluation. The protocol only states what conditions must be satisfied, not how. The recursive steps are handled by the roles of *eval* (evaluate) and *def* (defend) which are similarly constrained. Finally, the termination rule for the game is written as the last line in the 'evaluate' role. No more messages are sent when the remainder of the set of propositions is empty.

$agent(infoseek(P, B), A) ::$
$agent(provider(P, A), B)$ or
$agent(seeker(P, B), A).$

$agent(seeker(P, B), A) ::$
$question(P) \Rightarrow agent(provider(P, A), B)$ then
$assert(P) \Leftarrow agent(provider(P, A), B)$ then
$agent(eval(P, B), A)$ or
$assert(null) \Leftarrow agent(provider(P, A), B).$

$agent(provider(P, A), B) ::$
$question(P) \Leftarrow agent(seeker(P, B), A)$ then
$(assert(P) \Rightarrow agent(seeker(P, B), A) \leftarrow verify(P)$ then
$agent(def(P, A), B))$ or
$assert(null) \Rightarrow agent(seeker(P, B), A).$

$agent(eval([P|R], B), A) ::$
$accept(P) \Rightarrow agent(def([P|R], A), B) \leftarrow accept(P)$ or
$\begin{pmatrix} challenge(P) \Rightarrow agent(def([P|R], A), B) \text{ then} \\ assert(S) \Leftarrow agent(def([P|R], A), B) \text{ then} \\ agent(eval(S, B)A) \end{pmatrix}$
then
$\begin{pmatrix} null \leftarrow R = [] \text{ or} \\ agent(eval(R, B), A) \end{pmatrix}.$

$agent(def([P|R], A), B) ::$
$accept(P) \Leftarrow agent(eval([P|R], B), A)$ or
$\begin{pmatrix} challenge(P) \Leftarrow agent(eval([P|R], B), A) \text{ then} \\ assert(S) \Rightarrow agent(eval([P|R], B), A) \leftarrow justify(P, S) \end{pmatrix}$

.

Fig. 4. The agent clauses for the information-seeking protocol

Similar protocols can be written to express the other atomic dialogue types. Real world dialogues rarely consist of a single dialogue game type. [14] formally describe several combinations of dialogue types. *Iteration* is the initiation of a dialogue game immediately following the finishing of another dialogue game of the same type. *Sequencing* is the similar to iteration except that the following dialogue game can be of any type. In *Parallelisation* of dialogue games, agents make moves in more than one dialogue game concurrently. *Embedding* of dialogue games occurs when during play of one dialogue game another game is initiated and played to its conclusion before the agents continue playing the first. The example involves two agents; a doctor and a patient. The patient is trying to find out whether the proposition 'patient is ill' is true (i.e. looking for a diagnosis). This is the perfect scenario to play an information-seeking dialogue game and to use the dialogue game protocol. Figure 5 and 6 shows the dialogue state for the agents as it is rewritten during the course of the dialogue. The numbering reflects the ordering of the expansion of the dialogue state for each agent.

$$agent(infoseek(\text{``patient is ill''}, doctor), patient) ::$$
$$agent(seeker(\text{``patient is ill''}, doctor), patient) \qquad (1)$$

$$agent(infoseek(\text{``patient is ill''}, doctor), patient) ::$$
$$question(\text{``patient is ill''}) \Rightarrow agent(provider(\text{``patient is ill''}, patient), doctor) \qquad (2)$$

$$agent(infoseek(\text{``patient is ill''}, doctor), patient) ::$$
$$question(\text{``patient is ill''}) \Rightarrow agent(provider(\text{``patient is ill''}, patient), doctor) \; then$$
$$assert(null) \Leftarrow agent(provider(\text{``patient is ill''}, patient), doctor).$$
$$(3)$$

Fig. 5. The progression of the dialogue state for the patient

$$agent(infoseek(\text{``patient is ill''}, patient), doctor) ::$$
$$agent(provider(\text{``patient is ill''}, patient), doctor) \qquad (1)$$

$$agent(infoseek(\text{``patient is ill''}, patient), doctor) ::$$
$$question(\text{``patient is ill''}) \Leftarrow agent(seeker(\text{``patient is ill''}, doctor), patient) \; then$$
$$assert(null) \Rightarrow agent(seeker(\text{``patient is ill''}, doctor), patient).$$
$$(2)$$

Fig. 6. The progression of the dialogue state for the doctor

The patient begins the dialogue by taking the initial agent clause of *infoseek* which stands for information-seeking. This step is labeled *1*. The agent applies the rewrite rules to expand the seeker role and sends the *question* to the doctor agent, step *2*. The doctor receives the message and the protocol. The applies the rewrite rules and finds the only instantiation that is possible is the unfolding of the provider role (step *1* for the doctor). It applies the rewrite rules and comes to the *verify* constraint which it is unable to satisfy. It cannot determine the truth value of the proposition and is unwilling to defend the proposition. It takes the other half of the *or* operator and sends the *assert(null)* (step *2*). Let us assume the doctor agent is a bit more clever. It cannot currently assert that the patient is ill. It has a knowledge-base and an inference engine that allows it to figure whether the proposition is true or not, and it needs some more information from the patient. The particular kind of information would depend on each patient consultation. If this diagnosis scenario was part of an electronic institution, the institution would have to represent in a state diagram every possible permutation of a diagnosis scenario. This is not practical, if not impossible.

Instead, the doctor agent can use the patterns of dialogue games to structure the interaction but allow adaptations to handle any run-time dialogical needs that may arise. In the example, the doctor agent needs to ask about a different

$$A \xrightarrow{M_i, M_o, \mathcal{P}, O} A \text{ then } B$$
$$if \quad clause(P, B) \wedge isa(B, dialogue - type)$$

$$isa(infoseek, dialogue - type).$$

Fig. 7. Additional rewrite rule

$$agent(infoseek("patient\ is\ ill", patient), doctor) ::$$
$$question("patient\ is\ ill") \ \Leftarrow$$
$$agent(seeker("patient\ is\ ill", doctor), patient)\ then \qquad (2)$$
$$agent(infoseek("patient\ has\ a\ fever", patient), doctor).$$

$$agent(infoseek("patient\ is\ ill", patient), doctor) ::$$
$$question("patient\ is\ ill") \ \Leftarrow\ agent(seeker("patient\ is\ ill", doctor), patient)\ then$$
$$\textbf{question}("\textbf{patient has a fever}") \Rightarrow$$
$$\textbf{agent}(\textbf{provider}("\textbf{patient has a fever}", \textbf{doctor}), \textbf{patient})$$

$$(3)$$

$$\ldots$$

$$agent(infoseek("patient\ is\ ill", patient), doctor) ::$$
$$question("patient\ is\ ill") \ \Leftarrow\ agent(seeker("patient\ is\ ill", doctor), patient)\ then$$
$$\textbf{question}("\textbf{patient has a fever}") \Rightarrow$$
$$\qquad \textbf{agent}(\textbf{provider}("\textbf{patient has a fever}", \textbf{doctor}), \textbf{patient})\ then$$
$$\textbf{assert}("\textbf{patient has a fever}") \Leftarrow$$
$$\qquad \textbf{agent}(\textbf{provider}("\textbf{patient has a fever}", \textbf{doctor}), \textbf{patient})\ then$$
$$assert("patient\ is\ ill") \Rightarrow agent(seeker("patient\ is\ ill", doctor), patient).$$

$$(5)$$

Fig. 8. The progression of the dialogue state for the doctor with embedding

proposition before it can answer the patient's original query. This is achieved by an additional rewrite rule shown in figure 7.

This allows the agent to graft the infoseek agent clause between any term in the protocol. These rewrites can be expanded further to represent other dialogue combinations as well as domain specific rewrite rules. The doctor's dialogue clause with the use of the embedding is shown in figure 8. The expansions and dialogue begin the same, but rather than just sending the *assert(null)*. The agent inserts the agent definition *agent(infoseek("patient has a fever"),patient),doctor)*. The next instance of a information-seeking dialogue is begun. The moves of the embedded dialogue game are in bold text. In this instance the patient plays the provider role and the doctor plays the seeker. The game is finished by the patient asserting "patient has a fever". The doctor, now knowing this proposition to be true, has enough knowledge to assert the original proposition posed by the patient's first question. The first information-seeking game also concludes successfully by the doctor making the diagnosis and asserting the proposition "patient is ill" is true. The unusual numbering reflects, for brevity, that steps in the expansion of the dialogue state have been omitted.

6   Conclusions

The protocol language described in the paper is expressive enough to represent the most popular approaches to the agent communication. It is able to capture the various aspects of Electronic Institutions such as the scenes, performative structure, and normative rules. This enables agents to have structured and meaningful dialogues without relying on centralised control of the conversation. The language is also capable of facilitating agent-centric approaches to agent communication. Agents pass the protocol to their dialogical partners to communicate the social conventions for the interaction. Agents can adapt the received protocols to explore dynamic conversation spaces. The protocol language in this paper is not seen as a replacement for either model of agent communication. Instead, it synthesises the two approaches to gain the advantages of both. Protocols are used to coordinate and guide the agent's dialogue, but agents are able adapt the protocol by using an agent-centric model for communication. The use of this communicative model constrains transformation to the agent clauses in meaningful ways. The run-time delivery provides the mechanism for communicating the protocol as well as any adaptations that are made. We have begun developing a FIPA compliant agents which uses the ACL library and the protocol language. It is hoped that the verifiability and semantic problems associated with FIPA's ACL can be mitigated by the use of the protocol language to communicate the performative's semantics during their use.

This approach does raise new issues which have not been addressed in this paper. One issue concerns restricting changes to the protocols. There are certainly dialogues where certain agents will be restricted from modifying the protocols or dialogue which require portions of the protocol to remain unchanged. This remains for future work along with development of a vocabulary of generic transformations which can be proven *a priori* or verified to retain semantic and syntactical continuity of the protocols.

The protocol language has already been shown to be useful for a number of agent purposes. A scheduling program has been developed using the protocol written in Prolog and using LINDA [11]. A Java-based agent framework also exists which uses an XML representation of the protocols. Separating the protocol from the deliberative and communicative models of agency makes definition and verification simpler tasks. Tools have already been developed which use model-checking for automatic verification [23]. The protocol language has been used to implement the generic dialogue framework of [14] and the negotiation game described in [15].

References

1. Chris Walton, Dave Robertson: Flexible Multi-Agent Protocols. Technical report EDI-INF-RR-0164 November (2002)
2. David Robertson: A Lightweight Method for Coordination of Agent Oriented Web Services. Proceedings of AAAI Spring Symposium on Semantic Web Services. California, USA (2004)
3. David Robertson: A Lightweight Coordination Calculus for Agent Social Norms. Declarative Agent Languages and Technologies (AAMAS). New York, USA (2004) to appear
4. Marc Estava and Juan A. Rodriguez and Carles Sierra and Pere Garcia and Josep L. Arcos: On the Formal Specifications of Electronic Institutions. LNAI (2001) 126–147
5. Marc Esteva and Juan A. Rodrguez-Aguilar and Josep Ll. Arcos and Carles Sierra and Pere Garcia: Institutionalising Open Multi-agent Systems. proceedings of the Fourth International Conference on MultiAgent Systems (ICMAS'2000). (2000) 381–83
6. Robert A. Flores and R.C. Kremer: To Commit or Not To Commit: Modelling Agent Conversations for Action. Computational Intelligence **18:2** (2002) 120–173
7. Marc Esteva and David de la Cruz and Carles Sierra: Islander: an electronic institutions editor. Proceeding of the first International joint conference on Automomous agents and multiagent systems (2002) 1045–1052
8. Foundation for Intelligent Physical Agents: FIPA SL Content Language Specification. FIPA SL Content Language Specification (2000)
9. Foundation for Intelligent Physical Agents: Communicative Act Library Specification. FIPA communicative act library specification (2001)
10. Mark Greaves and Heather Holmback and Jeffrey Bradshaw: What is a Conversation Policy. Issues in Agent Communication (2000) 118–131
11. Nicholas Carriero and David Gelernter: Linda in context. Communications of the ACM **32:4** (1989) 444–458
12. Nicolas Maudet and Brahim Chaib-draa: Commitment-based and dialogue-game based protocols: new trends in agent communication languages. The Knowledge Engineering Review **17:2** (2002)
13. Nicolas Maudet and Fabrice Evrard: A generic framework for dialogue game implementation. Proceedings of the Second Workshop on Formal Semantics and Pragmatics of Dialog. (1998)
14. Peter McBurney and Simon Parsons: Games that agents play: A formal framework for dialogues between autonomous agents. Journal of Logic, Language and Information **11:3** (2002) 315–334
15. Peter McBurney and Rogier van Eijk and Simon Parsons and Leila Amgoud: A dialogue-game protocol for agent purchase negotiations. Journal of Autonomous Agents and Multi-Agent Systems (2002)
16. Jarred McGinnis and David Robertson and Chris Walton: Using Distributed Protocols as an Implementation of Dialogue Games. Presented EUMAS (2003)
17. Simon Parsons and Peter McBurney and Michael Wooldridge: The Mechanics of Some Formal Inter-agent Dialogues. Workshop on Agent Communication Languages (2003) 329–348
18. Philippe Pasquier and Nicolas Andrillon and Brahim Chaib-draa: An Exploration in Using The Cognitive Coherence Theory to Automate Agents's Communicational Behavior. Agent Communication Language and Dialogue workshop (2003)

19. Chris Reed: Dialogue frames in agent communication. Proceedings of the Third International Conference on Multi-Agent Systems (1998) 246–253
20. John Searle: Speech Acts. Cambridge University Press (1969)
21. Munindar P. Singh: A Social Semantics for Agent Communication Languages. Issues in Agent Communication (2000) 31–45
22. Chris D. Walton: Multi-Agent Dialogue Protocols. Proceedings of the Eighth International Symposium on Artificial Intelligence and Mathematics (2004)
23. Chris D. Walton: Model Checking Multi-Agent Web Services. Proceedings of the 2004 AAAI Spring Symposium on Semantic Web Services (2004)
24. Doug Walton and Eric C. W. Krabbe: Commitment in Dialogue: Basic Concepts of Interpersonal Reasoning SUNY press (1995)
25. Wamberto Vasconcelos: Skeleton-based Agent Development for Electronic Institutions. First International Joint Conference on Autonomous Agents and Multi-Agent Systems (2002)
26. Michael Wooldridge: Semantic Issues in the Verification of Agent Communication Languages. Autonomous Agents and Multi-Agent Systems **3:1** (2000) 9–31

Advice-Exchange Between Evolutionary Algorithms and Reinforcement Learning Agents: Experiments in the Pursuit Domain

Luís Nunes[1] and Eugénio Oliveira[2]

[1] ISCTE/FEUP/LIACC-NIAD&R ISCTE, Av. Forças Armadas,
1600-026 Lisbon, Portugal
Luis.Nunes@iscte.pt
[2] FEUP/LIACC-NIAD&R FEUP, Av. Dr. Roberto Frias,
4200-465, Porto, Portugal
eco@fe.up.pt

Abstract. This research aims at studying the effects of exchanging information during the learning process in *Multiagent Systems*. The concept of *advice-exchange*, introduced in previous contributions, consists in enabling an agent to request extra feedback, in the form of episodic advice, from other agents that are solving similar problems. The work that was previously focused on the exchange of information between agents that were solving detached problems is now concerned with groups of learning-agents that share the same environment. This change added new difficulties to the task. The experiments reported below were conducted to detect the causes and correct the shortcomings that emerged when moving from environments where agents worked in detached problems to those where agents are interacting in the same environment. New concepts, such as *self confidence, trust* and *advisor preference* are introduced in this text.

1 Introduction

The question that drives this research is: "(How) can learning agents cooperate during the learning process?". This question is broad, and parts of it were already addressed by other authors. For this reason, as well as for others that concern the applicability of the solution and the authors' research interests, we have drawn some restrictions to the type of problems and learning agents used in the experiments. In this work we will focus on agents with simple communication skills that are solving problems with the same structure, but possibly different local dynamics. The agents have only partial knowledge of the state-space and each learns using an algorithm of its choice, unknown to others. Agents may exchange information with peers that are cooperating to solve the same problem (its *partners*), or with agents that are solving similar problems in other environments with the same structure. For the moment we only consider non-malicious agents that always try to help others to the best of their knowledge. The en-

D. Kudenko et al. (Eds.): Adaptive Agents and MAS II, LNAI 3394, pp. 185–204, 2005.

vironment in which they act does not provide supervision information, only a measure of the quality of each action (or sequence of actions).

The approach taken in this work aims at improving the individual and global learning performance by providing learning-agents (hereafter referred to as "agents" for the sake of simplicity) with more feedback than the environment can give them. Agents, during their learning process, gather expertise in how to deal with the particular problem they are facing as well as information about the quality of their own actions. The knowledge of the performance achieved by others in similar problems can be used by an agent to detect how good its solution is. Also, the knowledge of how an agent would react to a given state of the environment may contain information that can improve the learning results of another agent, if the structure of the environment is similar enough.

The groups of agents referred to in this paper are heterogeneous in the sense that each team may use different learning techniques. The interest in cooperation amongst groups of heterogeneous agents lies in having different exploration techniques that may reach different solutions, or at least not become trapped in the same local-maxima, thus being able, by exchanging information, to help each other during the learning process. The main difficulty in having heterogeneous groups is that internal parameters cannot be exchanged, because agents are not aware of which learning algorithm their peers are using. This fact restricts communication. Only knowledge that has meaning outside the agents' internal context can be communicated. The simplest types of data with these characteristics are the ones generated by the environment itself, which all agents must understand in order to sense and act. This data can be either the state of environment, actions, or values of the quality function that agents are attempting to maximize. The exchange of other types of data, such as "trust agent X", was also found useful and it requires that all agents share a (small) common vocabulary. We will further assume that the agents are working in domains in which the problem has the same structure and is presented in the same way to the agent, i.e. the meaning and order of the variables that compose both state and actions, are known to be the same for all environments used in an experiment. Nevertheless, different environments in the same experiment may reward the same state-action pair differently and/or have different state transition dynamics.

The key questions of this research are: how to select, incorporate, and benefit-from all the available information without re-processing all the data gathered by each of an agent's peers (which is time and band-width consuming). The objective is to gain knowledge based on the synthesis that was done by others without exchanging the entire solution and adopting it blindly (which in some circumstances may even be a very poor option, if the dynamics of the advisee's environment are different enough from the advisor's, or if the agents are using different learning algorithms). To the best of the authors' knowledge there is no work that specifically addresses this problem in heterogeneous groups of agents.

The work reported in this paper focuses on exchanging episodic information consisting of state-action pairs and statistics on the performance of other agents. An agent requests information whenever it perceives that the current performance is relatively low when compared to that of its peers or when the agent is in a state for which the choice of the following action is unclear.

The amount of information exchanged is also controlled by a *self-confidence* parameter in each agent. This parameter is used in the decision of whether or not an agent should get advice for each new state of the problem. The decision of where to collect this information is based on knowledge regarding other agents' results and on the development of *trust* relationships between an agent and its peers. The exchanged information is used either as a desired output for *supervised learning* or as a different source of reinforcement in a process that was labelled *"learning from a teacher"* by Clouse in [1].

The objective of these experiments is to test solutions for the difficulties reported in [2] concerning the disturbances on the learning process caused by the interaction between agents and the exchange of advice during learning in social environments. In this work we compare the performance of four groups of agents in several versions of a task (the pursuit problem), thus providing the basis for an assessment of the advantages and drawbacks of *advice-exchange*. The discussion, based on these results, should provide clues on how techniques of this type can be improved to share information between agents efficiently. The four groups of agents used in the experiments are: Individual; Homogeneous cooperative groups; Heterogeneous cooperative groups and Heterogeneous cooperative groups plus Heuristic experts. The experts are a group of handcrafted agents that use a near-optimal heuristic (optimal in a single-agent scenario). This group of agents was introduced in the experiments to estimate the performance that can be obtained by agents that use optimal individual actions and verify the gain that can be achieved by the agents when they have near-optimal teachers.

In the following Sect. the reader can find a summarized review of the related work. Section 3 presents the learning algorithms used by the agents. In Sect. 4 the *advice-exchange* algorithm is explained, followed by the description of the experiments (Sect. 5). In Sect. 6 the results are presented and discussed, and finally, the last section presents the conclusions and some guidelines for future work.

2   Related Work

Quite a few researchers have contributed to answer the question stated above since the early 90's, especially in what concerns the transfer of learned information between *Q-Learning* agents (QL-agents). Without being exhaustive, due to the extent of the research that covers this and related topics, and trying simply to contextualize the work that will be presented below, the next paragraphs summarize the main contributions in the past decade. The work on information exchange between QL-agents, started in the early nineties with several contributions, namely [3, 4, 5, 6] and [7].

Whitehead [3] made several experiments with a cooperative learning architecture labelled *Learning By Watching* (LBW). In this architecture, the agent learns by watching its peers' behavior (which is equivalent to sharing series of state-action-quality triplets). The results presented in [4, 5] are reviewed and expanded in Clouse's Ph.D. thesis [1]. This important contribution reports the results of a technique labelled *Ask for Help* (AH), in which QL-agents learn by asking their peers for suggestions and then performing the suggested actions. This was labelled *learning from a teacher*. Clouse proposes two different approaches for the problem of deciding when to ask for help: in the first approach the advisee asks for help randomly for a given percentage of the actions it has to take; in a second approach the agent asks for help only when it is "confused" about what action to take next. Confusion is defined as having similar quality estimates for all possible actions that the agent can perform at a given stage.

Lin [6] uses an expert trainer to teach lessons to a QL-agent that is starting its own training. He experimented with several architectures, the most interesting for the current subject is QCON-T (*Connectionist Q-Learning with Teaching*). QCON-T records and replays both "taught" and "learned lessons", i.e. sequences of actions that led to a success. Some of these sequences (the "taught lessons") are given by an expert trainer (human or automatic), while others are recorded by the student agent as it explores the problem (the "learned lessons"). Results in variants of the maze problem show that teaching does improve learning performance in the harder task, although it seems to have no effect on the performance of the agents on the easier task.

Tan [7] addressed the problem of exchanging information between QL-agents during the learning process. This work reports the results of sharing several types of information amongst agents that are working in the pursuit (predator-prey) problem. Experiments were conducted in which QL-agents shared policies (internal solution parameters), episodes (series of state, action, quality triplets), and sensation (observed states). Although the experiments use solely *Q-Learning* in the pursuit domain, the author believes that: *"conclusions can be applied to cooperation among autonomous learning agents in general"*, [7], *(Sect. 8)*. Tan concludes that *"additional sensation from another agent is beneficial if it can be used efficiently"*, [7] (in *Abstract*).

Training of novice Q-learning agents by *implicit imitation* of pre-trained experts was studied and successfully applied by Price and Boutilier [8]. This work has some very interesting characteristics: the student agent has no knowledge of the actions done by the expert, it can only observe its state transitions; there is no explicit communication between the expert and the student and the goals and actions of both agents can be different. The student agent uses an augmented Bellman equation to calculate the utility of each state. This equation incorporates the information regarding the state transitions made by the expert. The technique was tested in several maze problems with very good results.

The work presented in this paper is focused on communication between teams of agents that use different learning algorithms. In these experiments we used Q-Learning and Evolutionary Algorithms to test the problems and benefits of exchanging information during learning in environments where the internal learning algorithm used by other agents is unknown.

3 Agents' Learning Algorithms

In this section we will briefly describe the variations on standard learning algorithms that were used in the experiments. Due to space constraints a full presentation of Q-Learning (QL) [10] and Backpropagation (BP) [11] is omitted. The version of QL used is the standard one-level Q-Learning with Boltzmann exploration and decaying temperature, described in [7,12]. Backpropagation is also a standard version with decaying learning rate. A fully detailed description, of the learning algorithms used along with their parameters can be found in [13].

The variant of *Evolutionary Algorithms* (EA) [14,15] used in these experiments deserves further attention. EA are a well known learning technique, with biological inspiration where the solution parameters are interpreted as a specimen (or phenotype), and its performance in a given problem as its fitness. An EA controls a population of specimens. In each generation-loop of the algorithm the fitness of all specimens in the population is evaluated and the best are selected for breeding.

The variant of EA used in these experiments works mainly based on mutation of parameters and a simple crossover strategy. It is based on the work presented in [18] that achieved good results in the task of navigation in a difficult maze-problem. The main characteristics of this variant are the following: the genotype is simply the set of real-valued matrixes that constitute an Artificial Neural Network (ANN) of fixed size; all specimens are ANN of the same size; the selection strategy is elitist, keeping a certain number of the best specimens untouched for the following generation; the remainder of the population is generated by mutation and crossover of randomly chosen specimens selected amongst the ones that achieved the best performances in the previous generation. Contrary to [18] this variant does not use tournament selection. Mutation is done by disturbing all the values of the parameters with random noise with zero average, and normal distribution. A mutation-rate parameter (m) controls the variance of the noise added to a neural network's weight when it is mutated. This parameter is decayed during training according to $m_{t+1} = m_t * (t_F - t)/t_F$, until it reaches a, pre-established, minimum value. In the previous equation t represents the current epoch and t_F is a parameter of the algorithm that determines the epoch at which the learning rate should drop to a minimum. The crossover strategy consists on choosing two parents from the selected pool and copy randomly from each of the parents sub-sets of parameters (in this case the allowed subsets are ANN sub-trees). Crossover is scarcely used because the approaches that were proved effective imply complex encoding and decoding schemes and their effectiveness is highly dependent on the problem being addressed. The crossover procedure applied in this case requires that all the ANN have the same structure and is done simply by choosing each unit (and all its incoming weights) randomly from one of the two selected parents.

Each agent contains a population of specimens, and exchanges its active specimen after a given number of epochs (3 in this case). After the evaluation of all the specimens, the selection process takes place, followed by mutation and

crossover of the selected specimens to generate a population of the same size as
the previous one.

4   Advice-Exchange

The first version of this algorithm was introduced in [19] where it was evaluated
in solving a simplified traffic-control problem. In these experiments, agents were
working on similar but detached problems. Recent work on this subject can also
be found in [2, 13]. *Advice-exchange* consists in presenting the current state of
the environment, as seen by a given agent (the advisee), to another agent that
has better performance in similar problems (the advisor) and in using the action
proposed by the advisor as desired response for a form of *supervised learning*.
This will enable an agent to learn, both, from the environment's reinforcement
and from its more successful partners, which will act as teachers/critics.

Table 1. Summary of the *advice-exchange* algorithm in the perspective of the advisee
agent i

While not train finished
Broadcast:
cq_i: relative current quality
bq_i: relative best quality, for $i \in$ Agents
While not epoch finished
1. Get state s for evaluation.
2. If *best quality not good enough* or
current quality not good enough or
uncertain/confused concerning state s
2.1 Select the best advisor (k).
2.2 Request advice to agent k for state s
2.3 Agent k: process request of agent i
producing advised action (a)
2.4 Process advised action (a)
3. Evaluate state s and produce response (r)
4. Receive reward for action taken
End epoch loop
Update cq_i, bq_i, $trust_{ij}$ and sc_i (*self-confidence*).
End train loop

The algorithm, described in Table 1 is based on the knowledge of two quantities for all peers involved in *advice-exchange*: the *relative current average quality*
(cq) and the *relative best average quality* (bq). These values are calculated as
follows: let $aq_{i,t}$ be the average quality of the actions of agent i in epoch t, then
$cq_{i,t+1} = (1 - \alpha)aq_{i,t} + \alpha cq_{i,t}$, with $\alpha \in]0, 1[$, and $bq_{i,t+1} = max(aq_{i,t}, \beta bq_{i,t})$,
with $\beta \in]0, 1[$. These measures of quality proved to be preferable to others, such
as the current average quality, because they are less subject to oscillation.

The *self-confidence* parameter is used in the decision of whether or not to get advice. This parameter was included to deal with the problem of the sudden withdrawal of advice and to prevent agents from getting unnecessary advice. When an agent is deciding if it needs advice it will compare its own quality statistics (cq and bq) with those of other peers. The *self-confidence* parameter is used as a weight, applied to its own quality values. If *self-confidence* is higher than 1.0 (meaning that in the recent past the agent was frequently one of the most successful) it will over-rate its own performance. If it is lower than 1.0 (meaning that in the recent past the agent was frequently one of the least successful) it will underrate its own performance.

This parameter can compensate the oscillations in performance, typical of dynamic domains. An agent that has recently been successful will not ask for advice because of one (or a few) bad epoch(s). The time it takes for self-confidence to decay to values lower that 1.0 allows an agent to recover from spurious bad results. Another problem that was mitigated by the introduction of *self-confidence* was that of sudden withdrawal of advice. When a low-performance agent is learning from a peer that obtains better results, the training ends when their performances reach the same level. It was observed that after advice was withdrawn some agents experienced a sudden drop in performance and had to restart the *advice-exchange* process. The analysis of this behavior, allowed us to conclude that the agents, after just a few epochs, had lost some of the capabilities that they were recently taught. The introduction of *self-confidence* gives the agent some time to solidify the lessons taught by others because it takes several epochs for a low-performance agent to regain its self-confidence when its performance improves.

Several variants of the update of *self-confidence* parameters were tested. In general the self-confidence (sc_i) for agent i is updated as follows: let hb_i be the number of agents for which $bq_j < bq_i$, for all agents $j <> i$; hc_i the number of agents for which $cq_j < cq_i$, for all agents $j <> i$; nc the total number of agents in the environment and k the agent with best cq. Then,

$$sc_{i,t+1} = \begin{cases} sc_{down} * sc_{i,t} & : \quad C1 \text{ is } true \\ sc_{up} * sc_{i,t} & : \quad C2 \text{ is } true \end{cases}, \qquad (1)$$

where $C1 = (hb_i > \gamma_{down}nc \vee cb_i > \gamma_{down}nc) \wedge cq_i < \rho_{down}cq_k$; $C2 = hb_i < \gamma_{up}nc \vee cb_i < \gamma_{up}nc \vee cq_i > \rho_{up}cq_k$; $sc_{down} \in]0,1[$ and $sc_{up} \in]1,2[$. The value of sc_i is not allowed to be greater than sc_{max} or smaller than sc_{min} taking up those values if the update has surpassed the maximum or minimum values, respectively. The values of γ_{up}, γ_{down}, ρ_{up}, ρ_{down}, sc_{min} and sc_{max} were, respectively (1/2, 3/4, 0.9, 0.8, 0.5, 2.0).

The *trust* parameters are used in the selection of the most suitable advisor for a given agent. It was observed that in certain situations the agent with the best quality statistics was not the best advisor for all its peers. The performance as an advisor depends not only on the performance of an agent, but also on other factors, such as: similarity of the dynamics of the advisor and advisee's environment and capability of the advisee to learn the advised behavior adequately. The introduction of the *trust* parameter, as a measure of "how much has the advice

from agent j helped to improve a given agent's performance in the recent past",
helps an agent to seek the most appropriate advisor for its own situation. The
update of the *trust* parameters is done in a similar way as for the *self-confidence*.
Trust will be increased if the relative current quality of the advisee increased in
the last epoch $(cq_{i,t} > cq_{i,t-1})$ and decreased otherwise.

Trust in a certain advisor can also be influenced by a partner. When a partner
changes advisors or when an advisor has proved successful an agent issues a
message to its own partner telling it to trust the partner of its own advisor. This
enables agents to learn joint strategies used by other teams by influencing each
of their partners to seek advice with a different member of a successful team.

The decision, made by a given agent i, on whether or not to get advice is
based on three conditions:

1. Best quality not good enough: $sc_i bq_i < bq_j$, for some $j <> i$,
2. Current quality not good enough: $sc_i cq_i < cq_j$, for some $j <> i$,
3. Confused about current state: An agent is said to be confused concerning
   a given state if its N best rated options differ in their estimated quality
   by less than a given number e. In these experiments the values used were
   $N = 4, e = 0.1$.

An agent will request advice if any of these conditions is true. If an agent
uses EA it will not get advice in the first epoch in which a specimen is being
tried. This prevents it from getting advice based on the performance achieved
by other specimens. When an agent (i) decides to request advice it selects the
peer with the highest product $cq_j * trust_{ij}, j <> i$, and sends its current state
to the selected agent. An agent will give preference of choice to the last advisor
when this agent's score is similar to the best. By similar, we mean that the
quality-trust product $(cq_j * trust_{ij})$ is higher than, for instance, 80% of the same
value for the agent with the highest quality-trust product. The introduction
of the preference given to the last advisor was necessary to avoid agents from
exchanging advisor too frequently, which leads to disturbances in the learning
process due to conflicting advice.

If the advisor is an EA-agent it will reload the weights used in the epoch when
the best score was achieved and run the state provided by the advisee as if it was
experiencing it in order to produce its best response to the request. If the selected
peer is a QL-agent it will run the state without using Boltzmann exploration
in the action-selection process. This way it will choose the action with highest
quality. The process of incorporating the received knowledge in an agent's current
hypothesis is also different for both types of agents. When the advisee is an EA-
agent it will back-propagate the advice as desired response using standard online
Backpropagation on the weights of the ANN. The selection process will work on
the specimens after they have been changed by the *Backpropagation* algorithm,
passing the knowledge acquired by *supervised-learning* to the next generation.
This can be interpreted as *Lamarckian* learning.

When the advisee is a QL-agent it will give a bonus of b_{up} to the advised
action and of b_{down} to all other actions starting at that state, with: $b_{up} > 0$,
$b_{down} < 0$ and $b_{up} \approx 10b_{down}$. A similar technique, labelled *Biasing-Binary*,

that uses the same absolute quantity both for positive and negative feedback is reported in [3]. It was observed that EA-agents took longer to incorporate the advised information into their current hypothesis than QL-agents. This is due to the particular characteristics of the learning algorithm and the fact that an EA-agent evaluates specimens in sequence. To overcome this problem it was necessary to store advice, which can be replayed before the beginning of a training epoch. The advice given during a training epoch is stored after being used, up to a limit of n_{stored} patterns (in this case we have used $n_{stored} = 450$). When the storage-space is filled, incoming advice will replace the oldest advice stored. At the beginning of a training epoch the advice is replayed to the specimen in evaluation prior to the taking of any actions. If the last advisor has lost the trust of the advisee the stored advice is thrown away. The next time an advisor is chosen the specimen that receives advice is re-initialized before replaying the advice. Replaying advice consists in performing *backpropagation* using the stored advice as desired response. This process is repeated until a given number of epochs is reached (usually 100) or the *Backpropagation* error falls below a certain threshold. The use of *advice-replay*, is still under study because it has the unwanted side-effect of reducing the diversity of the specimens by possibly pre-training an entire population with a similar set of examples. Another disadvantage of this approach is that online *backpropagation* is a time-consuming procedure, and training time may increase considerably when using this approach.

5   Experiments

The experiments this work refers to were conducted in the Pursuit Problem (a.k.a. Predator-Prey Problem).

This problem was first introduced in [20], although the version presented here has been inspired on several variations of this environment presented in [7] and [21]. The problem faced by the predator consists in learning to catch a prey in a square arena. A predator is said to have caught the prey if at the end of a given turn it occupies the same position as the prey. The arena is spherical and contains two agents (predators) and one prey. At the beginning of each turn all agents receive the state of the environment which consists solely of the relative position of the prey. The accuracy of the state received by the predator depends on its visual range. The predator perceives the correct position of the prey up to a limit defined by the visual range parameter (the value of this parameter in these experiments was 3). If the prey is at a distance greater than the visual range its relative position is disturbed (by Gaussian noise with null average) proportionally to the distance between predator and prey. The vision field is toroidal in the same way movement is.

Each predator has to choose between nine possible actions in each turn, i.e. it chooses either to move in one of the eight possible directions (four orthogonal and four diagonal), or to remain in its current position. Each predator moves one step in one direction in each turn. The prey moves before the predators. To decide in which direction to move, the prey detects the presence of the closest predator (closest in the sense of being at the shortest Euclidean distance) and moves in the opposite direction. If there is more than one predator at the same distance one of the predators is picked randomly and the prey moves away from it regardless if it is approaching the other predator(s). The prey moves only nine out of each ten turns. Any two units can occupy the same cell simultaneously at any time.

In each turn predators are given a reward that has both an individual and a global component. The individual component is based on their distance to the prey (d). This reward is equal to 1.0, if the predator has captured the prey or $(1.0 - d/d_{max})/10.0$ otherwise. The constant max_d represents the maximum distance between any two positions in the grid world. The global component of the reward is calculated by multiplying the partner's reward by a given number g, with $g < 1$. In these experiments we used $g = 0.25$. After a successful catch the predator that caught the prey is randomly relocated in the arena. This version of the pursuit problem does not involve either explicit cooperation or competition between the predators, although cooperative behavior has been detected in some experiments as will be explained below.

5.1   Agents and Scenarios

Agents in these experiments use either *Q-Learning* (QL) or *Evolutionary Algorithms* (EA) to learn the required skill. Heuristic agents perform a fixed (hand-coded) policy that always tries to reduce the distance to the prey as much as possible. These agents do not request advice, but they always reply to advice requests from other agents.

The scenarios used in these experiments are the following:

1. Individual: Four arenas, each with two predators and one prey. In each arena all predators use the same learning algorithm and they do not exchange any information with their peers.
2. Social Heterogeneous: Four arenas, each with two predators and one prey. In each arena all predators use the same learning algorithm and advice may be requested by a predator to any of its seven peers in the same or other arenas. Two arenas have EA-agents, the other two have QL-agents.
3. Social Heuristic: Similar to the Social scenario but with an extra arena where two Heuristic agents are performing the same task (hunting one prey) and may also be chosen as advisors.
4. Social Homogeneous: Four arenas, each with two predators and one prey. In all arenas all predators use the same learning algorithm (QL or EA) and advice may be requested by a predator to any of its seven peers in the same or other arenas.

For each of the above scenarios 11 trials were made (x4, or x8, agents of each type) with different random seeds. Each trial ran for 9000 epochs and each epoch has 150 turns. For each trial there is a corresponding test which runs for 1000 epochs without learning or exchange of advice. Each agent in the beginning of a test loads the parameters that the corresponding agent saved during training when it achieved its best absolute score. Partnerships were kept unchanged by this procedure.

Two experiments were made differing only in the dimension of the grid. In the first the grid was 10x10, and in the second 20x20 positions wide.

5.2   Experiment 1

The objective of the first experiment was to examine the behavior of *advice-exchange* in a problem where QL agents, when working individually, are clearly superior to Heuristic and EA-agents. In this experiment the dimension of the arena is 10x10 and *advice-exchange* is not allowed until mid trial (epoch 4500). Each point in the graphics (and value in the tables) is based on 44 (11 trials x 4 agents) or 88 (11 x 8) different trials of an agent using a particular algorithm in a particular scenario. For the training data the average quality per epoch of the agent's actions for all experiments was calculated and these values where averaged for every 200 epochs, for better understandability of the graphics.

Each graphic shows the results of an agent that uses a given learning algorithm (QL or EA) when not using *advice-exchange* (labelled: *Individual*), in a social heterogeneous environment with and without heuristic experts (*Social Heuristic* and *Social Heterogeneous*, respectively) and in a social homogeneous environment composed solely of other agents using the same learning algorithm (*Social Homogeneous*). The averaged results of the heuristic experts are presented in all figures to facilitate the comparisons between different graphics.

The agent that produced the best average score in test for each algorithm-scenario pair was chosen as representative and its average score during the 1000 epochs of testing is shown on the column labelled "Best test avg" of tables 2 and 3. The average score in test per agent-type and scenario is also presented in the last column of the same tables, and it is labelled "Avg in test".

One of the most interesting, and important, facts in this experiment is that QL-agents in individual scenarios learn to perform better than Heuristic and EA-agents. This performance is achieved by developing joint strategies. Notice that there is no explicit attempt to develop cooperative strategies and the agents have no information concerning their partners in their description of the state. Cooperation emerges spontaneously when one of the agents takes advantage of the other's strategy. Another interesting fact, and also of great importance to the following discussion, is that it is common to observe one of the QL-agents profit more than the other from these joint strategies. In certain cases this phenomenon resembles more a form of parasitism than actual cooperation. This also holds if agents do not share the reward and was observed in experiments documented in [2]. In these cases the joint strategy would often be destroyed because one of the members was not performing well enough and thus would seek advice (quite often from its own partner). When getting advice its strategy would change and the "parasite" would see its score drop to average/low levels in a few epochs simply because the dynamics of its environment had changed due to the change in its partner's behavior. In some cases the "parasite" agent's score would never reach the same levels as it had before its partner started to take advice.

Table 2. Best and average test results in experiment 1 for each scenario-algorithm pair, ordered by best test averages

Scenario	Alg.	Best test avg	Avg in test	Std. Dev.
Social Het.	QL	0.20740	0.18471	0.0167
Social Hom.	QL	0.20605	0.18803	0.0092
Social Heu.	QL	0.20447	0.17101	0.0131
Individual	QL	0.20413	0.19434	0.0063
Social Het.	EA	0.20358	0.17627	0.0169
Social Heu.	EA	0.19468	0.17118	0.006
Social Heu.	Heu.	0.17617	0.17345	0.0000
Individual	EA	0.16148	0.14368	0.0067
Social Hom.	EA	0.15850	0.14164	0.0069

One of the reasons for the introduction of a global component in the reward function was precisely to maintain these successful groups. The sharing of rewards was relatively successful in maintaining most of the groups together even if one agent would get only a small percentage of its partner's reward. The break-up of joint strategies can still be observed in the current experiments, although in a much smaller scale than in previous ones.

As seen in Table 2, QL-agents perform better in this experiment than either Heuristic or EA-agents. Curiously, although individual performances are better in terms of its average, the best tests are from QL-agents trained in social environments with *advice-exchange*. The difference is slight but this observation is consistent with previous tests. EA-agents perform considerably better in *Social Heterogeneous* and *Heuristic* environments than in the *Individual* trials, proving that *advice-exchange* does improve the scores of low-performance agents to levels that are close to those of the advisors. Nevertheless, interferences caused by trusting heuristic experts too much can be noticed in the difference between the results for EA-Agents in *Social Heterogeneous* and *Heuristic* environments. The exchange of advice in *Social Heterogeneous* scenarios produces the highest score in the best results column for EA-agents, although in *Homogeneous* scenarios it seems not to be very profitable, reaching slightly lower scores than in the *Individual* scenarios.

In Fig. 1 we can see the average evolution of the results of QL-agents in different scenarios during training. It is noticeable that at epoch 4500, when *advice-exchange* starts, social QL-agents suffer a small destabilization and in *Heuristic* scenarios start to take advice from heuristic experts, which leads them off their track and into a local maxima from which they do not seem able to escape.

In what concerns the performance of EA-agents in training, depicted in Fig. 2, we can notice that it is easier for an EA-agent to follow the performance of Heuristic agents (whose advice is more stable) than that of QL-agents. The number of advice-exchanged during training is relatively small. The highest value reported for both experiments is an average of 7 requests per epoch (150 turns) measured over the full trial (9000 epochs). It is important to notice however

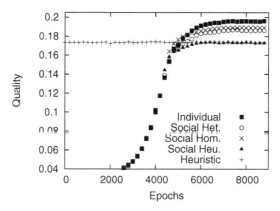

Fig. 1. Training results for QL agents in experiment 1

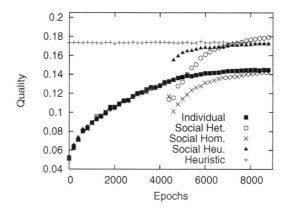

Fig. 2. Training results for EA agents in experiment 1

that advice is not allowed during at least half of these epochs and that the traffic generated is "bursty", concentrated between epochs 4500 and 5000.

5.3   Experiment 2

The objective of this experiment is to examine the behavior of *advice-exchange* in a problem where EA-agents (when working individually) are, in average, superior to QL-agents. This experiment is, in all respects, similar to experiment 1, except in the dimension of the arenas (in this case 20x20). Contrary to the previous experiment in this QL-agents have serious difficulties in learning an appropriate policy individually. In this experiment heuristic agents behave considerably better then their peers.

We can see in table 3, in the best results column, that agents in *Social Heterogeneous* and *Heuristic* environments have better results than their counterparts

Table 3. Best and average test results in experiment 2 for each scenario-algorithm pair, ordered by best test averages

Scenario	Alg.	Best test avg	Avg in test	Std. Dev.
Social Heu.	QL	0.12291	0.12176	0.0006
Social Heu.	Heu.	0.12227	0.12165	0.0000
Social Heu.	EA	0.12201	0.11940	0.0015
Social Het.	QL	0.11507	0.10721	0.0062
Social Het.	EA	0.11477	0.10822	0.0077
Individual	EA	0.11462	0.10661	0.0071
Social Hom.	EA	0.11290	0.10693	0.0040
Individual	QL	0.11079	0.08840	0.0059
Social Hom.	QL	0.10820	0.08990	0.0094

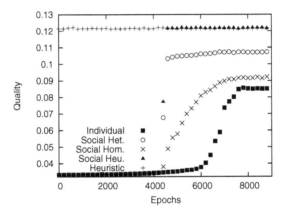

Fig. 3. Training results for QL agents in experiment 2

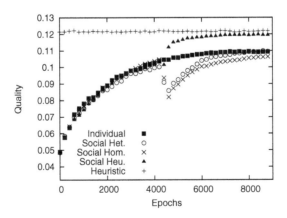

Fig. 4. Training results for EA agents in experiment 2

in *Individual* scenarios, and that when advised by heuristic experts, both QL and EA-agents achieve similar performances.

The average results are very similar to the best in terms of the ordering of agents and scenarios, although the ordering of *Individual* and *Homogeneous* trials is reversed for both types of agents. Also, QL-agents in *Heterogeneous* scenarios exhibit slightly better best performances than EA-agents (their teachers for a long period in these scenarios). The same type of phenomenon can be observed in *Social Heuristic* scenarios. This is, in a small measure, the type of effect we were hoping to find, which consists in the advisee surpassing its advisor and becoming itself the teacher for its peers (including, sometimes, its previous advisor).

In Fig. 3 we can clearly see the effects of *advice-exchange* in the average training behavior of QL-agents. The most interesting fact is that, contrary to the previous experiment, exchanging advice amongst agents of the same type improves considerably the performance of QL-agents, which means that by exchanging information they are able to learn better, in average, than when working individually. However, this effect is hardly noticeable in the best test results. This difference between train and test results can be attributed to a sharper definition of the best action for each state when using *advice-exchange* during training. This effect (the improvement in the scores in *Homogeneous trials*) is not noticeable in the learning curves of EA-agents (Fig. 4).

In summary, QL-agents benefit from *advice-exchange*, being able, not only to copy their teachers, but often to have slightly higher performances than the agents from which they received advice. This effect in QL-agents can be attributed to a more stable strategy or to a fine tuning of the solution proposed by their EA peers. EA-agents do not seem to benefit so clearly, in average, from *advice-exchange* as their QL-peers, although the best results are similar to those of the advisors. This indicates some instability in the training of social EA-agents. By observing the learning curves and the test logs we can conclude that some of this instability can be attributed to the change from Heuristic to QL advisors.

6   Discussion

One of the main reasons for the selection of these two algorithms (QL and EA) to test *advice-exchange* in the pursuit domain was that they have quite different internal structures and exploration strategies. EA usually climbs faster to a reasonable quality plateau. QL-agents often take very long to find a solution, in some cases failing to reach any solution within the experiment time-frame; However, after having solved the problem a few times, they quickly learn to perform at an expert level. The intended effect of exchanging advice would be that different agents could pull each other out of local maxima, thus achieving better performances than when trained in *Individual* scenarios.

The following paragraphs report and summarize the observations made, both in these, as well as in previous experiments reported in [2].

The use of absolute best and current quality measures in the decision of whether or not to get advice leads to worse results than the use of their relative counterparts (cq_i and bq_i) because a spurious good result can lead an agent that does not have a solid strategy to give others "bad advice".

The use of *advice-exchange* early in the training, although it improves the initial learning rate, may lead to local maxima, i.e. non-optimal strategies that are similar to the ones obtained by their advisors.

In problems where EA-agents reach a reasonable score and QL-agents are unable to solve the problem, the advice from EA-agents is beneficial and leads to considerably better average results for social QL-agents. In the reverse situation (problems where QL-agents perform better), most EA-agents benefit from the advice of their QL-peers near the end of the training, but some are unable to profit from the teachings and in some cases performance drops when agents fail to switch from their previous solution to the new one and use an in-between strategy, which is frequently very poor. This performance drop can also occur when agents are trying to learn a strategy that requires two cooperating partners, and the other partner is not be requesting advice, or is advised by the wrong advisor. In this case the "teamwork" that originated the good score of the advisor is never achieved.

The frequent exchange of advisor during training may cause severe instability in both types of agents. Being unable to concentrate on learning one strategy, and getting conflicting advice from several advisors frequently leads agents to long periods of low scores. Also, the sudden withdrawal of advice can hurt advisees. Its was observed that when an agent did not have a consolidated policy its performance could drop to low levels as soon as it stopped requesting advice. This happens mainly in experiment 2, which requires a long sequence of similar actions with low reward to achieve a capture.

To solve the problems mentioned above several new concepts were introduced. The measures in which agents base their decisions are not instantaneous but calculated using a window, or an infinite horizon technique, based on the values that need to be accessed. This contributes to the improvement of the decision of when to get advice and in the choice of advisors.

The problem of early convergence to local maxima due to exchange of advice was mitigated by the introduction of an initial period where agents are not allowed to exchange advice. At this time the period is still a pre-set parameter but it can easily be defined as a condition based on the derivative of the performance of an agent, similarly to many criteria for stopping training. When this derivative approaches zero for a certain number of epochs we can conclude that the agent will not be able to improve its performance any further alone, and proceed in the process of getting advice. It is important to mention that this solution, although it leads to better final scores, does so at the expense of a slower initial convergence in QL-agents.

Due to the specific nature of the learning algorithms we have noticed that QL-agents are much easier to advise than their EA peers. We have introduced *advice-replay* to cope with this disadvantage of EA-agents. Improvements in the time EA-agents take to incorporate advice and improve their scores were clearly noticeable. We are, nevertheless, fully aware that the more efficient the advice intake procedure is, the easier it is to have all agents rapidly going to the same area of the search-space with a consequent loss of diversity.

The problem of learning joint strategies from another group was solved by exchanging *advisor preferences*. This consists in one agent sending a message to its partner advising it to trust a given agent. This solution is reasonable for a problem where the partners are clearly identified, but refinements must be made for cases when it is unclear which are the cooperating partners.

Another problem was the frequent exchange of advisors. This was dealt with by giving preference to the last advisor. This simple strategy has clearly diminished the instabilities in training during *advice-exchange*.

The most important aspects in exchanging information are in the selection of when, and from where, to get this information. The decision of "when" is based on the relative quality statistics, mentioned above and in the concepts of *"self-confidence"* and *"confused about a given state"*. The first has a twofold effect, it prevents spurious bad results from leading an agent to seek advice (possibly abandoning a good strategy) and provides an advisee-agent the extra-time necessary to solidify its strategy after a sequence of advice. The second concept is a first step to define agents' learning stages. At some points an agent does not need continuous advice (because it has a relatively good score) but is sometimes unclear as to which is the best response for a given state. It is important, at this stage to ask for help only in some situations and be critical about the advice that is given. This may be considered an intermediate learning stage in which the agent makes the transition from continuous advice to autonomous exploration. The *"confused about state"* condition makes this transition easier and less turbulent.

The other important aspect that needs to be solved when dealing with exchange of information is: "where" to get it from. It was soon evident that in certain problems the agent with the best score was not the best advisor for all or part of its peers. This can happen due to a number of reasons, most of which were mentioned above: spurious good results, advisor is using a joint strategy, dynamics of the advisor's environment are not similar enough to the advisee, etc. To solve the problems that we have faced in the choice of advisors we used the concept of *trust*. Trust is a measure of how useful the advice of other agents was in the past to a given agent. This has also contributed to stabilize the *advice-exchange* process by helping agents to choose better advisors.

Table 4 presents a comparison of the average duration of a trial in several different scenarios. It is important to notice that in *Heuristic* scenarios there are 10 agents in 5 arenas, while other scenarios have only 8 agents in 4 arenas. As for all other characteristics all scenarios are in equal stand. The most time-consuming event in the trials is undoubtedly *advice-replay*, without which the difference between individual and social scenarios in terms of computation time would be considerably lower.

Table 4. Average time per trial (in seconds) measured in 11 trials on the 20x20 scenario

Scenario	Avg time (sec)
Individual	263
Social Heu.	970
Social Het.	1696

As mentioned above, there are still some problems that need to be addressed, namely:

– Improve procedures for coordinated learning of joint strategies.
– Consider options to adaptively balance the choice between individual exploration and reliance on advice.
– Automate the choice of values for the majority of the parameters that in these experiments are pre-set.
– Create the means to modify the learning behavior according to the phase of the training (initial, high climb, stabilization or fine-tuning).
– Study how to combine information from different sources.

One of the main expectations that drives this research is to create teams of agents that through communication may be able to learn more and faster than the same number of agents could when working individually. This was observed so far only in a minor scale and mostly in the harder problems with which we have experimented. It is important to assert if this behavior does occur in larger scale, and, if so, under which circumstances.

7   Conclusions and Future Research

The results obtained show that *advice-exchange* can be beneficial for the performance of learning agents even when the exchanged information is very simple. In both experiments, the type of agents that has lower performances achieves better scores when being advised. The use of *advice-exchange* in situations where the action of an agent depends on the strategy of others requires added capabilities on the part of agents to select and combine information from several sources, or to make better use of meta-learning information, such as the results of other agents or their effectiveness as advisors. The performance of most social agents can achieve levels similar or sometimes slightly higher than the best of the peers they have contact with, but clear improvements over the performance of the best of the members of a group were not observed in these experiments.

The process of human learning has several stages of growing autonomy: imitation; seeking advice for a complete solution; seeking advice for a particular step of a solution, or for how to relate a new problem with previous ones and, finally, a relatively autonomous stage where people simply request opinions to some trusted peers to increase the confidence in the solutions they have learned, or to adapt themselves to new situations. The introduction of these stages of evolution in the process of *advice-exchange* can be an interesting step towards the development of a technique that can autonomously shift the way in which advice is being used.

The application of similar methods to other type of learning agents, as well as other problems, is also an important step in the validation of this approach. The undergoing research in a traffic-control problem, as an extension of the work presented in [19], is of great importance to the validation of this technique in a more complex environment.

A development of the way *trust* is used by agents, associating it with agent-situation pairs, may allow the advisee to differentiate who is the expert on the particular situation it is facing and improve the effectiveness of *advice-exchange*. Another interesting issue is that humans usually offer unsolicited advice for some situations. Either great new discoveries or actions that may be harmful for the advisee seem to be of paramount importance in the use of advice. Rendering unsolicited advice at critical points, also seems like a promising approach to improve the skills of a group of learning agents. The same applies to the combination of advice from several sources.

Our major aim is to, through a set of experiments, derive some principles and laws under which learning in the Multiagent Systems framework proves to be more effective than, and inherently different from, just having agents learning as individuals.

References

1. Clouse, J.A.: On integrating apprentice learning and reinforcement learning. PhD thesis, University of Massachusetts, Department of Computer Science (1997)
2. Nunes, L., Oliveira, E.: Advice-exchange in heterogeneous groups of learning agents. Technical Report 1 12/02, FEUP/LIACC (2002)
3. Whitehead, S.D.: A complexity analysis of cooperative mechanisms in reinforcement learning. Proc. of the 9th National Conf. on AI (AAAI-91) (1991) 607–613
4. Clouse, J.A., Utgoff, P.E.: Two kinds of training information for evaluation function learning. In: Proc. of AAAI'91. (1991)
5. Clouse, J., Utgoff, P.: A teaching method for reinforcement learning. In: Proc. of the 9th Int. Conf. on Machine Learning. (1992) 92–101
6. Lin, L.J.: Self-improving reactive agents based on reinforcement learning, planning and teaching. Machine Learning **8** (1992) 293–321
7. Tan, M.: Multi-agent reinforcement learning: Independent vs. cooperative agents. In: Proc. of the Tenth Int. Conf. on Machine Learning. (1993) 330–337
8. Price, B., Boutilier, C.: Implicit imitation in multiagent reinforcement learning. In: Proc. of the Sixteenth Int. Conf. on Machine Learning. (1999) 325–334
9. Sen, S., Kar, P.P.: Sharing a concept. In: Working Notes of the AAAI-02 Spring Symposium on Collaborative Learning Agents. (2002)
10. Watkins, C.J.C.H., Dayan, P.D.: Technical note: Q-learning. Machine Learning **8** (1992) 279–292
11. Rumelhart, D.E., Hinton, G.E., Williams, R.J.: Learning internal representations by error propagation. Parallel Distributed Processing: Exploration in the Microstructure of Cognition **1** (1986) 318–362
12. Kaelbling, L.P., Littman, M.L., Moore, A.W.: Reinforcement learning: A survey. Journal of Artificial Intelligence Research **4** (1996)

13. Nunes, L., Oliveira, E.: Advice exchange between evolutionary algorithms and reinforcement learning agents: Experimental results in the pursuit domain. Technical Report 2 03/03, FEUP/LIACC (2003)
14. Holland, J.H.: Adaptation in Natural and Artificial Systems. University of Michigan Press (1975)
15. Koza, J.R.: Genetic programming: On the Programming of Computers by Means of Natural Selection. MIT Press, Cambridge MA (1992)
16. Salustowicz, R.: A Genetic Algorithm for the Topological Optimization of Neural Networks. PhD thesis, Tech. Univ. Berlin (1995)
17. Yao, X.: Evolving artificial neural networks. In: Proc. of IEEE. Volume 87. (1999) 1423–1447
18. Glickman, M., Sycara, K.: Evolution of goal-directed behavior using limited information in a complex environment. In: Proc. of the Genetic and Evolutionary Computation Conference, (GECCO-99). (1999)
19. Nunes, L., Oliveira, E.: On learning by exchanging advice. In: Proc. of the First Symposium on Adaptive Agents and Multi-Agent Systems (AISB'02). (2002)
20. Benda, M., Jagannathan, V., Dodhiawalla, R.: On optimal cooperation of knowledge resources. Technical Report BCS G-2012-28, Boeing AI Center, Boeing Computer Services, Bellevue, WA (1985)
21. Haynes, T., Wainwright, R., Sen, S., Schoenfeld, D.: Strongly typed genetic programming in evolving cooperation strategies. In: Proc. of the Sixth Int. Conf. on Genetic Algorithms. (1995) 271–278
22. Sen, S., Sekaran, M., Hale, J.: Lerning to coordinate without sharing information. In: Proc. of the National Conf. on AI. (1994) 426–431
23. Sen, S., Sekaran, M.: Individual learning of coordination knowledge. Journal of Experimental, Theoretical Artificial Intelligence **10** (1998) 333–356

Evolving Strategies for Agents in the Iterated Prisoner's Dilemma in Noisy Environments

Colm O'Riordan

Dept. of Information Technology,
National University of Ireland,
Galway, Ireland
colmor@it.nuigalway.ie

Abstract. In this paper, we discuss the co-evolution of agents in a multi-agent system where agents interact with each other. These interactions are modelled in an abstract manner using ideas from game theory. This paper focuses on the iterated prisoner's dilemma (IPD). We discuss properties that we believe to be of importance with respect to fitness of strategies in traditional environments and also in environments where noise is present. Specifically, we discuss the notion of *forgiveness*, where strategies attempt to forgive strategies that defect in the game, with the aim of increasing the level of cooperation present. We study these strategies by using evolutionary computation which provides a powerful means to search the large range of strategies' features.

1   Introduction

The prisoner's dilemma and the iterated prisoner's dilemma have received much attention in a number of domains [2], particularly since work by Axelrod in the 1980s [1]. Further research in the iterated prisoner's dilemma is still warranted as in many domains, for example, multi-agent systems, the assumption of cooperative behaviour is still made. Furthermore, a noise-free environment is often assumed which is not valid in certain domains. An *intended* cooperative gesture (a move in the game) by one participant may be interpreted as a non-cooperative gesture by the receiver due to a number of reasons (for example, ambiguity in the message; conflicting goals and differences in ontologies maintained by the participant). A transmitted gesture may be lost or damaged in transmission. These potential problems may result in a cooperative gesture being recognised by the receiver as a defective gesture and vice versa.

This problem has not been widely studied, with only a handful of researchers considering noise and errors in the iterated prisoner's dilemma [4, 11, 12, 13, 5].

Recent work in the iterated prisoner's dilemma has shown the usefulness of *forgiveness* in helping to overcome mutual defection on behalf of participants. This has been demonstrated in static environments playing against well known strategies [14] and also in fixed, noise-free evolutionary settings [15].

This paper presents recent results obtained in experiments dealing with the iterated prisoner's dilemma in both noise-free and noisy environments in a

D. Kudenko et al. (Eds.): Adaptive Agents and MAS II, LNAI 3394, pp. 205–215, 2005.

co-evolutionary setting. In these simulations, strategies play a finitely repeated game. However none of the strategies under investigation contain features to exploit end-game scenarios[1]. The approach taken in this research has been to design strategies based on heuristics, to validate these strategies in fixed environments and to search the range of properties of these strategies using co-evolutionary simulations. Populations of strategies playing the iterated prisoner's dilemma are co-evolved and the level of cooperation in these societies is studied. We compare the co-evolution of strategies which may *forgive* with the co-evolution of strategies that do not incorporate *forgiveness*.

Section 2 presents related research in the areas of the prisoner's dilemma, noisy environments and the *forgiving* strategy for noisy environments. Section 3 presents the experimental set-up and discusses results regarding the co-evolution of strategies. The paper concludes with some observations regarding the evolved strategies and their properties.

2   Related Research

2.1   Prisoner's Dilemma

In the prisoner's dilemma game, two players are both faced with a decision— to either cooperate(C) or defect(D). The decision is made by a player with no knowledge of the other player's choice. The game is often expressed in the canonical form in terms of pay-offs:

	Player 1	
	C	D
Player 2 C	(λ_1, λ_1)	(λ_2, λ_3)
D	(λ_3, λ_2)	(λ_4, λ_4)

where the pairs of values represent the pay-offs (rewards) for players Player 1 and Player 2 respectively. In order for a dilemma to the exist, the following must also hold: $\lambda_3 < \lambda_4 < \lambda_1 < \lambda_2$, where λ_2 is the temptation to defect, λ_3 is the sucker's payoff, λ_1 is the reward for mutual cooperation and λ_4 is the punishment for mutual defection. The constraint $2\lambda_1 > \lambda_2 + \lambda_3$ also holds.

In the iterated version, two players will play numerous games (the exact number not known to either player). Each player adopts a strategy to determine whether to cooperate or defect on each of the moves in the iterated game. A number of different classes of strategies can be identified:

- periodic strategies play C or D in a periodic manner. Common strategies include *all-c*, *all-d*, $(CD)^*$, $(DC)^*$, $(CCD)^*$, etc.
- random strategies which have some random behaviour. These can be totally random, or one of the other types of strategies, (e.g. periodic), with a degree of randomness.

---

[1] In a finite game of N iterations, it is rational for a player to defect on the last move, and, therefore, to defect throughout the game.

- strategies based on some history of moves, e.g. *tit-for-tat* (C initially, then D if an opponent defects, or C if an opponent cooperates), *spiteful* (C initially, C as long as an opponent cooperates, but if an opponent defects then D forever), *probers* (play some fixed string, example *(DDC)* and then decide to play *tit-for-tat* or *all-d* (to exploit non-retaliatory strategies)), *soft-majo* (C initially, then cooperate if an opponent is not defecting more than cooperating).

There are many variations on the above types of strategies.

In the iterated prisoner's dilemma, no best strategy exists; the success of a strategy depends on the other strategies present. For example, in a collection of strategies who defect continually (*all-d*) the best strategy to adopt is *all-d*. However, in a collection of strategies adopting a *tit-for-tat* strategy, an *all-d* strategy would not perform well.

2.2   Noisy Environments

The majority of work in the iterated prisoner's dilemma has concentrated on the game in a noise-free environment, i.e. there is no danger of a signal being misinterpreted by the opponent or of the signal being damaged in transit. However, this assumption of a noise-free environment is not necessarily valid if one is trying to model real-world scenarios. Different means can result in noise existing in an IPD environment:

- mis-implementation (when a player makes a mistake implementing its choice), or
- mis-perception (when a player misperceives another player's signal or choice).

Fudenberg et al. [8], argue that "if mistakes are possible, evolution may tend to weed out strategies that impose drastic penalties for deviations". Kahn and Murnighan [11] find that, in experiments dealing with the iterated prisoner's dilemma in noisy environments, the level of cooperation is affected when noise and uncertainty is present. Miller's experiments in genetic algorithms applied to the prisoner's dilemma result in the conclusion that cooperation is at its greatest when there is no noise in the system and that this cooperation decreases as the level of noise increases [12].

Hoffman [10] reports that results are sensitive to the extent to which players make mistakes (mis-implementation or mis-perception). For example, in a game between two *tit-for-tats*, a single error would trigger a series of alternating defections.

For example, where the fourth move by `tit-for-tat(2)` is the result of noise:

```
tit-for-tat(1): C C C C D C D  . . .
tit-for-tat(2): C C C D C D C  . . .
```

This results in the two strategies alternating between receiving the maximum payoff (λ_2) and the sucker's payoff (λ_3).

To further motivate the need to study strategies for the prisoner's dilemma in noisy environments, it is worth considering the effect of noise on well-known, well-researched strategies. If we consider two *tit-for-tat* strategies interacting in a noise free environment, we obtain an ongoing mutual cooperation. Introducing noise (=p, the probability that a cooperative move is implemented as a defection) we get four possible states—mutual cooperation, mutual defection and states where strategy is cooperating and the other defecting. This is illustrated in the state transition diagram in Figure 1.

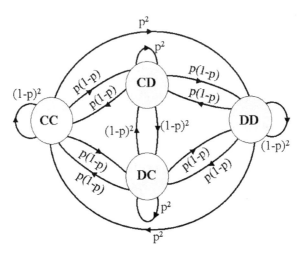

Fig. 1. State transition diagram for two *tit-for-tat* strategies in a noisy environment

This gives the following transition matrix (P):

$$\begin{pmatrix} (1-p)^2 & (1-p)p & (1-p)p & p^2 \\ p(1-p) & p^2 & (1-p)^2 & p(1-p) \\ p(1-p) & p^2 & (1-p)^2 & p(1-p) \\ p^2 & (1-p)p & (1-p)p & (1-p)^2 \end{pmatrix}$$

We can solve this (see Appendix), for any value of p greater than zero, to show that strategies will spend 25% of the time in a state of mutual cooperation, 25% of the time in mutual defection, 25% of the time receiving the sucker's payoff (λ_3) and the remainder of the time receiving the λ_2 (the temptation to defect). We can see, therefore, that the presence of noise is detrimental to the overall fitness of a society of *tit-for-tat* like strategies. We can do similar analysis for other simple strategies and derive the amount of time spent in each state, given an infinite game.

Empirical analysis of societies of homogeneous agents (i.e. all playing the same strategy) further illustrates the need to study forms of *forgiveness* in noisy environments. In Figure 2, we plot the fitness of three homogeneous societies of strategies: *tit-for-tat*, *all-c* and *spiteful*.

We see that *all-c* is not affected, to a large extent, by the introduction of noise and the fitness of the society remains high. This is as expected as *all-c*

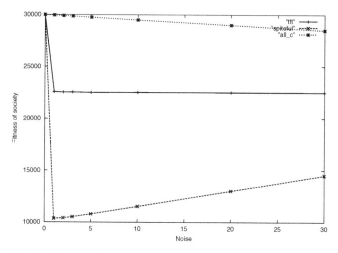

Fig. 2. Fitness of societies of strategies in noisy environments

does not retaliate and punish defections by the opposing strategy. The effect of noise would be similar for any periodic, non-reactive strategy. However, we see that the fitness in the society of *tit-for-tat* strategies falls dramatically with the introduction of noise. The society of *spiteful* strategies is seriously affected by the introduction of even a small amount of noise. The society will obtain low scores as strategies spend the majority of time in a state of mutual defection. If noise continues to increases, the overall fitness increases as strategies have a higher chance of obtaining scores other than the score for mutual defection.

2.3   The Forgiving Strategy

In earlier work [14], we explored the notion of *forgiveness*—the ability or readiness to play cooperatively in the game once *mutual* defection has been detected[2]. The type of *forgiveness* we reported was of a reactive nature, where cooperative gestures were played immediately following a defection. We argue, and demonstrate with empirical results, that in both clean and noisy environments, the willingness to break spirals of mutual defection by incorporating a degree of *forgiveness* is a useful trait.

Figure 3 shows the fitness of *forgiving* in comparison to the strategies of *tit-for-tat, all-c* and *spiteful*. We see that noise affects the fitness of the *forgiving* strategy, but that the decrease in fitness is not as dramatic as that for *tit-for-tat* and *spiteful*. The fitness of *all-c* is affected less by noise than *forgiving*. However, *all-c* will be exploited by other strategies whereas *forgiving* will not be exploited.

In previous work, we use an evolutionary approach to examine the behaviour of *forgiving* strategies. We encode, in each chromosome, several aspects of a strategy's behaviour. These include:

---

[2] Note that this differs from Axelrod's notion of contrition which is played by strategies to recover from the effect of their own defective behaviour.

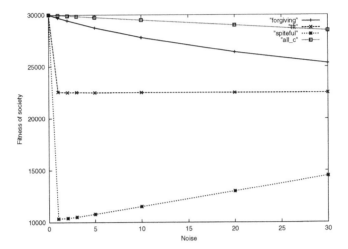

Fig. 3. Fitness of *forgiving* in noisy environments

1. behaviour on the first move,
2. behaviour following a defection by an opponent,
3. behaviour following a cooperation by an opponent,
4. whether the strategy *forgives* or not,
5. the number of mutual defections to allow before beginning the *forgiving* behaviour,
6. the number of successive cooperative gestures to make in order to *forgive*,
7. the number of times a strategy *forgives* in a game.

In the initial experiments, the evolved strategies played with a set of well-known fixed strategies which were not subjected to evolutionary pressures. On all trials the first genes corresponding to the first three features converge extremely quickly and confirm findings by many others—cooperate on first move, cooperate following a cooperation and defect following a defection.

The fourth gene converges to 1 (*forgiveness* is selected), indicating that a *forgiving* behaviour is a useful feature for any strategy to maintain. The degree of *forgiveness* and the length of the spiral varied in the trials. These experiments allowed us to explore a range of attributes of *forgiving* strategies.

Further experiments involved co-evolving a set of strategies where the initial set of strategies were created randomly and evolved in the environment of strategies playing the iterated prisoner's dilemma.

In these experiments, we see that *forgiving* quickly becomes the norm where strategies choose to forgive strategies with whom they are locked in a mutual spiral of defection. Furthermore, we see that cooperation on the first move is not always selected as the norm in all runs. We believe that the presence of *forgiveness* in the population reduces the evolutionary advantage conferred on those that initially cooperate, as the danger of mutual defection is not as costly to strategies that are likely to forgive.

3   Experimental Setup

Evolutionary computation approaches have been used previously by other researchers to explore the range of strategies. These include Beaufils [3], Harrald and Fogel [9], Cohen et al. [6] and Darwen [7]. In our experiments, we adopt a co-evolutionary approach where the fitness of a particular strategy is determined by its performance against the rest of the population. Hence, we have a changing environment where a strategy that is fit at a given time may not necessarily be fit at a future time. In effect, we have different selective pressures at different times.

We aim to identify the properties of the strategies that promote cooperation. In order to do this, we identify a set of features which define classes of strategies and utilise a genetic algorithm to search the space of strategies. The fitness of a given strategy, and its associated features, is dependent on the rest of the population, thus the fitness of the landscape changes from generation to generation.

All experiments are carried out in two different environments:

- noiseless environment, and
- noisy environment.

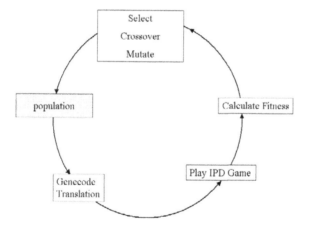

Fig. 4. Simulator Design

Figure 4 presents a high level view of the architecture of the simulator used. Following the creation of the initial population (randomly chosen) the following steps are repeated for a number of population generations:

1. Gene-code Translation: each gene-code is translated to a set of features which define a strategy. For example, the following gene-code:

   1101 00110 00101 00100

   would be interpreted as indicated in Table 1.

Table 1. Interpretation of genecodes

Gene code feature	Interpretation
1	Cooperate on first move
1	follow a defection with a defection
0	follow a cooperative gesture with a cooperation
1	forgive if in a spiral of defection
00110	the spiral will be of length 6
00101	the strategy will forgive by playing 5 cooperative gestures
00100	the strategy will forgive 4 times.

2. Play IPD Game: for the length of the game, each strategy plays a move.
3. Calculate Fitness: the fitness of each strategy (and its corresponding gene-code) is calculated based on its relative performance in the game.
4. Run Genetic Algorithm: A simple canonical genetic algorithm is utilised with the following parameters:
   (a) linear ranking selection.
   (b) operators of 1-point crossover and mutation.
   This generates a new population and the process repeats.

We run a number of simulations, varying the parameters which are fixed. For each simulation, we run the co-evolutionary model in a noise-free environment and in an environment with 1% noise. In our experiments we measure the average degree of cooperation over time by counting the number of cooperative gestures played per game per turn. Hence, the maximum average degree of cooperation is 2.

Four sets of experiments are run with the following parameters:

- a population size of 100,
- the number of generations is 3000,
- the degree of crossover is 90% and the degree of mutation is 1%.

The four experiments are as follows:

1. *tit-for-tat*-like strategies: A family of strategies with the first three of the parameters listed.
2. *forgiving* strategies: A family of strategies with all of the parameters listed.
3. fixed-*forgiving*(1) strategies: A family of strategies where *forgiving* is enforced but all parameters relating to *forgiveness* are evolved over time.
4. fixed-*forgiving*(2) strategies: A family of strategies where all parameters relating to *forgiveness* are fixed at constant values, but whether or not a strategy is *forgiving* is evolved.

The following table presents the average cooperation and standard deviation obtained in the experiments for each of the settings. The experiments were run 20 times.

Table 2. Experimental Results

Experiment	Noise Free Avg. Coop., St. Dev.	1 % noise Avg. Coop, St. Dev.
1 *tft*-family%	1.0312 (0.0007)	0.92745 (0.0007)
2 *forgiving*-family%	1.1109 (0.0002)	1.1381 (0.0005)
3 *forgiving*(1)%	1.1978 (0.0008)	1.2177 (0.0003)
4 *forgiving*(2)%	1.1069 (0.0003)	1.0075 (0.0006)

There is strong evidence (p value < 0.001) to suggest higher mean average co-operation with *forgiveness* (Experiment 2) over the *tit-for-tat*-family population (Experiment 1) (95% confidence interval) for both noisy and noise-free populations.

In individual runs, the existence of *forgiveness* is not stable. Cycle effects are noted in the population. Once *forgiveness* spreads in the population and cooperation increases, there is a selective pressure on strategies to exploit *forgiving* strategies by not forgiving. This leads to dramatic collapses in the number of forgiving strategies in the population. This can lead to a state of increased non cooperative behaviour. However, different features of the strategies interact in a complex manner and we can notice a shielding effect where features have little effect for generations due to the values of other genes. This in turn leads to a degree of genetic drift which can again, lead to the spread of cooperation and *forgiveness*.

4   Conclusion

The iterated prisoner's dilemma is an oft-studied game in many domains. This paper examined some features of strategies playing the game. Initially we explored the concept of *forgiveness* (the ability of a strategy to cooperate following a spiral of defections). We found that in a fixed environment, a designed *forgiving* strategy flourished, that in an evolutionary setting *forgiveness* was also selected for and finally, in a co-evolutionary setting, we showed that a selective advantage was conferred upon *forgiving* strategies.

We also investigated the effect of introducing noise into the system. The introduction of a low level of noise into the system has an immediate effect on well-known strategies and we demonstrated that their willingness to react to defections causes a decrease in their fitness. In the co-evolutionary experiments we see that *forgiveness*, although useful, does not result in a stable society.

References

1. R. Axelrod. *The Evolution of Cooperation*. Basic Books, New York, 1984.
2. R. Axelrod and L. D'Ambrosio. An annotated bibliography on the evolution of cooperation. *http://www.ipps.lsa.umich.edu/ipps/papers/coop/ Evol_of_Coop_Bibliography.txt*, October 1994.

3. B. Beaufils, P. Mathieu, and J.-P. Delahaye. Complete classes of strategies for the classical iterated prisoner's dilemma. In *Proceedings of Evolutionary Programming VII, LNCS vol 1447*, pages 33–41. Springer-Verlag, 1998.

4. J. Bendor, R.M. Kramer, and S. Stout. When in doubt cooperation in a noisy prisoner's dilemma. *Journal of Conflict Resolution*, 35(4):691–719, 1991.

5. S. Y. Chong and X. Yao. The impact of noise on iterated prisoner's dilemma with multiple levels of cooperation. In *Proceedings of the 2004 Congress on Evolutionary Computation (CEC'04)*, pages 348–355, 2004.

6. M.D. Cohen, R.L. Riolo, and R. Axelrod. The emergence of social organization in the prisoner's dilemma: How context-preservation and other factors promote cooperation. Technical report, SantaFe Institute, 1999.

7. P. Darwen and X. Yao. Co-evolution in iterated prisoner's dilemma with intermediate levels of cooperation: Application to missile defense. *International Journal of Computational Intelligence and Applications*, 2(1):83–107, 2002.

8. D. Fudenberg and E. Maskin. Evolution and cooperation in noisy repeated games. *The American Economic Review*, 80(2):274–179, 1990.

9. P. Harrald and D. Fogel. Evolving continuous behaviours in the iterated prisoner's dilemma. *Biosystems*, 37:135–145, 1996.

10. R. Hoffman. Twenty years on: The evolution of cooperation revisited. *Journal of Artificial Societies and Simulation*, 3(2), 2000.

11. L.M. Kahn and J.K. Murnighan. Conjecture, uncertainty, and cooperation in prisoner's dilemma games: Some experimental evidence. *Journal of Economic Behaviour & Organisation*, 22:91–117, 1993.

12. J.H. Miller. The coevolution of automata in the repeated prisoner's dilemma. *Journal of Economic Behaviour & Organisation*, 29:87–112, 1996.

13. U. Mueller. Optimal retaliation for optimal cooperation. *Journal of Conflict Resolution*, 31(4):692–724, 1988.

14. C. O'Riordan. A *forgiving* strategy for the iterated prisoner's dilemma. *Journal of Artificial Societies and Social Simulation*, 3(4), 2000.

15. C. O'Riordan. Forgiveness in the iterated prisoner's dilemma and cooperation in multi-agent systems. *UKMAS-4*, December 2001.

Solution to State Transition Diagram:

The state transition diagram gives the following transition matrix:

$$\begin{pmatrix} (1-p)^2 & (1-p)p & (1-p)p & p^2 \\ p(1-p) & p^2 & (1-p)^2 & p(1-p) \\ p(1-p) & p^2 & (1-p)^2 & p(1-p) \\ p^2 & (1-p)p & (1-p)p & (1-p)^2 \end{pmatrix}$$

$\Rightarrow$

$$\begin{pmatrix} (1-p)^2 & (1-p)p & (1-p)p & p^2 \\ p(1-p) & p^2 & (1-p)^2 & p(1-p) \\ p(1-p) & p^2 & (1-p)^2 & p(1-p) \\ p^2 & (1-p)p & (1-p)p & (1-p)^2 \end{pmatrix} \begin{pmatrix} \alpha_1 \\ \alpha_2 \\ \alpha_3 \\ \alpha_4 \end{pmatrix} = \begin{pmatrix} \alpha_1 \\ \alpha_2 \\ \alpha_3 \\ \alpha_4 \end{pmatrix}$$

$\Rightarrow$

$$(1 - 2p + p^2)\alpha_1 + (p - p^2)\alpha_2 + (p - p^2)\alpha_3 + p^2\alpha_4 = \alpha_1$$
$$(p - p^2)\alpha_1 + (p^2)\alpha_2 + (1 - 2p + p^2)\alpha_3 + (p - p^2)\alpha_4 = \alpha_2$$
$$(p - p^2)\alpha_1 + (p^2)\alpha_2 + (1 - 2p + p^2)\alpha_3 + (p - p^2)\alpha_4 = \alpha_3$$
$$(p^2)\alpha_1 + (p - p^2)\alpha_2 + (p - p^2)\alpha_3 + (1 - 2p + p^2)\alpha_4 = \alpha_4$$

Gathering terms for p^2, p and constants, $\Rightarrow$

$$p^2(\alpha_1 - \alpha_2 - \alpha_3 + \alpha_4) + p(-2\alpha_1 + \alpha_2 + \alpha_3) + \alpha_1 = \alpha_1 \quad \text{(i)}$$
$$p^2(-\alpha_1 + \alpha_2 + \alpha_3 - \alpha_4) + p(\alpha_1 - 2\alpha_3 + \alpha_4) + \alpha_3 = \alpha_2 \quad \text{(ii)}$$
$$p^2(-\alpha_1 + \alpha_2 + \alpha_3 - \alpha_4) + p(\alpha_1 - 2\alpha_3 + \alpha_4) + \alpha_3 = \alpha_3 \quad \text{(iii)}$$
$$p^2(\alpha_1 - \alpha_2 - \alpha_3 + \alpha_4) + p(\alpha_2 + \alpha_3 - 2\alpha_4) + \alpha_4 = \alpha_4 \quad \text{(iv)}$$

From (i) and (iv) above:

$$-2\alpha_1 + \alpha_2 + \alpha_3 = \alpha_2 + \alpha_3 - 2\alpha_4$$

$$\Rightarrow \alpha_1 = \alpha_4$$

Substituting α_4 for α_1 in (ii) and (iii), rewriting and equating, we get:

$$\alpha_1 = \alpha_3 \text{ and } \alpha_1 = \alpha_2$$

$$\Rightarrow \alpha_1 = \alpha_2 = \alpha_3 = \alpha_4$$

Given, $\Sigma_{i=1}^4 \alpha_i = 1$, we have $\forall \alpha_i, \alpha_i = \frac{1}{4}$

Experiments in Subsymbolic Action Planning with Mobile Robots

John Pisokas and Ulrich Nehmzow

Dept. of Computer Science, University of Essex, Wivenhoe Park,
Colchester CO4 3SQ, UK
{jpisso, udfn}@essex.ac.uk

Abstract. The ability to determine a sequence of actions in order to reach a particular goal is of utmost importance to mobile robots. One major problem with *symbolic* planning approaches regards assumptions made by the designer while introducing externally specified world models, preconditions and postconditions. To bypass this problem, it would be desirable to develop mechanisms for action planning that are based on the *agent's* perceptual and behavioural space, rather than on externally supplied symbolic representations. We present a subsymbolic planning mechanism that uses a non-symbolic representation of sensor-action space, learned through the agent's autonomous interaction with the environment.

In this paper, we present experiments with two autonomous mobile robots, which use autonomously learned subsymbolic representations of perceptual and behavioural space to determine goal-achieving sequences of actions. The experimental results we present illustrate that such an approach results in an embodied robot planner that produces plans which are grounded in the robot's perception-action space.

1 Introduction

Determining (Sequences of) Actions. Besides the ability to stay operational (e.g. obstacle avoidance *etc.*) and to navigate, action selection is the third major competence required for autonomously operating mobile robots.

One possibility for achieving action selection is to determine a world model manually, to specify permitted operators (actions) applicable to it, and to use standard artificial intelligence search techniques to find paths through the action space that will lead from an initial state to the goal state. STRIPS [1, 2] is an early example of this approach.

More recently hybrid architectures were developed which employ symbolic planning techniques. They attempt to tackle problems related with symbol grounding [3] by incorporating a reactive layer [4]. Well known examples are SOMASS [5] and ATLANTIS [6].

However, there are substantial weaknesses to approaches involving symbolic representations:

D. Kudenko et al. (Eds.): Adaptive Agents and MAS II, LNAI 3394, pp. 216–229, 2005.

- Because of the external identification of operators, only part of the behavioural space available to the robot may be exploited.
- Similarly, only part of the perceptual space available to the robot may be used, due to the difference of perception and experience of the world between robot and human designer.
- Finally, actual robot perceptions and actions may differ from those defined by the human designer (due to sensor and actuator noise), eventually leading to brittle and unreliable performance.

An alternative would be to let the robot acquire its own subsymbolic world representation, and to let it associate preconditions and postconditions with its behavioural repertoire autonomously.

Action Selection Versus Action Planning. The bulk of research on subsymbolic planning to date has focused on simulated agents, rather than situated, embodied mobile robots. In [7, 8], to name a recent example, simulated robots were able to select *one* optimal action (with respect to a fixed performance criterion), given a perceptual state. In contrast to such 'action selection' mechanisms, we present a mechanism for 'action planning' that allows the association of *multiple* actions with each perceptual state, and the selection of actions with respect to *variable* performance criteria.

Reaction-Diffusion Dynamics. To achieve this, we used the concept of reaction-diffusion dynamics, introduced by [9]. The use of reaction-diffusion dynamics to accomplish a search through a *symbolic* search space was proposed by [10], and has been used frequently in Artificial Intelligence for searching in artificial worlds. Applications such as Tower-of-Hanoi problem or abstract path planning are presented, for instance, in [11] and [12]. In contrast to this work, we use reaction-diffusion dynamics for searching through a *subsymbolic* search space.

Regarding applications in robotics, [13] for instance present a solution to a path planning problem for a real robot arm. However, heuristics were introduced *a priori* (in the form of a gradient descent search) adding *tacit knowledge*[1] component to the planner, making the planner task specific. A similar approach is taken by [12] in a simulated path planning task. In contrast to this approach, we avoid heuristics or other task specific knowledge altogether in the planner.

Contribution. In this paper we present experiments with a subsymbolic action planning mechanism that is based on *learned* representations of the robot's world. The agent autonomously explores its behavioural repertoire and learns its own world representation and precondition-action-postcondition associations. Specific information regarding the technical characteristics of the sensors and actuators is not introduced in the planner. Instead, we leave the mechanism to

---

[1] *Tacit knowledge* is the kind of knowledge that the system cannot reason about. A form of tacit knowledge is the procedural code in a program.

acquire its own representation of the robot's sensor-motor space, and later exploit this knowledge for making plans. Our hypothesis is that such knowledge doesn't need to be introduced to the planner and as we illustrate in sections 3.2 and 3.3 taking this approach we avoid introducing task specific assumptions by the designer and problems of scalability. Any specific sensor characteristics, or indeed difference between sensors of the same type, will be incorporated into the robot's knowledge automatically.

There are similarities here to biological systems, in that the signals transmitted through the nervous system do not convey information about the type of receptor, but merely the signal produced by the receptors [14].

2   The Action Planning Mechanism

The architecture of the subsymbolic planning mechanism is depicted in Figure 1. There are two layers: a perceptual space layer and a behavioural space layer. In the perceptual space layer a self-organising feature map [15] clusters sensory perception (section 2.1). In the behavioural space layer the clusters of the first layer are linked by actions available to the robot (section 2.2). To determine 'paths' between start and goal perceptions, reaction-diffusion dynamics are used (section 2.3).

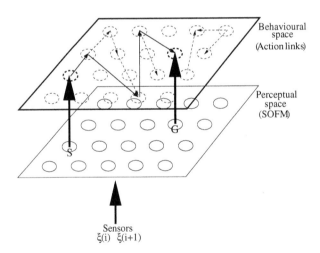

Fig. 1. Architecture of the subsymbolic action planning mechanism. A self-organising feature map clusters sensory perception (perceptual space layer). Action links — between pairs of perceptual clusters — are stored in a second layer (behavioural space layer). 'Goal' and 'start' clusters are denoted with the letters 'G' and 'S' respectively. The result of planning is a list of action links that link the perceptual clusters of start and goal location

2.1   Representation of Perceptual Space

To establish an internal representation of the robot's perceptual space through learning, we used a self-organising feature map (SOFM). There are two reasons for this choice: i) clustering is unsupervised, and therefore does not require clustering teaching signals to be supplied, and ii) clustering is topological, thus counteracting the effects of perceptual noise.

Initially, during the robot's exploration and learning phase, the robot is left to explore its environment executing random motor actions from its behavioural repertoire and collecting perception-action-perception triples. The acquired sensory perceptions are fed into the SOFM and organised in increasingly clear defined clusters. When this phase is completed, raw sensory perception is 'encoded' in a topological fashion by the SOFM.

The weight vectors of the SOFM are initialised as pseudo-random vectors of unit length. As similarity measure we use the Euclidean distance between the input vector $x(t_k)$ and each of the weight vectors $m_i(t_k)$.

$$\|x(t_k) - m_i(t_k)\| \; \forall \, i \in Units \tag{1}$$

where $m_i = \{\mu_{i,1}, \mu_{i,2}, \cdots, \mu_{i,n}\}$ is the weight vector of unit i, $x = \{\xi_1, \xi_2, \cdots, \xi_n\}$ is the input vector, and n is the number of input signals. The weight update rule is:

$$m_i(t_{k+1}) = m_i(t_k) + a(t_k)[x(t_k) - m_i(t_k)] \text{ for } i \in N_c \tag{2}$$
$$m_i(t_{k+1}) = m_i(t_k) \text{ otherwise.} \tag{3}$$

The learning rate a starts with value 1 and progressively decreases to 0, when training stops. $a(t_k)$ is the learning rate at iteration k. The weights update neighbourhood radius N_c starts from $N_c = \frac{\sqrt{Units\ number}}{2}$ and decreases to $N_c = 1$.

After each update the weight vectors are normalised again in order to be unit vectors, using the relationships:

$$\|m_i\| = \sqrt{\mu_{i,1}^2 + \mu_{i,2}^2 + \cdots + \mu_{i,n}^2} \; \forall \, i \in N_c \tag{4}$$

$$m_i = \left\{ \frac{\mu_{i,1}}{\|m_i\|}, \frac{\mu_{i,2}}{\|m_i\|}, \cdots, \frac{\mu_{i,n}}{\|m_i\|} \right\} \; \forall \, i \in N_c. \tag{5}$$

2.2   Representation of Behavioural Space

The robots used in our experiments were given a certain, defined behavioural repertoire of motor actions, e.g. 'move forwards', 'turn left' *etc.*

After the representation of perceptual space (see section 2.1) is completed, the robot uses the perception-action-perception triples acquired while exploring its environment — by executing corresponding actions — to train the behavioural space layer. Obviously, each action performed took the robot from an initial perceptual state to a resulting perceptual state.

Motor actions are therefore linked to perceptions encoded on the SOFM, and are consequently entered into the SOFM as directional action links between initial and final perceptual state labelled with the corresponding action (see figure 1).

In this manner, the robot develops a representation of perception-action-perception triples throughout the exploratory phase (which is terminated after a preset amount of exploratory actions has been performed).

2.3   The Action Selection Mechanism

Once the 'map' described in sections 2.1 and 2.2 is established, it is relatively straightforward to search the map for complete paths between the current (initial) sensory perception and an externally specified goal perception.

One major difficulty here is that either or both of the current physical location and the goal location may never have been visited before, meaning that no entry for them is found in the map. The way we tried to overcome this problem is by exploiting the topological nature of the map: we search for mapped similar (neighbouring) perceptual clusters, and use those for action planning.

The search mechanism used is one of diffusion. Placing an imaginary 'scent' at the start location and spreading it along all existing links pointing out of the start location, the 'scent' will eventually arrive at the goal location in perceptual space, indicating which neighbouring node to the goal (or the goal node itself) network node has a complete path from start to goal.

Once the robot has executed the first motor action of the plan, the planning algorithm as described above is invoked again. This is to avoid errors due to incorrect execution of a motor action (noise, *etc*).

3   Experiments

3.1   Experimental Method

Experiments were conducted with autonomous mobile robots. The robots were capable of moving in 2 dimensional metric space and had a repertoire of four distinct actions (e.g. 'move forwards 50 cm', 'move backwards 50 cm', 'turn left 40°', and 'turn right 40°'). During the experiments the robot's task was to stop at a specified position and orientation in its environment.

The experiments were divided into two distinct phases. During the initial *exploration phase*, the robot explored its environment performing predefined number of randomly selected actions out of its behavioural repertoire, and acquired (i) a subsymbolic representation of perceptual space, using the self-organising feature map (SOFM), and (ii) a representation of perception-action-perception associations. The self-organising feature map that we used was a two dimensional toroid with different size for each experiment, as described in the particular sections. The precondition-action-postcondition associations were stored as a list of labelled links (action links) between pairs of perceptual clusters of the SOFM.

In a subsequent *application phase*, the robot was initially placed at a 'goal' location (to obtain the sensory perception of the goal), then lifted to an arbitrary 'start' location and left to determine a sequence of motor actions that would take it to the goal. The robot achieved this through a mechanism of reaction-diffusion dynamics, as described in section 2.3. After finding a path to the goal the first of the actions of the plan was performed. Subsequently the planning process was repeated, until the current sensor perception activated the same perceptual cluster as the goal perception.

3.2   Experiments with Essex' Marvin Robot

Experimental Setup. In a first series of experiments we used an Essex' Marvin robot, which has eight ultrasonic range finders which were used as sensor inputs to the mechanism (figure 2).

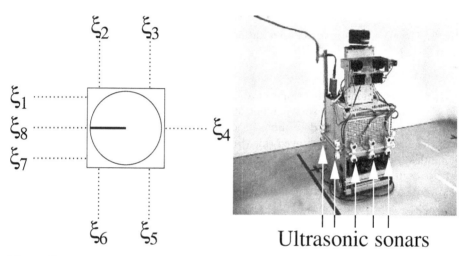

Fig. 2. Top view and side view of the Essex' Marvin robot. The robot has eight ultrasonic sensors, as indicated

The robot was placed in the experimental arena depicted in figure 3 and has a repertoire of four actions ('move forwards 50 cm', 'move backwards 50 cm', 'turn left 40°', and 'turn right 40°').

During the exploration phase, the robot explored its environment performing 294 randomly selected actions out of its behavioural repertoire. The self-organising feature map that we used was a two dimensional toroid with 7x7 units. During training each training example was presented to the SOFM 5000 times. The learning rate a starts from value 1 and decreases to 0 in steps of $\frac{1}{Training\ Cycles} = 0.0002$ after each training iteration. Therefore, after completing 5000 training cycles becomes 0 and the training stops. The weights update neighbourhood radius N_c starts from $N_c = 3$ and decreases to $N_c = 1$. The precondition-action-postcondition associations were stored *afterwards* as a list of action links (links labelled with the action taken) between pairs of perceptual clusters of the SOFM.

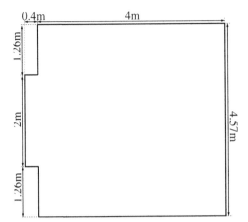

Fig. 3. The experimental arena used during the experiments with the Essex' Marvin robot

In the subsequent application phase, the robot was initially placed at a 'goal' location (to obtain the sensory perception of the goal), then lifted to an arbitrary 'start' location and left to determine a sequence of motor actions that would take it to the goal. The robot achieved this through a mechanism of reaction-diffusion dynamics, by which a marker propagated from the goal perceptual cluster *at even pace* in all directions until it reached the robot's current perceptual cluster. The sequence of actions that leads from the network node that is maximum activated when the robot is at the 'start' position to the node that corresponds to the 'goal' position will indicate the shortest path to the goal in terms of amount of actions — however, this does not mean that it will also indicate the shortest physical path to the goal. Nevertheless, as far as we are interested in *any* existing path to the goal, this shortcoming is not serious. As we will see in section 3.4 by introducing cost related to actions we can influence the planning to favour particular plans.

After finding a path to the goal the first of the actions of the plan was performed. Afterwards the planning process was repeated, until the current sensor perception activated the same perceptual cluster as the goal perception.

Experimental Results. An example of a typical experimental run is presented in figure 4.

Start and goal location shown in figure 4 differ both by angle (0° and 58° resp.) and distance to the nearest wall (90 cm and 70 cm resp.). Figure 5 shows the sequence of actions performed by the robot in order to move from start to goal.

Looking at figure 5, it might appear that the action sequence forwards-right-left-backwards partially cancels the effect of individual motor actions, returning the robot to the original position. On closer inspection one finds that this is not true. In fact, this simple experimental run clearly illustrates that the robot

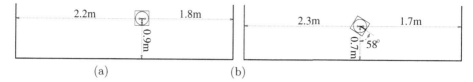

Fig. 4. Typical task in 2 dimensional experiment: the robot is placed at the goal location first (b), then lifted to an arbitrary start location (a) and instructed to determine a sequence of action that will take it to the goal

learned its own behavioural idiosyncracies, in this case the asymmetry between supposedly symmetric actions such as 'left' and 'right'.

This realisation illustrates that the subsymbolic planning mechanism avoiding use of symbolic representations produces grounded plans [3].

3.3   Experiments with a Magellan Pro

In a second set of experiments we transfered the subsymbolic action planning mechanism to a Magellan Pro robot (see figure 6), which has a larger and different sensor apparatus than the Marvin robot.

The sensors used in this setup were the 16 ultrasonic sonars employed as range sensors evenly placed around the robot. The 16 sonar input signals, each giving values in a range $0 - 4$, were used as an 16 dimensional input vector to the subsymbolic planning mechanism.

The different number of sensors, their different technical characteristics (different range and output values) and the different behaviour of actuators did not necessitate any changes to the planning mechanism, apart from a re-definition of the size of the input vector (sensor input signals) and output commands (motor actions). The reason for this (desirable) feature is the fact that we did not have to make assumptions about the nature and expected behaviour of the sensors and the actuators.

Experimental Setup. For the experiments presented here the experimental arena depicted in figure 7 was employed. It is a square area with side 2.80m and 4 cylindrical obstacles placed in order to give a variety of sensor perception through the field. During the training phase the robot selects random actions from its repertoire and performs them. Doing so it collects 400 training samples for training the subsymbolic planning mechanism. The SOFM we used was 9x9 units and toroid. During training each training example was presented to the SOFM 50 times. The learning rate a starts again from value 1 and decreases to 0 in steps of $\frac{1}{Training\ Cycles} = 0.02$ after each training iteration. The weights update neighbourhood radius N_c starts from $N_c = 4$ and decreases to $N_c = 1$.

Experimental Results. After training has been completed the application phase follows. In figures 7 and 8 one can see two different experimental runs of the application phase. The first one (figure 7) depicts the successful finding

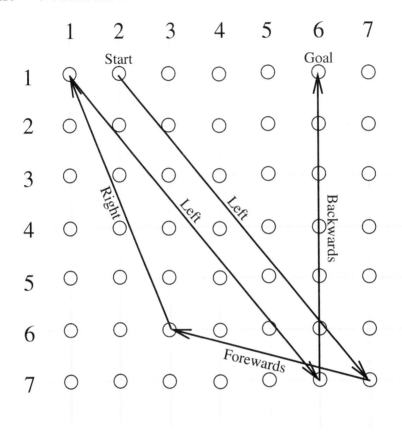

Fig. 5. Sequence of actions (shown in the perceptual space of the SOFM) performed to solve the task depicted in figure 4. Note that the circles represent units of the SOFM and that the SOFM we use is toroid

of the goal both in perceptual space and in Cartesian space. The second figure depicts another run. Here (figure 8), due to aliasing problem, the robot found the goal in perceptual space, but not in Cartesian space.

This second set of experiments confirms that the subsymbolic planning mechanism is able to learn the behavioural idiosyncrasies of the particular robot. Of course we should take into account that the specific hardware characteristics of a robot define and limit its abilities and suitability for a given task. This ability of the subsymbolic action planning mechanism to adapt to the idiosyncrasies of the particular robot makes it robust in real world applications, where sensors and motors do not have identical, predictable characteristics.

Furthermore, the experimental results presented in the two last sections vividly illustrate that the subsymbolic planning mechanism is embodied and the plans it creates are grounded [3, 16].

Fig. 6. The Magellan Pro robot has sixteen ultrasonic sonar sensors, sixteen bumper switches, and sixteen infrared proximity sensors placed around the body of the robot

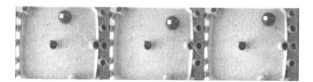

Fig. 7. The positions and orientations of the Magellan Pro robot in the arena during one of the experiments. The environment is a square arena with side length 2.80m and 4 cylindrical obstacles placed inside it. On the left the robot is placed on the start position. In the middle the robot is placed on the goal position. On the right the robot is on the goal it finally found

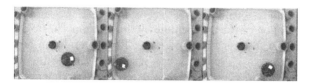

Fig. 8. The positions and orientations of the Magellan Pro robot in the arena during another experiment. On the left the robot is placed on the start position. In the middle the robot is placed on the goal position. On the right the robot is on the goal it finally found. Specified and found goals are perceptually identical, which is the reason for the outcome of this experiment

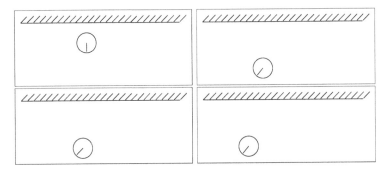

Fig. 9. The positions and orientations of the robot in the field during the experiments with the two cost functions. On the top left and top right the robot is placed on the start and goal positions respectively. The bottom left shows the goal found using cost favouring translation, the bottom right depicts the goal found using cost favouring turning. In both cases the goal was reached successfully, albeit using different plans (see figure 10)

3.4   Introducing 'Cost' Functions on the Planning Mechanism

Being able to determine *any* sequence of actions to take the robot to the goal is a useful property. However, in practical applications it is desirable to favour certain solutions over others.

We achieved this by introducing the notion of 'cost' to the planning process, assigning a 'cost' to each action link of the behavioural space layer (see figure 1). Specifically, we used two different cost functions, one that favoured translational movement, and one that favoured rotational movement of the robot.

The robot aims to execute the path with the minimum cost every time.

Experimental Setup. The Magellan robot was used for this experiments, it is again capable of performing four actions: 'move forwards 50 cm', 'move backwards 50 cm', 'turn left 40°', and 'turn right 40°'.

The robot is placed in front of a wall and the task is to obtain a specified distance and orientation. This environment was selected because it minimises the aliasing problem.

Initially, the robot performs random actions, from the four actions in its repertoire, moving in the arena and collecting 400 precondition-action-postcondition training data triples. This data was used for training the action planning mechanism. Drawings of the field we used for the experiments can be seen in figure 9.

The sensors used in this setup are 16 ultrasonic sonars employed as range sensors evenly placed around the robot. The task for the robot was again to move to a specified position and orientation in the environment, using a repertoire of the four actions. A two dimensional toroid self-organising feature map of size 13x13 units was used for perception clustering. By using smaller SOFM the aliasing problem increases because there is not enough resolution to the perception clustering. The learning rate a starts again from value 1 and decreases

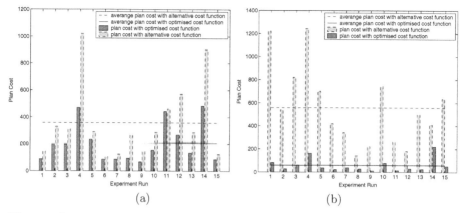

Fig. 10. Comparison of optimised (dark bars) and alternative (light bars) path cost functions of 2 x 15 experimental runs. Figure (a) shows the optimisation favouring translational moves, figure (b) that for optimisation favouring rotational moves. Average costs for the optimised (solid line) and the alternative cost function (dashed line) are also displayed

to 0 in steps of $\frac{1}{Training\ Cycles} = 0.02$ after each training iteration. The weights update neighbourhood radius N_c starts from $N_c = 6$ and decreases to $N_c = 1$. During training we presented the training examples 50 times to the SOFM, subsequently storing a list of action links. In contrast to the earlier experiments, 'cost' was associated with each action link.

The reaction-diffusion dynamics now incorporated the cost, in that the marker travelled more slowly along links with higher cost. During diffusion dynamics search the cost of an *action* link is translated to propagation time, and therefore the "scent" arrives first at the goal along the "cheapest" path. This shortest path is then a plan towards the goal and the first *action* of this plan is executed.

Once a link between goal and current perceptual cluster was found, the first action of the sequence was executed, and the entire planning process repeated until current and goal perceptual cluster were identical.

Costs are assigned to action links after training has been completed and thus cost functions can vary as desired.

Experimental Results. Figure 10 shows the results of 30 independent experiments, 15 of which favoured translational moves of the robot[2] (part *a* of the figure), and 15 which favoured rotational moves[3] (part *b* of the figure).

For all 2x15 runs, the cost of the path followed (dark bars) in each run and the cost if the other measure had been used (light bars) are depicted in pairs of bars. Also the average of the costs of all runs are displayed as a measure of comparison, it shows clearly that the action planning mechanism plans and executes a minimal cost path. Applying t-tests on the data presented on each

---

[2] Here the cost was '1' for translational moves and '20' for rotational ones.
[3] Here the same cost values were used, but with the allocation reversed.

of the graphs illustrates that there is a significant difference between the path costs using the optimisation function and an alternative function (p=0.0021 and p<0.0001 respectively).

The experiments demonstrated that the robot, starting from the same location and having the same goal, is able to pursue the task with different plans each time. This is of great advantage because in real world where we should not assume a specific perceptual postcondition following the execution of an *action*. Planning now is more flexible and tolerant to environmental, sensor, and motor noise[4]. Therefore we have a robust system tolerant to noisy data during training and application, and designed to plan in the real world.

4   Discussion

The subsymbolic planning mechanism presented in section 2 was able to determine task-achieving sequences of actions, without using symbolic representations, but instead applying previously acquired knowledge in new ways, essentially 'assembling' novel plans from smaller components which had previously been learned (section 2.3).

Transferring the mechanism to another robot demonstrated that the subsymbolic planning mechanism does not depend on specific assumptions about the technical characteristics of the robot (section 3.3). Furthermore, subsymbolic planning proved to be capable to employ cost functions and plan optimum paths (section 3.4) with respect to different performance criteria (cost functions).

These experimental results illustrate that such a subsymbolic planning approach lead to an embodied robot planner that produces grounded plans.

One weakness of the proposed mechanism is that only plan components that have explicitly been encountered previously can become part of a plan. In other words, the mechanism as proposed here is unable to generalise regarding the behavioural space.

Ongoing work at Essex addresses this weakness, aiming to enable the robot to make plans towards and from areas of the perceptual space that the robot has not explored before.

Acknowledgements

John Pisokas is sponsored by IKY (State Scholarship Foundation of Greece), whose support is gratefully acknowledged.

References

1. Fikes, R., Nilsson, N.: Strips: A new approach to the application of theorem proving to problem solving. Artificial Intelligence **2** (1971) 189–208

---

[4] With the term *noise* here we mean all the unpredictability involved with operation in real world.

2. Nilsson, N.J.: Shakey the robot. Technical Report 323, SRI International (1984)
3. Harnad, S.: The symbol grounding problem. Physica D **42** (1990) 335–346
4. Arkin, R.: Behavior-Based Robotics. MIT Press (1998)
5. Malcolm, C.: Behavioural modules in robotic assembly. Lecture Notes (2000) Division of Informatics, University of Edinburgh.
6. Gat, E.: Integrating planning and reacting in a heterogeneous asynchronous architecture for controlling real-world mobile robots. In: Proceedings AAAI-92. Volume 4. (1992) 809–815
7. Baldassarre, G.: A planning modular neural-network robot for asynchronous multi-goal navigation tasks. In: Proceedings of the 2001 Fourth European Workshop on Advanced Mobile Robots - EUROBOT-2001. (2001) 223–230
8. Baldassarre, G.: Planning with neural networks and reinforcement learning. PhD thesis, University of Essex (2001)
9. Turing, A.: The chemical basis for morphogenesis. Phil. Trans. Roy. Soc. **37** (1952) 129–152
10. Steels, L.: Steps towards common sense. In: Proceedings ECAI 1988. (1988) 49–54
11. Fleuret, F., Brunet, E.: DEA: An architecture for goal planning and classification. Neural Computation **12** (2000) 1987–2008
12. Fomin, T., Rozgonyi, T., Szepesvári, C., Lörincz, A.: Self-organizing multi-resolution grid for motion planning and control. International Journal of Neural Sciences **7** (1996) 757–776
13. Zeller, M., Sharma, R., Schulten, K.: Topology representing network for sensor-based robot motion planning. In: Proceedings of the 1996 World Congress on Neural Networks, INNS Press (1996) 100–103
14. Kandel, E.R., Schwartz, J.H., Jessell, T.M., eds.: Essentials of neural science and behavior. Appleton and Lange, Stanford (1995)
15. Kohonen, T.: Self-Organization and Associative Memory. Springer-Verlag (1984)
16. Sun, R.: Symbol grounding: A new look at an old idea. Philosophical Psychology **13** (2000) 149–172

Robust Online Reputation Mechanism by Stochastic Approximation

Takamichi Sakai[1], Kenji Terada[2], and Tadashi Araragi[1]

[1] NTT Communication Science Laboratories, NTT Corporation,
2–4 Hikaridai Seika-cho Soraku-gun Kyoto 619–0237, Japan
{sakai, araragi}@cslab.kecl.ntt.co.jp
[2] NTT East Research and Development Center, NTT East Corporation,
3–19–2 Nishi-shinjuku Shinjuku-ku Tokyo 163–8019, Japan
kenji.terada@rdc.east.ntt.co.jp

Abstract. Recently, online reputation mechanisms have attracted much attention in many areas. They have been widely adopted and worked well, although their reliability is still a major concern. Because of online properties such as openness and anonymity, it is necessary to consider rating errors, noise and unfair lies. Furthermore, these disturbances (attacks) have a significant effect on multi-agent systems containing malicious agents who tell lies or engage in strategic manipulations. Current online reputation mechanisms are not sufficiently robust against such disturbances. In an attempt to solve this problem, we propose a stochastic approximation-based online reputation mechanism. Our mechanism assigns one global trustworthiness value to each agent and updates estimates of these values dynamically from mutual ratings of agents. Experimental results show that our mechanism is able to identify good and bad agents effectively under condition of the above disturbances and also trace the changes in agents' true trustworthiness values adaptively.

1 Introduction

Recently online reputation mechanisms have attracted much attention in many areas, such as multi-agent systems, peer-to-peer systems, and electronic commerce. In such areas, there is an enormous number of unfamiliar potential trading partners, so *reputation information* of partners can take a central role in selecting partners to contact. Here, reputation information is a collection of many users' ratings about trustworthiness of the specified partner. The role of reputation information is larger for an agent than for human, because an agent has difficulty in feeling the partner's trustworthiness from the partner's advertising statements, responses and so on. Furthermore, an online reputation mechanism is more cost-effective than establishing an authentic oversight mechanism like a law-enforcement agency [1].

The basic mechanism of an online reputation mechanism is that users rate each other, and their ratings (i.e. reputation information) become publicly available [2, 3]. For example, the mechanism of the major Internet auction site eBay

D. Kudenko et al. (Eds.): Adaptive Agents and MAS II, LNAI 3394, pp. 230–244, 2005.

(www.ebay.com) is as follows. When a transaction between a seller and a buyer finishes, the seller and the buyer rate each other: they choose one level from positive, neutral or negative, and they can add a comment, too. These ratings are subsequently collected and made publicly available. Each user's reputation information consists of a table and a sheet. The table shows the total counts of each rating level that the user has acquired during past 1, 6 and 12 months, and the sheet lists ratings the user acquired in the newest-first order, where each rating consists of a rating level, a comment and a rater. In this way each user can estimate the trustworthiness of an unfamiliar partner by referring to the partner's reputation information. Furthermore, the effect of suppressing a user's bad behaviors can be expected because they receive bad ratings in feedback when they behave badly.

Online reputation mechanisms have been widely adopted and worked well, although their reliability is still a major concern. Because of online properties such as openness and anonymity, the online reputation mechanism has to be robust against rating errors, noise and unfair lies. Furthermore, these disturbances (attacks) by malicious agents or groups of them, who tell lies or engage in strategic manipulations, have a significant effect on multi-agent systems where human do not intervene. Current online reputation mechanisms are not sufficiently robust against such disturbances, so developing a secure online reputation mechanism remains a significant challenge in multi-agent systems.

In this paper, we propose a stochastic approximation-based online reputation mechanism in multi-agent systems. Our mechanism assigns one global trustworthiness value to each agent as its reputation information and updates estimates of this value dynamically from mutual ratings of agents. Experimental results show that our mechanism is able to identify good and bad agents effectively under conditions of the above disturbances. Moreover, our mechanism is able to trace the changes in agents' true trustworthiness values adaptively, which is the situation where agents with good behaviors suddenly start performing manipulations.

This paper's structure is as follows. First, we discuss works related to online reputation mechanisms and present the position of this paper in Sect. 2. Then, we show our framework of the online reputation mechanism and define the problem in Sect. 3. We then propose our solution to the problem, stochastic approximation-based algorithms, in Sect. 4, and provide experimental results of these algorithms in Sect. 5. Finally, we conclude in Sect. 6.

2   Related Work

There are many related works about online reputation mechanisms. In this section we focus on the related works concerning mechanism design that propose novel mechanisms or algorithms in terms of robustness or other aspects. Furthermore, we clarify the position of this paper by classifying related works from the perspective of the representation of trust (Sect. 2.1) and the subjectivity of trust (Sect. 2.2). By the way, for clarity, let agent A's trust in agent B (agent B's trustworthiness for agent A) be $T(A, B)$, from now on.

2.1   Representation of Trust

When designing online reputation mechanisms, we have to decide the representation of trust $T(A, B)$ at the beginning. If its user is human, using natural language is possible for the representation of trust $T(A, B)$. However, if its user is an agent, a computer-friendly representation format of trust is suitable. In this paper and [4, 5, 6], trust $T(A, B)$ is represented by one (real or natural) number. The bigger this number is, the more agent A trusts agent B. Basically this representation can include eBay's ratings of three levels, except for comments. This representation is easy to handle, although it does feature a limitation. For example, this representation cannot handle trust in the manner that "I can trust her about computers, but I cannot trust her about cooking," or that "the seller provides high quality goods but the seller's delivery is late." In general, trust should be rated by many viewpoints, and in order to represent such detailed trust, more complex representation formats are suitable. Indeed, [6] proposes to represent trust by a vector. And [7] uses the Dempster-Shafer theory-based basic probability assignment, [8] uses Bayesian network, as a representative format of trust.

2.2   Subjectivity of Trust

One major role of the online reputation mechanism is estimating the trustworthiness of an unfamiliar agent. There are main two approaches to this estimation. We explain the two approaches using Fig. 1. Figure 1 shows the situation where agent C wants to know the agent A_1's trustworthiness $T(C, A_1)$ in the existence of agents A_1, A_2, B_1, B_2, B_3 and C. For example, this is a situation where A_1 and A_2 are seller agents providing a similar service, and C is a buyer agent who wants to know the trustworthiness of A_1 and A_2 to decide which seller agent C receives the service from. If C traded with A_1 directly in the past, C can estimate $T(C, A_1)$ from C's experiences by itself. Here, however, it is assumed that A_1 is unfamiliar with C. In this case, C receives trustworthiness of A_1 from other agents. Here, we assume B_1, B_2, B_3 traded with A_1 directly in the past and has the rating $T_1 = T(B_1, A_1)$, $T_2 = T(B_2, A_1)$, $T_3 = T(B_3, A_1)$, respectively. Then C can estimate trustworthiness $T(C, A_1)$ by integrating T_1, T_2 and T_3. However, the method of this integration differs by two approaches.

The first approach (this paper and [4, 5]) assumes the existence of a *global* trustworthiness $T_g(A_1) = T(\text{agency}, A_1)$ for each agent. Here, $T_g(A_1)$ represents the trustworthiness of A_1 for agency (all agents). $T_g(A_1)$ is an objective and absolute rating; that is, the trustworthiness of A_1 for B_1 is the same as for B_2, and for every different agent. $T_g(A_1)$ is computed by integrating (e.g. averaging) all agents' trust in A_1, and C uses this $T_g(A_1)$ as the estimation of $T(C, A_1)$. Although the assumption of the existence of a global trustworthiness is arguable, this approach has a merit in that a newly arriving agent can use this $T_g(A_1)$ immediately to estimate the trustworthiness of an unfamiliar agent (here, A_1).

The second approach [6, 7, 8] does not assume the existence of a global trustworthiness $T_g(A_1)$. Instead, this approach considers that trust is personal, subjective, and relative, not global. That is, the trustworthiness of A_1 for B_1 is

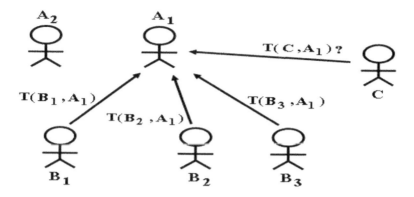

Fig. 1. Estimating the trustworthiness of an unfamiliar agent

different from that for B_2, and for every different agent. Therefore, in order to estimate $T(C, A_1)$, we should search agents whose ratings or preference is similar to C. Here, we assume B_2 and B_3 are searched as the similar agents to C. Then the estimation of $T(C, A_1)$ is computed by integrating only these trusts T_2 and T_3. Although this approach requires a reasonable measure of similarity between agents, the estimated trust can be relatively meaningful.

2.3   Position of This Paper

This paper use one real number as a trust representation and assumes the existence of a global trustworthiness.

Some related works [4, 5] have already adopted the same framework as this paper. However, they [4, 5] derive estimation algorithms of global trustworthiness values in an ad-hoc style, and their theoretical support is not strong enough (see "Discussion of Other Algorithms" in Sect. 4.1). This paper presents stochastic approximation-based algorithms and, in particular, analytical and experimental results about robustness against disturbances.

3   Online Reputation Mechanism

In this section, we show our framework of the online reputation mechanism, and define the problem.

We assume an Internet-based multi-agent system where there is an enormous number of autonomous agents interacting with each other, and some agents may enter or leave in real time. When agent j obtains a service from agent i, agent j rates agent i, for instance, on the basis of the quality of agent i's service, and reports the rating value $R_{ji} \in [0, 1]$ to the online reputation mechanism (see Fig. 2), where $R_{ji} = 1(0)$ means that agent j thinks agent i is quite good (bad). (Although the online reputation mechanism in Fig. 2 is depicted by centralized form for the sake of simplicity, it is also possible for our proposed algorithms to be implemented by decentralized form.) R_{ji} should be treated as a random (stochastic) variable, since there exist rating errors and noise. In addition, the value of R_{ji} is not always true, since malicious agents may tell lies as a tactic of manipulation.

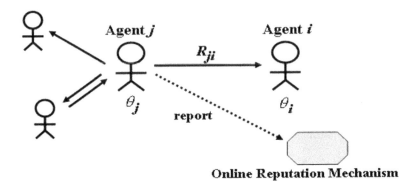

Fig. 2. Framework of the online reputation mechanism

The online reputation mechanism assigns a *global* trustworthiness value of each agent $k(k = 1, \ldots, r)$, and has its estimate $\theta_k \in [0, 1]$. Here, r is the number of agents and also dimensions of θ, and $\theta_k = 1(0)$ means that agent k is quite good, honest (bad, malicious). And, the online reputation mechanism provides this estimate θ_k when it receives inquiry of agent k's trustworthiness. The problem of the online reputation mechanism, therefore, is how to update the trustworthiness values' estimates $\theta = (\theta_1, \ldots, \theta_r)$, which converge to the *true* trustworthiness values $\bar{\theta} = (\bar{\theta}_1, \ldots, \bar{\theta}_r)$, dynamically from the sequence of the reports $\{R_{ji}\}$, especially where $\{R_{ji}\}$ contains rating errors, noise and unfair lies by malicious agents.

Note that in our framework an agent's global trustworthiness is represented by only one real number, even though it has two meanings. That is, $\bar{\theta}_k$ represents both the trustworthiness of agent k's "service" and the trustworthiness of agent k's "rating" for other agents (i.e. whether agent k is a liar or not). Strictly speaking, these two trustworthiness factors are independent. For example, there can exist agents whose "service" is good, but whose "rating" is bad (that is, they are liars). However, these two trustworthiness factors are identical in many cases, and in addition, the needs of users are knowing agents that offer both a good "service" and "rating". Hence we define the true trustworthiness value $\bar{\theta}_k$ as a conjunction (AND, $\wedge$) of these two trustworthiness factors. That is to say, in our framework, a good agent ($\bar{\theta}_k = 1$) means that both agent k's "service" and "rating" are good, and a bad agent ($\bar{\theta}_k = 0$) means either agent k's "service" or "rating" is bad, or both are bad. Conversely, we are unable to distinguish, for instance, whether $\bar{\theta}_k = 0$ indicates that agent k's "service" is bad, agent k's "rating" is bad, or both. To handle this type of trustworthiness factors precisely, we have to employ an even more complex representation of trust, such as vectors (see Sect. 2.1). However, we think our simple representation by one real number is usually sufficient for many applications.

4   Stochastic Approximation-Based Algorithm

In this section, we provide three algorithms that update the trustworthiness values' estimates θ recursively from the mutual ratings $\{R_{ji}\}$. Each algorithm is obtained in a similar fashion from the corresponding rating model. Then we explain about asynchronous algorithms suitable for practical use, and introduce the adaptive algorithm to adjust step-size parameters automatically.

4.1   Stochastic Gradient Descent Algorithm

Rating Model. To obtain the algorithms, we set a *rating model* first. The rating model is a function $u(\bar{\theta})$ describing our expectations of how R_{ji} is generated, i.e. we define $u_{ji}(\bar{\theta}) = E[R_{ji}]$ where $E[\,]$ denotes the expectation operator. In this paper, we use the following three typical rating models. However, these three models are just examples, and the following developments hold true even when using other rating models.

$$\text{LLS} \quad u_{ji}^{\text{LLS}}(\bar{\theta}) = \bar{\theta}_i, \tag{1}$$

$$\text{Joint} \quad u_{ji}^{\text{Joint}}(\bar{\theta}) = \bar{\theta}_j \bar{\theta}_i, \tag{2}$$

$$\text{Lie} \quad u_{ji}^{\text{Lie}}(\bar{\theta}) = 2\bar{\theta}_j \bar{\theta}_i - \bar{\theta}_j - \bar{\theta}_i + 1 \ . \tag{3}$$

The *Linear Least-Squares (LLS)* model is the simplest model, which predicts that R_{ji} reflects the agent i's true trustworthiness value $\bar{\theta}_i$ on average, and will lead to a linear least-squares estimate of $\bar{\theta}_i$. The *Joint* model assumes that the transaction between agent j and agent i will succeed ($R_{ji} = 1$) if both agents j and i are good ($\bar{\theta}_j = 1 \wedge \bar{\theta}_i = 1$). The *Lie* model deals with lying agents that always express the complementary (NOT, $\neg$) rating. Indeed, when rater agent j's true trustworthiness value $\bar{\theta}_j$ is 0 ($\bar{\theta}_j = 0$), this model expects the agent j's rating of agent i (that is, R_{ji}) to be $1 - \bar{\theta}_i$, which is complementary of the agent i's true trustworthiness value $\bar{\theta}_i$. A more general form of the Lie model is $(1 - 2\bar{\theta}_i)(1 - \bar{\theta}_j)^a + \bar{\theta}_i$, which leads to (3) when $a = 1$.

Table 1 shows the output value of the function $u_{ji}(\bar{\theta})$ of each model when two input values $(\bar{\theta}_j, \bar{\theta}_i)$ are (1,1), (1,0), (0,1) and (0,0).

Derivation of Algorithms. Next, to estimate $\bar{\theta}$, we choose the mean square error (MSE) criterion as a cost function to minimize. Here we define

$$\text{MSE} = E\left[\sum_{i,j(i\neq j)} \left(R_{ji} - u_{ji}(\theta) \right)^2 \right] \ . \tag{4}$$

That is, we treat R_{ji} as desired outputs and adjust θ to output these desired outputs. In addition, here we assume many R_{ji} are obtained synchronously, and

Table 1. The output value of the function $u_{ji}(\bar{\theta})$

$\bar{\theta}_j$	$\bar{\theta}_i$	$u_{ji}^{\text{LLS}}(\bar{\theta})$	$u_{ji}^{\text{Joint}}(\bar{\theta})$	$u_{ji}^{\text{Lie}}(\bar{\theta})$
1	1	1	1	1
1	0	0	0	0
0	1	1	0	0
0	0	0	0	1

we imply that the summation $\sum_{i,j(i\neq j)}$ is done only by the set of R_{ji} obtained in each synchronization round (we mention an asynchronous case at Sect. 4.2). We also define the *sample* MSE

$$e(\theta, R) = \frac{1}{2} \sum_{i,j(i\neq j)} \left(R_{ji} - u_{ji}(\theta) \right)^2 \tag{5}$$

and the *sample* error

$$e_{ji} = R_{ji} - u_{ji}(\theta) . \tag{6}$$

The gradient values of the MSE are not known, although these "noise-corrupted" observations can be taken. Then we can use the stochastic approximation (Robbins and Monro) method [9] to obtain this *stochastic gradient descent algorithm*:

$$\theta'_k = \theta_k - \epsilon_k \frac{\partial e(\theta, R)}{\partial \theta_k}$$
$$= \theta_k + \epsilon_k \sum_{i,j(i\neq j)} e_{ji} \frac{\partial u_{ji}(\theta)}{\partial \theta_k}, \quad k = 1, \dots, r, \tag{7}$$

where θ'_k denotes the next time step's value of θ_k, and ϵ_k is the kth component of the *step-size parameter (learning rate)*. If ϵ_k's sequence $\{\epsilon_{k,n}(n = 1, \dots)\}$ satisfies

$$\epsilon_{k,n} > 0, \quad \sum_n \epsilon_{k,n}^2 < \infty, \quad \sum_n \epsilon_{k,n} = \infty, \tag{8}$$

θ is converged to the minimum point with the probability of one (w.p.1).

Substituting $u_{ji}(\theta)$ in (7) by the models $u_{ji}^{\text{LLS}}(\theta)$, $u_{ji}^{\text{Joint}}(\theta)$ and $u_{ji}^{\text{Lie}}(\theta)$, we obtain concrete algorithms for each model, respectively:

LLS $\quad \theta'_k = \theta_k + \epsilon_k \sum_{j(j\neq k)} (R_{jk} - \theta_k),$ $\tag{9}$

Joint $\quad \theta'_k = \theta_k + \epsilon_k \sum_{j(j\neq k)} \theta_j \big((R_{jk} - \theta_j\theta_k) + (R_{kj} - \theta_k\theta_j) \big),$ $\tag{10}$

Lie $\quad \theta'_k = \theta_k + \epsilon_k \sum_{j(j\neq k)} (2\theta_j - 1)\big((R_{jk} - 2\theta_j\theta_k + \theta_j + \theta_k - 1) +$

$$(R_{kj} - 2\theta_k\theta_j + \theta_k + \theta_j - 1) \big) . \tag{11}$$

Here we supplement one item. The domain of θ_k is constrained by $[0,1]$; therefore, equation (7) is used by the following *projected* form in practice,

$$\theta'_k = \prod_{[0,1]} \left[\theta_k + \epsilon_k \sum_{i,j(i \neq j)} e_{ji} \frac{\partial u_{ji}(\theta)}{\partial \theta_k} \right], \tag{12}$$

where $\prod_H(\theta)$ denotes the closest point in H to θ. If θ is one-dimensional and H is $[a, b]$, $\prod_H(\theta)$ is the same as

$$\prod_{[a,b]} (\theta_k) = \min(\max(\theta_k, a),\ b)\ . \tag{13}$$

We do not indicate this clearly just for simplicity: we always assume that the right side of θ_k's updating equations including (9), (10), and (11) are projected by $\prod_{[0,1]}$ implicitly.

Discussion of Other Algorithms. Equation (9) shows that the finite difference in the estimate θ_k can be interpreted as the sum of the product of the "estimation error" $R_{jk} - \theta_k$ and the coefficient of "reliability" ϵ_k [9]. Therefore, we can derive another algorithm by incorporating the rater agent j's trustworthiness value θ_j into the coefficient of "reliability":

$$\text{Weighted} \quad \theta'_k = \theta_k + \epsilon_k \sum_{j(j \neq k)} \theta_j (R_{jk} - \theta_k)\ . \tag{14}$$

This *Weighted* algorithm forms the basis of the algorithms used in the related works [4, 5]. However, we can derive more effective algorithms as described below.

First, we consider a more general MSE than (4):

$$\text{MSE}^\dagger = E \left[\sum_{i,j(i \neq j)} w_{ji} \left(R_{ji} - u_{ji}(\theta) \right)^2 \right], \tag{15}$$

where w_{ji} denotes the coefficient of each square error's weight. We treat all square errors' weights as an equal ($w_{ji} = 1$) in (4). Now, however, we place a special weight (influence) on square errors' weights associated with rater agents of high trustworthiness, i.e. we set $w_{ji} = \theta_j$ here (we can use a step function or a logistic function also). Then we define the sample $\text{MSE}^\dagger$

$$e^\dagger(\theta, R) = \frac{1}{2} \sum_{i,j(i \neq j)} w_{ji} \left(R_{ji} - u_{ji}(\theta) \right)^2, \tag{16}$$

and employ the stochastic approximation method to obtain this stochastic gradient descent algorithm:

$$\theta'_k = \theta_k - \epsilon_k \frac{\partial e^\dagger(\theta, R)}{\partial \theta_k}$$

$$= \theta_k + \epsilon_k \sum_{i,j(i \neq j)} \left(w_{ji} e_{ji} \frac{\partial u_{ji}(\theta)}{\partial \theta_k} - \frac{1}{2} e_{ji}^2 \frac{\partial w_{ji}}{\partial \theta_k} \right)$$

$$= \theta_k + \epsilon_k \sum_{i,j(i \neq j)} \left(\theta_j e_{ji} \frac{\partial u_{ji}(\theta)}{\partial \theta_k} - \frac{1}{2} e_{ji}^2 \delta_{j,k} \right), \quad k = 1, \ldots, r . \tag{17}$$

Here, $\delta_{j,k}$ is the Kronecker delta, which becomes 1 when $j = k$ and 0 when $j \neq k$. In addition, we used $w_{ji} = \theta_j$ to change the equation of the second line to that of the third line in (17).

Substituting $u_{ji}(\theta)$ in (17) by the model $u_{ji}^{\mathrm{LLS}}(\theta)$, we obtain the concrete algorithm (we omit concrete algorithms of Joint^{W} and Lie^{W}):

$$\mathrm{LLS}^{\mathrm{W}} \quad \theta_k' = \theta_k + \epsilon_k \sum_{j(j \neq k)} \left(\theta_j (R_{jk} - \theta_k) - \frac{1}{2} (R_{kj} - \theta_j)^2 \right) . \tag{18}$$

Comparing this $LLS^{\mathcal{W}}$ algorithm (18) with the Weighted algorithm (14), we see that the only difference between (18) and (14) is the second term in $\sum_{j(j \neq k)}$. This term indicates the error between R_{kj} (agent k's rating of another agent j) and agent j's trustworthiness value θ_j is reflected to agent k's own trustworthiness value θ_k. For this reason, we can interpret this term as the reflection effect as [4] mentioned. This term enables the LLS^{W} algorithm to perform better than the Weighted algorithm (see Sect. 5.2).

4.2 Asynchronous Algorithm

In the preceding Sect. 4.1, we dealt with the synchronous case in which many R_{ji} are obtained synchronously. There exist many applications working synchronously, like a sensor network [4]. However, the online reputation mechanism's framework of this paper assumes that each R_{ji} is obtained asynchronously. In this section, we derive asynchronous algorithms and discuss problems like the order and frequency of updating estimates, which arise in the asynchronous case.

Derivation of Asynchronous Algorithms. When each R_{ji} is obtained asynchronously, the most simplest way of updating θ is to update θ every time each R_{ji} is obtained. So here we derive asynchronous algorithms by defining this MSE* as a cost function to minimize:

$$\mathrm{MSE}^* = E \left[w_{ji} (R_{ji} - u_{ji}(\theta))^2 \right] . \tag{19}$$

We also define the sample MSE*

$$e^*(\theta, R_{ji}) = \frac{1}{2} w_{ji} (R_{ji} - u_{ji}(\theta))^2, \tag{20}$$

and employ the stochastic approximation method to obtain this stochastic gradient descent algorithm:

$$\theta_k' = \theta_k - \epsilon_k \frac{\partial e^*(\theta, R_{ji})}{\partial \theta_k}$$

$$= \theta_k + \epsilon_k \left(w_{ji} e_{ji} \frac{\partial u_{ji}(\theta)}{\partial \theta_k} - \frac{1}{2} e_{ji}^2 \frac{\partial w_{ji}}{\partial \theta_k} \right), \quad k = 1, \ldots, r . \tag{21}$$

However, both $u_{ji}(\theta)$ and w_{ji} are usually the function of θ_i and θ_j only. In this case,

$$\frac{\partial u_{ji}(\theta)}{\partial \theta_k} = \frac{\partial w_{ji}}{\partial \theta_k} = 0 \quad (k \neq i \ \wedge \ k \neq j),$$

and the equation (21) is expanded as follows:

$$\theta_i' = \theta_i + \epsilon_i \left(w_{ji} e_{ji} \frac{\partial u_{ji}(\theta)}{\partial \theta_i} - \frac{1}{2} e_{ji}^2 \frac{\partial w_{ji}}{\partial \theta_i} \right), \tag{22}$$

$$\theta_j' = \theta_j + \epsilon_j \left(w_{ji} e_{ji} \frac{\partial u_{ji}(\theta)}{\partial \theta_j} - \frac{1}{2} e_{ji}^2 \frac{\partial w_{ji}}{\partial \theta_j} \right), \tag{23}$$

$$\theta_k' = \theta_k \quad (k \neq i \ \wedge \ k \neq j) . \tag{24}$$

That is, we have to update at most two components θ_i and θ_j at each R_{ji}, and need not update (sweep) all components of θ.

Substituting $u_{ji}(\theta)$ in (22)–(24) by the models $u_{ji}^{\mathrm{LLS}}(\theta)$, $u_{ji}^{\mathrm{Joint}}(\theta)$ and $u_{ji}^{\mathrm{Lie}}(\theta)$, we obtain concrete algorithms for each model, respectively. That is, in the case of $w_{ji} = 1$:

$$\text{LLS} \quad \theta_i' = \theta_i + \epsilon_i (R_{ji} - \theta_i), \tag{25}$$

$$\text{Joint} \quad \theta_i' = \theta_i + \epsilon_i \theta_j (R_{ji} - \theta_j \theta_i), \tag{26}$$

$$\theta_j' = \theta_j + \epsilon_j \theta_i (R_{ji} - \theta_j \theta_i), \tag{27}$$

$$\text{Lie} \quad \theta_i' = \theta_i + \epsilon_i (2\theta_j - 1)(R_{ji} - 2\theta_j \theta_i + \theta_j + \theta_i - 1), \tag{28}$$

$$\theta_j' = \theta_j + \epsilon_j (2\theta_i - 1)(R_{ji} - 2\theta_j \theta_i + \theta_j + \theta_i - 1) . \tag{29}$$

Furthermore, in the case of $w_{ji} = \theta_j$:

$$\text{LLS}^{\mathrm{W}} \quad \theta_i' = \theta_i + \epsilon_i \theta_j (R_{ji} - \theta_i), \tag{30}$$

$$\theta_j' = \theta_j - \frac{1}{2} \epsilon_j (R_{ji} - \theta_i)^2, \tag{31}$$

$$\text{Joint}^{\mathrm{W}} \quad \theta_i' = \theta_i + \epsilon_i \theta_j^2 (R_{ji} - \theta_j \theta_i), \tag{32}$$

$$\theta_j' = \theta_j + \epsilon_j \big(\theta_j \theta_i (R_{ji} - \theta_j \theta_i) - \frac{1}{2} (R_{ji} - \theta_j \theta_i)^2 \big), \tag{33}$$

$$\text{Lie}^{\mathrm{W}} \quad \theta_i' = \theta_i + \epsilon_i \theta_j (2\theta_j - 1)(R_{ji} - 2\theta_j \theta_i + \theta_j + \theta_i - 1), \tag{34}$$

$$\theta_j' = \theta_j + \epsilon_j \big(\theta_j (2\theta_i - 1)(R_{ji} - 2\theta_j \theta_i + \theta_j + \theta_i - 1) - \frac{1}{2} (R_{ji} - 2\theta_j \theta_i + \theta_j + \theta_i - 1)^2 \big) . \tag{35}$$

Discussion About Asynchronous Algorithms. In the asynchronous case, the strategy of updating is important for the effective performance of the algorithms, just as asynchronous dynamic programming (DP) or Q-learning is [10]. If exactly the same set of ratings R_{ji} are given, the difference between synchronous algorithms and asynchronous algorithms is that synchronous algorithms update θ from this set of ratings R_{ji} all at once, whereas asynchronous algorithms update θ many times as each rating R_{ji} is given, where updated θ are used at each update. Therefore, we can ignore this difference if the step-size parameters are adequately small. However, there is the possibility that the ratio of unfair ratings by malicious agents increases in the asynchronous case because malicious agents may wage an intensive attack in a short period of time. Thus, we have to constrain the frequency of each agent's rating reports per specified time interval.

4.3   Adaptive Algorithm

When we use the stochastic approximation-based algorithms, the choice of the sequence $\{\epsilon_{k,n}\}$ is an important issue [9]. For the convergence of θ, (8) is required; however, to track the time-varying parameter $\bar{\theta}$, we usually use the fixed $\epsilon_{k,n} = \epsilon$. In general, if the $\bar{\theta}$ changes faster, ϵ should be larger, and if the observation noise is greater, ϵ should be smaller, though the optimal value of ϵ is unknown in many cases. Here we adopt a useful approach suggested by [11]. The idea is to use the stochastic approximation method again to estimate the correct step-size parameter ϵ. By differentiating $e(\theta, R)$ with respect to ϵ_k, we obtain the stochastic gradient descent algorithm of ϵ_k (although we use $e(\theta, R)$ here, we can derive adaptive algorithms of $e^{\dagger}(\theta, R)$ and $e^{*}(\theta, R_{ji})$ in a similar fashion):

$$
\epsilon'_k = \prod_{[\epsilon_-, \epsilon_+]} \left[\epsilon_k - \mu \frac{\partial e(\theta, R)}{\partial \epsilon_k} \right]
$$

$$
= \prod_{[\epsilon_-, \epsilon_+]} \left[\epsilon_k + \mu \sum_{i,j(i \neq j)} e_{ji} \frac{\partial u_{ji}(\theta)}{\partial \theta_k} V_k \right], \quad k = 1, \ldots, r, \tag{36}
$$

where ϵ'_k denotes the next time step's value of ϵ_k, ϵ_- and ϵ_+ are coefficients to constrain the domain of ϵ_k, and μ is the step-size parameter. Additionally, $V_k = \partial \theta_k / \partial \epsilon_k$ and we can obtain its updating equation by differentiating (7) with respect to ϵ_k:

$$
V'_k = V_k + \sum_{i,j(i \neq j)} \left[e_{ji} \frac{\partial u_{ji}(\theta)}{\partial \theta_k} + \epsilon_k V_k \left(e_{ji} \frac{\partial^2 u_{ji}(\theta)}{\partial \theta_k^2} - \left(\frac{\partial u_{ji}(\theta)}{\partial \theta_k} \right)^2 \right) \right], \tag{37}
$$

$k = 1, \ldots, r$, where V'_k denotes the next time step's value of V_k and the initial value of V_k ($V_{k,0}$) is 0. The set of (7), (36) and (37) forms the adaptive algorithm.

5   Experimental Results

In this section, we provide the experimental results to evaluate the algorithms proposed in the preceding Sect. 4.

5.1   Setting of Simulation

First, we explain the formation of agents. We simulated 100 agents, including 70 good agents ($\bar{\theta}_k = 0.9$) and 30 bad ones ($\bar{\theta}_k = 0.1$). The ratings R_{ji} by good agents are generated by

$$R_{ji} = \prod_{[0,1]} \left[\bar{\theta}_i + 0.1N(0,1) \right], \tag{38}$$

where $N(0,1)$ denotes a normally distributed random variable with zero mean and unit variance. As for bad agents, there are two types. The ratings R_{ji} by the first type (15 agents) are generated randomly (an uniform random variable), whereas the ratings R_{ji} by the second type (15 agents) are generated by

$$R_{ji} = \prod_{[0,1]} \left[1 - \bar{\theta}_i + 0.1N(0,1) \right] . \tag{39}$$

That is, bad agents of the second type are lying agents whose ratings are always complementary.

Furthermore, we assumed the asynchronous situation where R_{ji} were reported asynchronously. At each time step, we randomly selected two agents, and they rated each other and reported their ratings to the online reputation mechanism. We always used asynchronous algorithms in our simulation.

We set the parameters $\theta_{k,0} = 0.7$ ($\forall k$), $\epsilon_{k,0} = 0.05$ ($\forall k$), $\mu = 0.01$, $\epsilon_- = 0$, and $\epsilon_+ = 0.3$. We can't set $\theta_{k,0} = 0$ ($\forall k$) and $\theta_{k,0} = 0.5$ ($\forall k$), because the former is a fixed point of Weighted, Joint, LLS^W, Joint^W and Lie^W algorithms and the latter is a fixed point of the Lie algorithm.

5.2   Performance Comparison of Algorithms

Here we provide the experimental results. Figure 3 shows the changes in the squared error of 7 algorithms, that is Weighted, LLS, Joint, Lie, LLS^W (LLS_w), Joint^W (Joint_w) and Lie^W (Lie_w) (all algorithms are of the asynchronous type). The squared error is defined as

$$\sum_k (\theta_k - \bar{\theta}_k)^2, \tag{40}$$

and each path of the squared errors represents the average of 30 simulations.

Until time step 10,000, we can see that all algorithms, except for the LLS and Weighted algorithms, learn the true trustworthiness values $\bar{\theta}$ gradually and converge within the bounds of $[0, 2]$. The Weighted algorithm is more effective than the simplest LLS algorithm. However, LLS^W is much more effective than the Weighted algorithm, as we noted in "Discussion of Other Algorithms" of Sect. 4.1.

Continuously, at the time step 10,000, we changed the true trustworthiness values $\bar{\theta}_k$ of 10 good agents from 0.9 to 0.1, and these 10 agents started to express complementary ratings defined by (39). It is clear that again the LLS and

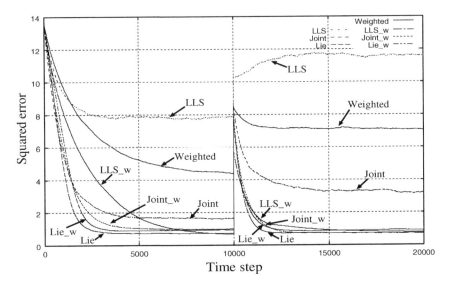

Fig. 3. Changes in squared error

Weighted algorithms do not work well and indeed make things worse. Moreover, this time we can see that the Joint algorithm cannot trace this change appropriately, although other algorithms, Lie, LLS^W, Joint^W and Lie^W, can adapt to this change immediately.

5.3   Effectiveness of Adaptive Algorithm

Here we present more results to show the effectiveness of the adaptive algorithm (see Sect. 4.3). Figure 4 shows the changes in squared error of 6 algorithms under the same condition in Sect. 5.2. Joint, Lie and LLS^W are exactly the same as in Fig. 3, and Joint(a), Lie(a) and LLS^W(a) represent the corresponding algorithms with the adaptive algorithm.

We can see that the adaptive algorithm improves the convergence rate of all three algorithms, not only in time steps before 10,000, but also after 10,000. We omitted the case of other algorithms, LLS, Joint^W and Lie^W, for the sake of a clear graph. However, improvements in the convergence rate by the adaptive algorithm are equally observed.

5.4   Discussion

In our simulation, all agents including malicious agents, have the static strategy of ratings. If the majority of agents are good, we consider that our proposed algorithms still work well under the situation containing malicious agents who dynamically change their rating strategies. However, empirical analysis is needed to examine the robustness against attacks by malicious agents with more intelligent manipulation strategies. Furthermore, (evolutionary) game theory-based

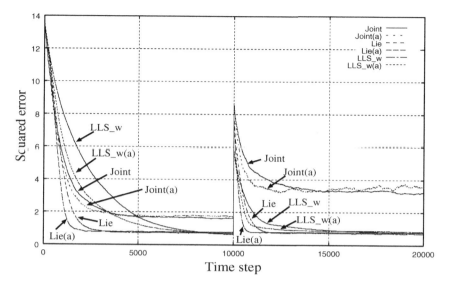

Fig. 4. Changes in squared error (adaptive)

analysis will also help this robustness analysis. We may characterize our problem of online reputation mechanism as the nonzero-sum (general-sum) game between the online reputation mechanism and the intelligent malicious agents. This is future work.

6   Conclusion

We proposed stochastic approximation-based algorithms on our framework of the online reputation mechanism. These algorithms are obtained in a similar fashion from the corresponding rating models and cost functions. We extended these algorithms by introducing the adaptive algorithm of the step-size parameter, in addition to deriving asynchronous algorithms.

Experimental results show that the proposed algorithms can identify good and bad agents effectively under the conditions of the disturbances and also trace the changes in agents' true trustworthiness values adaptively.

References

1. Kollock, P.: The production of trust in online markets. In Lawler, E.J., Macy, M., Thyne, S., Walker, H.A., eds.: Advances in Group Processes (Vol. 16), Greenwich, CT: JAI Press (1999)
2. Resnick, P., Zeckhauser, R., Friedman, E., Kuwabara, K.: Reputation systems. Communications of the ACM **43** (2000) 45–48
3. Dellarocas, C.: The digitization of word-of-mouth: Promise and challenges of online reputation systems. In: Management Science. (2003)

4. Ishida, Y.: An immune network approach to sensor-based diagnosis by self-organization. Complex Systems **10** (1996) 73–90
5. Zacharia, G., Moukas, A., Maes, P.: Collaborative reputation mechanisms in electronic marketplaces. In: Proceedings of the 32nd Hawaii International Conference on System Sciences (HICSS-32). (1999)
6. Dellarocas, C.: Immunizing online reputation reporting systems against unfair ratings and discriminatory behavior. In: Proceedings of the 2nd ACM Conference on Electronic Commerce (EC'00). (2000)
7. Yu, B., Singh, M.P.: Detecting deception in reputation management. In: Proceedings of Second International Joint Conference on Autonomous Agents and Multi-Agent Systems (AAMAS'03). (2003)
8. Wang, Y., Vassileva, J.: Bayesian network-based trust model. In: Proceedings of the IEEE/WIC International Conference on Web Intelligence (WI'03). (2003)
9. Kushner, H.J., Yin, G.G.: Stochastic Approximation and Recursive Algorithms and Applications (Second Edition). Springer-Verlag (2003)
10. Sutton, R.S., Barto, A.G.: Reinforcement Learning. The MIT Press (1998)
11. Benveniste, A., Métivier, M., Priouret, P.: Adaptive Algorithms and Stochastic Approximations. Springer-Verlag (1990)

Learning Multi-agent Search Strategies

Malcolm J.A. Strens

Future Systems & Technology Division, QinetiQ Ltd.
G020/A9, Cody Technology Park, Farnborough, Hants. GU14 0LX. U.K.

Abstract. We identify a specialised class of reinforcement learning prob
lem in which the agent(s) have the goal of gathering information (identifying the hidden state). The gathered information can affect rewards
but not optimal behaviour. Exploiting this characteristic, an algorithm
is developed for evaluating an agent's policy against *all possible* hidden
state histories at the same time. Experimental results show the method
is effective in a two-dimensional multi-pursuer evader searching task. A
comparison is made between identical policies, joint policies and "relational" policies that exploit relativistic information about the pursuers'
positions.

1 Introduction

We address the reinforcement learning problem [1] for episodic tasks in partially
observable environments. These tasks are characterised by the presence of 'hidden state' which is not observable by the agent, although it may be revealed over
the course of a trial.

For example, suppose the task is to search an area of the ground using a
robotic vehicle (the *pursuer*, under the learning agent's control). Initially, the
pursuer may only know that the evader (another vehicle perhaps) is within some
given uncertainty area. The pursuer may also have available a dynamics model
that determines how the evader could move over the course of a trial. The goal is
simply to bring the evader within detection range of the pursuer's sensors (and
at this point the trial ends). Therefore the only use that the pursuer can make
of its sensor measurements during the course of the trial is to eliminate regions
of the search area: *i.e.* the pursuer must reason about *where the evader could
be*. This is an extreme example of a *dual control* problem: an agent must take
actions to gather information on the way to its goal.

If the means available to the agent for observing the environment (*e.g.* sensors) do not allow the agent to gather instantaneously all the information that
is relevant to its decision-making, then the task is a *partially observable* (PO)
one. In PO tasks, reactive policies based on only the instantaneous observations
are rarely effective: it is necessary for the agent to fuse information over time
to make best use of the observations (and initial information). The searching
task is a good example: the instantaneous observations are identical at every
time step until the evader is found, and so no useful memoryless policy could
be found. However, if the agent uses the observations to modify a longer-term

D. Kudenko et al. (Eds.): Adaptive Agents and MAS II, LNAI 3394, pp. 245–259, 2005.

memory representing where the evader could be at the current time, it can use this memory as the foundation for decision-making.

A standard model for reasoning about PO environments is the Partially Observable Markov Decision Process (POMDP). This models the transition dynamics of the (full) environment state, the expected return for every (state, action) pair, and a stochastic function mapping states to observations. Most success for large POMDP problems has come from restricting the complexity of learning by choosing the agent's policy from a parameterised family (our approach), rather than estimating state-action values for every information state. The learning problem becomes one of finding appropriate policy parameters. However, even with parameterised policies there remains a difficulty in how to define the 'inputs' to the policy. In fully observable problems, these inputs should be a compact representation of the state (a *feature vector*) that carries with it all information relevant to decision-making. Similarly, in PO problems the inputs can be *information features* that encode aspects of the belief relevant to decision-making. For example, in the detection task where the belief is an evader uncertainty area (EUA), candidate sets of features might include informative points in the EUA (center of mass, extrema of boundaries) or spatial moments of the distribution.

Section 2 gives formal descriptions for a POMDP and the proposed specialisation, an *information gathering problem*. Section 3 introduces recursive Bayesian filters for tracking beliefs, including the particle filter used in the experiments. Section 4 describes a set of appropriate information features for the searching task, and three types of policy parameterisation (individual, joint, and relational). Section 5 describes a fast way of learning in information gathering problems that exploits conditional independence between the true hidden state and the optimal behaviour, given the belief. Section 6 describes direct search methods for finding effective policy parameters. Section 7 describes evaluation of the approach using a multi-pursuer evader task, and section 8 concludes.

2   A Special Class of POMDP

Before describing a specialised version of the POMDP for information gathering problems, we give a formal description of the existing MDP and POMDP models. An MDP is a discrete-time model for the stochastic evolution of a system's state, under control of an external input (the agent's actions). It also models a stochastic reward that depends on the state and action.

> *Definition* A Markov Decision Process is given by $\langle X, A, T, R \rangle$
> where X is a set of states and A a set of actions. T is a stochastic
> transition function defining the likelihood the next state will be
> $x' \in X$ given current state $x \in X$ and action $a \in A$: $P_T(x'|x, a)$.
> R is a stochastic reward function defining the likelihood the imme-
> diate reward will be $r \in \mathbf{R}$ given current state $x \in X$ and action
> $a \in A$: $P_R(r|x, a)$.

A POMDP is a general-purpose discrete-time mathematical model for reasoning about single-agent interaction in the presence of partial observability. The POMDP assumes that the agent receives observations that do not necessarily convey the full hidden state of the environment.

> *Definition* A POMDP $\langle X, A, T, R, Y, O \rangle$ builds upon a MDP $\langle X, A, T, R \rangle$ by adding a set of observations Y and an observation function O that generates stochastic observations from the hidden state according to $P_O(y|x)$.

2.1 Optimal Behaviour in POMDPs

Reinforcement learning for partially observable problems is generally more difficult than for fully-observable ones. The reason for this can be seen by analysing optimal behaviour in a POMDP (assuming all parts of the POMDP are known[1]). Optimal behaviour is given not by a policy that maps observations to action probabilities, but by a policy that maps *beliefs* to action probabilities. The agent's belief or *information state* is its representation for uncertainty in the hidden state at the current time. This belief is a probability distribution $P(x|H)$ over X, where H is the complete interaction history. It is possible to find the agent's optimal policy by constructing a MDP from the POMDP but with a much larger state space corresponding to the set of possible beliefs. This larger MDP can, in theory, be solved by standard RL methods. In practice, however, the belief space is usually so large that the methods are intractable without some kind of approximation. For example Thrun estimated state-action values for a discrete set of belief 'exemplars', each corresponding to a particle filter estimate of the belief [2]. The KL divergence was used as a distance-measure between information states, to allow the nearest neighbor exemplar to be found for each information state encountered during learning. In the worst case, the belief space has size exponential in the number of time steps of interaction.

2.2 Information Gathering Problems

Now we investigate special cases where part of the state is *fully* hidden. By *fully* hidden we mean that observations that depend on this state do not affect optimal behaviour (and are therefore excluded from the model). Firstly, suppose that the fully hidden state represents the location of a physical entity (*e.g.* a vehicle) and that the agent's *only goal* is to discover this information. When the information is discovered the trial ends. In this case the agent knows its own physical state, and observations convey no information about the hidden state until the end of the trial. Therefore optimal searching behaviour is not dependent on these observations. More generally, consider an agent that aims to discover some part of the hidden state, but passes the information on to another agent for action. The trial does not end, but from that point on the agent has "no interest" in

---

[1] If the observation, transition and reward functions of the POMDP are not known *a priori* an even more difficult learning problem is encountered.

that part of the state. An example would be a remote surveillance system (e.g. a relocatable satellite) that must plan its own course to gather imagery at a set of locations, and report this information for interpretation by another system (e.g. a ground station). This is an example of a *continuing* information gathering problem (IGP) for which the following definition is proposed:

> *Definition* An IGP is given by $< X, S, A, T^h, T^s, R >$. The fully hidden part of the state $x \in X$ evolves according to a transition function $P_{T^h}(x'|x, s, a)$. The observable part of the state $s \in S$ evolves separately according to a transition function $P_{T^s}(s'|s, a)$. R defines the stochastic immediate reward $P_R(r|x, s, a)$ which may depend on both the hidden part and the observable part of the state.

Note that there is no observation function because the observations are identical to the observable part of the state (s). The observable state could incorporate the physical state of the agent(s) and any other observable scenario information. A stationary policy for the agent is now a stochastic function of (i) the belief $b \equiv P(x|H)$ over the fully hidden state and (ii) the fully observable state:

$$\pi(b, s, a) \equiv P(a|b, s)$$

The benefit of this new formulation is that the belief b evolves independently of the actual fully hidden state x. (There are no observations to convey information about it.) The belief b is obtained simply by a recursive Bayesian filter that has no information update step.

3   Recursive Bayesian Filtering

Bayesian filtering is the process of estimating the distribution of possible values (belief) for the state of a dynamic system, given a sequence of noisy measurements. A *recursive* Bayesian filter implements this process by using only the current measurement to update the belief at each time step; it never refers back to previous measurements. Consider first the non-interactive case where the agent is simply observing the dynamic system. Implementation requires a way to represent the current belief $P(x_t|Y_t)$ where x_t is the state vector and Y_t is the sequence of measurements so far. There are many possible implementations. The Kalman filter approximates the belief by a multivariate Gaussian distribution. Particle filters use a 'cloud' of samples as the representation, allowing multi-modal distributions to be represented. Grid-based filters discretise the state space and store a probability at each grid point.

The filter has two updates at each step: *prediction* applies the known dynamics $P(x_{t+1}|x_t)$ to obtain a prior distribution $P(x_{t+1}|Y_t)$ for the state at next time step; *information update* uses Bayes' rule to account for the new observation y_{t+1}, yielding a posterior distribution (the belief at $t + 1$):

$$P(x_{t+1}|Y_{t+1}) \propto P(y_{t+1}|x_{t+1})P(x_{t+1}|Y_t)$$

This states that the likelihood of a new state (x_{t+1}) is proportional to ($\propto$) the likelihood of the observation (y_{t+1}) given that state, weighted by its prior probability given previous observations (Y_t).

For example, a recursive Bayesian filter can be applied to the problem of tracking the location of an aircraft using noisy sensor measurements from a radar. The state is the aircraft's location, pose, and speed. The dynamics is determined by the aircraft's acceleration capability. The measurement model $P(y_t|x_t)$ describes the radar's performance (e.g. typical error) and must be known. Applying the filter yields a belief that represents the uncertainty in the aircraft's state at each time step, and allows decisions to be made.

3.1   Formulation for Interactive Systems

In many sequential decision problems it is feasible to estimate the belief (even when it is not feasible to enumerate the space to represent a value function). Using the POMDP notation, the vector x_t represents the full state of the environment (e.g. the position and motion of one or more objects). The belief is a probability density for x_t given the interaction history $H_t \equiv (A_{t-1}, Y_t)$ where $A_{t-1} \equiv (a_1, \ldots, a_{t-1})$ is the action history and Y_t is the observation history. The initial information is $P(x_0)$. The recursive Bayesian filter makes use of a dynamics model $P_T(x'|x, a)$ and an observation model $P_O(y|x)$ to recursively estimate the belief:

$$\underbrace{P(x_{t+1}|A_t, Y_t)} = \int_{x_t} P(x_t|H_t) P_T(x_{t+1}|x_t, a_t) dx_t$$

$$P(x_{t+1}|H_{t+1}) \propto P_O(y_{t+1}|x_{t+1}) \overbrace{P(x_{t+1}|A_t, Y_t)}$$

3.2   The Particle Filter

Our experiments make use of the particle filter [3] because it is very easy and convenient to work with: it represents the belief as a sum of weighted hypotheses $\{(x_t^i, w_t^i)\}$:

$$P(x_t|H_t) = \sum_{i=1}^{N} w_t^i \delta(x_t^i, x_t)$$

The update can be implemented (separately for each particle) by importance sampling, using some proposal density $q(x_{t+1}^i|x_t^i, H_{t+1})$ then re-weighting the particles according to:

$$w_{t+1}^i \propto w_t^i \frac{P_O(y_t|x_t^i) P_T(x_{t+1}^i|x_t^i, a_t)}{q(x_{t+1}^i|x_t^i, H_{t+1})}$$

Over the course of time, the weights of the particles may become imbalanced causing the set of particles to be a poor representation of the true belief. To overcome this problem, *resampling* is usually necessary. Resampling makes all weights equal, but there tend to be more copies in the new population of the particles that had the largest weights.

3.3   Particle Filter for Fully Hidden State

The full recursive Bayesian filter is not required in information gathering problems. In particular, there are no observations conveying information about the hidden state, and so the belief depends only on the initial distribution $P(x_0)$ and on the dynamics expressed as a transition model $P_T^h(x_{t+1}|x_t, a_t)$ (now using IGP notation). The update becomes a single step:

$$P(x_{t+1}|H_{t+1}) = \int_{x_t} P(x_t|H_t)P(x_{t+1}|x_t, s_t, a_t)dx_t$$

where $H_t \equiv (A_{t-1}, S_t)$ and $S_t \equiv (s_1, \dots, s_t)$ is the observable state history. We will be use this "history filter" for two different purposes: representing an agent's beliefs and representing an ensemble of scenarios for evaluation.

A detection event in the pursuer-evader problem will lead to the weight of the corresponding hypothesis being set to 0. If resampling were then to take place, these zero-weight hypotheses would be replaced in the filter by duplicates of other hypotheses; i.e. the computational effort of the whole particle filter would be focussed on cases where the evader would not yet have been intercepted. However, there is a strong argument for not resampling[2]. Given that no computational effort is expended on zero-weight particles, the processing requirement will be proportional to the likelihood that the evader has not yet been detected. This implies that, without resampling, computational load is matched to the maximum change in total return from the trial. Therefore, in the pursuer-evader problem, the particle filter has been reduced to a very simple update for each hypothesis, implementing the evader's instantaneous motion.

4   Policy Parameterisation

Our goal is for the learning agent to acquire effective control policies (searching behaviours). A policy is a means for selecting an appropriate action, given the current situation. For large problems, there are two main approaches: policy search and value function approximation. In policy search, the designer provides the agent with a parameterised control policy, and the parameters are the objective for learning. In contrast, value function approximation approaches (common in reinforcement learning) estimate a mapping from states to values. This allows an agent to exploit a known (or sampled) transition function to reason about the values of future states (using Bellman's "backup" operator within the learning rule), and to *derive* a control policy. The advantage of representing and exploiting the state information in this way is faster learning. The disadvantage is that it is difficult to meet the assumptions required by the Bellman operator (especially in the presence of large state spaces or partial observability).

---

[2] However, resampling *is* required if the transition function does not assign similar probabilities to all feasible outcomes.

The method used here is best described as "direct policy search" because it does not exploit Bellman's operator in learning (even though it does represent the policy intrinsically as a parameterised value function). The uncertainty in the evader's location is given at any instance in time by a belief consisting of $N_H = 256$ hypotheses (particles in the filter). To pose the problem as one of direct policy search, a set of information features is required that summarises the set of particles adequately for robust decision-making. This process is sometimes called *belief compression* [4]. The features described here make use only of the position part of each particle's state.

4.1   Information Features

Let (x_i, y_i) be the position vector for hypothesis i expressed in a coordinate system of a pursuer of interest[3]. To obtain a compact set of information features, we integrate over the particles using a small number of basis functions ϕ_{jk} for $j \in \{1, 2\}$ and $k \in \{1, 2, 3, 4\}$. A suitable set is given by the regularised spatial derivatives:

$$\phi_{jk}(x, y) = H(j, 2k - 2)$$

where:

$$H(m, n) = \frac{\partial^m}{\partial x} \frac{\partial^n}{\partial y} \exp(-\frac{x^2 + y^2}{2})$$

These basis functions are all derivatives of a Gaussian distribution placed at the origin (of the pursuer's coordinate system). They are mutually orthogonal and (multiplicatively) separable in the two axis directions. Only even derivatives are selected in the y-direction; the odd ones are of no interest as a result of symmetry in the problem. This yields a set of information features:

$$z_{jk} = \frac{1}{N_H} \sum_i \phi_{jk}(x_i, y_i)$$

We then define an information-state value function:

$$V_\alpha(x_i, y_i) = \sum_{j,k} \alpha_{jk} C_{jk} z_{jk}$$

C_{jk} is a constant that ensures the magnitudes of the information features are balanced:

$$C_{jk}^{-1} \equiv \int_x \int_y \phi_{jk}^2(x, y) \mathrm{d}y \mathrm{d}x$$

---

[3] This coordinate system has its x-axis parallel to the pursuer's velocity vector. A nonlinear transformation is also applied: a displacement of (u, v) in the pursuer's coordinate system is mapped to $(x, y) \equiv (u/\{R_0 sqrt|u|\}, v/\{R_0 sqrt|v|\})$, in order to provide more spatial resolution close to the agent. R_0 is a constant that will determine the effective spatial extent of the basis functions, and is chosen equal to 512 in our evaluation.

The 2x4 parameter matrix α will be the target for learning. We make use of the smooth dynamics to avoid computing V explicitly. Instead, each pursuer selects its action (turn left or turn right) according to the sign of the gradient of V with respect to the angle θ of its velocity vector. The gradient is given here without proof:

$$\frac{\partial V}{\partial \theta} \equiv \sum_i \sum_{j,k} C_{jk}\{x_i H(j, 2k-1) - y_i H(j+1, 2k-2)\}$$

Since only the sign of the gradient is used to determine the pursuer's action, an arbitrary scaling of α will not affect its behaviour. This redundancy is eliminated by requiring $\|\alpha\| = 1$.

4.2   Joint and Relational Policies

In general, every pursuer need not be given the same policy. Instead, the problem can be regarded as a search for the joint policy $(\alpha_1, \ldots, \alpha_{N_p})$ which has $8N_P$ dimensions. We will evaluate whether the extra representational freedom (and complexity) of a joint policy can be exploited.

In order to allow any number of pursuers to *cooperate* without the policy size increasing, a simple relational policy has also been designed. Every pursuer has a copy of the policy which consists of two components: α (as before) and β which contains information about the relative positions of the pursuers. β affects the value function in the same way as α except that the basis functions are summed over pursuer locations instead of particle locations:

$$z_{jk}^{rel} = \frac{1}{N_P - 1} \sum_l \phi_{jk}(x_l, y_l)$$

$$V_\beta(x_l, y_l) = \sum_{j,k} \beta_{jk} C_{jk} z_{jk}^{rel}$$

where (x_l, y_l) is the location of pursuer l expressed in the coordinate system of the pursuer for whom the decision is to be made. Using relational policies, it is the gradient of the combined value function $V_\alpha + V_\beta$ that determines each pursuer's action. The dimension of this policy is 16 nomatter how many pursuers are present. (Also, the number of pursuers taking part in the search could change dynamically during a trial.) This approach will be evaluated to determine whether pursuers are aided by taking account of each other's locations.

5   Dual Particle Filter Method

One major benefit of identifying the problem as an "information gathering process" rather than (the more general) POMDP is that specialised solution methods can be derived. In the pursuer-evader problem, the pursuers' locations are the fully observable state (s) and the evader's location is the hidden state. When the evader comes within detection range of a pursuer, the trial ends. Therefore, the hidden state is never used to determine future actions: i.e. observation of the hidden state conveys no information about optimal behaviour (pursuer policy). The implication of this is that *any proposed policy can be tested against all possible hidden state histories in parallel*. The outcome of a parallel trial is not success or failure (evader detected or not) but instead the *proportion* of the histories in which the evader was detected.

The method proposed here uses one particle filter to represent the pursuers' beliefs about the location of the evader, and a separate particle filter to represent hidden state histories for parallel evaluation. Although it may not be immediately obvious, the two particle filters are estimating the same distribution: the possible state of the evader at each time step. Nevertheless, it is essential that they are kept separate because if the approximation errors (inevitable in a particle filter) were correlated, a grossly overoptimistic estimate of the performance of a policy would be obtained.

We found that 256 particles in each filter were sufficient, whereas using a single filter for both estimation tasks means that over 4000 particles are required for similar performance. Each trial does not end until the evader has been detected in every parallel scenario, or a maximum duration has expired. This approach is also very efficient compared with the naive alternative: running 256 separate trials; one for each possible trajectory taken by the evader.

6   Direct Policy Search

Suppose that the agent's policy has a parameter vector w of size m; for example $w \equiv \alpha$ for pursuers with identical policies; $w \equiv (\alpha_1 :: \ldots :: \alpha_{N_P})$ for joint policies (where :: indicates concatenation of vectors); or $w \equiv \alpha :: \beta$ for relational policies. A single simulation trial in which w defines the pursuers' behaviours will lead to a stochastic return. The aim of learning is to find a w that maximises the expected return. *Direct policy search* methods attempt to optimise expected return without reference to performance gradient information. Some methods use a large number of trials for each proposed w to obtain a near-deterministic evaluation, then apply a deterministic optimization procedure (e.g. downhill simplex method). However, here we use a method that can work with unreliable policy comparisons [5].

6.1   Differential Evolution

Our approach is a variant of *differential evolution*, an evolutionary method that operates directly on a population of real-valued vectors (rather than binary strings) [6]. Proposals are obtained by linear combination of existing population members.

Initially, the population is chosen randomly from some prior density on w. To generate each proposal, one candidate in the population is chosen (systematically) for improvement. Then the vector difference between two more randomly[4]

---

[4] All vectors used in the process of generating a proposal are mutually exclusive.

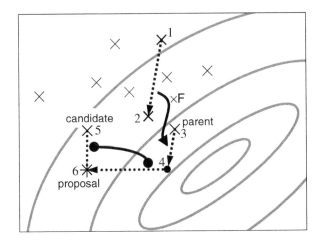

Fig. 1. Obtaining a new proposal in differential evolution

chosen members, weighted by a scalar parameter, F, is added to a third randomly chosen 'parent'. Crossover (see below) takes place between this and the candidate, to obtain a proposal point. The proposal is compared with the candidate by running a small set of new simulation trials for each. To reduce variance in this comparison, the same set of scenarios[5] is used for every comparison. According to the outcome *either* the proposal replaces the candidate *or* the population remains unchanged. In either case, a new candidate for replacement will be selected on the next iteration.

Crossover is implemented here by selecting each element of the proposal vector from either the candidate or the new vector with equal probability. Crossover helps to prevent the population from become trapped in a subspace. For each proposal, $\log_2 F$ was chosen uniformly from the range $[-10, 0]$ and the result was scaled by a value $F_{max}(t)$ that decreased with time. ($\log_2 F_{max}(t)$ was reduced uniformly from 0 to -10 during learning.) This ensures convergence of the population.

6.2   Illustration

Figure 1 illustrates this process in more detail: the weighted difference between two population members (1,2) is added to a third population point (3). The result (4) is subject to crossover with the candidate for replacement (5) to obtain a proposal (6). The proposal is evaluated (using a number of trials) and replaces the candidate if it is found to be better. Note that the proposal could be identical to (4) or (5), depending on the outcome of crossover.

This form of DE has a very useful property; replacing any one population member due to an occasional incorrect comparison is not catastrophic. It suf-

---

[5] A scenario is an initial configuration for the pursuers' locations.

fices that the comparison be unbiased, and correct with probability only slightly better than chance (0.5) in large populations [7]. This means that it is possible to use only a small number of simulation trials (4 in this case) per proposal.

7   Evaluation

We perform a comparison between individual, joint and relational policies for different numbers of pursuers. The aim is to demonstrate the effectiveness of the dual particle filter method and to collect some evidence about the best way to structure a policy for this type of task.

7.1   Multi-pursuer Evader Task

We consider a multi-pursuer evader task in which the observable state is the location and velocity of each pursuer, and the hidden state is the location and goal direction of an evader. The pursuers must cooperate to detect the evader before the uncertainty in its position becomes too large.

- **States.** Each pursuer's state is a location on the 2-dimensional plane and a motion direction. The evader's state is a location in the plane and a preferred direction; therefore each particle in the filters will be a 3-vector.
- **Scenarios.** The initial belief for the evader's location is an uncertainty area given by a Gaussian distribution with standard deviation 100, located at the origin. The pursuers all start at a distance from the origin chosen uniformly from [2000, 3000]. Their angular separation (subtended from the origin) is 30 degrees. Note that rotational and translational invariance of our formulation will mean that the policy obtained will work just as well for any rotated or translated versions of this set of scenarios.
- **Dynamics.** The pursuers can move at a speed of 24 (length units per time step) and the evader at 1. The evader can instantaneously change its direction whereas the pursuers have a maximum turn angle of $\pi/8$ at each time step. In our implementation, each pursuer selects either $+\pi/8$ or $-\pi/8$ according to the information-state value function's gradient. It remains possible for a pursuer to follow an almost straight course by alternating between these two actions. The evader's behaviour is given by a stochastic policy: with equal probability it either moves in its preferred direction or moves in a direction that takes it away from the nearest pursuer (ensuring the problem is non-trivial[6]). If the evader's position is within detection range (24 units) of a pursuer, it is deemed to have been found.
- **Termination.** The maximum trial duration is 256 steps. With a naive implementation in which only one evader trajectory (history) is used in each trial, detection would often be completed within this time limit. However, using the dual particle filter method, the trial will not end until detection

---

[6] In particular it ensures there is a dependency between the pursuers' actions and the evolution of the hidden state; otherwise it would be possible to pre-compute evader trajectories.

takes place in *every* hypothesis for the evader's trajectory. Therefore, often the maximum duration will be reached (but with a diminished number of active particles in each filter.)
– **Returns.** The return at the end of a simulation trial is the proportion of the original probability mass within the evaluation filter that has been eliminated during the course of the trial. This represents the expected return over the 256 parallel scenarios described above, and can be interpreted simply as the probability that the evader is found within the trial duration. The differential evolution method uses this return as the (stochastic) evaluation of the weight vector associated with that trial.

Figure 2 shows the trajectories of 3 pursuers during a trial as sequences of connected circles. The radius of each circle is the area within which the evader can be detected. A more detailed view of the central circle (radius 400 units) is also given, for a different learning trial. It shows a strategy has been learnt for the 3 pursuers that covers the central part of the space very well. By this stage in the trial the pursuers have moved towards the edge of this central circle, because the evader could have reached these areas. The plotted markers indicate the states of one particle filter at the end of a trial. The grey points indicate particles that have been detected. These are frozen in the locations at which they were detected, for illustration. The outer (black) points represent hypotheses for the current location of an evader that has not yet been captured.

7.2   Configuration of Learning System

Differential evolution used a population size of 16 and F was chosen as described in section 1. 256 particles were used in each filter. 4 trials were performed for each policy evaluation (with pursuers at distances of 1125, 1375, 1625 and 1875 from the origin). Therefore 8 trials were needed for each policy comparison, and so 512 policy comparisons were possible in the total budget of 4096 trials. (This is a relatively small number of function evaluations for an evolutionary algorithm.) The best policy within the population was tested at the end of learning, using a set of 512 scenarios, in which the initial pursuer positions were uniformly distributed in the interval [2000,3000]. A baseline performance was obtained using a very simple policy in which $\alpha_{11} = 1$ and all other elements are 0. This causes each pursuer to turn towards the centre of probability mass of the evader's position distribution, taken under the weighting function $H(0,0)$.

7.3   Results

Table 1 shows the performance of the baseline policy and three types of learnt policy as a percentage (likelihood of detecting evader), for different number of pursuers. The error bounds given are at one standard deviation: the standard errors ($n = 500$) are about 20 times smaller so a difference of 2% is significant, using Gaussian statistics.

The task is sufficiently difficult that no method is able to obtain 100% success, even with 4 pursuers. This is not surprising, because the uncertainty in the

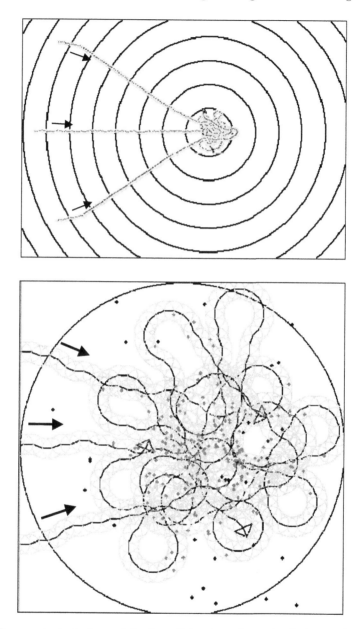

Fig. 2. Pursuer trajectories and final particle states in a simulation trial. Full trial (top); detail from a different trial (below)

evader position expands at a rate that increases rapidly with time. The baseline strategy (no learning) provides performance that increases with the number of pursuers: this indicates that the pursuers do not all converge onto the same trajectories even though they are acting independently according to a simple

Table 1. Success rate (%) for different policy types

N_P	1	2	3	4
Baseline	46 ± 4	64 ± 3	75 ± 4	81 ± 3
Identical	47 ± 7	72 ± 3	80 ± 2	88 ± 2
Joint	NA	73 ± 6	79 ± 3	85 ± 2
Relational	NA	72 ± 6	86 ± 3	93 ± 1

strategy. Introducing learning improves performance (significantly) for 2 or more pursuers even though the pursuers continue to ignore each others' positions in their decision-making. The learnt joint policy, in which each pursuer has a separate set of policy parameters performs very similarly: it seems there is no great advantage in allowing each to have a different strategy. There is actually a performance decrease with 4 pursuers, probably because the joint strategy has 32 parameters and so could be expected to take much longer to learn than the identical (8 parameter) strategies.

The learnt relational policies are equally effective (compared with the other learnt strategies) for 2 pursuers, but show major benefits with 3 or more pursuers. This indicates pursuers that are aware of each others' positions can "divide and conquer" the search problem in a more systematic way. The gains that have been obtained are very significant: with 4 pursuers the chance that the evader escapes has been halved (compared with the other learnt policies) and reduced by nearly 3 times compared with the baseline policy.

8   Conclusions

Some information gathering problems such as searching tasks have special structure. Although there is hidden state, and beliefs must be tracked, the actual hidden state does not affect optimal behaviour. In other words, optimal behaviour is conditionally independent of the true hidden state given the belief. Therefore it is possible to evaluate a policy against any number of hidden state trajectories in a single learning trial.

The implementation described here matches the computational burden of agent reasoning (belief revision) and simulation (generating hidden state histories) exactly: a particle filter can be used for each of these processes. Furthermore, these two particle filters are performing the same estimation task. They are kept separate in the learning algorithm only because there are benefits if errors are not correlated. When the learnt strategy is transferred into a real environment (not a simulation) only the particle filter representing agent beliefs would be retained: the second filter is part of the learning algorithm rather than the agent itself.

When learning policies for multiple homogeneous agents, it is not necessary to learn separate policies for each agent (the joint policy option); however it is important that the agents make use of relational information (e.g. relative position) in order to divide the workload effectively. The "relational policy" achieved this by applying the same set of basis functions (used for obtaining evader information features) to represent the relative positions of the other pursuers. The deterministic structure of the pursuers' dynamics was also exploited in the policy formulation, that might otherwise have required a state-action value function to be estimated.

Acknowledgements

This research was funded by the UK Ministry of Defence Corporate Research Programme in Energy, Guidance and Control. © Copyright QinetiQ Limited, 2004.

References

1. Sutton, R.S., Barto, A.G.: Reinforcement Learning. MIT Press, Cambridge, MA (1998)
2. Thrun, S.: Monte carlo POMDPs. In Solla, S., Leen, T., Müller, K., eds.: Advances in Neural Information Processing Systems 12, MIT Press (2000) 1064–1070
3. Doucet, A., de Freitas, J.F.G., (Eds.), N.J.G.: Sequential Monte Carlo Methods in Practice. Springer-Verlag, New York (2001)
4. Roy, N., Gordon, G.: Exponential family PCA for belief compression in POMDPs. In: Advances in Neural Information Processing Systems. (2002)
5. Strens, M.J.A., Moore, A.W.: Direct policy search using paired statistical tests. In: Proceedings of the 18th International Conference on Machine Learning, Morgan Kaufmann, San Francisco, CA (2001) 545–552
6. Storn, R., Price, K.: Differential evolution - a simple and efficient adaptive scheme for global optimization over continuous spaces. Technical Report TR-95-012, International Computer Science Institute, Berkeley, CA (1995)
7. Strens, M.J.A., Moore, A.W.: Policy search using paired comparisons. Journal of Machine Learning Research **3** (2002) 921–950

Combining Planning with Reinforcement Learning for Multi-robot Task Allocation

Malcolm Strens and Neil Windelinckx

Future Systems & Technology Division, QinetiQ G020/A9, Cody Technology Park, Farnborough, Hampshire. GU14 0LX. U.K.

Abstract. We describe an approach to the multi-robot task allocation (MRTA) problem in which a group of robots must perform tasks that arise continuously, at arbitrary locations across a large space. A dynamic scheduling algorithm is derived in which proposed plans are evaluated using a combination of short-term lookahead and a value function acquired by reinforcement learning. We demonstrate that this dynamic scheduler can learn not only to allocate robots to tasks efficiently, but also to position the robots appropriately in readiness for new tasks (tactical awareness), and conserve resources over the long run (strategic awareness).

1   Introduction

Dynamic scheduling is a resource allocation problem in which the plan must be reviewed constantly in response to exogenous events (*e.g.* user-specified tasks entering the system). A plan consists of an ordered allocation of robots to tasks, together with any associated parameters.

A "heterogeneous task stream" contains tasks of several types (possibly from many different users/clients). The tasks may have individual constraints on their successful completion (*e.g.* earliest or latest start or finish times), or joint constraints (*e.g.* completion of task A before starting task B).

This paper describes a part of a proprietary QinetiQ software suite for dynamic scheduling in multi-agent systems. We focus here on the case where the resources are physical robots (vehicles or robots) and the tasks arise at various locations across the space in which they operate. For example, an on-demand transport system consisting of many individual road vehicles will be required to review its planned schedule whenever a new journey request enters the system.

We view the problem as one of optimal control (sequential decision making) in a partially observable environment. Boutilier *et al.* [1] survey existing work in this topic area, which links operations research (OR), reinforcement learning (RL) and planning. This contrasts with the usual formulation of multi-robot task allocation (MRTA) as a static optimisation problem [2]. The problem with the latter approach is that it does not account for the likelihood that new tasks will enter the system (before *or* beyond the planning horizon).

Partial observability arises from not being able to predict what new tasks will arise in the stream of tasks that is provided to the robots. Therefore it

D. Kudenko et al. (Eds.): Adaptive Agents and MAS II, LNAI 3394, pp. 260–274, 2005.

is not possible to *plan* beyond the tasks that are already known. To obtain a near-optimal solution requires the robots not only to complete the known tasks as rapidly as possible, but also to remain well-positioned for new tasks, and to preserve resources (*e.g.* fuel or battery power).

From a decision-theoretic viewpoint, the state of the system is high-dimensional, because it includes the state of each robot, the known tasks, and the distribution of unseen tasks. The actions available to the decision-maker are assignment of robots to tasks. The cost function that is to be optimised consists of the accumulated "rewards" received for successful completion of tasks.

1.1   Paper Outline

Section 2 introduces sequential decision theory formulations of the problem, and identifies the need for approximate solution methods. Section 3 describes the hybrid planning/learning approach and its underlying assumptions. Section 4 provides an evaluation of the hybrid approach, comparing with short-term planning and a heuristic approach. This is followed by a discussion (section 5) and conclusions (section 6).

2   Theoretical Foundations

A formal description is given of the Markov Decision Process (MDP) model that underlies dynamic programming, reinforcement learning and optimal control. Models for partial observability are introduced, and the need for approximate solution methods is identified.

2.1   Markov Decision Process

An MDP is a discrete-time model for the stochastic evolution of a system's state, under control of an external input (the agent's action or agents' joint action). It also models a stochastic reward that depends on the state and action.

> *Definition* A Markov Decision Process is given by $< X, A, T, R >$ where X is a set of states and A a set of actions. T is a stochastic transition function defining the likelihood the next state will be $x' \in X$ given current state $x \in X$ and action $a \in A$: $P_T(x'|x,a)$. R is a stochastic reward function defining the likelihood the immediate reward will be $r \in \mathbb{R}$ given current state $x \in X$ and action $a \in A$: $P_R(r|x,a)$.

2.2   Optimal Policy

Combining an MDP with a determistic control policy $\pi(x)$, that generates an action for every state gives a closed system. A useful measure of policy performance, starting at a particular state, is the expected value of the *discounted return*:

$$r_t + \gamma r_{t+1} + \gamma^2 r_{t+2} + \dots$$

$\gamma < 1$ is a discount factor that ensures (slightly) more weight is given to rewards received sooner. For a given policy π and starting state x, we write $V_\pi(x)$ for this expectation. If a trial has finite duration, then the infinite sum is truncated, and we can allow the case $\gamma = 1$ (finite horizon undiscounted return).

A very useful quantity for deriving optimal control policies is the state-action value $Q_\pi(x, a)$ which is the expected discounted return in state x when taking action a initially, then following policy π for action selection thereafter. Given an MDP and a discount factor, there exist optimal value functions Q^* and V^* that satisfy:

$$V^*(x) = \max_a Q^*(x, a)$$

$$Q^*(x, a) = R(x, a) + \gamma \sum_{x'} P_T(x'|x, a) V^*(x')$$

where $R(x, a)$ is the expected instantaneous reward for action a in state x, determined by $P_R(r|x, a)$. The optimal policy is to select the action a that maximises the state-action value:

$$\pi^*(x) = \arg\max_a Q(x, a)$$

2.3   Reinforcement Learning

Dynamic programming [3] is a simple process for finding π^* for a *known* MDP, using repeated updates such as:

$$Q'(x, a) \leftarrow R(x, a) + \gamma \sum_{x'} P_T(x'|x, a) \max_{a'} Q(x', a')$$

This causes Q to converge to Q^* when applied repeatedly in every state-action pair (x, a).

Reinforcement learning (RL) attempts to find the optimal policy for an *unknown* MDP by trial-and-error interaction with the system [4]. *Model-based* RL methods estimate the MDP, then solve it by dynamic programming. "Conventional" reinforcement learning methods such as Q learning [5] and *SARSA* estimate Q^* (and hence π^*) directly without estimating P_T explicitly. *Policy search* reinforcement learning methods parameterise π and search directly for values of these parameters that maximise trial returns (*e.g.* [6]).

2.4   The Need for Approximate Solution Methods

Partially observable problems in which the agents cannot observe the full system state are much more challenging. These can be formulated using an extended model called a *partially observable* Markov Decision Process (POMDP) that adds an observation process to the MDP. The optimal policy can be derived in the same way as for the fully observed case (above), but replacing the MDP's state-space with the POMDP "belief space" [7]. An agent's *belief* is its estimate for the probability density over the true system state, given the observation history. Unfortunately the set of beliefs has infinite size, and so methods that enumerate the state space (*e.g.* dynamic programming and Q learning) cannot be applied directly. Policy search, however, remains feasible.

In dynamic scheduling domains the partial observability usually arises not from noisy measurements of the physical system state, but in the unknown tasks that have not yet been presented to the agents. Even without this uncertainty, approximate solution methods would be required, because the state space is continuous and high dimensional. (The state consists of robots' physical states and the known task descriptions.) The MDP and POMDP models that are so useful in theory are too general, in practice, to find solutions to even the simplest dynamic scheduling problem. However, they offer a "perfect solution" against which approximate methods can be judged.

3   Hybrid Planning and Learning Algorithm

Although partial observability and large state spaces make dynamic scheduling a very difficult problem, it should be possible to simplify the solution by exploiting specific problem structure. It is natural to attempt to *factor* the "full" MDP representing the multi-agent, multi-task system into many smaller sub-problems that can be individually solved. It is also appropriate to exploit as much prior knowledge about the problem as possible, to ensure best use is made of (trial-and-error learning) simulation runs. This prior knowledge will be made available to the system in the form of "task models" that predict the time taken to perform known tasks, and "state features" that compress the state-space into a compact description for learning.

3.1   Short-Term Predictability Assumption

The special form of partial observability found in dynamic scheduling leads to an approach in which we assume that the short-term future is *predictable* and can be treated as a static planning problem, but the long-term future is unpredictable and requires an approximate method that accounts for uncertainty. Hence we propose a hybrid planning/learning system in which short-term planning ignores the exogenous events (new tasks entering the system) up to some "planning horizon", but a value function is learnt to represent the medium and long term benefits of being in a particular joint state when the planning horizon is reached.

This assumption allows replanning to be viewed as a search over a discrete set of plans (ordered allocations of robots to tasks). A planning mechanism must be made available that takes as input the current joint state x (of the robots) and a proposed plan P, and yields an end state x' and an expected discounted return $R(x, P)$, up to the planning horizon τ. The total value of the plan is given by:

$$Q(x, P) = R(x, P) + \gamma^\tau V(x')$$

where $V(x')$ is a state-value function that will account for the "goodness" of being in state x'; *i.e.* a prediction for the expected discounted return from the planning horizon to the end of the trial. As we expect predicted rewards to become less reliable with time, another discount factor, λ can be introduced to discount more severely (in short-term planning). Suppose plan P predicts that reward r will be obtained at time t (from the time at which the plan is formed). The contribution to $R(x, P)$ is now given by $(\gamma\lambda)^t r$. In the experiments here, we used $\gamma = 1$ (undiscounted finite horizon return) and $\lambda = 0.9986$.

Normally it will not be possible to evaluate every possible plan, but many methods are available for searching over this discrete space. (Our search method is based on making local changes to the current plan.)

3.2   The Weak-Coupling Assumption

Once an allocation decision (of robots to tasks) has been made, the tasks essentially become independent in terms of rewards received and end states [8]. For example, if robot A is assigned to task 3 and robot B to task 5, the effectiveness of A in task 3 is assumed to be independent of the individual steps taken by B in performing task 5. (This assumption cannot be made in all scheduling domains.) This suggests a two-level planning process in which the top level (allocation of robots to tasks) is "globally" aware, but the lower level planning (execution of individual tasks) can be achieved in a *local* context (a particular robot and particular task).

We introduce *task performance models* to provide the lower-level planning capability. Given a particular allocation decision (robot to task), the task performance model predicts both the time taken to complete the task, and the likely final location of the robot after completion. The task performance model is also responsible for predicting the rewards (performance feedback signals) that will be obtained on task completion. Using these performance models, it is possible to estimate the short-term rewards that will accrue from a particular assignment of tasks to robots. Such an assignment is called a "short-term plan" (Figure 1).

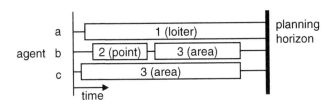

Fig. 1. A plan is an assignment of tasks to robots

Strictly, a task performance model takes as input the state of a single robot x_j, the parameters y_k describing a particular task instance (k), and any allocation parameters α_{jk}. It provides as output a new state x'_j, a duration t_{jk} and an expected discounted return r_{jk}. More generally the task model can sample from stochastic outcomes:

$$P(x'_j, t_{jk}, r_{jk} | x_j, y_k, \alpha_{jk})$$

For each robot, a series of these predictions can be performed to plan for the ordered list of tasks that are assigned to it. If a prediction takes the total time

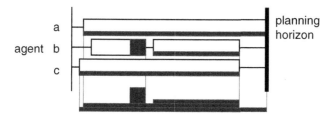

Fig. 2. Short-term planning

beyond the planning horizon, then the actual end state must be interpolated. By appropriately discounting and summing the individual returns ($\{r_{jk}\}$) associated with each task allocation in a plan P, the short-term value $R(x, P)$ of that plan is obtained. For tasks that require robots to cooperate, *group* task models can be used to predict the outcome of assigning multiple robots to a single task.

3.3   Short-Term Plans

A short-term planning approach makes use of the approximate task performance models to predict the return $R(x, P)$ that will accrue from a particular plan P. Figure 2 illustrates how instantaneous rewards (solid blocks) may be predicted by the task models. The prediction is performed only up to the planning horizon. These are summed[1] over all robots to give a reward profile (lower chart in the figure). The area under this profile measures the expected return for the short-term plan.

The short-term planning approach is to search for an assignment of tasks to robots that maximises the short-term expected return. This is better than simply selecting the closest robot for each new task. However, short-term planning is not optimal because it ignores several important factors in decision-making: a. the need for positioning of the robots in readiness for new tasks; b. the preservation of energy and other resources (*e.g.* robot battery life); c. the approximate nature of the task performance models.

In the short-term planning, we can also make use of a set of default behaviours that can be selected when no tasks are scheduled. These allow the robots to reposition, ready for new tasks to enter the system. There are no rewards associated with performing the default behaviours (but they will often be selected because they have an influence on the position value function at the planning horizon).

3.4   Value Function Learning

Positioning of the robots ("readiness") is essential in problem domains where there are tight time constraints on the completion of tasks. This means that robots should be positioned so as to minimise the time taken to reach new task locations, and is a form of *tactical awareness*. Resources have a value that depends on the type of problem domain. In long-endurance domains, learning

---

[1] The rewards should first be discounted if $\gamma\lambda \neq 1$.

strategies that minimise energy consumption may be essential for effectiveness. If robots are operating in a group, there will often be an additional benefit to balancing the use of resources as equally as possible between them during a trial. This is a form of *strategic awareness*; another instance of this would be the avoidance of low-probability, high-risk events (such as lightening strikes.)

The representation for learning is a state-value function, that will be evaluated at the planning horizon indicated in Figure 1. The value function provides an approximate mapping from the state (of the robots) to the expected discounted return from that time onward. For example states in which the robots are well-positioned (and have full energy stores) will have the highest values. The value function is always evaluated at the planning horizon (a time in the future), rather than the current time. This simplifies the decision-making process because *known* tasks are assumed to have no influence beyond the planning horizon. Therefore it is the predicted state x' of the robots, rather than the status of *tasks*, that determines the state-value $V(x')$ at the planning horizon.

Learning takes place at the end of each trial, and aims to reduce (by gradient descent) the residual error between the actual return received during the trial and predictions that were made during the trial using the value function. The gradient descent rule is simple to derive for the linear function approximator used here (*e.g.* [4]), and for nonlinear generalisations such as the multilayer perceptron. Training instances are obtained each time replanning takes place. This occurs whenever a new task enters the system or an existing task is completed, and at regular time intervals during the trial. (Other learning rules can be considered if the function approximator or task models are known to be inaccurate: direct policy search or policy gradient descent are more robust, but potentially slower.)

Suppose replanning has taken place N times during a trial. Let $(i = 1, \ldots N)$ index these instances. The predicted value (for the chosen plan) is given by the weighted sum of m state features:

$$v_i = \sum_{j=1}^{m} w_j x_j^{(i)}$$

where $x_j^{(i)}$ is state feature j for instance i. Suppose that the recorded discounted return (from that instance onward) is r_i. Then the residual error is given by:

$$e_i = (v_i - r_i)$$

Summing the squared error over instances, and differentiating with respect to the weights yields a steepest descent direction in weight-space. This leads to an update rule:

$$w_j' \leftarrow w_j - \beta \frac{1}{N} \sum_{i=1}^{N} e_i x_j^{(i)}$$

The learning rate β for the feature weights was decayed during the experiments, to force convergence of the value function.

4   Evaluation

Evaluation of the hybrid planning/learning approach requires a high-speed simulation that allows repeated trials to be performed (for value-function learning). We describe the simulation software that achieves this, a set of state features, a challenging test scenario with 3 task types, and the evaluation results.

4.1   Performance System

An asynchronous discrete event simulation has been developed to support machine learning and optimisation of agent behaviours. In most simulations, the majority of computational cost is involved in the update of the dynamic parts of the system (*e.g.* the robots). Simulations are normally clocked at regular intervals ("synchronously") to ensure an adequate level of accuracy (and also for simplicity). In contrast, we aim to update the state of each simulation element only when it is needed for decision-making or graphical output. Where possible the update is performed analytically (*i.e.* by direct calculation) but it may be necessary to apply numerical integration in some cases. An example of analytical update is the calculation of robot paths as a sequence of arcs (corresponding to periods of constant turn rate).

At the core of the model is a scheduler that processes events in the simulation in order. Each event is sent to a simulation element (or higher level process) where some processing is performed. For example, the process controlling an robot in a loiter pattern will send a short sequence of events to the scheduler; each event, when processed by the robot's simulation model, causes it to update its state (position, motion, energy store) to the current time, and the new turn rate (demanded by the event) is set.

Built upon this event handling mechanism is the ability for processes within the simulation to send messages to each other. These messages are themselves events, but they represent the actual information that would be passed across a communications network (or bus) within an operational system. Delays and failure modes can also be simulated. Therefore the simulation is built up from a set of processes that operate by receiving, processing and sending messages to each other. Some of these processes are used to represent simulated physical systems (the robots) and others form part of the operational software.

The system has a graphical user interface which allows basic control of the learning system. Although learning trials are normally executed without graphical display, it is possible to inspect occasional trials, through two or three dimensional display, as shown in Figure 3. Here the robot positions are indicated by small triangles. Their short-term plans are indicated by lines. Markers indicate the fixed set of reference locations (w0 to w4) and locations of known tasks (all others). Detailed implementation of the performance system (dynamics, low-level control, task constraints, *etc.*) is beyond the scope of this paper.

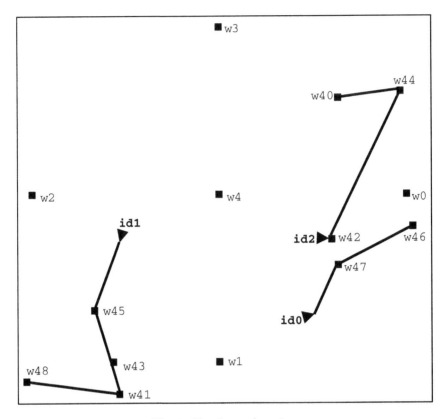

Fig. 3. Simulator plan view

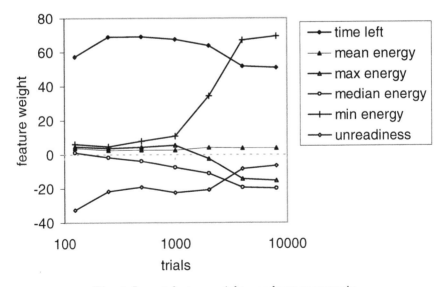

Fig. 4. Learnt feature weights: endurance scenario

4.2   State Features

The state-value function was chosen to be a linear combination of state features. The state features are intended to represent, in a compact form, the aspects of the robots' state that are relevant for subsequent decision-making. Some are simply averages over the group of robots, whereas others represent relational or relativistic information. A set of reference locations were used to define the operating area for each trial. All the features are listed here:

1. **Time left**: proportion of maximum trial duration remaining

2. **Bias**: a constant additive term

3. **Mean energy**: the average of the robots' energy levels.

4. **Max energy**: the maximum of the robots' energy levels.

5. **Median energy**: the median of the robots' energy levels.

6. **Min energy**: the minimum of the robots' energy levels.

7. **Unreadiness**: the average (over the reference locations) of the distance of the closest robot to that location.

The 7 values to be learnt are the weights for each of these features in the value function. A positive weight for a feature will mean that situations in which the feature is large are preferred. For example we expect one of the energy features to have a large positive weight to reflect the remaining endurance of the group. The **time left** and **bias** features have no effect on decisions between alternative plans, because they are independent of the robots' states, but they can improve the accuracy of the value function.

4.3   Example Scenarios

The simulator was configured for repeated trials with 5 robots. The state of each robot is its 2D position, direction of travel, speed and energy level. Each robot is allowed only two possible speeds (40 and 60). For these speeds, energy is consumed at 1 unit per step and 2 units per step respectively. Each robot is able to turn at a maximum constant rate of 0.1 radians per step.

Replanning takes place whenever a new task enters the system, a known task is completed, and at regular intervals (300 steps). The trial time is limited to 10,000 steps. For "endurance" scenarios energy is limited to 10,000 units, but for "non-endurance" scenarios it is essentially infinite.

The planning horizon was 2000 steps and the planning discount factor $\lambda = 0.9986$. At trial number k, the learning rate was chosen to be $\beta = \beta_0 \exp(-0.003k)$, where the initial value is $\beta_0 \equiv 0.85$.

4.4   Three Task Types

Three types of task have been identified:

1. Point tasks (*e.g.* sensing): send one of the robots to a location; upon arrival the task is deemed complete.

2. Area tasks (*e.g.* searching): move to a location, then systematically move around the region surrounding that location.

3. Loiter tasks: move to a location and stay there for a period of time.

The specific instance of area task used here, is to visit 4 locations arranged in a unit square; a loiter task required one robot to move to the specified location and stay there (moving in a figure-of-eight pattern) for a specified period of time. The actual task mix (Table 1) is diverse in terms of duration (and rewards) but the three types contribute almost equally to overall trial returns (*i.e.* summed rewards). The default behaviours, also available to the planner, are effectively the same as a slow-speed loiter, in which the robot moves to (then waits at) one of the reference locations.

Table 1. Major task types, frequencies of occurrence and rewards

Task type	Frequency	Reward
Point	80%	1
Area	18%	4
Loiter	2%	30

There is a random delay between successive tasks, given by $1000u^{10}$ where u is uniformly distributed in the range $[0, 1]$. Each task has a 1 in 10 chance of having a precondition. This precondition has equal change of being (completion of) each of the five preceding tasks. Every task must be completed within a specified time period given by 2^u where u is drawn uniformly in the range $[9, 9.65]$. The location of each task is uniformly distributed across the area of operation (a 100,000-unit square).

4.5   Results

Results were obtained using 8 runs for each approach. Standard errors were computed and are shown as error bars on the plots. First we give results for "endurance" scenarios in which the group of robots may not survive until the end of the trial unless they choose the more efficient (lower) speed and balance effort between themselves. Once one robot has run out of energy, it can play no further part in the trial, and so the remaining robots must travel further (on average) to reach new tasks.

Figure 5 shows (a decaying average of) returns at the end of each trial for three methods: hybrid planning/learning system, the short-term planning system, and a simple heuristic policy (assign each task to the closest available robot). We observe that short-term planning alone makes a big difference to the efficiency with which the tasks are performed. Note that short-term planning depends strongly on the availability of task performance models: that is the ability to make approximate predictions about the time that a task will take and the final robot states.

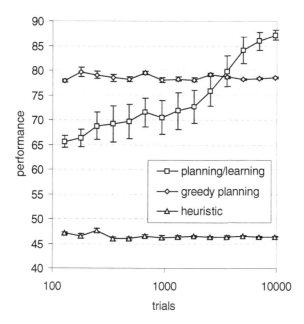

Fig. 5. Performance comparison: endurance scenario

Complementing the short-term planning with a learnt value function to form a hybrid planning/learning approach clearly offers a major additional advantage, and the difference is significant after 5000 trials (paired t-test, $p = 0.03$). The robots can (for example) make rational decisions about whether it is better to move fast to complete a task sooner, or to preserve energy. This is certainly not possible in the short-term planning approach.

Figure 4 shows learning curves for the feature weights in the value function. We note that `time left` is a significant state feature: clearly, the expected return to the end of the trial depends strongly on the time remaining. However it should be noted that this feature cannot directly affect behaviour because it will have the same value when comparing two plans with the same planning horizon. Of the various features describing the energy status of the robots, `min energy` is the most significant. It has positive weight, indicating that situations with large minimum energy have higher value. The robots learn to take actions which

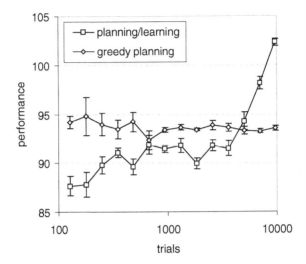

Fig. 6. Performance comparison: non-endurance scenario

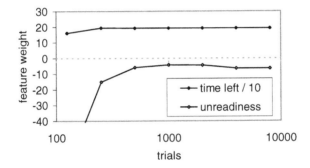

Fig. 7. Learnt feature weights: non-endurance scenario

maximise the energy of the one with least remaining, to balance the burden of tasks.

This provides evidence that the group as a whole is more effective than its individual components: if some robots "drop-out" before the end of the trial, the others have difficulty responding effectively to the incoming task stream. In contrast, mean energy has little importance. The remaining two energy features (max energy and median energy) have negative weight, but no obvious conclusions can be drawn because there may be a complex interaction with the min energy feature: removing one feature from the value function can often change the signs of lesser features.

A second scenario that does not require endurance was also studied. The only difference is that robots are given enough initial energy to complete each 10000-step trial at maximum speed, and so the energy features have very little part to play. The performance results (Figure 6) follow the same pattern as for the previous scenario: planning outperforms the simple heuristic, and learning increases performance further. (The heuristic performance remained below 50 and is not shown.) The benefit of learning is significant ($p < 0.01$) after 7000 trials, and does not level-off within the experiment duration (10000 learning trials).

The analysis of feature weights in Figure 7 shows that time remaining is the strongest feature. However, the positional feature **unreadiness**, which measures mean distances of closest robots to reference points, plays the most important role because it can affect behaviour. A large negative weight was learnt. This was expected because a high value of **unreadiness** causes robots to take longer to reach new tasks that appear within the operational area. There is scope for additional features to be added which encode more detailed information about the relative positioning of the robots. The remaining (energy) features have been omitted from this figure because they have little influence on learnt behaviour: negative weights are obtained because this encourages robots to select the maximum speed.

5   Discussion

These results have shown that a hybrid planning/learning method offers major advantages over simple heuristic rules such as assigning the closest robot to each task. In the scenarios given, performance has been approximately doubled. The performance improvement will depend strongly on the nature of the task stream. If there are few tasks entering the system, every task can be completed successfully using a naive policy. If there are many tasks, the need to limit energy consumption through speed control and effective positioning becomes important. Furthermore, if there are tight time constraints on individual tasks, it is likely that robot positioning will become very important, and have a major impact on performance.

The experimental evaluation highlighted the need to learn different value functions for different classes of problem instance. For "endurance" problem instances, where the aim is to operate the group of robots for as long as possible, the value function will be sensitive to the preservation of resources (*e.g.* energy). In contrast, for "rapid response" problem instances that require tasks to be completed within tight time constraints, *positioning* features will be the major influence in the learnt value function.

We have presented a centralised solution that assumes adequate communication for the robots to form joint plans. This is not unreasonable, because some communications are required to inform the robots of new tasks. A copy of this centralised processing could be executed on each robot to avoid failure of one robot being catastrophic to behaviour of the whole system. Furthermore, instances of the dynamic scheduler can naturally be used as planning components within a hierarchical task execution system, enabling distribution and specialisation of the scheduling functionality. Another argument for de-centralised processing is the growth in computational costs with numbers of resources and tasks; a hierarchical decomposition would also address this issue.

6   Conclusions

We have developed a hybrid planning/learning system that allows scheduling of a group of robots for a heterogeneous stream of tasks. It was assumed that the task stream would be unpredictable, preventing planning beyond a short time horizon. The risk of using planning alone is that tactical factors (positioning of robots in readiness for new tasks) and strategic factors (preserving resources) are ignored. Therefore reinforcement learning (exploiting a fast system simulation) was applied to obtain a value function for taking these factors into account.

A short-term planning element remained necessary because it is able to properly take account of the actual tasks that are currently known to the system. This short-term planning uses task performance models that are able to predict the end-state and reward for each task, given a robot assignment. Initial experiments indicated a benefit from both the short-term planning and the learning elements of the system, compared with a naive heuristic approach that assigns the closest available robot to each task.

Acknowledgements

This research was funded by the UK Ministry of Defence Corporate Research Programme in Energy, Guidance and Control. © Copyright QinetiQ Limited, 2004.

References

1. Boutilier, C., Dean, T., Hanks, S.: Decision-theoretic planning: Structural assumptions and computational leverage. Journal of Articial Intelligence Research 11 (1999) 1–94
2. Gerkey, B.P., Mataric, M.J.: A formal framework for study of task allocation in multi-robot systems. Technical Report CRES-03-13, University of Southern California (2003)
3. Bellman, R.E.: Dynamic Programming. Princeton University Press. (1957)
4. Sutton, R.S., Barto, A.G.: Reinforcement Learning. MIT Press, Cambridge, MA (1998)
5. Watkins, C.J.C.H.: Models of Delayed Reinforcement Learning. PhD thesis, Psychology Department, Cambridge University, Cambridge, United Kingdom (1989)
6. Strens, M.J.A., Moore, A.W.: Policy search using paired comparisons. Journal of Machine Learning Research 3 (2002) 921–950
7. Martin, J.J.: Bayesian Decision problems and Markov Chains. John Wiley, New York (1967)
8. Meuleau, N., Hauskrecht, M., Kim, K.E., Peshkin, L., Kaelbling, L.P., Dean, T., Boutilier, C.: Solving very large weakly coupled Markov decision processes. In: Proceedings of the 15th National Conference on Articial Intelligence (AAAI-98), Menlo Park, AAAI Press (1998) 165–172

Multi-agent Reinforcement Learning in Stochastic Single and Multi-stage Games

Katja Verbeeck[1], Ann Nowé[1], Maarten Peeters[1,*], and Karl Tuyls[2]

[1] Computational Modeling Lab, Vrije Universiteit Brussel, Belgium
[2] Theoretical Computer Science Group, University of Limburg, Belgium
{kaverbee, mjpeeter}@vub.ac.be
asnowe@info.vub.ac.be
Karl.Tuyls@luc.ac.be

Abstract. In this paper we report on a solution method for one of the most challenging problems in Multi-agent Reinforcement Learning, i.e. coordination. In previous work we reported on a new coordinated exploration technique for individual reinforcement learners, called Exploring Selfish Reinforcement Rearning (ESRL). With this technique, agents may exclude one or more actions from their private action space, so as to coordinate their exploration in a shrinking joint action space. Recently we adapted our solution mechanism to work in tree structured common interest multi-stage games. This paper is a roundup on the results for stochastic single and multi-stage common interest games.

1 Introduction

Coordination is an important issue in multi-agent reinforcement learning research, because it is often a requirement when agents want to maximize their revenue. In many real-world applications the problem of coordination becomes even harder because of system limitations such as, partial or non observability, communication costs, asynchronism etc. For instance in systems where resources are limited as in job scheduling and routing these assumptions certainly apply. Predefined rules are not feasible in complex and changing environments, and communication can be costly. Therefore we are interested in how independent reinforcement learning agents can learn how to coordinate. More specifically in this paper we are interested in whether independent agents are able to coordinate in stochastic single and multi-stage common interest games.

Common interest games are special types of multi-agent systems (MAS), in the sense that the individual utility of the agents coincides with the joint utility of the group. This reduces some of the difficulties individual reinforcement learning agents experience in a multi-agent environment, such as not knowing the other

---

* Research funded by a Ph.D grant of the Institute for the Promotion of Innovation through Science and Technology in Flanders (IWT Vlaanderen).

D. Kudenko et al. (Eds.): Adaptive Agents and MAS II, LNAI 3394, pp. 275–294, 2005.

agents' payoff. However convergence to the optimal Nash equilibrium is still not guaranteed, not even for single stage common interest games see [3, 5, 6].

As opposed to joint action learners, independent agents only get information about their own action choice and pay-off. As such, they neglect the presence of the other agents. Joint action learners, [3, 4] do perceive the actions of the other agents in the environment and are therefore able to maintain models on the strategy of others. However in the light of the applications we have in mind the assumptions joint action learners make are too strong. We assume here that observations are not reliable, the environment is unknown to the agents and only limited communication is allowed. Because of the latter we will call our agents pseudo independent.

In this paper we report on a new exploration technique for independent reinforcement learning agents which is called Exploring Selfish Reinforcement Learning (ESRL) [18, 19]. In the first part of this paper, ESRL is developed for single decision problems that are formalised by common interest normal form games well known in game theory [11]. The idea of ESRL is to let independent RL agents explore as many joint actions as possible. They achieve this by excluding actions from their private action space, so that the joint action space shrinks more and more. In combination with random restarts the algorithm is proved to converge in the long run to the optimal joint action of a single stage common interest game, [19]. ESRL agents are based on the theory of learning automata, more in particular learning automata games, [9]. Modeling independent agents as learning automata is easily motivated. Learning automata are updated strictly on the basis of the response of the environment and not on the basis of any knowledge regarding other automata or their strategies. Moreover their behavior is already studied thoroughly both in a single automata setup as in interconnected systems, see [9, 15].

Single stage games are useful testbeds for some real world problems such as job scheduling [10, 12]. However in most real world problems a sequence of decisions has to be learned. So in the second part of this paper, we scale ESRL up to multi-stage problems. For now we restrict ourselves to multi-stage common interest games for which the corresponding state graph is a tree, i.e. it shows no loops and has disjunct paths. But we also assume that rewards can be stochastic. The extension of ESRL agents to multi-stage games is done using hierarchical learning automata agents from [8]. Originally, this learning automata scheme was used for hierarchical multi-objective analysis. A hierarchical learning automata agent (a hierarchical agent for short) consists of several learning automata. Particularly, an agent has a new learner for every state or node in the multi-stage tree. A hierarchical agent is enhanced with the exploration and exclusion abilities of the ESRL agents, so that they will be able to converge to an optimal path in multi-stage common interest trees. The resulting algorithm is called Hierarchical Exploring Reinforcement learning (HESRL).

In the next section we start with explaining the related game theoretic background needed to understand how the agents interact and how the games are addressed. In Section 3 we introduce the learning automata theory on which our exploration techniques are founded. Section 4 explains ESRL and HESRL, while sections 5 and 6 report on their results. In a final section we conclude and propose further research.

2   Game Theoretic Background

In this section some basic game theory terminology is introduced. For a detailed overview see [11].

2.1   Single Stage Games

Assume a collection of n agents where each agent i has an individual finite set of actions A_i. The number of actions in A_i is denoted by $|A_i|$. The agents repeatedly play a single stage game in which each agent i independently selects an individual action a from its private action set A_i. The actions of all agents at any time step, constitute a joint action or action profile $\boldsymbol{a}$ from the joint action set $\mathbb{A} = A_1 \times \ldots \times A_n$. A joint action $\boldsymbol{a}$ is thus a vector in the joint action space $\mathbb{A}$, with components $a^i \in A_i, i : 1 \ldots n$. With each joint action $\boldsymbol{a} \in \mathbb{A}$ and agent i a distribution over possible rewards is associated, i.e. $r_i : \mathbb{A} \to \mathbb{R}$ denotes agent i's expected payoff or expected reward function. The payoff function is often called the utility function of the agent, it represents a preference relation each agent has on the set of action profiles.

Definition 1. *The tuple* $(n, \mathbb{A} = A_1 \times, A_n, r_{1\ldots n})$ *defines a single stage strategic game, also called a normal form game.*

A strategy $s : A_i \to [0,1]$ for agent i is an element of the set of probability distributions over agent's i action set A_i, i.e. $\mu(A_i)$. As a consequence, $\sum_{a_j \in A_i} s(a_j) = 1$. A strategy s is called pure or deterministic when $s(a_j) = 1$ for some $a_j \in A_i$ and zero for all other actions in A_i. Strategy profiles can then be defined as follows:

Definition 2. *A strategy profile* $\boldsymbol{s}$ *is a vector in the set* $\mu(A_1) \times \ldots \times \mu(A_n)$. *For all* $i \in \{1 \ldots n\}$ *component* s^i *is a strategy in* $\mu(A_i)$.

When all strategies in $\boldsymbol{s}$ are pure, $\boldsymbol{s}$ is actually a joint action $\boldsymbol{a}$ in $\mathbb{A}$ and an expected reward can be directly associated with it. For mixed strategies we have:

Definition 3. *The expected reward for a strategy profile* $\boldsymbol{s}$ *for agent* i *is calculated as follows:*

$$r_i(\boldsymbol{s}) = \sum_{\boldsymbol{a} \in \mathbb{A}} \prod_{j=1}^{n} s^j(a^j) r_i(\boldsymbol{a})$$

A reduced strategy profile $\boldsymbol{s}_{-i}$ for agent i is a strategy profile $\boldsymbol{s}$ for all agents minus the strategy of agent i, so $\boldsymbol{s}_{-i} \in \mu(A_1) \times \ldots \times \mu A_(i-1) \times \mu(A_{i+1}) \times \ldots \times \mu(A_n)$. Reduced profiles are introduced to define best responses and *Nash equilibria.*

Definition 4. *Given a reduced profile* s_{-i}, *a strategy* $s \in \mu(A_i)$ *is a best response for agent* i *if the expected value for the strategy* $s_{-i} \cup \{s\}$ *is maximal for agent* i; *i.e.*

$$r_i(s_{-i} \cup \{s\}) \geq r_i(s_{-i} \cup \{s_k\}) \text{ for all } s_k \in \mu(A_i)$$

So there is no other strategy s_k for agent i, which yields a strictly better expected payoff for agent i than strategy s.

Definition 5. *When for each agent* i *component* s^i *of strategy* s *is a best response,* s *is a mixed strategy Nash equilibrium and vice versa, i.e. for all* i *we have :*

$$r_i(s_{-i} \cup \{s^i\}) \geq r_i(s_{-i} \cup \{s_j\}) \text{ for all } s_j \in \mu(A_i)$$

A Nash equilibrium s *is said to be pure, when all strategies in* s *are pure.*

It is proved that every strategic game, which has finitely many actions has at least one possibly mixed Nash equilibrium [11]. Another concept introduced to account for group rationality is *Pareto optimality*,

Definition 6. *A strategy profile* s_1 *is said to be Pareto optimal if there is no other strategy profile* s_2 *in which all players simultaneously do better and at least one player is doing strictly better.*

In this paper we are interested in learning pure common interest games. In a pure common interest game the agents' rewards are drawn from the same reward distribution. As such the individual utility of the agents coincides with the joint utility of the group. As a consequence, in a common interest game (at least) one Pareto optimal Nash equilibrium exists. All *identical payoff games* belong to the class of common interest games. In an identical payoff game, all players get exactly the same reward for each joint action played, e.g. the games of Figure 1. In this case, the Pareto optimal Nash equilibrium is a *coordination equilibrium*, it gives every player his maximal possible outcome. Figure 1 shows 2 interesting examples of identical payoff games. Both problems are difficult to solve from the viewpoint of agent coordination. In the first game the punishment for miscoordination in the neighborhood of the optimal joint action (a, a) is extremely high, and therefore convergence to it is very difficult for agents using only limited communication. In the penalty game 2 different optimal joint actions co-exist, however when the agents each choose to play the other optimal action, this miscoordination is punished by a penalty term k. In both games the agents may be

	a	b	c			a	b	c
a	11	−30	0		a	10	0	k
b	−30	7	6		b	0	2	0
c	0	0	5		c	k	0	10

Fig. 1. Left: The climbing game from [3]. The Pareto optimal Nash equilibrium (a, a) is surrounded by heavy penalties. Right: The penalty game from [3]. Mis-coordination at the Pareto optimal Nash equilibria (a, a) and (c, c) is penalized with a penalty value k

tempted to play the safe, non-optimal actions, which is (c, c) for the climbing game and (b, b) for the penalty game.

2.2   Tree Structured Multi-stage Games

Until now we only showed examples of single stage problems. To represent common interest multi decision problems we use Multi-agent Markov decision processes (MMDP's). Formally an MMDP is a tuple $< \mathbb{S}, \alpha, < A_i >_{\forall i \in \alpha}, Pr, R >$ where $\mathbb{S}$ is a set of states, α a set of n agents, A_i a finite set of actions available to agent i, $Pr : \mathbb{S} \times A_1 \times \ldots \times A_n \times \mathbb{S} \to [0, 1]$ a transition function and $R : \mathbb{S} \to \mathbb{R}$ a reward function. Figure 2 gives an example of a simple MMDP

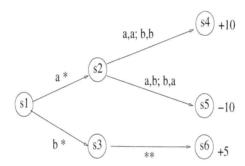

Fig. 2. The Opt-In Opt-out game: A simple MMDP with a coordination problem and two stages from [1]. Both agents have two actions, a or b. A $*$ can be either action a or b

	aa	ab	ba	bb
aa	10	−10	10	−10
ab	−10	10	−10	10
ba	5	5	5	5
bb	5	5	5	5

	aa	ab	ba	bb
aa	10	−10	5	5
ab	−10	10	5	5
ba	5	5	10	−10
bb	5	5	−10	10

Fig. 3. Left: Translation of the multi-stage tree of Figure 2 in the equivalent single stage common payoff game. A path in the multi-stage tree becomes a joint action in the single stage game. Right: Translation of the multi-stage tree of Figure 4 in the equivalent single stage common payoff game

with two stages. It can be viewed as a standard MDP in which the actions are implemented in a distributed fashion. Similar to an MDP a credit assignment problem is present, however there is also a coordination problem. In the above problem the first agent should decide to play a in the first stage, no matter what the other agent decides. Next both agents have to coordinate their actions in the second stage to reach the high payoff state s_4. We could still view the tree of Figure 2 as a single stage game. Every sequence of two actions, an agent can take can be considered as a single action of that agent's action space. A path in the

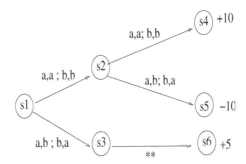

Fig. 4. A simple MMDP with a coordination problem in both stages

tree will thus be a joint action in the single stage game. In Figure 3 (Left) the corresponding game matrix is given. The optimal joint actions or Nash equilibria are $(aa, aa), (aa, ba), (ab, ab)$ and (ab, bb). The Nash equilibria of the equivalent single stage game are called equilibrium paths in the tree. The problem with this single stage view is that the equivalent single stage game can become very large.

Typical coordination problems can now occur on every stage of the game. Consider for instance the multi-stage tree of Figure 4 which is a variant of the tree in Figure 2.In this case a coordination issue also applies in the first stage of the game, i.e. as well as in the first stage as in the second stage both agents should agree on the same action. So again 4 equilibrium paths exists which lead to state $s4$. Non coordination in the first stage is less worse than non-coordination in the second stage. The corresponding single stage game is given in Figure 3 (Right). Another issue related to sequential coordination arises when a reward is also given after the first stage, instead of only a delayed reward at the end of the path. Just as in an MDP, cumulating rewards becomes important. A path of which the first link gives bad reward, may belong to a path which receives high reward at the end. What will be the equilibrium path depends on how important immediate reward is opposed to for instance global or average reward on the whole path. Usually a discount factor $\gamma \in [0, 1]$ weights the importance of the immediate reward versus the future reward.

In summary, we are concerned with learning in common interest single stage games and multi-stage trees. The objective of learning for the agents is to coordinate on a Pareto optimal Nash equilibrium or path. We will focus on identical payoff games and trees, however our approach can be applied to more general common interest games.

3 Learning Automata

In this section the theory of learning automata is reviewed. We are especially interested in automata games and hierarchical learning automata as these form the basis for respectively ESRL and HESRL agents.

3.1   Learning Automata Theory

A learning automaton formalizes a general stochastic system in terms of states, actions, state or action probabilities and environment responses, see [9, 15]. The design objective of an automaton is to guide the action selection at any stage by past actions and environment responses, so that some overall performance function is improved. At each stage the automaton chooses a specific action from its finite action set and the environment provides a random response. In a variable structure stochastic automaton action probabilities are updated at every stage using a reinforcement scheme. The automaton is defined by a quadruple $\{\alpha, \beta, p, T\}$ for which α is the action or output set $\{\alpha_1, \alpha_2, \ldots \alpha_r\}$ of the automaton, the input β is a random variable in the interval $[0, 1]$, p is the action probability vector of the automaton and T denotes an update scheme. The output α of the automaton is actually the input to the environment. The input β of the automaton is the output of the environment, which is modeled through penalty probabilities c_i with $c_i = P[\beta \mid \alpha_i], i : 1 \ldots r$.

A linear update scheme that behaves well in a wide range of settings is the linear reward-inaction scheme, denoted by L_{R-I}[1]. The philosophy of this scheme is essentially to increase the probability of an action when it results in a success and to ignore it when the response is a failure. The update scheme is given by:

$$\begin{cases} p_i(n+1) = p_i(n) + a(1 - \beta(n))(1 - p_i(n)) & \text{if } \alpha_i \text{ is chosen at time } n \\ p_j(n+1) = p_j(n) - a(1 - \beta(n))p_j(n) & \text{if } \alpha_j \neq \alpha_i \end{cases}$$

The constant a is called the reward parameter and belongs to the interval $[0, 1]$. In stationary environments $p(n)_{n>0}$ is a discrete-time homogeneous Markov process and convergence results for L_{R-I} are obtained. Despite the fact that multiple automata environments are non-stationary, the L_{R-I} scheme is still appropriate in learning automata games.

3.2   Learning Automata Games

Automata games were introduced to see if automata could be interconnected in useful ways so as to exhibit group behavior that is attractive for either modeling or controlling complex systems. A play $\alpha(t) = (\alpha^1(t) \ldots \alpha^n(t))$ of n automata is a set of strategies chosen by the automata at stage t. Correspondingly the outcome is now a vector $\beta(t) = (\beta^1(t) \ldots \beta^n(t))$. At every instance all automata update their probability distributions based on the responses of the environment. Each automaton participating in the game operates without information concerning payoff, the number of participants, their strategies or actions. In [9] it is proved that when a team of automata use the L_{R-I} update scheme in identicall payoff games, convergence is established around Nash equilibria. When more than one

---

[1] L_{R-I} is what is called absolutely expedient and ϵ optimal in all stationary random environments. This means respectively that the expected average penalty for a given action probability is strictly monotonically decreasing with n and that the expected average penalty can be brought arbitrarily close to its minimum value.

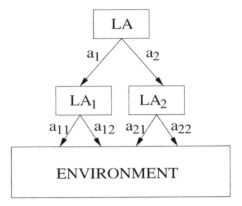

Fig. 5. A simple hierarchical system of learning automata with two stages, from [8]

equilibrium exists, the solution converged to obtained depends on the initial conditions.

3.3   Hierarchical Learning Automata

A simple hierarchical system of learning automata as in Figure 5 can be thought of as a single automaton (or agent) whose actions are the union of actions of all automata at the bottom level of the hierarchy. We call this agent a hierarchical agent. Two hierarchical agents as given in Figure 5 can interact at two different levels. An example is given in Figure 6. They receive an environment response on each level. These agents will be able to play two stage game trees as we will show below. The interaction of the two hierarchical agents of Figure 6 goes as follows. At the top level (or in the first stage) agent 1 and agent 2 meet each other in the stochastic game M. They both take an action using their top level learning automata A and B. Performing actions a_i by A and b_j by B is equivalent to choosing automaton A_i and B_j to take actions at the next level. The response of environment $E1$, $\beta_1 \in \{0, 1\}$, is a success or failure, where the probability of success is given by m_{ij}. At the second level the learning automata A_i and B_j choose their actions a_{ik} and b_{jl} respectively and these will elicit a response β_2 from environment $E2$ of which the probability of getting a positive reward is given by $m'_{ik,jl}$. At the end all the automata which were involved in the games, update their action selection probabilities based on the actions performed and the response of the composite environment, i.e. $\beta(n) = \lambda\beta_1(n) + (1 - \lambda)\beta_2(n)$, where $\lambda \in [0, 1]$.

To let these agents play for instance the tree game of Figure 2, we have to map the immediate rewards in the tree to the environment responses of the hierarchical learning automaton system. We translate the rewards of Figure 2 in stochastic rewards, i.e. we scale the rewards of the tree in Figure 2 between

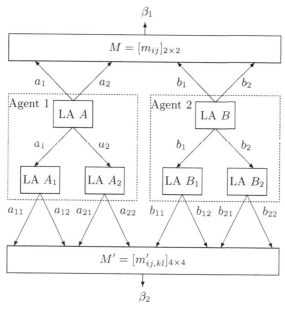

Fig. 6. An interaction of two hierarchies of learning automata at 2 stages [8]

$$M = \begin{pmatrix} 0.0 \ 0.0 \\ 0.0 \ 0.0 \end{pmatrix}, \quad M'(0,0) = \begin{pmatrix} 1.0 \ 0.0 \\ 0.0 \ 1.0 \end{pmatrix}, \quad M'(0,1) = \begin{pmatrix} 1.0 \ 0.0 \\ 0.0 \ 1.0 \end{pmatrix}$$

$$M'(1,0) = \begin{pmatrix} 0.75 \ 0.75 \\ 0.75 \ 0.75 \end{pmatrix}, \quad M'(1,1) = \begin{pmatrix} 0.75 \ 0.75 \\ 0.75 \ 0.75 \end{pmatrix}$$

Fig. 7. Translation of the multi-stage tree of Figure 2 in environment responses for the hierarchical learning automata. The joint action chosen at the first stage, decides the game that is played at the second stage

0 and 1 and use these results as a probability of success[2] in the update of the learning automata. In Figure 2 no rewards are given after the first stage, so M becomes the null matrix as is shown in Figure 7. After the second stage possible rewards are $10, -10$ and 5, which gives scaled probabilities of $1, 0$ and 0.75 for M' respectively. The actions taken by the agents in the first stage are important, as they determine the game of the next stage and the learning automata which are going to play it. In the tree of Figure 2 all rewards are given at the end, therefore we should set the weight factor $\lambda = 0$. In general the hierarchical agent should have as many levels of automata as there are stages in the tree

---

[2] The reason for this is that we use what is called a P-model learning automata. This means that the reward they receive from their environment is binary, i.e. the action was a success or a failure. This is however no limitation, as other richer learning automata exist for which the P-model algorithms are extended.

and suitable weights λ^l should be chosen. The matrices are not known to the agents, i.e. learning is model-free. When every automaton of the hierarchy uses a linear reward inaction scheme and the step sizes of the lower levels automata vary with time, convergence around Nash paths is established [8]. However in the experiments we will see that hierarchical agents will not always converge to optimal equilibrium paths.

4   Coordinated Exploration in MARL

In this section we explain how coordinated exploration can let the agents jointly converge to the optimal equilibrium point or path. First the ESRL algorithm is presented for single stage games. Next hierarchical agents are extended with the exploration abilities of ESRL.

4.1   ESRL

The technique of Exploring Selfish Reinforcement Learning was introduced in [10] and [19] for respectively single stage games of conflicting interest and single stage games of common interest[3]. We focus on the common interest version of the algorithm here. The main idea of the technique is to explore the joint action space $< A_i >_{i \in \alpha}$ of the agents as efficient as possible by shrinking it temporarily during different periods of play. At the beginning of learning, agents behave selfish or naive; i.e. they ignore the other agents in the environment and use a L_{R-I} reward-inaction learning automata update scheme to maximize their payoff. The first period of play ends when the multi-stage agents have found a Nash equilibrium. As mentioned in Section 3.2 an L_{R-I} scheme will converge to one of the Nash equilibria of the learning automaton game, with a suitable step size. So the agents do converge after a certain number of iterations[4]. Which Nash equilibrium the agents will find is not known in advance, it depends on the initial conditions and the basin of attraction of the different equilibria. Next all the agents exclude the action they converged to in the previous period of play. If the average payoff for this action was better than the average payoff they received so far for that action, they store this average as a new best payoff so far for that action. We call this part of the algorithm the synchronization phase. A new period of selfish play, which we call an exploration phase can now restart in a smaller joint action space and convergence to a new joint action will take place. As such agents alternate between playing selfish and excluding actions. When the agents have no actions left over in their individual action space, the original action space is restored and learning restarts in the full joint action space[5]. To enlarge the possibility that they shrink the joint action space

---

[3] In these references we did not call our technique ESRL yet.

[4] In this paper the number of iterations done in one period (we call it the period length) is chosen in advance and thus a constant. In a newer version of the algorithm, the agents themselves learn when they are converged.

[5] At least for symmetric games in which all agents have the same number of actions.

in as many ways as possible, and thus collecting information about as many joint actions as possible[6], they take random restarts, i.e. they initialize their action probabilities (of the not excluded actions) randomly at the start of a new period. As agents remember the best payoff they received for each action, ESRL was proved to converge in fully cooperative games to the optimal solution without needing communication, even in stochastic environments [17, 19]. Algorithm 1 and Algorithm 2 give the exploration respectively synchronization phases of ESRL agents for stochastic common interest games with binary output. In these games, each joint action has a probability on succes, i.e. reward 1.

In Section 5 some experimental results of ESRL are discussed.

Algorithm 1 Exploration phase for ESRL agent j in stochastic common interest games

---

   Initialize
time step $t \Leftarrow 0$,
average payoff $average(t) \Leftarrow 0$ and
for all actions i that are not excluded:
initialize action probability $p_i(t)$ randomly
   repeat
      $t := t + 1$
      choose action a_i in A_j probabilistically using p_t
      take action a_i, observe immediate reward r in $\{0, 1\}$
      if action a_i successfully **then**
         update action probabilities $p(t)$ as follows: L_{R-I}

$$p_i(t) \Leftarrow p_i(t-1) + \alpha(1 - p_i(t-1)) \text{ for action } a_i$$
$$p_{i'}(t) \Leftarrow p_{i'}(t-1) - \alpha p_{i'}(t-1)$$
$$\text{for all actions } a_{i'} \text{ in } A_j \text{ with} : a_{i'} \neq a_i$$

     set $average(t) \Leftarrow \frac{t-1}{WINDOW} average(t-1) + \frac{r}{WINDOW}$
   until $t = N$

4.2   HESRL

Thanks to action exclusions and random restarts, ESRL agents avoid to converge to local optima. We will enhance hierarchical agents with the same abilities to let them avoid to converge to a suboptimal path in the multi-stage tree. The idea for HESRL agents is to let them converge to a path in the multi-stage tree and then exclude that path or a part of that path from the tree. In a new period of play other paths can then be explored in a smaller joint path space, i.e. the space of all possible paths. So initially HESRL agents behave as common hierarchical agents from Section 3.3; and after enough iterations they will converge to one path in particular, though not necessarily the optimal one. As the actions for

---

[6] Actually this means that there should be enough exploration.

Algorithm 2 Synchronization phase for ESRL agent j in stochastic common interest games

if $T \leq M$ (M = total number of exploration phases to be played) **then**
    $T \leftarrow T + 1$
    get action a_i in A_j for which the action probability $p_i \approx 1$
    update action values vector q as follows:

$$q_i(T) \Leftarrow max\{q_i(T-1), average(N)\}$$
$$q_{i'}(T) \Leftarrow q_{i'}(T-1)$$
$$\text{for all actions } a_{i'} \text{ in } A_j \text{ with} : a_{i'} \neq a_i$$

    if $q_i(T) > q_{best}(T)$ **then**
        set $best \Leftarrow a_i$ {keep the best action until now in the parameter $best$ and its value
        in q_{best}}
    if $|A_j| > 1$ **then**
        temporarily exclude action $a_i : A_j \Leftarrow A_j \backslash \{a_i\}$
    else
        restore the original action set: $A_j \Leftarrow \{a_1, \ldots, a_l\}$ with $l = |A_j|$
else if $T = M$ **then**
    set $A_j \Leftarrow \{best\}$

the hierarchical agents in multi-stage trees are sequences of local actions, the exclusion phase can now be defined in different ways.

A first approach could be a *top-down* method of excluding. This means that the agents exclude only the first link of the path. More concrete this means that the learning automata of the first stage of every agent excludes the action that it converged to. So all paths which start from that link will be excluded. After only a few periods of selfish play, all actions of the first level automata, and thus also all paths are excluded. At this point, all actions should be included again and play can continue in the original joint path space. The action probabilities of all learning automata are randomly initialized after every exploration period, so that as many paths as possible can be found. The pseudo code of top-down exclusions is given in Algorithm 3. Alternatively, an agent could randomly decide to exclude any action involved in the path. In a second approach the agents exclude the action from that learning automaton, that was involved on the bottom level. We call this approach a *bottom-up* exclusion method. Of course after a while all the actions of an automaton on the bottom level could become excluded. In that case the action of the automaton of the previous level, which leads to the corresponding bottom level automaton should also be excluded. So after the first period of selfish play, exactly one path becomes excluded. After several periods of play more paths become excluded and when eventually exclusions reach the first level automaton of the agent, all paths will be excluded. Again the action probabilities of all learning automata are randomly initialized after every exploration phase. The pseudo code of bottom-up exclusions is given in Algorithm 4. In Section 6 hierarchical agents and HESRL agents are tested

---

Algorithm 3 Synchronization phase for HESRL agent j with top-down exclusions in a level L multi-stage tree

---

if $T \leq M$ (M = total number of exploration phases to be played) **then**
  $T \Leftarrow T + 1$ and $l \Leftarrow 0$
  get path $(a_{i_0}^0 \ldots a_{i_L}^L)$ for which corresponding action probabilities $p_i^l \approx 1$
  repeat
    update action values vector q^l of level l automaton A^l that was active in the
    path. Assume that $\tau^l \leq T$ was the last time that the action value vector q^l was
    updated then:

$$q_{i_l}^l(T) \Leftarrow max\{q_{i_l}^l(\tau^l), average(N)\}$$
$$q_{i'}^l(T) \Leftarrow q_{i'}^l(\tau^l)$$
$$\text{for all actions } a_{i'}^l \text{ in } A^l \text{ with : } a_{i'}^l \neq a_{i_l}^l$$

    if $q_{i_l}^l(T) > q_{best}^l(T)$ **then**
      set $best \Leftarrow a_{i_l}^l$ {for each automaton on each level l keep the best action in the
      parameter $best$ and its value in q_{best}^l}
    $l \Leftarrow l + 1$
  until $l = N$
  if $|A^0| > 1$ (exclusions only in the top level automaton) **then**
    temporarily exclude action $a_{i_0}^0 : A^0 \Leftarrow A^0 \backslash \{a_{i_0}^0\}$
  else
    restore the original action set: $A^0 \Leftarrow \{a_1^0, \ldots, a_k^0\}$ with $k = |A^0|$
else if $T = M$ **then**
  set path: $a^0 \Leftarrow best \in A^0$
    $a^1 \Leftarrow best \in A^1 =$ the automaton reached via action a^0 ...
    $a^L \Leftarrow best \in A^L =$ the automaton reached via action a^{L-1}

---

against the multi-stage trees of Section 2.2. Furthermore, top-down and bottom-up exclusions are evaluated and compared.

5 Experiments in Single Stage Games

In Figure 8 average results are given for ESRL agents using Algorithm 1 and 2 in randomly generated stochastic common interest games. Using both exclusions as multi-starts, assures that a good proportion of the Nash equilibria are visited. Almost 100% in small joint action spaces an still about 94% in the larger ones. It may seem strange that although the optimal Nash equilibrium is visited, the players sometimes do not recognize it. This is a consequence of the fact that rewards are stochastic and when payoffs are very close to each other[7], the sampling technique used here by the agents is not able to separate them. So actually when convergence is not reached, agents still find extremely good solutions which are almost inseparable from the optimal one. We tested this by

---

[7] Very close means here, they only differ in the third or fourth decimal.

Algorithm 4 Synchronization phase for HESRL agent j with bottom-up exclusions in a level L multi-stage tree

---

if $T \leq M$ (M = total number of exploration phases to be played) **then**
$\quad$ $T \Leftarrow T + 1$ and $l \Leftarrow 0$
$\quad$ get path $(a_{i_0}^0 \ldots a_{i_L}^L)$ for which corresponding action probabilities $p_i^l \approx 1$
$\quad$ **repeat**
$\quad\quad$ update action values vector q^l of level l automaton A^l that was active in the
$\quad\quad$ path. Assume that $\tau^l \leq T$ was the last time that the action value vector q^l was
$\quad\quad$ updated then:

$$q_{i_l}^l(T) \Leftarrow max\{q_{i_l}^l(\tau^l), average(N)\}$$
$$q_{i'}^l(T) \Leftarrow q_{i'}^l(\tau^l)$$
$$\text{for all actions } a_{i'}^l \text{ in } A^l \text{ with} : a_{i'}^l \neq a_{i_l}^l$$

$\quad\quad$ if $q_{i_l}^l(T) > q_{best}^l(T)$ **then**
$\quad\quad\quad$ set $best \Leftarrow a_{i_l}^l$ {for each automaton on each level l keep the best action in the
$\quad\quad\quad$ parameter $best$ and its value in q_{best}^l}
$\quad\quad$ $l \Leftarrow l + 1$
$\quad$ **until** $l = N$
$\quad$ temporarily exclude action $a_{i_l}^l : A^l \Leftarrow A^l \backslash \{a_{i_l}^l\}$ {$l = L$ at this point, exclusions
$\quad$ start at the end of the path}
$\quad$ **while** $A^l = \emptyset$ **do**
$\quad\quad$ temporarily exclude action $a_{i_{l-1}}^{l-1} : A^{l-1} \Leftarrow A^{l-1} \backslash \{a_{i_{l-1}}^{l-1}\}$
$\quad\quad$ $l \Leftarrow l - 1$
$\quad$ if $A^0 = \emptyset$ **then**
$\quad\quad$ restore all action sets of all LA on all levels
$\quad$ **else if** $T = M$ **then**
$\quad\quad$ set path: $a^0 \Leftarrow best \in A^0$
$\quad\quad\quad$ $a^1 \Leftarrow best \in A^1 =$ the automaton reached via action $a^0 \ldots$
$\quad\quad\quad$ $a^L \Leftarrow best \in A^L =$ the automaton reached via action a^{L-1}

#agents	#actions	#joint actions	% of convergence	% of nash equilibria found
2	3	9	97	99.67
2	5	25	95	100
3	3	27	96	98.38
3	5	125	87	93.67
5	3	243	78	94.51
5	5	3125	36(0.001)	94.39
5	5	3125	68(0.0001)	94.39

Fig. 8. Average results for ESRL agents in different sized joint action spaces. Convergence is redefined in the last run. It suffices that the difference between the payoff of the optimal joint action and that of the one converged to is not greater than 0.0001

redefining convergence in the last experiment of Figure 8. We agreed the agents had converged when the difference in payoff of the joint action they recognized as the best and the true optimal one was no more than 0.0001. This improves the results considerable as can be seen in Figure 8. We also tested ESRL on stochastic versions of difficult testbed problems, i.e. the climbing game and penalty game of Figure 1. A convergence of 100% was reached after only 3 exploration phases, this is exactly the number of actions in the agents' action space [17, 19].

6   Experiments in Tree Structured Multi-stage Games

In this section we report on the results of hierarchical agents and HESRL agents playing different multi-stage games. In a first subsection we test how well the agents can cope with typical coordination problems. The next subsection studies the effect of discounted rewards. In the last subsection top down exclusions and bottom-up exclusions are compared. In all experiments the reward parameter a is initially set to 0.05. Note that the experiments with the HESRL agents only show the exploration phase, i.e. after enough periods are played in which different joint actions are found an exploitation phase should be added in which the agents play the best path they found.

6.1   Hard Coordination Problems

The multi-stage game of Figure 2 combines two hard coordination problems. A first problem is that multiple equilibrium paths exists, so that agents have to coordinate on the same equilibrium. Secondly the equilibrium path is surrounded by low reward paths. The average payoff hierarchical agents[8] receive for the game of Figure 2 is approximately 0.8. This means that in almost every run of the game the hierarchical agents converge to one of the suboptimal paths of the tree, which gives on average a payoff of 0.75. In only a few runs an optimal path, which gives payoff 1.0 is reached.

Figure 9 gives the average of a typical run of HESRL agents using respectively top-down and bottom-up exclusions. The period length is set to 1000 iterations, i.e. after 1000 iterations of playing selfish, the agents run their synchronisation phase of which the pseudo code is given in Algorithms 3 and 4. Since the learning time is set to 5000 time steps, only 5 paths can be explored, while there are 16 possible paths present in the game tree. In both experiments an optimal path is reached. The top-down HESRL agent in Figure 9 find an optimal path in the first and fourth period of selfish play. The bottom-up HESRL agents find an optimal path in the third and fourth period. Over 20 different runs both types of HESRL agents find an optimal path in all runs.

The game tree of Figure 4 has 2 coordination problems, one at both stages of the game. Hierarchical agents now reach an average of approximately 0.93. The results for HESRL agents are given in Figure 10 . Again both types find an optimal path. The same period length is used, i.e. 1000 iterations. Again a 100% converge to one of the equilibrium paths is reached when different runs are

---

[8] The average is calculated over 100 different runs.

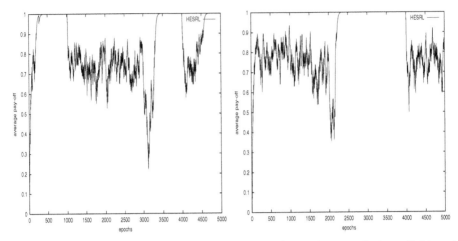

Fig. 9. The average payoff for HESRL agents with top-down exclusions (left) and bottom-up exclusions (right) playing the multi-stage tree of Figure 2

played. In Figure 10 (left) you can see that after the first two periods, i.e. from epoch 2000 until 5000, the agents are reaching a suboptimal path, whereas in Figure 10 (right) the agents find an optimal path in the first 4 periods. This is because the agents use a different exclusion technique. Indeed, in Figure 10 (left) the agents have found 2 equilibrium paths, i.e. $(aa, **)$ and $(bb, **)$, but after these 2 periods, the agents have excluded all paths that begin with action aa and action bb, so only suboptimal paths are left over in the joint path space, while actually there 4 different joint equilibrium paths. With bottom-up exclusions only one path is excluded from the joint path space at a time, so the bottom-up HESRL agents can find all equilibrium paths in sequential periods, that is exactly what happens as is shown by Figure 10 (right).

6.2   Discounting Rewards

Figure 11 gives the reward matrices of a sequential game problem which gives immediate reward after every stage. It was already reported in [8]. We played it with hierarchical agents and HESRL agents using a weight factor of $\gamma = 0.5$. The equivalent single stage game is given in Figure 12. Important to notice is that the equilibrium of this game is situated at the joint action (aa, bb) with an average reward of 0.725. So in the first stage agent 1 should choose action a and agent 2 should choose action b. However this is not the optimal joint action of the first stage game M, i.e. joint action (a, b) gives an average payoff of 0.6, while joint action (a, a) gives an average payoff of 0.7. Notice that there is only one optimal path in this game, the equivalent single stage game has a unique Nash equilibrium. This explains why hierarchical agents always converge to the optimal path in this game. Their average payoff is approximately 0.725, which is exactly the Nash equilibrium payoff of the equivalent single stage game. From a coordination point of view, is this an easy coordination problem. This is also

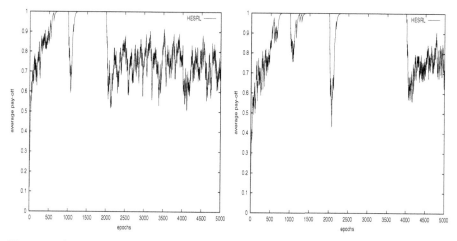

Fig. 10. The average payoff for HESRL agents with top-down exclusions (left) and bottom-up exclusions (right) playing the multi-stage tree of Figure 4

$$M = \begin{pmatrix} 0.7 & 0.6 \\ 0.1 & 0.1 \end{pmatrix}, \quad M'(0,0) = \begin{pmatrix} 0.6 & 0.2 \\ 0.3 & 0.1 \end{pmatrix}, \quad M'(0,1) = \begin{pmatrix} 0.3 & 0.85 \\ 0.2 & 0.2 \end{pmatrix}$$

$$M'(1,0) = \begin{pmatrix} 0.4 & 0.1 \\ 0.2 & 0.1 \end{pmatrix}, \quad M'(1,1) = \begin{pmatrix} 0.3 & 0.2 \\ 0.2 & 0.2 \end{pmatrix}$$

Fig. 11. A sequential stage game from [8]. The joint action chosen at the first stage, decides the game that is played at the second stage. $\lambda = 0.5$

shown by the results of the HESRL agent, see Figure 13. Convergence to the optimal path happens always in the first period.

6.3   Large Joint Path Space

To put the HESRL exclusion techniques to the test and to make a comparison between top-down and bottom-up exclusions, we experimented with a larger joint path space. We scaled the game of Figure 4 up to three players, all with three actions, i.e. a, b or c. This results in $27^2 = 729$ different paths possible. The equilibrium paths are reached when all players play the same action in every stage, for instance (abc, abc, abc) is an equilibrium path. In total there are 9 equilibrium paths. On average over 10 runs of $120,000$ iterations the top-down technique managed to converge to an equilibrium path in 80% of the runs. The length of the exploration phase was set to be 3000, so at most 40 paths could be explored during learning. This good result is due to the fact that the large joint path space is quickly reduced with this technique. And because only interesting paths are attracted during learning. We also ran this experiment with the bottom-up technique. Here we only reached an equilibrium path 4 out of 10 times. The bottom-up exclusion technique causes a slower reduction in the number of paths resulting in a lower percentage of optimal runs.

	aa	ab	ba	bb
aa	0.65	0.45	0.45	0.725
ab	0.5	0.4	0.4	0.4
ba	0.25	0.1	0.2	0.15
bb	0.15	0.1	0.15	0.15

Fig. 12. The equivalent single stage game of the sequential game given in Figure 11 with $\lambda = 0.5$

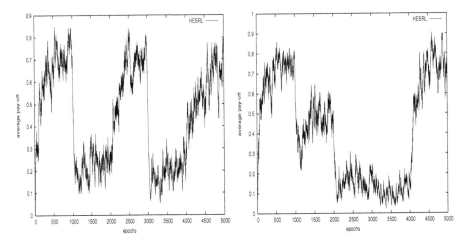

Fig. 13. The average payoff for HESRL agents with top-down exclusions (left) and bottom-up exclusions (right) playing the sequential game problem of Figure 11

7   Conclusion

The issue of learning in MAS has gained a lot of interest the last few years, [1, 2, 3, 5, 6, 7, 14, 16, 20]. Previously we introduced ESRL, a coordinated exploration technique for independent agents to coordinate on the Pareto optimal Nash equilibrium of common interest games. More recently we reported on an extension of this technique, HESRL, that enables agents to coordinate in tree-structured multi-stage games. ESRL has been studied intensively and has been tested in a broader range of games such as pure conflicting interest games [10]. The technique has also been applied to real-life experiments such as adaptive load-balancing of parallel applications and job scheduling [12, 10]. For the extended HESRL research is still ongoing. Recently we reported on preliminary results for conflicting two level games [13]. Although these results are just a first step in the direction of independent agents learning a sequence of actions, the results look promising. Further research should also point out how scalable the HESRL technique is. ESRL was tested in a joint action space of 3125 actions and still resulted in a high percentage of Nash equilibria found.

Summarized, ESRL and HESRL are state-of-the-art exploration techniques for independent agents with limited communication in a multi-agent setting. These techniques overcome major pitfalls in current multi-agent reinforcement learning research, i.e. the assumptions and limitations made by some of the other multi-agent reinforcement learning approaches, like complete information, no communication cost, static environments and the possibility of modeling other agents.

References

1. C. Boutilier. Sequential optimality and coordination in multiagent systems. In *Proceedings of the International Joint Conference on Artificial Intelligence*, pages 478 – 485, Stockholm, Sweden, 1999.
2. M. Carpenter and D. Kudenko. Baselines for joint-action reinforcement learning of coordination in cooperative multi-agent systems. *LNCS, Adaptive Agents and Multi-Agent Systems II Editors: Daniel Kudenko, Dimitar Kazakov, Eduardo Alonso*, (this volume), 2004.
3. C. Claus and C. Boutilier. The dynamics of reinforcement learning in cooperative multiagent systems. In *Proceedings of the fiftheenth National Conference on Artificial Intelligence*, pages 746 – 752, 1998.
4. J. Hu and M.P. Wellman. Nash q-learning for general-sum stochastic games. *Journal of Machine Learning Research*, 4:1039 – 1069, 2003.
5. S. Kapetanakis, D. Kudenko, and M. Strens. Learning to coordinate using commitment sequences in cooperative multi-agent systems. *LNCS, Adaptive Agents and Multi-Agent Systems II Editors: Daniel Kudenko, Dimitar Kazakov, Eduardo Alonso*, (this volume), 2004.
6. M. Lauer and M. Riedmiller. An algorithm for distributed reinforcement learning in cooperative multi-agent systems. In *Proceedings of the Seventeenth International Conference on Machine Learning*, pages 535 – 542, 2000.
7. M.L. Littman. Markov games as a framework for multi-agent reinforcement learning. In *Proceedings of the Eighteenth International Conference on Machine Learning*, pages 322 – 328, 2001.
8. K.S. Narendra and K. Parthasarathy. Learning automata approach to hierarchical multiobjective analysis. Technical Report No. 8811, Electrical Engineering. Yale University., New Haven, Connecticut., 1988.
9. K.S. Narendra and M.A.L. Thathachar. *Learning Automata: An Introduction.* Prentice-Hall International, Inc, 1989.
10. A. Nowé, J. Parent, and K. Verbeeck. Social agents playing a periodical policy. In *Proceedings of the 12th European Conference on Machine Learning*, pages 382 – 393, Freiburg, Germany, 2001. Springer-Verlag LNAI2168.
11. J.O. Osborne and A. Rubinstein. *A course in game theory.* MIT Press, Cambridge, MA, 1994.
12. J. Parent, K. Verbeeck, A. Nowe, K. Steenhaut, J. Lemeire, and E. Dirkx. Adaptive load balancing of parallel applications with social reinforcement learning on heterogeneous systems. *Scientific Programming*, to appear, 2004.
13. M. Peeters, K. Verbeeck, and A. Nowé. Multi-agent learning in conflicting multi-level games with incomplete information. In *Proceedings of the 2004 American Association for Artificial Intelligence (AAAI) Fall Symposium on Artificial Multi-Agent Learning*, 2004.

14. P.J. 't Hoen and K. Tuyls. Analyzing multi-agent reinforcement learning using evolutionary dynamics. In *Proceedings of the 15th European Conference on Machine Learning*. Springer-Verlag LNCS, 2004.

15. M.A.L. Thathachar and P.S. Sastry. Varieties of learning automata: An overview. *IEEE Transactions on Systems, Man, and Cybernetics, Part B: Cybernetics*, 32 (6):711 – 722, 2002.

16. K. Tuyls, A. Nowe, T. Lenaerts, and B. Manderick. An evolutionary game theoretic perspective on learning in multi-agent systems. In *Synthese, section Knowledge, Rationality and Action, Volume: 139, Issue 2, pages 297-330*, 2004.

17. K. Verbeeck, A. Nowé, J. Parent, and K. Tuyls. Exploring selfish reinforcement learning in non-zero sum games. *submitted*, 2004.

18. K. Verbeeck, A. Nowé, and M. Peeters. Multi-agent coordination in tree structured multi-stage games. In *Proceedings of the Fourth Symposium on Adaptive Agents and Multi-agent Systems, (AISB04) Society for the study of Artificial Intelligence and Simulation of Behaviour, pages 63–74*, 2004.

19. K. Verbeeck, A. Nowé, and K. Tuyls. Coordinated exploration in stochastic common interest games. In *Proceedings of the Third Symposium on Adaptive Agents and Multi-agent Systems, (AISB03) Society for the study of Artificial Intelligence and Simulation of Behaviour*, 2003.

20. David H. Wolpert, Kevin R.Wheller, and Kagan Tumer. General principles of learning-based multi-agent systems. In Oren Etzioni, Jörg P. Müller, and Jeffrey M. Bradshaw, editors, *Proceedings of the Third International Conference on Autonomous Agents (Agents'99), pages 77–83*, Seattle, WA, USA, 1999. ACM Press.

Towards Adaptive Role Selection for Behavior-Based Agents

Danny Weyns, Kurt Schelfthout, Tom Holvoet, and Olivier Glorieux

AgentWise, DistriNet,
Department of Computer Science, K.U.Leuven,
Celestijnenlaan 200A, B 3001 Leuven, Belgium
{Danny.Weyns, Kurt.Schelfthout, Tom.Holvoet}@cs.kuleuven.ac.be

Abstract. This paper presents a model for adaptive agents. The model describes the behavior of an agent as a graph of roles, in short a *behavior graph*. Links between roles provide conditions that determine whether the agent can switch roles. The behavior graph is assigned at design time, however adaptive role selection takes place at runtime. Adaptivity is achieved through factors in the links of the behavior graph. A factor models a property of the agent or its perceived environment. When an agent can switch roles via different links, the factors determine the role the agent will switch to. By analyzing the effects of its performed actions the agent is able to adjust the value of specific factors, adapting the selection of roles in line with the changing circumstances. Models for adaptive agents typically describe how an agent dynamically selects a behavior (or action) based on the calculation of a probability value as a function of the observed state for each *individual* behavior (or action). In contrast, the model we propose aims to dynamically adapt logical *relations* between different behaviors (called roles here) in order to dynamically form paths of behaviors (i.e. sequences of roles) that are suitable in the current state. To verify the model we applied it to the Packet-World. In the paper we discuss simulation results that show how the model enables the agents in the Packet-World to adapt their behavior to changes in the environment.

1 Introduction

Adaptability is a system's capacity to take into account unexpected situations. Multi-agent systems in particular are characterized by the property that not everything can be anticipated in advance. In the context of cognitive agent systems the problem of adaptation is tackled by introducing learning techniques. Traditional learning techniques are based on the agents' symbolic models of the environment. This however, does not fit the approach of behavior-based agents since these agents do not build a symbolic model of their environment [1, 2, 3].

To deal with the problem of adaptation, an agent has to take into account the quality of the effects realized by its past decisions. Several techniques for behavior-based agent architectures have been proposed to realize adaptation, some examples are [4, 5, 6]. In our research group we also developed two architectures for adaptive agents [7, 8]. All these models typically describe how an

D. Kudenko et al. (Eds.): Adaptive Agents and MAS II, LNAI 3394, pp. 295–312, 2005.

agent dynamically selects a behavior (or action) based on the calculation of a probability value in function of the observed state for each *individual* behavior (or action). The contribution of this paper is a model that aims to dynamically adapt logical *relations* between different behaviors (called roles here) in order to dynamically form paths of behaviors (i.e. sequences of roles) that are suitable in the current state.

This paper is structured as follows. Section 2 introduces the basic model for agent behavior. In section 3 we extend the model for adaptive behavior. Section 4 evaluates the model for the Packet-World application. We show how the model enables the agents in the Packet-World to adapt their behavior to changes in the environment. Section 5 compares Markov models and Belief nets with behavior graphs. Finally, we draw conclusions in section 6.

2   Basic Model for Agent Behavior

In this section we introduce the basic model for agent behavior. The basic model describes the behavior of an agent as a graph, in short a *behavior graph*. A behavior graph consists of *roles* that are connected by means of *links*. An agent executing a certain behavior graph is "moving" through this graph, executing actions in a role and moving to the next role via links connecting the roles. We now describe these concepts in detail.

2.1   Roles

A role is an abstract representation of a sequence or combination of actions the agent executes when it is in that role. A role abstracts from the number and details of its actions as well as the applied action selection mechanism within the role. At each moment in the agent's lifetime there is exactly one active role, called the *current role*. All other roles are inactive.

We choose the term role instead of task for the reason that a role is an organizational concept: it captures the fact that an agent is part of a multi-agent system, and thus part of an organization. We also introduce the concept of *dependency roles* later to explicitly model both inter-agent dependencies, as well as a form of intra-agent parallelism.

The decision which combination of actions is grouped into a role is left to the human designer. He or she can choose to use atomic actions as a role: this leads to agents consisting of many small roles, and thus many links between those roles. It is likely that such a design generates a lot of overhead when executed. On the other hand, the designer can choose to group many actions into a few big roles. This makes the behavior graph look very comprehensive, while hiding a lot of complexity in the roles themselves. In practice the designer should balance the tradeoff between the overhead of minimal roles and the complexity of weighty roles.

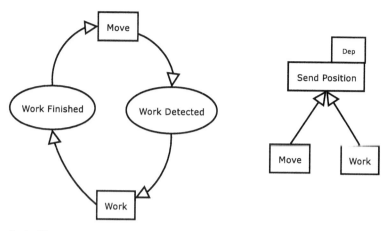

Fig. 1. Left: Example of a simple behavior graph, boxes are roles, ellipses are links. Right: the representation of a dependency role

2.2   Links

Besides roles, the behavior graph consists of directed links that connect roles. A link starts at a *source role* and points to a *goal role*. Several links can start from the same role and several links can point to the same role. When an agent is executing a certain role, it can decide that it wants to switch roles to any role that is linked with the current role.

Additionally, a *condition* is associated with each link, that determines whether the link is *open* or *closed*. The condition is evaluated at runtime, and influences the selection of the next role the agent can execute: if a condition closes a link, the agent cannot switch to that link's goal role. An agent can only switch roles via open links.

These conditions are used to model that during execution, certain goal roles can not be executed (or it makes no sense executing them) from certain source roles. Links represent a logical connection between roles, based on the current context of the agent. Some roles are independent of each other - these are not connected at all, or only through intermediate roles. The links in the behavior graph represent all possible paths the agent can follow through the graph in order to reach its goals.

2.3   Role Pre-conditions

The condition of a link determines whether roles can be switched via that link, i.e. whether the goal role can become current role. Often however, a role requires certain general conditions before it can be activated. For example a role may require particular resources in the environment to become active. We call such general conditions the *pre-conditions* of that role.

It is possible to integrate pre-conditions as conditions in each link that points to the role. However, this would require a copy of the pre-condition in each link. Therefore we decided to integrate pre-conditions in the roles themselves. Putting pre-conditions in roles promotes reuse of the role since it uncouples the links from the context of the roles (since the latter can be integrated in the pre-condition).

In summary, a switch from role A to role B is only possible if

- role A is the current role
- there is a link L from A to B;
- link L's condition is true, and L is thus open;
- role B's pre-condition is true.

2.4   Dependency Roles

It is obvious that in general an agent must be able to perform identical actions in several different roles, as well as be able to respond to events that occur asynchronously with the agent's current activities. An example is an agent that is able to respond to requests for information. When the agent receives a request it should be able to answer, no matter in which particular role the agent is at that moment. If we wanted to model this in the approach described above, we would have to duplicate the answering functionality in each role.

To avoid this duplication a new role can be introduced that is responsible for handling requests. All roles in which the agent is able to answer requests are connected to this new role. Because requesting agents *depend* on the answers produced by this new role we call such role a *dependency role*. Dependency roles are similar to roles in the dependencies layer of the Cassiopeia approach [9].

Fig. 1 depicts a simple example of a behavior graph. In this example, the agent has two roles, *Move* and *Work*. An agent without work to do is in the *Move* role. In this role the agent moves around looking for work. When it detects work, the *Work Detected* link opens and the agent switches to the *Work* role. As soon as the work is finished the agent again switches to the *Move* role via the *Work Finished* link. The right part of Fig. 1 illustrates the common dependency of both roles to answer a request for the agents' current location. This functionality is modelled as the *Send Position* dependency role on top of the behavior graph.

Whereas a role of the behavior graph becomes active through role switching via a link, a dependency role becomes active via the connection with the current role when a dependency is detected. The dependency role then gets priority over the current role to resolve the dependency after which the underlying role takes over again. If the dependency role is not connected to the current role the moment the dependency appears, the resolution of the dependency is delayed until a role connected to the applicable dependency role becomes active.

2.5   Refreshment of Information

A final aspect of our basic model concerns the refreshment of information. When new information becomes available to the agent it may switch roles. In the proposed model it is only necessary to update the information in the links that start from the current role. After all, only the goal roles of these links are candidates to become the next current role. This approach not only saves computation time, more important is its impact on the scalability of the model. Since the refreshment of information happens only locally it is independent of the number of roles and the size of the behavior graph.

3   Model for Adaptive Behavior

In this section we extend the basic role-based model towards adaptive agents. An adaptive agent dynamically changes its behavior according to altering circumstances it is faced with. First we introduce dynamic links for behavior graphs, based on factors. Then we zoom in on adaptive factors.

3.1   Dynamic Links Based on Factors

In the basic model a link can be open or closed, allowing role switching or not. Now we extend a link to have a certain *relevance* to switch roles. The relevance is determined through a set of relevant *factors*. A factor models a property of the agent or its perceived environment. An example of a factor is the distance to a target (when the agent is close to the target the factor is high and the other way around). When the link is evaluated each factor returns a value that indicates the current strength of the property of that factor. Based on a mathematical function the agent then calculates (using the values of all the factors of the link) the relevance to switch roles via that link.

A simple approach is to use a linear sum, i.e. the relevance to switch roles is then:

$$R = \sum_i w_i.f_i \ \ (\%)$$

$0 \leq w_i \leq 1$ is the weight of factor i and f_i its current value, with $\sum_i f_i = 100$. A disadvantage of this simple model is that none of the factors is able to dominate the result and so force a role switch along the link. To resolve this problem we can give a link a standard relevance to switch roles. This relevance can then be influenced by the factors as follows:

$$R = [\ R_{standard} + \sum_i w_i.f_i \ ]_0^{100} \ \ (\%)$$

$R_{standard}$ is the pre-defined standard relevance, w_i the weight of factor i and $-100 \leq f_i \leq 100$ the value of the factor. The calculated value of R is normalized from 0 to 100. This method is more flexible, e.g. it supports the negative influence of a factor. However it suffers from another problem: saturation. A link with a normalized relevance of 95 % has almost the same relevance to switch roles as a link with a relevance of 100 %, although the absolute relevance of this latter may be much higher. More complex calculations can also be used, such as Boltzmann exploration [10], however they are out of the scope of this paper.

Based on the relevances of all links that start from the current role (and for which the preconditions of the goal role hold) the agent then calculates to which role it will switch. The simplest approach selects the link with the highest relevance, alternatively a stochastic probability over the candidate links can be used to calculate a decision.

3.2 Adaptive Factors

As stated above, factors model conditions to switch roles via one of the candidate links. We introduce two kind of factors, pre-defined and learning factors.

Pre-defined factors allow a designer to express relative preferences for role selection. The definition of pre-defined factors requires a thorough knowledge of the problem domain. The designer has to identify the relevant properties of the agent or its surrounding environment that affect its role selection. Based on the values of the factors in the links that start from the current role, the agent dynamically calculates to which role it will switch.

Learning factors go one step further and allow an agent to adapt its behavior over time. Learning factors take into account the good or bad experiences of recent role selections. The result of a role selection is determined by the past performance of the goal role. The calculation of the performance can be done locally, by the goal role itself (e.g. the success of getting an answer to a request) or globally, i.e. a general evaluation function can be used that takes into account macroscopic information (e.g. an agent that follows an alternative route to a target to avoid a blockade). During refreshment, the result of the performance calculation is returned back to the link that uses it to adjust the values of its learning factors.

Sometimes however the result of actions is not immediately available, e.g. the answer to a question sent to another agent may be delayed. Meanwhile the agent may have left its previous role. To deliver late results at the right links we introduce a *graph manager*. The graph manager is a module internally to the agent that handles the delivery of late results of performance calculations. Learning factors can subscribe themselves at the graph manager when they expect a late result of a goal role. As soon as the result is available the goal role returns it to the graph manager. During the next refreshment, the graph manager passes the result to the correct link which updates the learning factors to which the result applies.

Contrary to most traditional models for adaptive selection of behavior that dynamically select a behavior based on the calculation of a probability value as a function of the observed state for each *individual* behavior, learning factors enable an agent to construct logical *relations* between different roles in order to dynamically form paths of roles that are suitable in the current state. When the circumstances change, the agent dynamically adjusts its learning factors and shifts its paths of roles accordingly.

For example, in Q-learning [10], a value is learned for every possible action in a certain state. In our model, every role represents an abstract action or group of actions, that are linked with each other using various kinds of pre-conditions on the state. In a sense, whereas Q-learning links all states through an action–value pair, we link actions through a condition on the state. Thanks to the introduction of factors, we are able to change the influence of a certain property of the environment on the agent's actions adaptively. Because actions are linked, it is easier to learn paths of actions, rather than paths of states.

In one extreme, the behavior graph can be completely linked, so that the agent can learn all useful paths himself during execution. However, usually some human designer knowledge is already encoded in the graph, so that obviously useless links can be avoided beforehand.

4   The Model Applied to the Packet-World

In this section we apply the model for adaptive behavior to the Packet-World. First we introduce the Packet-World application and describe a basic behavior graph for agents in the Packet-World. Next we discuss the problem of the "sparse world" in the Packet-World. To resolve this problem, we extend the basic behavior graph to enable the agents to adapt their behavior when the world gets sparse. Finally, we show simulation results that demonstrate the improved performance of the adaptive agents over the basic agents for a sparse world.

4.1   The Packet-World

The Packet–World [11, 12] consists of a number of different colored packets that are scattered over a rectangular grid. Agents that live in this virtual world have to collect these packets and bring them to the correspondingly colored destination. We call a *job* the task of the agents to deliver all packets in the world. The left part of Fig. 2 shows an example of a Packet–World of size 10x10 which 8 agents. Colored rectangles symbolize packets that can be manipulated by the agents and circles symbolize destinations.

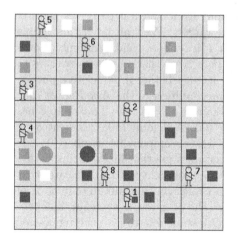 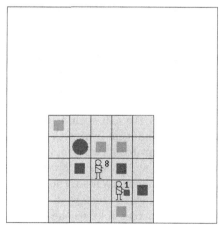

Fig. 2. Example of the Packet–World

In the Packet–World agents can interact with the environment in a number of ways. An agent can make a step to one of the free neighbor fields around him. If an agent is not carrying any packet, it can pick up a packet from one of its neighbor fields. An agent can put down a packet it carries at one of the free neighbor fields, or of course at the destination point of that particular packet. Finally, if there is no sensible action for an agent to perform, it may wait for a while and do nothing. Besides acting into the environment, agents can also send messages to each other. In particular agents can request each other for information about packets or the destination for a certain color of packets.

It is important to notice that each agent of the Packet–World has only a limited view on the world. The view–size of the world expresses how far, i.e. how many squares, an agent can "see" around him. The right part of Fig. 4.1 illustrates the limited view of agent 8, in this example the view–size is 2.

We monitor the Packet–World via two counters that measure the efficiency of the agents in performing their job. A first counter measures the energy invested by the agents. When an agent makes a step without carrying a packet it consumes one unit of energy, stepping with a packet requires two units of energy. The energy required to pick up a packet or to put it down is also one unit. Finally, waiting and doing nothing is free of charge. The second counter measures the number of sent messages. This counter simply increments for each message that is transferred between two agents. The overall performance can be calculated as a weighted sum of both counters.

4.2   A Behavior Graph for Agents in the Packet-World

Fig. 3 depicts a behavior graph for a basic agent in the Packet–World. The accompanying dependency role to answer questions is depicted in Fig. 4. The behavior of a basic agent is simple, it moves to the nearest packet, picks it up and brings it to its destination. If the agent does not perceive any packet (or the destination it is looking for), it searches randomly. However, if it perceives another agent it asks if the other agents knows the target. We translated this simple behavior into six roles. In the role *Search Packet* the agent randomly moves around looking for packets. However, if it perceives other agents it switches to the role *Ask Packet* requesting the farthest agent whether it perceives a packet. Perceiving another agent is modelled as a precondition of the *Ask Packet* role. The link to switch from the *Search Packet* role to the *Ask Packet* role has no condition. We call such a link a *default link*. A default link is indicated by an arrow without an oval with a condition. The accompanying number $(0 \dots 1)$ denotes the probability for an agent to switch roles via that link[1]. A link with a probability 1 will always be open. A link with a probability of 0.33 indicates that if all other conditions hold, the agent changes roles via that link in only 33 % of the cases. When the requested agent receives the question, it switches, independent of its current role, to the *Answer to Question* role to give the requesting agent an answer. Since the requesting agent *depends* on the requested agent, the *Answer to Question* role is modelled as a dependency role. When the requested agent receives the location of a packet, it switches via the *See Packet* link to the role *To Packet*, otherwise it continues to execute the *Search Packet* role. In

---

[1] The default value for a probability is 1, this value is not annotated.

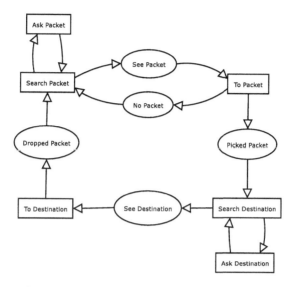

Fig. 3. A behavior graph for a basic agent in the Packet-World

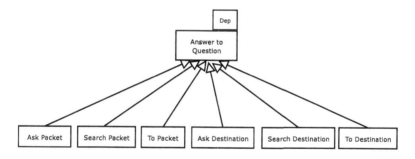

Fig. 4. Representation of the dependency role to answer questions

the role *To Packet* the agent moves straight on to the packet. If meanwhile the packet is picked up by another agent, the agent returns via the *No Packet* link to the *Search Packet* role to look for another packet. If it perceives other packets it switches again to the *To Packet* role and moves to the nearest perceived one. If no other packet is visible the agent keeps searching for a packet in the *Search Packet* role. Finally when the agent succeeded in picking up a packet it switches via the *Picked Packet* link to the *Search Destination* role. In a similar way the agent then searches for the destination of the packet it carries. When the agent finally delivers the packet it enters the *Search Packet* role to look for the next packet.

4.3   The Sparse World Problem

We observed the behavior of the basic agents in the Packet-World and noticed a particular problem for the agents. When the agents deliver packets at the destination the number of remaining packets in the environment decreases. When the world gets sparse, i.e. when only a couple of packets are left, we observed that the behavior of the agents becomes inefficient. We called this the "sparse world" problem.

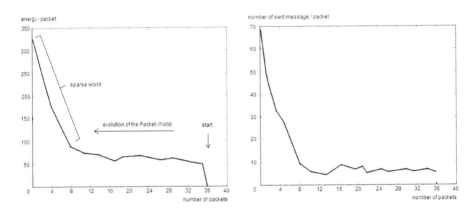

Fig. 5. Left: energy usage during the evolution of the Packet-World. Right: the number of sent messages

Fig. 5 shows simulation results that illustrate the effects on energy consumption and communication traffic when the world gets sparse. As the number of packets in the environment decrease, the graphs have to be read from the right to the left side. The left graph shows the energy used by the agents for each packet that is delivered. From the start (in this case the number of initial packets was 36) until approximately 8 packets the energy consumption is fairly constant. However the required energy to deliver the remaining packets strongly increases. The right graphs shows the number of messages sent for each packet that is delivered. Similarly to the energy consumption, the number of sent messages increases remarkably when the number of remaining packets becomes less then 8.

From the observations, we identified three kinds of problems for the agents when the world got sparse:

1. The number of requests for packets explodes while most agents can not give a meaningful answer. We call this the *request explosion* problem.
2. Most agents keep searching aimlessly for packets wasting their energy. We call this the *energy waste* problem.
3. When several agents detect one of the few packets all of them run at it while in the end only one agent is able to pick it up. We call this the *storming* problem.

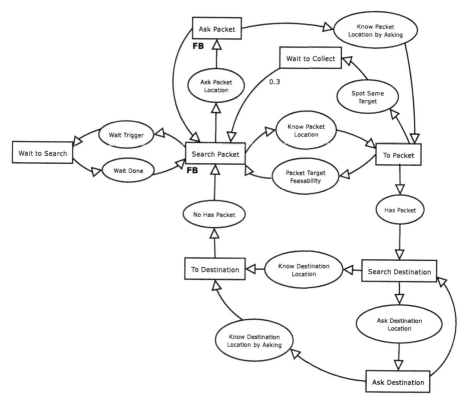

Fig. 6. Behavior graph for an adaptive agent that deals with the sparse world problem

4.4   A Behavior Graph for Adaptive Agents

To resolve the problems with the sparse world, we designed an adaptive agent according to the model described in section 3. Fig. 6 depicts the behavior graph of the adaptive agent.

We reused the roles of the basic agent for the adaptive agent. We added two extra waiting roles, *Wait to Search* and *Wait to Collect*. Similarly as to the basic agent, the adaptive agent has a dependency role *Answer to Question* to answer questions sent by other agents (this dependency role is not depicted). As for the basic agent, the adaptive agent is able to answer questions from all roles of the behavior graph. The symbol *FB* denotes that feedback (for learning factors) is passed from a goal role back to the connected link.

Now we explain the adaptive behavior of the agent. First we discuss how the agent adapt its behavior to cope with the request explosion problem. Then we look at the energy waste problem. Finally we discuss how the agent adapts its behavior to deal with the storming problem.

The request explosion problem. We start with the role *Search Packet*. As long as the agent does not perceive a packet it searches randomly for one. However, if it perceives one or more agents it *may* switch to the *Ask Packet* role to request the farthest agent for the location of a packet (the chance that this agent perceives a packet is highest). The decision whether the agent requests another agent for information depends on the state of the *Ask Packet Location* link. In this link we introduce a *Success* factor. The value of this factor determines the probability whether the agent sends a request or not. The value of the *Success* factor is affected by the previous success of the goal role *Ask Packet*. If a request is answered with a requested information, the *Ask Packet* role returns a positive feedback to the *Success* factor of the *Ask Packet* link, otherwise a negative feedback is returned. It is not difficult to see that the learning *Success* factor enables the agent to adapt its behavior to cope with the request explosion problem. If the number of successful requests decreases, the probability that the agent will send new questions decreases too.

The energy waste problem. Besides searching randomly or asking another agent for a packet location, the agent may also switch from the *Search Packet* role to the *Wait to Search* role. In the *Wait Trigger* link we added the *Search Period* factor that reflects the time the agent searches for a packet. The *Search Packet* role measures the search time for packets. When the search time exceeds the value of the *Search Period* factor the agent switches to the *Wait to Search* role. As such the agent enters the *Wait to Search* role more frequently when the time to detect a packet increases. The link *Wait Done* determines when the agent restarts searching, i.e. when it returns back from the *Wait to Search* role to the *Search Packet* role. We introduced a factor *Wait Period* in the *Wait to Search* link that reflects the usefulness of waiting. If the agent after a waiting period returns to the *Seach Packet* role and then again fails to find a packet (before it switches to the *Wait to Search* role), the *Search Role* returns negative feedback to the *Wait Period* factor. As a consequence the agent increases the time it waits in the *Wait Search* role. However if the agent quickly discovers a new packet the *Search Packet* role returns positive feedback, decreasing the next waiting time. The *Wait Search* role enables the agent to deal with the energy wasting problem.

The storming problem. As soon as the agent finds a packet, it switches to the *To Packet* role. In addition to the basic behavior we introduced the *Wait to Collect* role. The *Spot Same Target* link from the *To Packet* role to the *Wait to Collect* role is influenced by the behavior of the other agents within the perceptual scope of the agents. The *Spot Same Target* link contains two dynamic factors: *Same Target* and *Nearest to Target*. The *Same Target* factor increases the probability to switch to the *Wait to Collect* role when the agent suspects that other agents move to the packet it is looking for. Therefore the agent compares (in the *To Packet* role) for each visible agent the distance to the packet it is looking for with the distance to the nearest (visible) packet for the other agent. The second factor *Nearest at Target* decreases the probability to switch to the *Wait to Collect* role when the agent believes it is nearer to the targeted packet than the other agents inside its perceptual scope. Therefore the agent simply compares its own distance to the target packet with the distance of

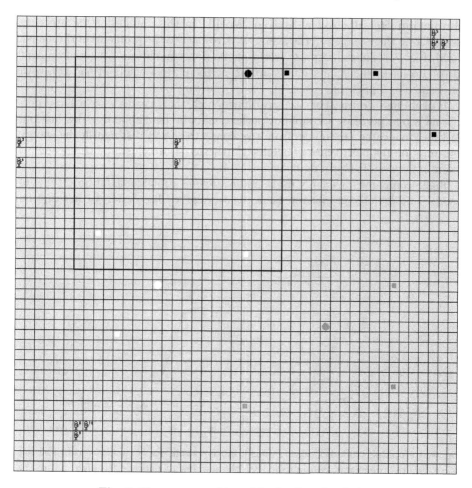

Fig. 7. The sparse world used in the first simulation

each visible agent to the packet. From the *Wait to Collect* role the agent returns to the *Search Packet* role via a default link. In Fig. 6 the probability to switch back is set to 0.3. The *Wait to Collect* role enables the agent to deal with the storming problem. Especially when only a few packets are left, the factors in the *Spot Same Target* link work very efficient.

When the agent picks up a packet it switches to the *Search Destination* role. From then on, until the packet is delivered, the adaptive agent behaves the same way as the basic agent does.

4.5   Simulation Results

To verify whether the adaptive agents behave as desired we did two types of simulations. First we compared the behavior of the basic agents with the adaptive agents in a sparse world. Then we put the agents in a homogeneous world and looked at a the behavior of both types of agents when the world gets sparse.

Simulation Results for a Sparse World. In this simulation we are only interested in the behavior of the agents with respect to the problems of the sparse world. Fig. 7 depicts the sparse world of the first simulation. The environment size is 45x45. In the simulation environment there are 3 colors of packets, with for each color 3 packets.

Packets and destinations are positioned such that agents with a large perceptual scope perceive a couple of packets and the corresponding destination. Packets are located far enough from the agents to clearly distinguish the energy consumption for both types of agents. Furthermore, we clustered the agents to accentuate possible storming behavior.

Fig. 8 compares the energy usage and communication traffic for both types of agents. The depicted graphs represent the average results of energy consumption

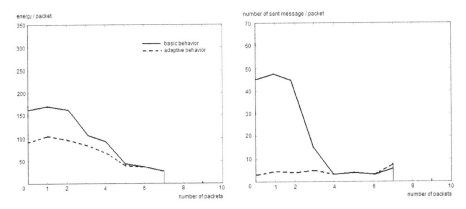

Fig. 8. Comparison non-adaptive versus adaptive agent for a sparse world. The left figure denotes the energy consumption vs. the number of packets, the right figure the number of sent messages vs. the number of packets

(on the left) and requests for packets (on the right) for 80 runs. The right figure illustrates the significant reduction of requests for packets for adaptive agents. The left figure illustrates the decreased energy consumption to deliver the packets. The simulation results demonstrate the improved behavior of the adaptive agents in the sparse world. The adaptation of the behavior appears very quickly, in the example the effects of adaptation are already noticeable after two of the last 8 packets where delivered.

Simulation Results for a Homogeneous World. In this section we show how adaptive agents change their behavior while the environment changes and the world becomes spare. Fig. 9 depicts the test world we used in this simulation.

In the environment of size 32x32 we put 25 packets of 2 different colors, homogenously scattered. 10 agents spread over the world have to collect the packets and bring them to the correct destination.

The average simulation results for 80 runs are depicted in Fig. 10 (in the graphs only the results for the collection of the last 40 packets are depicted).

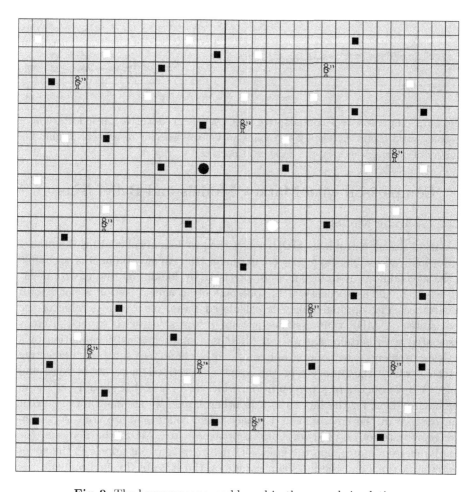

Fig. 9. The homogeneous world used in the second simulation

The figure shows that adaptation starts to work when approximately 10 packets are left in the environment. From that point on, the energy consumption as well as the communication is significantly lower for adaptive agents. The simulation results demonstrate that adaptive agents recognize the changes in the environment and change their behavior accordingly. As an overall result, we calculated an expected gain of 12 % for the adaptive agents in the second simulation.

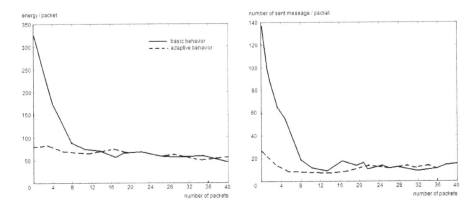

Fig. 10. Comparison of a non-adaptive agent versus an adaptive agent for a homogeneous world. Left: the energy consumption vs. the number of packets. Right: the number of messages sent vs. the number of packets

5   Comparison with Markov Models and Belief Nets

5.1   Markov Models

A Markov decision problem (MDP) solves the problem of calculating an optimal policy in an accessible, stochastic environment [13]. An environment is accessible if the agent knows it's current state precisely by looking at the environment. An environment is stochastic if the outcome of an agent's action is not known in advance. The optimal policy is calculated based on a utility value of the goal states. A MDP thus assumes a state–action space with explicit utilities associated with certain states – an MDP is a mathematical formulation of a decision problem. A behavior graph, on the other hand, is a software engineering artefact, where the *behavior* of the agent is described in terms of roles and links. A link consists of a precondition, which is a state that should be true in the environment for the link to fire; in other words, we assume that the agent can observe in the environment whether these conditions are true. A graph-like representation is used for both approaches: in a MDP, the nodes in the graph represent states, and the links actions; whereas in our approach the nodes represent actions and the links constraints on the state of the environment.

5.2   Belief Nets

A belief network (Bayesian net) summarizes the beliefs of an agent about possible events in the environment in a graph–like representation [13]. Each node in a belief network is a possible event or process that can occur in the environment, and each link represents the probability that the source event of the link influences the target event. A belief network by itself does not describe behavior of an agent: it instead summarizes the beliefs the agent has about the environment, which in turn are used to determine the agent's behavior. So, although the representation of belief networks and our approach is both similar (a graph–

like representation), the meaning and goal of each is different: a belief network models the agent's beliefs; a behavior graph models an agent's behavior.

6   Conclusions

In this paper we proposed a role-based model for adaptive agents. The model describes the behavior of an agent as a graph of roles. Adaptivity is achieved through factors in the links of the graph. Pre-defined factors express relative preferences for role selection. Learning factors reflect the extent of success of recent role selections, enabling an agent to dynamically form paths of roles that are suitable in the current state. Adapting the logical *relations* between different roles contrasts to most existing approaches for adaptive behavior selection that dynamically selects a behavior based on the calculation of a probability value for each *individual* behavior. The model is similar to a reinforcement learning approach, with the notable difference that it allows a designer to logically group large numbers of state together in a role, and thus avoids a state-space explosion. It also allows easy integration of "common knowledge" through the pre-defined factors.

A prerequisite to apply the proposed model is sufficient knowledge of the domain. To design a behavior graph, the designer must first be able to identify the roles for the agents and all the possible and necessary switches between roles. Conditions for a role to become active have to be modelled as pre-conditions, dependencies between roles are modelled as separate dependency roles. Second, to identify the factors in the links, the designer has to identify the relevant properties for the agent to switch roles. And finally, to define learning factors, the designer needs a notion of the relevance of the performance of roles. On the other hand the designer does not have to manage the problems all alone. Adaptivity adds value by adjusting the behavior of the agent at runtime according to the changing (not explicitly foreseen) circumstances.

To illustrate that the model works, we applied it to the Packet-World. We discussed simulation results that demonstrate that the model enables the agents to adapt effectively to a changing environment.

References

1. Maes, P.: Modeling adaptive autonomous agents. Artificial Life, I **1-2** (1994)
2. Bryson, J.J.: Intelligence by design: Principles of modularity and coordination for engineering complex adaptive agents. In: PhD thesis, MIT, Department of EECS, Cambridge, MA. AI Technical Report 2001-003. (2001)
3. Bruemmer, D.: Adaptive robotics, behavior-based robotics, muti-agent control, http://www.inel.gov/adaptiverobotics/behaviorbasedrobotics/multiagent.shtml. (2004)
4. Maes, P., Brooks, R.: Learning to coordinate behaviors. Autonomous Mobile Robots: Control, Planning and Architecture **2** (1991) IEEE Computer Society Press, CA.

5. Drogoul, A.: De la simulation multi-agent a la résolution collective de problémes. Ph.D thesis, Université Paris 6, France (1993)

6. Bonabeau, E., Henaux, F., Guérin, S., Snyers, D., Kuntz, P., Theraulaz, G.: Routing in telecommunications networks with "smart" ant-like agents. In: Intelligent Agents for Telecommunications Applications '98 (IATA'98). (1998)

7. Schelfthout, K., Holvoet, T.: To do or not to do: The individual's model for emergent task allocation. In: Proceedings of the AISB'02 Symposium on Adaptive Agents and Multi-Agent Systems. (2002)

8. De Wolf, T., Holvoet, T.: Adaptive behavior based on evolving thresholds with feedback. In D. Kazakov, D.K., Alonso, E., eds.: Proceedings of the AISB'03 Symposium on Adaptive Agents and Multiagent Systems. (2003)

9. Drogoul, A., Zucker, J.: Methodological issues for designing multi-agent systems with machine learning techniques: Capitalizing experiences from the robocup challenge. Technical Report 041, LIP6 (1998)

10. Kaebling, L., Litmann, L., Moore, A.: Reinforcement learning: a survey. Journal of Artificial Intelligence Research **4** (1996)

11. Huhns, M., Stephens, L.: Multi-agent systems and societies of agents. Ed. G. Weiss, Multi-agent Systems, MIT Press **2** (1999)

12. Weyns, D., Holvoet, T.: The packet–world as a case to investigate sociality in multi-agent systems. Demo presented at the 1st International Conference on Autonomous Agents and Multiagent Systems, AAMAS'02, Bologna (2002)

13. Russell, S., Norvig, P.: Artificial intelligence, a modern approach. Prentice Hall International Editions (2004)

Author Index

Lecture Notes in Artificial Intelligence (LNAI)

Vol. 3209: B. Berendt, A. Hotho, D. Mladenic, M. van Someren, M. Spiliopoulou, G. Stumme (Eds.), Web Mining: From Web to Semantic Web. IX, 201 pages. 2004.

Vol. 3206: P. Sojka, I. Kopecek, K. Pala (Eds.), Text, Speech and Dialogue. XIII, 667 pages. 2004.

Vol. 3202: J.-F. Boulicaut, F. Esposito, F. Giannotti, D. Pedreschi (Eds.), Knowledge Discovery in Databases: PKDD 2004. XIX, 560 pages. 2004.

Vol. 3201: J.-F. Boulicaut, F. Esposito, F. Giannotti, D. Pedreschi (Eds.), Machine Learning: ECML 2004. XVIII, 580 pages. 2004.

Vol. 3194: R. Camacho, R. King, A. Srinivasan (Eds.), Inductive Logic Programming. XI, 361 pages. 2004.

Vol. 3192: C. Bussler, D. Fensel (Eds.), Artificial Intelligence: Methodology, Systems, and Applications. XIII, 522 pages. 2004.

Vol. 3191: M. Klusch, S. Ossowski, V. Kashyap, R. Unland (Eds.), Cooperative Information Agents VIII. XI, 303 pages. 2004.

Vol. 3187: G. Lindemann, J. Denzinger, I.J. Timm, R. Unland (Eds.), Multiagent System Technologies. XIII, 341 pages. 2004.

Vol. 3176: O. Bousquet, U. von Luxburg, G. Rätsch (Eds.), Advanced Lectures on Machine Learning. IX, 241 pages. 2004.

Vol. 3171: A.L.C. Bazzan, S. Labidi (Eds.), Advances in Artificial Intelligence – SBIA 2004. XVII, 548 pages. 2004.

Vol. 3159: U. Visser, Intelligent Information Integration for the Semantic Web. XIV, 150 pages. 2004.

Vol. 3157: C. Zhang, H. W. Guesgen, W.K. Yeap (Eds.), PRICAI 2004: Trends in Artificial Intelligence. XX, 1023 pages. 2004.

Vol. 3155: P. Funk, P.A. González Calero (Eds.), Advances in Case-Based Reasoning. XIII, 822 pages. 2004.

Vol. 3139: F. Iida, R. Pfeifer, L. Steels, Y. Kuniyoshi (Eds.), Embodied Artificial Intelligence. IX, 331 pages. 2004.

Vol. 3131: V. Torra, Y. Narukawa (Eds.), Modeling Decisions for Artificial Intelligence. XI, 327 pages. 2004.

Vol. 3127: K.E. Wolff, H.D. Pfeiffer, H.S. Delugach (Eds.), Conceptual Structures at Work. XI, 403 pages. 2004.

Vol. 3123: A. Belz, R. Evans, P. Piwek (Eds.), Natural Language Generation. X, 219 pages. 2004.

Vol. 3120: J. Shawe-Taylor, Y. Singer (Eds.), Learning Theory. X, 648 pages. 2004.

Vol. 3097: D. Basin, M. Rusinowitch (Eds.), Automated Reasoning. XII, 493 pages. 2004.

Vol. 3071: A. Omicini, P. Petta, J. Pitt (Eds.), Engineering Societies in the Agents World. XIII, 409 pages. 2004.

Vol. 3070: L. Rutkowski, J. Siekmann, R. Tadeusiewicz, L.A. Zadeh (Eds.), Artificial Intelligence and Soft Computing - ICAISC 2004. XXV, 1208 pages. 2004.

Vol. 3068: E. André, L. Dybkjær, W. Minker, P. Heisterkamp (Eds.), Affective Dialogue Systems. XII, 324 pages. 2004.

Vol. 3067: M. Dastani, J. Dix, A. El Fallah-Seghrouchni (Eds.), Programming Multi-Agent Systems. X, 221 pages. 2004.

Vol. 3066: S. Tsumoto, R. Słowiński, J. Komorowski, J.W. Grzymała-Busse (Eds.), Rough Sets and Current Trends in Computing. XX, 853 pages. 2004.

Vol. 3065: A. Lomuscio, D. Nute (Eds.), Deontic Logic in Computer Science. X, 275 pages. 2004.

Vol. 3060: A.Y. Tawfik, S.D. Goodwin (Eds.), Advances in Artificial Intelligence. XIII, 582 pages. 2004.

Vol. 3056: H. Dai, R. Srikant, C. Zhang (Eds.), Advances in Knowledge Discovery and Data Mining. XIX, 713 pages. 2004.

Vol. 3055: H. Christiansen, M.-S. Hacid, T. Andreasen, H.L. Larsen (Eds.), Flexible Query Answering Systems. X, 500 pages. 2004.

Vol. 3048: P. Faratin, D.C. Parkes, J.A. Rodríguez-Aguilar, W.E. Walsh (Eds.), Agent-Mediated Electronic Commerce V. XI, 155 pages. 2004.

Vol. 3040: R. Conejo, M. Urretavizcaya, J.-L. Pérez-de-la-Cruz (Eds.), Current Topics in Artificial Intelligence. XIV, 689 pages. 2004.

Vol. 3035: M.A. Wimmer (Ed.), Knowledge Management in Electronic Government. XII, 326 pages. 2004.

Vol. 3034: J. Favela, E. Menasalvas, E. Chávez (Eds.), Advances in Web Intelligence. XIII, 227 pages. 2004.

Vol. 3030: P. Giorgini, B. Henderson-Sellers, M. Winikoff (Eds.), Agent-Oriented Information Systems. XIV, 207 pages. 2004.

Vol. 3029: B. Orchard, C. Yang, M. Ali (Eds.), Innovations in Applied Artificial Intelligence. XXI, 1272 pages. 2004.

Vol. 3025: G.A. Vouros, T. Panayiotopoulos (Eds.), Methods and Applications of Artificial Intelligence. XV, 546 pages. 2004.

Vol. 3020: D. Polani, B. Browning, A. Bonarini, K. Yoshida (Eds.), RoboCup 2003: Robot Soccer World Cup VII. XVI, 767 pages. 2004.

Vol. 3012: K. Kurumatani, S.-H. Chen, A. Ohuchi (Eds.), Multi-Agents for Mass User Support. X, 217 pages. 2004.

Vol. 3010: K.R. Apt, F. Fages, F. Rossi, P. Szeredi, J. Váncza (Eds.), Recent Advances in Constraints. VIII, 285 pages. 2004.

Vol. 2990: J. Leite, A. Omicini, L. Sterling, P. Torroni (Eds.), Declarative Agent Languages and Technologies. XII, 281 pages. 2004.

Vol. 2980: A. Blackwell, K. Marriott, A. Shimojima (Eds.), Diagrammatic Representation and Inference. XV, 448 pages. 2004.

Vol. 2977: G. Di Marzo Serugendo, A. Karageorgos, O.F. Rana, F. Zambonelli (Eds.), Engineering Self-Organising Systems. X, 299 pages. 2004.

Vol. 2972: R. Monroy, G. Arroyo-Figueroa, L.E. Sucar, H. Sossa (Eds.), MICAI 2004: Advances in Artificial Intelligence. XVII, 923 pages. 2004.

Vol. 2969: M. Nickles, M. Rovatsos, G. Weiss (Eds.), Agents and Computational Autonomy. X, 275 pages. 2004.

Vol. 2961: P. Eklund (Ed.), Concept Lattices. IX, 411 pages. 2004.

Vol. 2953: K. Konrad, Model Generation for Natural Language Interpretation and Analysis. XIII, 166 pages. 2004.